BEGINNING

Rust® Programming

Ric Messier

wrox

A Wiley Brand

Beginning Rust® Programming

Copyright © 2021 by John Wiley & Sons, Inc., Indianapolis, Indiana

Published simultaneously in Canada

ISBN: 978-1-119-71297-8
ISBN: 978-1-119-71298-5 (ebk)
ISBN: 978-1-119-71287-9 (ebk)

Manufactured in the United States of America

Library of Congress Control Number: 2020937958

SKY10024588_012921

BEGINNING
RUST PROGRAMMING

BEGINNING

Rust® Programming

ABOUT THE AUTHOR

RIC MESSIER is an author, consultant, and educator who holds CCSP, GCIH, GSEC, CEH, and CISSP certifications and has published several books on information security and digital forensics. With decades of experience in information technology and information security, Ric has held the varied roles of programmer, system administrator, network engineer, security engineering manager, VoIP engineer, consultant, and professor. He is currently a Principal Consultant with FireEye Mandiant.

ABOUT THE TECHNICAL EDITOR

JESSICA ROCCHIO has been in the information technology industry for over a decade and is currently an incident response consultant at Mandiant. Over the last few years, she has worked with various programming languages. She has spent most of her career in incident response, forensics, intelligence, insider threats, and vulnerability management. Jessica has worked on a wide range of incidents, including espionage, cybercrime, fraud, data theft, and insider threats.

ACKNOWLEDGMENTS

Without my tech editor, Jessica, and my project editor, Kim, I might not have made it through this book, so many thanks to them!

CONTENTS

CHAPTER 15: ODDS AND SODS

INTRODUCTION

Save me from another "hello, world" book. Don't make me have to skim or skip through a half dozen chapters before I can get to something that's going to be useful to me. Or you, in this case. I can't tell you the number of programming books I've purchased over the decades, hoping to actually learn the language, only to end up just not using the book because it wasn't presented in a way that made a lot of sense to me. Instead of a dry explanation of how the language is constructed so you can try to put it all together in meaningful ways yourself, the purpose of this book is to jump straight into writing hopefully interesting or useful programs. Once we have the program, we can take a look at how it's constructed. You'll be learning by doing—or learning by example, if you prefer. I hope you'll find this a more useful and practical way of learning Rust.

Rust is an interesting language, as it turns out. Like so many other languages, it claims a C-like syntax, which is roughly correct but misses out on many important elements. Where Rust really shines is where C has introduced bad behavior in programming practices. This is more apparent as more have been using C as a language. Where C provides you with the gun and the bullets to shoot yourself in the foot, Rust provides you with necessary protections to keep you from injuring yourself or, from the perspective of the application, keeps the application from crashing. Rust is focused on protecting the memory space of the program, in part to provide a better ability for concurrent programming. After all, Rust is considered to be a systems programming language, meaning it is intended for applications that are lower level than those that a user directly interacts with.

In addition to protections provided to the programmer, Rust has a reasonably active community that can be used not only for support but also to get additional functionality for your programs. There are a lot of third-party libraries. These libraries can make your life easier by introducing you to functionality without you needing to write it yourself.

The idea behind this book is to introduce you to Rust in context, rather than via snippets that, by themselves, don't work. You need all the surround to fully understand what is happening in the program. You'll find this out when you are looking at example code sometimes. This is true with the Rust documentation: it's like you need to fully understand the language to understand the examples you are looking at. This book doesn't take that approach. It assumes that you don't know the language, so every line in every program is explained in as much detail as is necessary to pull it all apart, since Rust can be a dense language in some ways. This means single lines can pack a lot of meaning and functionality.

The one thing this book does not assume, though, is that you are coming to programming completely fresh. You will see examples for the programs written in Rust also presented in other programming languages. This may be helpful if you come from another language like C or Python, for instance, but want to learn Rust. Seeing the approach in a language you know before translating it into Rust may be beneficial. If you don't know those other languages, you can skip through those examples and jump to the explanation of how to write a program for the problem under discussion in Rust. You can still compare the other languages to Rust as you are going through so you can better understand Rust and how it is different from other languages.

OBTAINING RUST

Rust is a collection of programs that you will use. While a big part of it is the compiler, that's not the only program that will get installed. First, of course, is the compiler, `rustc`. This program will compile any Rust source code file, but more than that, it will compile complete executables. With some compiler programs, you have to compile source code files individually and then perform a step called *linking,* where you link all the source code files together along with any needed libraries to create the executable. If there is a reference to another source code file you have written as a module, the Rust compiler will compile all the modules and generate an executable without any additional intervention.

In practice, though, you probably won't use the Rust compiler directly. Instead, you'll use the `cargo` program. You'll want to get used to using `cargo` because it not only compiles your source code but also will manage any external dependencies. You will probably have libraries that are not part of the standard library. With languages like C and Python, you'd typically need to go get the library yourself and get it installed. You'd need to make sure it was installed in the right place, and then, in the case of C, you'd probably need to call the compiler in a way that made it clear you wanted to link in the external library so all the external references could get resolved and put into the resulting executable.

Rust is also a newer program, which means there are changes being made to it. You'll generally want to keep up-to-date on the newest Rust compiler. Your third-party libraries may be keeping up with the latest Rust changes, and if you aren't up-to-date, your program won't compile. You'll want the `rustup` utility to help manage your Rust installation.

If you are working on a Linux distribution, you may be inclined to use whatever package manager you have to install Rust. There's a better-than-good chance that your distribution has the Rust language in it. The problem is, once you install using the package manager, you may be held back by the package manager. The latest Rust software may not be available to you. It's easier to just install Rust without the Linux package manager. With operating systems like macOS and Windows, you don't even have a built-in package manager, so installing that way wouldn't be an option anyway.

The best approach is to go to the Rust website (`www.rust-lang.org`). For Unix-like operating systems, including Linux and macOS, there is a command-line string you will probably use to install. Because there is a chance this approach may change, it's best to just go to the website to get the right way. As of the writing of this book, the command used to install Rust on those operating systems follows. If you are on Windows, you can download an installer from the Rust website:

```
curl --proto '=https' --tlsv1.2 -sSf https://sh.rustup.rs | sh
```

Once you have the Rust toolchain installed, you can keep it updated by using the command `rustup update`. This will always get the latest version of the Rust toolchain and make sure it is installed. You will also need to use a good source code editor. There are several available that will support Rust extensions, including Visual Studio Code, Atom, and Sublime. You should make sure you have installed the Rust extensions, which will help you with syntax highlighting and other features.

GETTING THE SOURCE CODE

As you work your way through this book, you will see primarily complete programs that are explained in context. You can certainly retype the programs from the book, and most are not that long. There is some value in retyping because it helps to ingrain the code and approach to programming used by Rust. However, it can be tedious to stare at a program and try to retype it. You may want to just start with the source code. It's all available on GitHub. GitHub is a source code repository site using the `git` source code management software. It was originally written to be used with the Linux kernel, as previous source code management software was not considered to be feature-rich enough. While there is other software available, `git` is most widely used today because public repositories like GitHub use `git`. To get the source code for this book, you can use the following command:

```
git clone https://github.com/securitykilroy/rust.git
```

If you have a `git` client that you prefer to the command line, you can certainly use it. The command line is going to be the most common approach to grabbing source code from a `git` server.

> **NOTE** *The files are also available at* www.wiley.com/go/beginningrust.

WHAT YOU WILL LEARN

The approach in this book is to write complete programs that are useful in some way, even if they are very simple starting points to more interesting programs. The idea is not to try to deconstruct enormous programs, so each chapter will tackle important ideas, but the programs presented may be limited. You will get important building blocks but maybe not large, complex programs. Each chapter will present some essential ideas in Rust and, sometimes, programming in general. Many chapters build on ideas from previous chapters. You can certainly read individual chapters since, in most cases, the program is still explained in detail, not always assuming you have read previous chapters.

The book doesn't exclusively cover the Rust programming language. Programming is about far more than language syntax. There is much more to programming than just how a language is constructed. This is especially true if you ever want to write software on a team—working with an open source project or being employed as a programmer. You need to be aware of how larger programs are constructed and ways to write software in a way that is readable and maintainable, as well as ways to write tests of your software. You can see the topics covered in each chapter here.

Chapter 1

We get started with a partially functional implementation of Conway's Game of Life, a classic computer science program. Along the way, you will learn how to use `cargo` to create a new program with all the files and directories needed for `cargo` to build the program for you. You'll also learn about data types and some initial control structures, as well as creating functions in Rust.

Chapter 2

The reason for making the program in Chapter 1, "Game of Life: The Basics," only partly functional is that the complete program is larger, and there are a lot of concepts to introduce to implement everything. By the end of this chapter, you will have a fully functional program that will implement Conway's Game of Life. You will also learn about the use of a collection data type that is good for dynamically sized collections. You will also learn about performing input/output to interact with the user. One of the most important concepts in Rust is introduced in this chapter, and it will keep recurring in several subsequent chapters. Ownership is foundational to Rust and is part of what makes it a good language for systems programming. Rust is designed to be a safe language, unlike a language like C.

Chapter 3

This chapter works with another essential concept in Rust—the struct. This is a complex data structure, defined entirely by the programmer. It underpins data abstraction in Rust, so it will be covered across multiple chapters in different ways. You'll also be working with writing to files as well as working with JavaScript Object Notation (JSON), a common approach to store and transmit complex data structures in a way that is self-describing. We'll also extend the idea of ownership by talking about lifetimes.

Chapter 4

The struct is an important concept in Rust because it provides a way to abstract data. *Data abstraction* is hiding the data behind a data structure and a set of functionality that acts on the data. This is done using traits in Rust, and this chapter introduces those traits. We'll spend a lot of time in subsequent chapters looking at traits in more detail. We'll also talk about error handling, which is another dense and important topic that will be covered in unfolding detail across several chapters. Additionally, we'll cover another control structure that allows you to make different decisions based on the contents of an identifier. Identifiers in Rust are similar to variables in other languages, although there are some subtle nuances, which is why it's easier to refer to them as identifiers. We'll also look at how to take input from a user.

Chapter 5

This chapter covers concurrent programming, sometimes called parallel programming. This is where a program ends up breaking into multiple, simultaneous execution paths. There are a lot of challenges with concurrent programming, not least of which is the way the different execution paths communicate with one another to keep data and timing synchronized. We'll also look at how to interact with the operating system to get information from the filesystem. And we'll take an initial pass at encryption, although this is not the last time encryption will be covered.

Chapter 6

We'll start on network programming, although this will also be spread across additional chapters. There are a lot of different ways to write programs for network communication because there are so many protocols that are used over networks. We'll look at some additional interactions with the operating system in this chapter as well. This is the first of a pair of chapters that are linked. In this chapter, we implement a network server that requires a client to talk to it. This chapter also talks about different ways to design your program so you'll have thought about all the elements and features the program needs before you start writing it.

Chapter 7

This is the chapter that covers the client that communicates with the server from the previous chapter. We will also cover using encryption to communicate over the network. Additionally, we'll use regular expressions, which can be a powerful pattern-matching system. While they have a lot of other uses, we're going to use regular expressions in this chapter to help us make sure we have the right input from the user.

Chapter 8

This is the first chapter that talks about database communications. This chapter covers the use of relational databases, which are traditional ways to store structured information. If you've seen the use of MySQL, PostgreSQL, Microsoft SQL Server, Oracle, SQLite, or other databases, you've seen relational databases in action. You may be working with a database server or an embedded database. This chapter will cover those two techniques so you will be able to talk to a server or store data in a searchable way in a local file.

Chapter 9

Relational databases have been around for decades; but the way forward is using other database types, since data isn't always so well structured that you know exactly what properties will be associated with it. Additionally, there may be documents involved that need to be dealt with. This chapter covers the use of NoSQL databases, which are databases that use something other than traditional relational techniques to store and retrieve data. This chapter also covers assertions, which are ways to ensure that data is in the state it is expected to be in before being handled by a function. This is a way of protecting the program, allowing it to fail gracefully.

Chapter 10

Many applications are moving to the web. This means you need to be able to write programs that can communicate over web-based technologies, including the HTTP protocol. This chapter will cover not only how to write web client programs but also extracting data from web pages and asynchronous communication, where you may send a request and not wait for the response but still be able to handle the response when it comes back. This chapter also covers how to use style guides to make your programs more consistent and readable.

Chapter 11

Where the last chapter talked about writing web-based clients, this program presents a couple of different ways to write a web server. This is useful if you want to write an application programming interface (API) that can be consumed by clients remotely. This gives Rust the ability to be on the server end of a multitier web application as well as on the client side. Additionally, this chapter will talk about considering offensive and defensive programming practices to make your programs more resilient and more resistant to attack. This includes the idea of design by contract, guaranteeing that a program acts exactly the way it is expected to.

Chapter 12

Rust is considered a systems programming language, so we will investigate how to interact with the system. We'll start by writing programs to extend data structures, including some built-in data structures. We'll also take a look at how to interact with the Windows Registry to store and retrieve information. Finally, we'll introduce functionality to get information about the system, including process listings.

Chapter 13

We're going to take the systems programming idea and talk about an essential aspect of programming that is often overlooked; whether you are writing a system service or something that is user-focused, you should always be generating logs. We'll take a look at how to write to both syslog as well as the Windows Event Log. On top of that, we'll take a look at how to write directly to hardware on a Raspberry Pi using the General Purpose Input Output (GPIO) header on the single-board computer.

Chapter 14

Early in the book, we covered data collections in the form of arrays and vectors. Data collections are such a useful feature, though, that we spend this chapter on different types of data collections, including linked lists, queues, stacks, and binary search trees.

Chapter 15

There are some fun and useful ideas that are left over and covered in this chapter. First, recursion is a common way to tackle programming problems, so we take a look at how to address some problems using recursion. We'll also look at how to use Rust to write machine learning programs using third-party libraries. Finally, we will be writing unit tests in Rust, which are ways to ensure that a function does what it is meant to do. This can also be a way to try to break a function. A library included in Rust makes it easy to write tests, which should be a practice always used when writing programs.

PROVIDING FEEDBACK

We hope that *Beginning Rust Programming* will be of benefit to you and that you create some amazing programs with Rust. We've done our best to eliminate errors, but sometimes they do slip through. If you find an error, please let our publisher know. Visit the book's web page, `www.wiley.com/go/beginningrust`, and click the Errata link to find a form to use to identify the problem.

Thanks for choosing *Beginning Rust Programming*.

1

Game of Life: The Basics

IN THIS CHAPTER, YOU WILL LEARN THE FOLLOWING:

➤ How to create a new project using Cargo

➤ How to use variables in Rust

➤ How to use basic functions in Rust, including returning values and passing parameters

➤ How basic control mechanisms work

In 1970, British mathematician John Horton Conway devised a game using cellular automata. In October of that year, Martin Gardner wrote about the game in his monthly column Mathematical Games in *Scientific American*. It's a game with simple rules, which can be played on paper, but honestly, it's more fun to write programs that implement the game. We're going to start the dive into Rust by writing a simple implementation of *Conway's Game of Life*. First we'll talk about the rules so that when we get to implementing it, you'll know what you are looking at.

Imagine a two-dimensional space that consists of cells on both the horizontal and vertical axes. Maybe it's just easier to think about graph paper—row upon row and column upon column of little boxes. Each of these little boxes contains, or at least has the potential to contain, a living creature—a single-celled organism living in a single cell. The game is evolutionary, meaning we cycle through one generation after another, determining whether each cell lives or dies based on the rules of the game. Speaking of those rules, they are as follows:

➤ If a cell is currently alive but it has fewer than two neighbors, it will die because of lack of support.

➤ If a cell is currently alive and has two or three neighbors, it will survive to the next generation.

➤ If a cell is currently alive and has more than three neighbors, it dies from overpopulation (lack of resources).

➤ If a cell is currently dead but has exactly three neighbors, it will come back to life.

To turn this game into code, we need to do a couple of things. First, we need a game grid where all of our little cells are going to live. Second, we need a way to populate the game grid with some living cells. An empty game board won't lead to anything good. Once we have a game board, we can run generations using these rules.

The following is the complete program that will create the game board and also run the checks for whether different cells live or die. Don't worry—you don't have to take it all in at once. We'll go through it step-by-step as we introduce you to Rust.

GAME OF LIFE: THE PROGRAM

The program in this section will create the game board for *Conway's Game of Life* and populate it with an initial generation. This portion of this program will be more than enough to get us started talking about how to begin a Rust program. However, this is not a complete program in the sense that it won't fully implement a useful *Conway's Game of Life*. It's primarily missing the output and generational functions.

```rust
extern crate rand;
use std::{thread, time};

fn census(_world: [[u8; 75]; 75]) -> u16
{
    let mut count = 0;

    for i in 0..74 {
        for j in 0..74 {
            if _world[i][j] == 1
            {
                count += 1;
            }
        }
    }
    count
}
fn generation(_world: [[u8; 75]; 75]) -> [[u8; 75]; 75]
{
    let mut newworld = [[0u8; 75]; 75];

    for i in 0..74 {
        for j in 0..74 {
            let mut count = 0;
            if i>0 {
                count = count + _world[i-1][j];
            }
```

```
                if i>0 && j>0 {
                    count = count + _world[i-1][j-1];
                }
                if i>0 && j<74 {
                    count = count + _world[i-1][j+1];
                }
                if i<74 && j>0 {
                    count = count + _world[i+1][j-1]
                }
                if i<74 {
                    count = count + _world[i+1][j];
                }
                if i<74 && j<74 {
                    count = count + _world[i+1][j+1];
                }
                if j>0 {
                    count = count + _world[i][j-1];
                }
                if j<74 {
                    count = count + _world[i][j+1];
                }

                newworld[i][j] = 0;

                if (count <2) && (_world[i][j] == 1) {
                    newworld[i][j] = 0;
                }
                if _world[i][j] == 1 && (count == 2 || count == 3) {
                    newworld[i][j] = 1;
                }
                if (_world[i][j] == 0) && (count == 3) {
                    newworld[i][j] = 1;
                }
            }
        }
    newworld
}

fn main() {
    let mut world = [[0u8; 75]; 75];
    let mut generations = 0;

    for i in 0..74 {
        for j in 0..74 {
            if rand::random() {
                world[i][j] = 1;
            } else {
            world[i][j] = 0;
            }
        }
    }
}
```

STARTING WITH CARGO

Although you can certainly use just the Rust compiler, `rustc`, Rust comes with a utility that can be used to create the files and directory structure necessary to build a program that could go beyond a single file if needed. To get started, we can run `cargo new life` to create everything we need initially.

What you will get is a directory named `src`, which contains a single file, `main.rs`. Initially, you will have a simple hello, world program in that file, which means there is at least one line of code you will need to delete if you want to do something interesting. The file does, though, contain the bones of a main function. If you are familiar with C programming, you are familiar with the main function. This is the entry point for your program. When the compiler runs, the resulting executable will point to the chunk of code that results from whatever is in your main function. This function is essential for your program to do anything, because the compiler will look for it in order to know where to link the entry point (which is just an address in the `.text` segment of the resulting assembly language code).

In addition to the `src` directory and the `main.rs` file, where you will be doing all your development work initially, there is a `Cargo.toml` file. This is the configuration file used by Cargo, written in Tom's Obvious, Minimal Language (TOML). It's an easy language to use, and Cargo will put almost everything you will need into it. We will eventually get into making changes to it, but what you will see initially is metadata about the resulting executable, including your name, your email address, and the version number. Everything is in text, as you can see here in what was created when I ran `cargo new life`:

```
[package]
name = "life"
version = "0.1.0"
authors = ["Ric Messier <kilroy@mydomain.com>"]

[dependencies]
```

You will get something that looks slightly different, of course, since you have neither my name nor my email address. The version will be 0.1.0 initially, and if you actually use *life* as the name of your program, you will get that configured in your `Cargo.toml` file. Cargo takes care of all that for you.

> **NOTE** Don't get too fancy with your naming. This is going to be the name given to the executable that results from building your program. If you get too fancy and try using something like camel case, Cargo will complain. It expects simple naming. If you are unfamiliar, camel case is mixing upper and lowercase letters, usually with the uppercase letter coming in the middle of the word, as in `myProgram`.

Cargo is also used to build your project. To build your executable, you just run `cargo build`. By default, Cargo will build a debug version, which will be dropped into the target/debug folder. If you want a release version rather than a debug version, you have to run `cargo build --release`. This will place your executable into the target/release directory. You can run your program from there, should the build succeed. You will get more than the executable in the target directories.

Here, you can see the contents of the debug directory from a build of the Life program:

DEBUG DIRECTORY LISTING

```
kilroy@milobloom:~/Documents/rust/life/target$ cd debug
kilroy@milobloom:~/Documents/rust/life/target/debug$ ls
build        examples     life         life.dSYM
deps         incremental  life.d       native
```

The file named `life` is the executable, and the debug symbols are in the file named `life.dSYM`. This is useful in the case where you need to perform debugging using a debugger that will make use of these symbols to keep track of where in the program it is so that it can show not only the assembly language representation of the program but also the source code, which is likely far more meaningful than assembly language to most people. For our purposes, you won't need the debug symbols, unless you really want them, since I'll have done all the debugging to ensure all the code compiles and runs on the version of Rust that is current as of this writing.

PUTTING THE PIECES TOGETHER

Once you have created your new project using Cargo, you can start adding code, typically to the `main.rs` file. Everything we're doing going forward will be in the `main.rs` file unless specified otherwise. We'll go through the program a little at a time to explain it all. We're going to try to keep the bouncing around the program to a minimum, though there will be a little of that. To begin with, though, we'll start at the top of the file.

Bringing In External Functionality

No matter what kind of program you're writing, you'll likely need to bring in functionality from outside your own code. There are a couple of different ways to do that. We can talk about both of them here since both are in use in our Life program. The relevant code fragment is shown here. You will notice that a few different things are going on here that may be slightly different from what you're used to in other programming languages.

```
extern crate rand;
use std::{thread, time};
```

Rust uses libraries called *crates* to store external, reusable functionality. No one should be reinventing the wheel every time they write a program, so you'll probably use a lot of crates as you go. The difference between the previous two lines is the first one refers to an external crate, meaning it's a package available outside of the standard library. The library we're using here is one that will give us the ability to generate random numbers. When it comes to populating the game board on the initial world creation, you can (1) do it by hand as the programmer, (2) allow a user to do it by hand using some configuration, or (3) generate the world using random values. We'll choose the third approach on this initial pass through the world, so we need to have functions that can generate random values for us. This is not functionality included in the standard library. The `extern` keyword indicates the compiler needs to be looking elsewhere for the library.

Speaking of the standard library, the second line in the previous code brings in functionality from the standard library. We are pulling in two separate modules from the standard library, but rather than taking up two lines to do it, we're compressing it onto a single line. The { } you see are borrowed from Unix and they are used to mean "insert each of the values in the set contained within these brackets to complete the expression." What we are doing is just a shorthand notation that will achieve the same results as if we'd written the following two lines. This works only if you are importing functionality from the same location.

```
use std::thread;
use std::time;
```

You may be familiar with the idea of importing functionality. In a language like C, you'd include the same functionality from the C libraries using these lines:

```
#include <threads.h>
#include <time.h>
```

Other languages have the same concept of importing external functionality. In Objective-C, for instance, you can use @import. In Swift, you would just use import. C++ inherits the same include statements that C uses. One of the differences between C/C++ and other languages is that C/C++ makes use of a preprocessor that replaces directives like #include with actual C code. The compiler never sees the #include statement because it gets replaced by the preprocessor before the compiler gets to it. C++ is really just another preprocessor. All C++ code gets converted to actual C, which is then passed into the C compiler. Not all languages have a preprocessor. Rust makes use of these import statements in conjunction with Cargo, which acts less as a preprocessor and more as a coordinator.

As mentioned, the extern keyword indicates we are using an external library. We rely on Cargo to make sure that the library is in place and built so that when it comes time to compile the program, all external references can be successfully resolved. This means we need to add a line to our Cargo.toml file. In the [dependencies] section, we need to tell Cargo that we're going to require a library. As you can see in the following code, we provide the name of the library as well as the version number necessary for our program to work. This last part can be replaced with an * to indicate that any version will work, but you may need a specific version, since different versions will sometimes have different functionality, as well as different signatures.

```
[dependencies]
rand = "0.7.2"
```

The signature is important, because it identifies the parameters a function expects to receive as well as the value or values the function will return. If the program we're writing doesn't make use of the function in the same way as it is specified in the library version being used, the compilation will fail. As a result, it's important to know which version of the library you're using to ensure that you're using functions in the same way as they're specified in that one version.

Namespaces

This brings up the idea of namespaces, though this is not what Rust calls them. It's a useful concept to talk about, though, even if it's not terminology that Rust uses. Namespaces are common things, and they are especially used in object-oriented languages like C# or C++. They are also used in containers, which are ways of virtualizing applications. A namespace really is just a container. It's a way of placing a lot of related things into the same place in order to make referring to those things consistent. This is why bringing up namespaces here makes some sense. Earlier, we brought in functionality from modules. You can think of all the properties and functions within those modules as belonging to the same namespace, by which I mean that in order to refer to them, you'd use the same naming structure.

One of the guidelines for writing programs is that we try to name functions and variables in ways that will make sense to people who are writing programs using the functions and variables we've created. In doing that, unfortunately, many modules or libraries will have functions or properties that use the same names. We need a way to differentiate one from another.

Consider your house. You have a number of rooms in your house. Each room has at least one light switch. If I were to tell you to turn off the light switch, how would you know which light switch to turn off? The room provides the context, or the namespace, that will help us make sense of the request. Then I can say turn off the light switch in the living room, and you'll know exactly what to do. You've already seen something along these lines in the previous code. When we brought in functionality from the standard library, we used `std::thread`, as one example. That expression provides us the namespace, essentially, to differentiate a thread out of the standard library from a thread from a different library.

We can take this example a little bit further, which will also move us ahead a bit. Using the Rust syntax, I can tell Rust to turn off the light in the living room using something like `livingroom::switch.off()`. This gives me the context, or namespace, up front. I'm using `livingroom` as the module I want to use functionality from. I'm going to switch out of the `livingroom` module, and then I'll call `off()` as a function or method on that switch object.

We have to keep using the namespace to refer to any object we use from modules we're making use of (`livingroom::`) in order to ensure we're clear about exactly which object we'll be using. That way, the compiler has nothing to guess about, and perhaps as importantly, when it comes to any other programmer reading what we've written, it's clear. This explicitness is something we'll keep coming back to when using Rust. Everything is explicit and is required to be explicit so that there are no guessing games or misunderstandings when it comes to what we've written versus what the compiler is generating for us. It's, frankly, one of Rust's charms.

GENERATING THE GAME GRID

With our functionality imported, we can get started writing the program. As mentioned, this is mostly going to be a linear process from the standpoint of reading the source code. As best as we can, we'll go from the top to the bottom of the source code. The one deviation is going to be that we'll start with the main function, or the entry point to the program.

One reason for putting the main function at the bottom of the source code, even though it's really the start of the program, is a holdover from C. In the C programming language, as well as with many other programming languages, you can't use something that hasn't been defined. When you write your main function, you're going to be calling other functions. If you try to call them before they've been defined or implemented (which is a definition, by definition), you'll get a compiler error because the compiler doesn't know what it is in order to match it up against how you're using it. This is that signature thing again. If I define a function as taking two integers but you try calling it with an array of characters, that's not going to work well. The compiler should flag that, but it can't if it doesn't know what it's supposed to look like before it's used.

In Rust, you can put the main function at the top of your source code since it will hold off on passing judgment on whether you've called a function correctly until it actually sees the definition. As an exercise, take the source code from this chapter and move the main function starting with `fn main` all the way to the last } and put it at the top of the file, right under where we pull in the modules we're going to be using. When you build, it will build successfully. As we go forward and you start writing your own Rust programs, you can feel free to put the main function, or any function for that matter, wherever in the file you want. The compiler won't error on you simply because of that.

DISSECTING MAIN

We're going to the bottom of the file and looking at the main function, but in pieces because it's a fairly long function. There are also some critical components of the main function here, so we'll try to keep it slow and manageable so you'll easily understand not only the syntax of the language but also the important features that separate Rust from other languages. Where it's helpful, we'll take a look at how Rust compares with other common languages that you may be familiar with.

Defining Functions

Functions are a common feature of most languages today, though you may hear the term *method* used sometimes to describe the same sort of feature. A function is a way of putting code and data together in a smallish block. When we create functions, we create the ability to reuse a set of code over and over without having to rewrite the same code every time we want to use it. Typically, functions take parameters and may also return values. This means we can pass data into the function to operate on, and then the function can return the result of any work done to the calling function.

Rust requires the use of functions, which differs from some languages you may be familiar with. Python, for instance, does not require that you use any function. If you want, you can write a Python script without using any functions at all. Other scripting languages, similarly, don't require the use of any function. Of course, Rust isn't a scripting language like Python is. Unlike Python, Perl, or other scripting languages, Rust uses a compiler to generate an executable that is used when a user wants to run the program. Even if you do use functions when you're writing a Python program, you don't have to create a main function, which explicitly tells the interpreter (the compiler in the case of Rust) where to start the program execution.

```
fn main() {
```

Here, you can see the definition of the main function in Rust. This is a basic definition. We use `fn` to indicate that what is coming is a function. This is similar to a language like Python, which uses `def` to indicate the definition of a function. Swift uses `func` to indicate what is coming is a function. Even though these languages are said to be C-like—because some of the syntax and control structures are similar between C and languages like Swift, Python, and Rust—the function definition in C is different. A C main function is defined as follows:

```
int main (int argc, char **argv) {
```

Rather than indicating up front that what we have is a function, we start with the variable type that the function will return at the end. In C, you have to specify some datatype to return, even if it's void, which is no datatype, indicating there is no return value. Languages like Rust may never return a value and if there's no value being returned, there's no indication of a value being returned, as you can see in the declaration of the main function earlier. We can absolutely return values from any function we want, and you'll see how that works later on in this chapter when we take a look at some other functions in our program. Similarly, the C declaration of the main function includes command-line parameters being passed into the main function. This is not required, just as it's not required in our Rust program. When it's not required, we simply don't include it.

Functions, as much as anything, are scope definitions. When we have data in a function, the data stops being available once we pass outside of the function. This means we need a way to indicate where the function starts and where it stops. Python likes the idea of using white space to clearly define scope. It's part of the language definition. There are no begin/end blocks with Python. You simply have to pay attention to the level of indentation. Personally, I'm not a fan of using white space as part of the syntax or definition of the language. Fortunately, Rust again follows C here. C uses curly braces (or brackets) to indicate the beginning and ending of any block of code. We start a function with a { and close it with a }. This may be harder to parse visually than the white space used in Python, but you can just use good indentation practices to give you that visual parsing ability without it being forced on you.

At this point, we have a declaration of our main function as well as the start of the code block. We can move right into the rest of the function.

Defining Variables

Some languages are really picky about where you define variables. It's usually a good practice to define all your variables at the top of a function, but it's not required by the language definition or the compiler. It makes it easier to understand what is going on if you know exactly where to look for the different elements of a function. Defining variables mid-function can make it harder to debug or read the program later on because you might miss the declaration to know what datatype is being used when you read through complex or longer functions. Using this guidance, the declarations (with one exception, which we'll get to later) are done at the top of the function.

```
let mut world = [[0u8; 75]; 75];
let mut generations = 0;
```

We're defining two variables in our main function. One of these is the game grid, which is a multidimensional array. Before we get to that aspect of the definition, we should address the rest of it, starting from the left side. First, we declare a variable using the keyword let. If we want, we can do a simple declaration of a variable by saying something like let count = 0;. This indicates that we have a variable named count that we have set to an initial value of 0. Rust will infer the datatype because we haven't specified it. Since it's defined, we can go on our merry way using the variable count.

> **NOTE** *When it comes to naming variables, you can use letters, digits, or the underscore character. You can't use special characters in the name of a variable. There are some conventions when it comes to naming, which the compiler will help you with, making suggestions when you aren't following the naming conventions. The starting character in a variable name has to be either a letter or an underscore. It's also worth noting that variable names are case sensitive. Camel case is commonly used in Java and other languages, but it is used in Rust only in specific situations, which you'll learn about in later chapters.*

This is a bit of a gotcha, however, which brings us to the second keyword in our declaration lines. It's important to note that Rust uses what the developers call *immutable variables* by default. You can quibble, like me, with the term immutable variable since variable, by definition, means changing and immutable means not changing. The term immutable variable means something that's going to change but that isn't going to change. Essentially, if you have an immutable variable, you have a constant, because it won't change. From a language and compilation perspective, an immutable variable is different from a constant.

Linguistic quibbles aside, this is an important aspect to the language. Because it's such a subtle thing, you'll see it come up a lot as we talk about different variables and how they're used throughout the rest of this book. A constant, from the perspective of the language and the compiler, is essentially an alias. Compilers, like those commonly used in the C language, will go through and simply replace the term for what it refers to. For instance, again using C as an easy way to demonstrate this concept, here's how we would declare a constant in a C program:

```
#define MYCONST 42
```

This indicates that we have a term, MYCONST, that refers to the value 42. The C preprocessor will run through all the code where this definition applies and replace anywhere it finds MYCONST with the value 42. The only purpose MYCONST serves is to make it easier to change the value MYCONST at any point and have that change be made across an entire program. It also provides some self-documentation if you give it a meaningful name. If you were to use MAX_X, for instance, you'd know that it would be the maximum value along the x-axis on a graph, potentially. This is more useful than just a raw number.

A variable that can't be changed is different. For a start, you can't set a constant to the result of a function call, because it's not known at compile time. You can set a variable to the return value from a function call, though once the value is set it can't be changed. A variable that can't be changed is also protected from modification, so you can always be sure that the value you expect to be there will be there—or at least that the value that was set at one point hasn't been corrupted. This helps with any concurrent programming since you can use a variable without fear of it being modified mid-use by another thread.

> **NOTE** There is a concept in programming called a pure function. A pure function is one that will return the same value every time the function is called, given the same set of inputs. Additionally, a pure function causes no side effects, meaning there is no alteration of variables or arguments. Using non-mutable variables can help with the implementation of pure functions because we can protect against side effects. A pure function, because it has predictable outcomes, can be "proved," meaning we can test against the output to be sure the function is working as expected. This testing repeatability using automation can result in more robust programs.

To make a change to a variable during program execution, we have to specify that it is mutable, meaning we expect it to change. We set a mutable variable with the mut keyword. Both of the variables being declared in the main function in this program are mutable. One of these variables is the game grid. This has to be mutable because we're going to keep changing all the values as we go through one generation to another. Cells are going to die and be born, so we need to change values in each of the positions of the array. The other variable is the generation count. This is not an absolutely necessary value other than it's interesting to keep track of what generation number we're in as the game iterates through generation after generation. Since we're going to increment that value after each generation, it has to be mutable.

It's always worth considering whether you have to have a value that is mutable or not mutable. If you're going to set it once and not touch it again, you don't need to have it mutable. You can protect your program by just leaving it immutable. This is where the compiler is helpful. If you set a value once on a variable you have indicated is mutable and then don't change it, the compiler will prompt you that it should probably be left immutable. Similarly, if you have a value that simply should not change at all, leave it immutable and if any part of the program tries to change it, the compiler will complain about it.

This compiler error can help you track down bugs faster since your compile will simply fail, and you'll have to decide whether the variable can be mutable or if the change in value should simply never have happened to begin with. If the compiler hadn't errored on you, you would've had a bug in your program later on when a value you didn't expect to change got changed. It's this explicit programming that can lead to more robust programs—if you want to change a value, you have to think about it and then indicate that the value is going to change at some point.

Datatypes

The game grid itself is where we get explicit about the type of data that is going to be used. As discussed earlier, Rust may infer the datatype based on the value that's being put into a variable, but we can also be explicit about it, and you can see this in the declaration of the world variable. In addition to being an array, which we'll deal with shortly, you can see that the world identifier has an interesting notation where the datatype could or should be. What you'll see there is `0u8`. Rust is a strongly typed language, and you can't just move from one type to another willy-nilly.

The `0u8` is saying that we'll populate this variable with a 0 value but that the 0 value is going to be an unsigned 8-bit integer. This allows us to initialize the value at the same time we tell Rust (the compiler in this case) the datatype to expect. This means we never expect to get a value larger than 255 in this field. Because it's unsigned, we aren't ever going to have to accommodate a signed bit, so we can take values from 0 to 255 in a u8 datatype. As you might expect, if we can support unsigned, we can support signed as well. A signed 8-bit integer would be declared by i8.

This is another area where Rust lets you be as explicit as you want to be. Depending on your memory requirements, you can pick whatever size you want for your integer values. You can use 8-, 16-, 32-, 64-, or 128-bit values, both signed and unsigned. This means that you can declare variables to be i8, i16, i32, i64, i128, u8, u16, u32, u64, or u128. You can also specify the size of your floating-point values, though you get the choice of f32 and f64 only. The default floating-point size is 64 bits because it has no performance penalty on modern processors but has considerably more precision.

We are not limited to just numbers, though. We can also create *char* values. A char in Rust is a 4-byte value, which allows for support of Unicode values as well as accents and emoji characters. It's perfectly legal in Rust to do the following, assuming your editor allows you to enter this character:

```
let emo_char = '☺';
```

Another common datatype is the Boolean value. A Boolean value, used for logic operations, will evaluate to true or false. If we wanted to create a Boolean value and use explicit type annotation, we'd use the following statement:

```
let yes_no: bool = true;
```

This statement lets us declare the datatype while setting the value at the same time. Someone who is accustomed to other languages may find it difficult to get used to using the `variable: datatype` notation ahead of an equal sign to set the value. It can also be challenging to read initially if you're accustomed to languages like C, C++, Java, C#, and others where you indicate the datatype on the left-hand side, ahead of the variable name. In this case, Rust uses the keyword `let` to indicate there's a variable here, and so it needs another way of declaring variables. It might be even more awkward to use `let datatype variable = value`. Either way, we don't get a vote here, so you'll have to accept `let datatype variable = value` as the way you declare and set initial values on variables.

It's worth noting that, just because you don't want this to turn into a gotcha, the variables we created are immutable. The value can't be changed. This also raises the importance of naming. Using a variable name yes_no on a Boolean value that can't change after it's been set to true isn't really a good way of naming it. It is always going to, effectively, be yes and will never be no. So, two lessons from our earlier declarations. Always think about whether you are going to make a variable mutable and then make sure you are giving the variable a meaningful name so that you can read and understand it later. Or, perhaps, someone else can read and understand it.

Arrays

One of the variables we are going to work with is an array. More specifically, it's a multidimensional array. An array isn't a datatype itself. It's a primitive data structure. There are better ways of handling data that is tightly related and you want to be able to address it directly, as in either walking through the entire data stream or just going straight to a particular value. The problem is that none of the other ways of handling this data structure can handle multiple dimensions. Imagine a single-dimension array, or even better, just take a look at Figure 1.1, which shows a single-dimension array. This would be a chunk of contiguous memory where you would store a number of values.

One important aspect to consider here is that when we are working with arrays, all the values will have the same datatype. In our case, we have a collection of unsigned 8-bit values. In reality, we're only going to be using two values. We could use an array of Boolean values, true or false, but using unsigned integers means we can do arithmetic directly with the values we have. This gives us a couple of ways of keeping track of how many neighbors our cells have—we just add up all the values or we check to see whether there is a value and then increment. For our "world," we are going to be using a multidimensional array, which in practice is going to look like Figure 1.2, though in reality it will just be a contiguous section of memory, just like a single-dimension array.

FIGURE 1.1: Single-dimension array

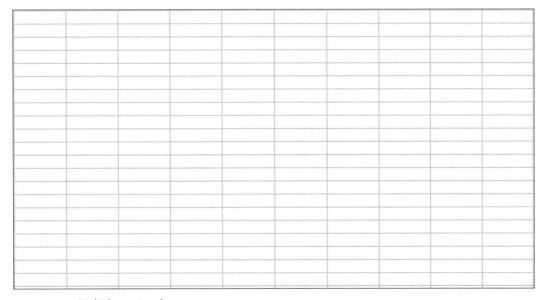

FIGURE 1.2: Multidimensional array

If we were going simple, we could define a one-dimensional array using the following declaration. It creates an array of 15 integers. Notice the way we indicate the datatype being used. Rather than using *variable: datatype* as we have done previously, we indicate that it's an array using the square brackets (`[]`). Inside the square brackets we include the datatype, followed by a semicolon, then the size of the array. If you wanted, you could also include a set of initial data. That could be done with a comma-separated list of values inside square brackets, such as [3, 6, 9, 14, 2, 15, 16, 90, 145]. You then have an initialized array of values. Again, without the `mut` keyword, we can't change any values once they have been set, though you don't have to set them when you declare the array. However, one thing you do need to do is make sure you have filled the array to the size you have declared.

```
let list: [i32; 15];
```

If you were to use the following code, you'd get a compiler error. The error would tell you that an array was defined with 15 elements but that only 8 elements were found. Rust expects a fixed-size array to be populated to the length of the array. If you are going to use only 8 values, you should declare an array with only 8 values. Rust sees a declaration of an array as essentially a datatype. `i32; 15` is the datatype the variable is defined as. Anything that doesn't exactly match that fails the type check.

```
let array: [i32; 15];
array = [3, 43, 12, 18, 90, 32, 8, 19];
```

In our case, we are working with a multidimensional array. If you wanted to declare a multidimensional array in C, you could use `int array[10][10]`. This says you have an array that is 10 values wide by 10 values deep. If you wanted a three-dimensional array, you would just tack on an additional number in square brackets. In Swift, it would look like `var array = Int[][]`, which is an unbounded multidimensional array. No size is specified in either direction. In Rust, we don't close the square brackets to create the additional dimension. A multidimensional array is created using the following code:

```
let array: [15]; 15];
```

This is an array where no datatype has been specified. If you want to specify a datatype, you need to initialize the array. Pick a value and then the datatype, as we did here. This means something like `[[95u16; 10]; 10]` if you want an unsigned 16-bit integer array with the value 95 placed in all the cells. The other option is to simply not declare the datatype and let Rust infer it when you initialize it for real. We'll get to one way to initialize the array momentarily.

To access array elements, you use the `[]` notation. If you wanted to get to position 5 in your array, you'd use `array[4]`, keeping in mind that arrays are 0-based, meaning you start accessing arrays starting with an index of 0. If you had an array you had defined as `[15]`, you'd access the 15 elements using the values 0–14. Trying to use `[15]` to get to a value in that array would generate an error because you would've gone beyond the defined bounds of the array.

Control Structures

Any programming language needs to have control structures. Programmers cannot live by variables and declarations and functions alone. We need things like conditionals where we compare something and make a decision based on that comparison. This might be an `if` statement, for instance. We also need loops. For the main function here, we are going to look at one type of loop, which is a `for` loop.

A `for` loop might use a counter that gets incremented each pass through the loop. When it comes to arrays, we can make use of the loop counter as an index into the array. You can see that in the following code:

```
for i in 0..74 {
    for j in 0..74 {
        if rand::random() {
            world[i][j] = 1;
        } else {
            world[i][j] = 0;
        }
    }
}
```

Let's deconstruct just one of these and then talk about why there are two here. The line is `for i in 0..74 {`. The `0..74` is a set of all integer values starting with 0 and ending with 74. The `..` indicates a range of values. Since we are going to use the variable *i* as an index to the array, we need to start at 0. We don't have to start at 0 just because it's a `for` loop. This would be similar to a C loop that looked like the following, which does the same thing but just expresses the range using less than or greater than:

```
for (i=0; i<75; i++) {
```

Rust is closer to Python than it is to C when it comes to writing for loops. In Python, the same loop would look like the line that follows. In Rust, the range is more elegantly expressed with `0..75`, where Python uses the keyword `range`, which generates a range of values starting at 0, ending at the value passed to `range` and incrementing by 1 each pass through the `for` loop. The behavior is the same as the `for` loop written in Rust earlier.

```
for i in range(74):
```

We are using nested loops, which means we have two separate `for` loops. Without the nested loops, we'd end up with a diagonal line through our two-dimensional array, because the same value would be used on the x-axis as the y-axis. In this case, we use *i* as our row counter and *j* as our column counter. For every iteration of *i*, we run through the entire row by running through each possible column using the *j* variable. Speaking of variables, the `for` statement automatically declares and creates our *i* and *j* for us. You'll also note that the `mut` keyword is implicit in the creation of the two variables, since the value has to change as we iterate over the range of values. The loop wouldn't work well if the loop index didn't iterate. Think about the C implementation of the same loop. If you left off the i++, which increments the index value, the loop would just keep going endlessly because the condition that keeps the loop going (i<74) would always be met since *i* never increases. It remains at 0 without that incrementing.

The heart of creating the world is inside the loops we have used. The code for that follows, and it uses random values to determine whether the cell is alive or dead in the initial generation. We call the function `random()` out of the `rand` crate, which we included at the top of the program. This function generates a Boolean. And this brings us to another control structure. We are using `if` as a decision point. If we get a true out of `rand::random()`, then we set the cell with a value of 1. Otherwise, we set the cell with a value of 0. The `else` keyword indicates that if the first condition is not true, then the enclosed block of code is executed. Using `else` saves us from having to use another condition. The only thing we care about with an `else` statement is whether or not the first condition is true.

```
if rand::random() {
    world[i][j] = 1;
} else {
    world[i][j] = 0;
}
```

You may notice that the initial condition doesn't have parentheses around it. You will find this is common in Rust programming. In fact, the Rust compiler will let you know that you don't need them if you include them. As someone who has been writing programs in multiple languages over multiple decades, I find the use of parentheses clarifies the logic of my expression. Some languages require that you put the expression in parentheses. Rust is not one of those languages. Leave the parentheses out unless you absolutely have to have them to get the right value out of a complex Boolean expression.

To set the value of each cell in our multidimensional array, we use the two sets of square brackets to indicate the row and column of the cell. Again, we use the index values *i* and *j* to indicate where we are in the "world" we are creating.

Although this is the end of the main function in this version of the program, there are pieces missing to create a fully functional program. We have a pair of functions left to talk about, and neither of them get called. The fact that you have written code that never gets called will also generate warnings from the Rust compiler. Rust wants you to know that you should probably call the functions you have taken the time to write, just to make sure you put the functions into the right program. However, even if we aren't yet going to call these functions, we are going to move into talking about them so that you have a broader palette of colors to write your own programs with after just this chapter.

LOOKING AT MORE FUNCTION FUNCTIONS

We'll look at two additional functions for our Game of Life program. This will bring up two additional features of functions you will need to understand. The first of these is returning values from the function. This is a common feature of functions in programming languages. You don't just call a function to introduce a chunk of code, even if it's code you want to reuse. Ultimately, that function may create a new value that needs to be returned to the calling function. The calling function needs that returned value to make a decision. Of course, in order for the function to perform a meaningful task, it needs data. This means we must be able to pass data into the function so that it can act on it. We have to pass parameters into our functions, which is something we didn't do with our main function.

Returning Values

The next function we'll look at is the one called `census()`, which takes a count of all the living cells in the world. This doesn't have any direct relation to the necessary functionality for the Game of Life program, but it's a useful statistic. We want to know when our world becomes unpopulated, if it should ever get to that point. If our world did become fully unpopulated, it would probably be a good point to stop running through successive generations since it's not possible, given the rules of the game, for cells to spring to life without any neighbors. The return value could be checked to see when it becomes 0 and the game could be stopped at that point, just as an example of the use of census from a pure game play perspective.

For our purposes, it gives us a chance to talk about return values. The following is the census function, which includes the line at the top that tells us we are returning a value. The important part from that perspective is at the end of the function declaration, -> u16. This tells us the function is going to return an unsigned 16-bit integer. This is a simple return type. In practice, you can return essentially any value you can make use of as a variable.

```
fn census(_world: [[u8; 75]; 75]) -> u16
{
    let mut count = 0;

    for i in 0..74 {
        for j in 0..74 {
            if _world[i][j] == 1
            {
                count += 1;
            }
        }
    }
    count
}
```

In languages like C, you have to indicate that you are returning a value using something like a return keyword. Rust doesn't use that. To return a value from a function, you just provide the value or variable you are returning on a line by itself at the end of the function. This is because Rust is considered an expression-oriented language. In an expression-oriented language, every construction or block is considered an expression, and as an expression, it yields a value. Because a function is an expression in Rust, it yields a value. The value the expression evaluates to for a Rust function is the last line of that function.

> **NOTE** We haven't talked about an important construct as yet, but since it's not essential to developing programs, we can just drop it in here as a note. When you are writing programs, you should be commenting. This is not a necessary task, because as you can see none of the Rust code provided thus far has been commented in any way inside the code. All the comments are coming in the text of the book, so code comments seem redundant to this point. Writing comments is simple, and we use a common approach. When you want to insert a line comment, you use // and then place the comment after them. From the // to the end of the line is a comment, regardless where on the line the // are placed. You can also use /// if you want to use a document comment. Using document comments, where you can use Markdown for formatting, gives you the ability to generate documentation for your project by just running cargo doc. The cargo utility creates your documentation for you, placing it in target/ doc.

Think about it this way, since you may be less familiar with expression-oriented languages. Everything you do in Rust is intended to create a result of some sort. All of the "things" you are doing—setting variables, introducing control structures, calling functions—are expressions when they return a value. Most programming languages you may be familiar with use statements. A statement doesn't return a value. In Rust, we can and do use statements. One difference between an expression and a statement is the use of the semicolon. You may have noticed that there is no semicolon at the end of the line that just says count at the end of the function. That's because the function is an expression and the return value is whatever is in the variable named count. Because expression-oriented languages are, or at least can be, different from other languages, we'll keep returning to the concept so that you can understand the differences between expression-oriented languages and statement-oriented languages.

The rest of the function provided here is fairly straightforward, especially since it includes the nested loops we've already looked at to work through the entire world, or game grid. One note, if you aren't familiar with it, is the line where we increment the number of cells that are alive in the variable count. We use count += 1, which is a shorthand way of saying count = count + 1. Rather than type additional characters, especially repeating the name of the variable, we just use a shorthand notation, which evaluates to the same thing. In the end, we get the same result, no matter which way we write it. Either one will work just fine. This is a way of writing incrementing variables that has been used in C for decades and has been borrowed by several other C-like programming languages.

One thing we can do in Rust that isn't possible in other languages, like C, is to return multiple values. This is done through the use of tuples. A *tuple*, speaking mathematically, is a finite ordered list. For our purposes, it's a list and it's finite. The ordered part is relevant only in the sense that you need to know which order the values are in. This isn't to say that it has to be ordered in the way that ordered often means (smallest integer to largest or alphanumeric order). What we need to be able to do is just pull the values back since we aren't naming them.

To return a value as a tuple, you can just use a comma-separated list bracketed with parentheses: (val1, val2, val3). When it comes to retrieving the values on the other side, where you are calling the function you can use a tuple in the same way you did at the end of the function. Here, you can see how you'd retrieve values from a function that returned a tuple:

```
let i: i32;
let b: bool;
(i, b) = function1();
```

The one other aspect of this function we didn't talk about is also in the declaration line, but we can save that for the next section.

Passing Parameters

This will be the last function for this pass at the Life program. We're going to look at how we run through the entire world to determine what cells live and die based on the rules of the game. There are a couple of ways we can go about this. This implementation assumes the world is bounded rather than wrapping around on itself. This is primarily the case because I simply can't imagine how you'd take a two-dimensional grid and connect the left end with the right end while simultaneously connecting the top and bottom. This is the problem with using Cartesian coordinates, assuming the top left of the two-dimensional array is the fixed point that everything else is relative to. This is one reason we end up with a longish implementation, because we always have to check to see whether we are at the boundary of the grid.

```
fn generation(world: [[u8; 75]; 75]) -> [[u8; 75]; 75]
{
    let mut newworld = [[0u8; 75]; 75];

    for i in 0..74 {
        for j in 0..74 {
            let mut count = 0;
            if i>0 {
                count = count + world[i-1][j];
            }
            if i>0 && j>0 {
                count = count + world[i-1][j-1];
            }
            if i>0 && j<74 {
                count = count + world[i-1][j+1];
            }
            if i<74 && j>0 {
                count = count + world[i+1][j-1]
            }
            if i<74 {
                count = count + world[i+1][j];
            }
            if i<74 && j<74 {
                count = count + world[i+1][j+1];
            }
            if j>0 {
                count = count + world[i][j-1];
            }
            if j<74 {
                count = count + world[i][j+1];
            }

            newworld[i][j] = 0;

            if (count <2) && (world[i][j] == 1) {
                newworld[i][j] = 0;
            }
            if world[i][j] == 1 && (count == 2 || count == 3) {
                newworld[i][j] = 1;
            }
            if (world[i][j] == 0) && (count == 3) {
                newworld[i][j] = 1;
            }
        }
    }
    newworld
}
```

We're going to focus, to start with, on the function declaration, since that's where we pass parameters. However, there are some serious gotchas here that will unfold over time because they are such complex issues. Simply, to pass a parameter into a function, you essentially declare the parameter in the function declaration. You indicate the name of the variable being passed in so that it can be referred to later by name. You also need to indicate the datatype being used.

When you are calling functions, remember that calling parameters (the things we are talking about here) are placed on the stack so the called function can access them. Local variables are also on the stack, as well as other important data. I'm bringing this up here because one of the reasons for declaring the parameter is so that the compiler knows how much space to allocate on the stack for the parameter when the function is called. Additionally, of course, the compiler needs to be able to match the declared function (its signature) with the function call. If the parameters passed in the function call don't match the function's signature, the compiler will generate an error.

Note that in the declaration we are not only taking a multidimensional array in as a parameter, we're also returning a multidimensional array. There is a reason for this. Rust is a language that is built around memory safety. Some languages use the ideas of pass by reference or pass by value. Pass by value means that the value itself is passed into the function. Pass by reference means the memory location of the data is passed into the function. Pass by value is essentially read-only. With only the value, the function can't make any changes to the data, so there are no side effects. The variable that is passed into the function is untouched when the function is done and execution is passed to the calling function.

Pass by reference allows the called function to make changes to the data because direct access to the memory location where the data is stored is provided to the called function. This would allow the called function to make changes to that memory location so that when execution passes back to the calling function, the changed value is available in that variable in the calling function. You can see a simple representation of this idea expressed in C, since the C programming language allows this type of behavior, in Figure 1.3. In this example, a variable named *x* is created that has a storage location, shown in the box in the center. Initially, that box contains the value 10. We pass the address of that box (the & in front of *x* indicates we are passing the address, not the value) to the function foo. In foo, we make it clear that we are getting an address by putting an * in front of *x*. In the function body, we dereference the variable, meaning we are assigning the value 15 to that address location.

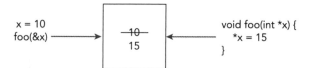

FIGURE 1.3: Passing by reference in C

This is much harder in Rust, and it will take a few passes through to explain so that you can grasp the implications. There are ways to pass values back and forth in Rust, but there is a fundamental design decision in Rust as a language that makes it a lot harder. In Rust, only one function can ever own a variable, though ownership can change hands. Before we discuss the implications of ownership in the context of this program, you will need to better understand scope.

Scope

Scope is generally an easy concept, especially since most if not all programming languages implement scope in one way or another. Scope, simply, is the space in which you can refer to a variable and have it be understood. A simplified version of one of the loops earlier would be as follows. The variable i here has a clearly defined scope. Anything inside the { } block is the scope of the variable i. This means we can make use of the variable i, and our program will happily compile and run.

```
for i in 0..74 {
    println!("{}", i);
}
```

If we try to make use of the variable outside the block of code inside the brackets, the compiler will generate an error indicating that there is no variable named i in the scope where it is being referred to. Here, you can see the error generated from compiling a Rust program with the for loop from the previous code followed by a println!("{}", i); statement. Not only will the code not run, it simply won't compile.

```
error[E0425]: cannot find value `i` in this scope
  --> test.rs:5:20
   |
5  |     println!("{}", i);
   |                    ^ not found in this scope

error: aborting due to previous error
```

The rules of scope aren't always straightforward, though once you learn them, they are easy enough to remember. Typically, you can say that a variable is contained in a block of code denoted by { }. In a function, any variable defined at the top of the function will go out of scope when the function ends. If you have a block of code that is contained within an if statement, as seen in the function named generation earlier and shown next, the brackets after the if statement define a scope. In the example, the code in that block is just the incrementing of the count variable. If the count variable had been defined inside those brackets, the scope of that variable would be only within those brackets. The variable passes out of scope, as we say, when the brackets close.

```
if i>0 {
    count = count + world[i-1][j];
}
```

In Rust, we have an additional complication. The complication is because of variable ownership. When we call a function with a variable as a parameter, that variable—more specifically, the memory location where the data the variable refers to is stored—becomes the property of the called function. Keep in mind that as soon as a function ends, all variables in that function go out of scope, meaning they are no longer available. In the function definition for generation, you can see we are passing in a variable called world. This is a multidimensional array. As soon as the function generation ends, the memory space allocated for that variable is freed automatically. Because the memory is freed, there is no way to get to the contents of that memory location any longer.

In this case, we can solve it by simply creating a whole new variable. This is done at the top of the function in the line you can see below. We create a new multidimensional array that gets populated with the next generation of our game grid. The current generation will simply disappear once we are done calculating who is going to live, who is going to die, and who is going to be born. In our case, this is a better solution anyway, since we can't make changes to the current world without impacting the rest of the world. If we make a change to any cell in our grid, it will change the determination for subsequent cells. So, instead, we create a brand-new game grid and just swap out the existing one for the new one once we've figured out what the next generation looks like.

```
let mut newworld = [[0u8; 75]; 75];
```

To return the new game grid back to the calling function, we place the variable on a line by itself. Most languages use an explicit return. In C, just as with many other languages, if I want to pass a value back from a function to a calling function, I use the keyword `return`, as in `return x`. Rust, instead, uses an implicit return. The last value in a function becomes the returned value. It goes on a line by itself and does not include a semicolon because it is not a statement. Instead, it's an expression. Expressions don't use semicolons to terminate them as statements do.

Because this is another complex topic in Rust, we'll continue to return to it in coming chapters. There are other ways to return values in Rust. We're just not going to address them here, so we'll save them until later.

COMPILING PROGRAMS

We have a working program at this point. Well, we have working code that needs to be compiled into a program. Rust is not an interpreted language, so we need to generate an executable. In Rust, there are two different ways to handle that task. First, Rust comes with a compiler that can be used to compile any source code. The Rust compiler is a program named `rustc`. This program can be used to generate an executable from any basic Rust source code file. This means that if you don't have any external functionality, you can compile your program with the Rust compiler and you will get an executable.

You may be familiar with some compilers that don't use the name of the program you want as the name of the output executable. Traditionally, for example, C compilers will generate a file called `a.out` when you compile without specifying an output filename. This is an artifact of the executable format that was commonly used on the Unix operating system when C compilers were first developed. Today, we don't usually use the `a.out` executable format, though many C compilers will still default to the traditional output filename. The Rust compiler will generate a file named for the file you are compiling. Here, you can see how that would work using a file named `life.rs`:

```
kilroy@milobloom:~/Documents$ rustc life.rs
kilroy@milobloom:~/Documents$ ls -la life
-rwxr-xr-x  1 kilroy  staff  288052 Jan 29 20:33 life
kilroy@milobloom:~/Documents$ file life
life: Mach-O 64-bit executable x86_64
```

However, if you used `cargo` to create your source code file and the associated directory structure, your source code file won't be named `life.rs`. It will be named `main.rs` by default. We can also use `cargo` to create the executable for us. This is generally a good habit to get into anyway since not only will `cargo` do the compilation, it will also bring in all the external functionality needed.

We'll get more into using external functionality in later chapters. For now, though, we want to build an executable from the project we have with just one source file. If we just run `cargo build` in the project directory, `cargo` will take care of doing the compiling and generating the executable, as you can see here:

```
kilroy@milobloom:~/Documents/rust/life$ cargo build
    Finished dev [unoptimized + debuginfo] target(s) in 0.07s
kilroy@milobloom:~/Documents/rust/life$ cd target/debug/
kilroy@milobloom:~/Documents/rust/life/target/debug$ ls -la
total 1720
drwxr-xr-x@ 12 kilroy  staff     384 Jan 15 19:57 .
drwxr-xr-x   5 kilroy  staff     160 Jan  8 19:08 ..
-rw-r--r--   1 kilroy  staff       0 Dec  3 20:12 .cargo-lock
drwxr-xr-x  26 kilroy  staff     832 Dec  5 19:40 .fingerprint
drwxr-xr-x   8 kilroy  staff     256 Dec  5 19:40 build
drwxr-xr-x  56 kilroy  staff    1792 Jan 15 19:57 deps
drwxr-xr-x   2 kilroy  staff      64 Dec  3 20:12 examples
drwxr-xr-x   5 kilroy  staff     160 Dec  5 19:40 incremental
-rwxr-xr-x   2 kilroy  staff  875812 Jan 15 19:57 life
-rw-r--r--   1 kilroy  staff      99 Jan  9 20:23 life.d
lrwxr-xr-x   1 kilroy  staff      31 Dec  5 19:45 life.dSYM -> deps/life-
1a787212c1e544bc.dSYM
drwxr-xr-x   2 kilroy  staff      64 Dec  3 20:12 native
```

If you are looking closely, you will see that the dev target is what is built and the directory shown is the debug directory. This is the default build target. You can easily build the release target, which is a much cleaner build directory, shown next. Missing is all the debug information, including the file with the debug symbols in it, shown in the previous directory listing but not the one that follows:

```
kilroy@milobloom:~/Documents/rust/life/target/debug$ cd ../release
kilroy@milobloom:~/Documents/rust/life/target/release$ ls -la
total 608
drwxr-xr-x@ 10 kilroy  staff     320 Jan  8 19:08 .
drwxr-xr-x   5 kilroy  staff     160 Jan  8 19:08 ..
-rw-r--r--   1 kilroy  staff       0 Jan  8 19:08 .cargo-lock
drwxr-xr-x  17 kilroy  staff     544 Jan  8 19:08 .fingerprint
drwxr-xr-x   6 kilroy  staff     192 Jan  8 19:08 build
drwxr-xr-x  34 kilroy  staff    1088 Jan  8 19:08 deps
drwxr-xr-x   2 kilroy  staff      64 Jan  8 19:08 examples
drwxr-xr-x   2 kilroy  staff      64 Jan  8 19:08 incremental
-rwxr-xr-x   2 kilroy  staff  305392 Jan  8 19:08 life
-rw-r--r--   1 kilroy  staff     101 Jan  8 19:08 life.d
```

You may notice that both listings show an incremental directory. This is because the Rust compiler is capable of doing incremental builds to speed up the build process. In an incremental compilation, the Rust compiler builds the changes only in the source files.

We now have working source code and two ways of building our source files into executables. If you like, you can run the program that results from building it. It won't do anything interesting, but it can be executed. We have a good starting point to build additional projects on top of with the different Rust languages features we've discussed.

SUMMARY

Rust is a language that is said to be C-like, but significant differences exist between C and Rust, as there are between Rust and other C-like languages like Python. When we say C-like, what we mean is that the syntax is similar, meaning the keywords you use to cause behaviors or actions in your program are essentially the same. This includes control structures like `for` and `if`. There are some minor differences, though not significant.

One of the biggest differences between C-like languages and Rust is in variables. First of all, when we are declaring variables, we use the keyword `let` rather than just using a datatype and then the variable name. More importantly, variables cannot be changed by default. To make any changes to a variable after it has been declared, you need to declare it as mutable by using the `mut` keyword. This tells the Rust compiler that the variable can be changed later, meaning the compiler won't generate an error if it sees any attempt to change the variable.

Alongside this, an important concept in Rust is that of ownership. Remember that one of the foundational concepts in the development of Rust is memory safety. As a language that was developed knowing concurrent or parallel processing would be a possibility, those who created the Rust language determined that only one function could ever own a variable at any given time. This means that any variable essentially goes out of scope once it has been passed to another function. This doesn't mean the value goes away—just the ability to refer to the value using the alias that is the variable name.

Speaking of functions, Rust of course has functions. As you'd expect, the functions can take parameters and return values, including tuples, which are ordered collections of values. Rust can be an expression-oriented language. When it comes to programming languages, there are statements and expressions. An expression is something that evaluates to a value. A statement performs an action. A statement doesn't evaluate to a value. Even setting a variable doesn't evaluate to a value. A value gets placed into the memory location that the variable name refers to, but that's not the same as actually evaluating to a value. If you were to use a statement like `x = 10;`, the value 10 gets placed into `x`, but there is no resulting value that is residual from that.

If you are familiar with the Unix command line, you may be aware that if you were to run a program, you'd get a return value when the program was done running. This leaves a value, whether or not it gets used. This isn't a perfect analog, but it's similar. If `x = 10;` left a value that could be checked—say, a 1 or 0 indicating success or failure of the assignment—it might be considered an expression.

All of this is a long way of saying that Rust uses implicit returns through expressions. There is no `return` statement to explicitly return a value at the end of the function. Instead, you leave anything that could evaluate to a value, including a bare value or a variable, on a line by itself. Also, keep in mind that expressions do not use the semicolon to terminate the line. An expression does not get terminated like a statement does.

In the next chapter, we're going to extend Life and spend some more time looking at the ramifications of ownership on function calls and trying to reuse a variable after a function is called.

EXERCISES

1. Change the size of the grid to something other than 75×75. Keep in mind that you will need to find all the places where you have declared the life grid.

2. Call the `generation` function once. Remember that the `generation` function returns a value, so you will need to create a variable to hold the new grid that results from calling `generation`.

ADDITIONAL RESOURCES

Conway's Game of Life (from Scientific American) - `www.ibiblio.org/lifepatterns/october1970.html`

Conway's Game of Life - `pi.math.cornell.edu/~lipa/mec/lesson6.html`

What is the Game of Life? - `www.math.com/students/wonders/life/life.html`

Computer Programming - Variables - `www.tutorialspoint.com/computer_programming/computer_programming_variables.htm`

Computer Programming - Functions - `www.tutorialspoint.com/computer_programming/computer_programming_functions.htm`

2

Extended Life

IN THIS CHAPTER, YOU WILL LEARN THE FOLLOWING:

➤ How to create file input/output operations

➤ How to use the vector datatype

➤ How to use terminal input/output operations

➤ Ownership and borrowing variables

➤ How to include command-line arguments in your program

If you grabbed the source code from the previous chapter and compiled it, you have a Rust program. However, it's not the most interesting program since it's utterly silent. It doesn't ask for anything, and it doesn't give anything. You can run it as much as you like and not get any satisfaction out of it, other than you have a compiled Rust program that runs without error. Not the most fun thing in the world, for sure.

In this chapter, we'll correct that by adding a number of other functions that make it far more interesting. First of all, we're going to actually run through generations and be able to watch the changes to each generation. If you read up on the game of *Life*, you'll see there are some patterns that are well-known among people who have spent time running the game. This is especially true for those who have set up the game grid in a particular way, rather than the completely random way that we've done it so far.

We'll address that as well. We'll move away from just a random approach to populating the world, and you'll learn how to create your own population, laid out exactly as you'd like. With this ability, you can create gliders, blinkers, toads, pulsars, and others.

Along the way, of course, we're going to introduce some additional Rust capabilities, such as file input/output (I/O). Most importantly, we'll spend more time talking about ownership and how you can move data between functions.

UNDERSTANDING OWNERSHIP

Since we have to address this topic in a fair amount of detail because of the functionality of the program we're working on, we should spend a little more time talking about ownership in Rust. To do that, we need to first explain how identifiers in Rust work—which is similar to how other languages handle variables, except that it's more explicit and in some ways disconnected in terms of how the different elements are concerned. When I say elements, we really have three elements to be concerned with. The first is the name of the identifer; the second is the memory location the identifier name points out, which means you may think of the name of the identifier as an alias for that memory location. Finally, we have the value that is stored in the memory location. Let's say we have the following line of code in Rust:

```
let var1 = 42;
```

We have a variable name (called an identifier), `var1`. We don't see the second element explicitly in this line of code, but it's there. As soon as we say `let`, we indicate that memory must be allocated to hold whatever value we'll place into that memory. The name of the variable is a convenience for the programmer, especially since the programmer has no idea what the memory address would be when the program is being written. Even if they did, `var1` is far easier to remember than `0x4890ba45`, for instance. So, it's a convenience for readability, as well as being an alias for a piece of information we don't know when we're writing the program. You will see the words *variable* and *identifier* sometimes used interchangeably here. To be clear, identifier refers to the name of the variable while variable really is the contents or the memory location where the contents are stored. You can see a visual representation of that in Figure 2.1.

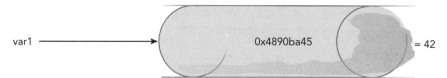

var1 ──────────────────────▶   0x4890ba45   = 42

FIGURE 2.1: Visual representation of variables

Where Rust differs from other programming languages is there can be only a single alias that refers to any memory address at any one time. Additionally, whenever you make use of one of these aliases, you are using it by reference rather than by value. Looking at the following lines of code, you can see exactly how that works:

```
let var1 = 42;
let var2;
var2 = var1;
```

On its face, we create a new variable with the name of `var1` and stick the value 42 into the memory location that `var1` points to. We then create a new variable that doesn't have any value associated with it. This means we've allocated memory for this variable but nothing goes into the memory location. Finally, we assign `var1` to `var2`. You may think that `var2` gets the value of 42 and `var1` remains available to us. In Rust, that's not the case. If you know the C programming language, the previous Rust code is similar to the following:

```
int var1 = 42;
int *var2;
var2 = &var1;
var1 = 0;
```

In the C code, we create a variable and assign the value 42 to it. This allocates memory and stuffs the value 42 into that memory location. We then create a pointer, which is a value that contains only a memory location, though no memory location is initially assigned to it. This is done in the next line. The variable var2 is then assigned the address of var1. This means we now have two variables that point to the same location. In the next line, we essentially deallocate the variable named var1. This is what happens in Rust. Figure 2.2 shows what this looks like. As soon as we assign var1 to var2, only var2 can point at the memory location. The variable named var1 no longer points to anything.

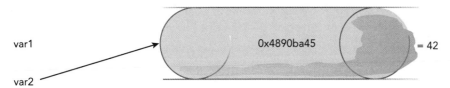

FIGURE 2.2: Assigning variables

If you tried to do anything with var1 after the line var2 = var1, you'd get a compiler error because the compiler knows the memory location has been moved (not copied) from one alias to another. You may be wondering why it's a move and not a copy. Remember that memory safety is an important part of Rust development. As soon as we have two different aliases, or variable names, that refer to the same location, potential exists for unexpected changes being made to the contents of the memory location.

More than that, though, it simplifies the design of the language and the runtime of the program. In languages like Java, there is a garbage collector. The garbage collector runs through, returning unused memory segments to the pool of available memory that can be allocated. Some languages use a technique called reference counting in order to know when the memory allocation is no longer used. Figure 2.3 shows a memory location with four different variables that point to the same location. There is a count associated with the memory location. When any of these four variables is freed or pointed somewhere else, the reference count—the number of variables that refer to the memory location—is decremented. When that count becomes 0, the memory can be returned for use.

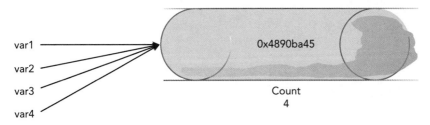

FIGURE 2.3: Reference counting

Rust avoids reference counting and the need to have garbage collectors by allowing only a single variable name or alias if you like to own a memory location at any point in time. You can move the ownership from one variable name to another, but you can't have two variable names pointing to the same memory address. Doing so ends up having consequences for how we have to program, since it goes beyond just two variable names within a function. You can't have a variable name in one function owning a memory location while simultaneously passing that variable name (memory location) to another function.

We get around this with various tactics, including borrowing. However, rather than piling onto an already deep discussion about ownership, we can postpone any conversation about borrowing until later on. Instead, we can start looking at extending the Game of Life program we started in the previous chapter.

EXTENDING LIFE

The functions introduced in the previous chapter remain essentially the same, with the exception of the main function. The reason for this is we are extending what the program does, so we have to add to the main function. The other functions don't change, however. The rest of the program is shown next, though we'll work through each of the functions, explaining what is happening and providing detailed explanations of the elements of the Rust language that we'll be making use of.

Here, you'll see the new functions as well as the top section of the source file, with additional modules added. Finally, there's the extended main function.

```
extern crate rand;
extern crate termion;
use std::{env, thread, time};
use std::fs::File;
use std::io::{BufRead, BufReader};
use termion::clear;
use termion::color;

fn main() {
    let mut world = [[0u8; 75]; 75];
    let mut generations = 0;

    let args: Vec<String> = env::args().collect();

    if args.len() < 2 {
        for i in 0..74 {
            for j in 0..74 {
                if rand::random() {
                    world[i][j] = 1;
                } else {
                    world[i][j] = 0;
                }
            }
        }
    } else {
```

```rust
        let filename = env::args().nth(1).unwrap();
        world = populate_from_file(filename);
    }

    println!("Population at generation {} is {}", generations, census(world));
    for _gens in 0..100 {
        let temp = generation(world);
        world = temp;
        generations += 1;
        println!("{}", clear::All);
        displayworld(world);
        println!("{blue}Population at generation {g} is {c}", blue =
color::Fg(color::Blue), g = generations, c = census(world));
        thread::sleep(time::Duration::from_secs(2));
    }

}

fn populate_from_file(filename: String) -> [[u8; 75]; 75]
{
    let mut newworld = [[0u8; 75]; 75];
    let file = File::open(filename).unwrap();
    let reader = BufReader::new(file);
    let mut pairs: Vec<(usize, usize)> = Vec::new();
    for (index, line) in reader.lines().enumerate() {
        let l = line.unwrap();
        let mut words = l.split_whitespace();
        let left = words.next().unwrap();
        let right = words.next().unwrap();
        pairs.push((left.parse::<usize>().unwrap(),
right.parse::<usize>().unwrap()));
    }

    for i in 0..74 {
        for j in 0..74 {
            newworld[i][j] = 0;
        }
    }

    for (x,y) in pairs {
        newworld[x][y] = 1;
    }
    newworld
}

fn displayworld(world: [[u8; 75]; 75])
{
    for i in 0..74 {
        for j in 0..74 {
            if world[i][j] == 1
            {
                print!("{red}*", red = color::Fg(color::Red));
            }
```

continues

```
(continued)
            else
            {
                print!(" ");
            }
        }
        println!("");
    }
}
```

Adding Modules

We'll make use of another external crate with this version of Life. In addition to the random number generator we need, we'll include the ability to do console output with colors. This requires a terminal that can support that sort of functionality, but one thing at a time. First, let's get the crate added that we need to support this terminal functionality. This happens in the `cargo.toml` file. In addition to the `rand` crate we used in the first version of Life, we need to add the `termion` crate. Make sure your `cargo.toml` file includes the following lines:

```
[dependencies]
rand = "0.7.2"
termion = "*"
```

You'll see that with the `rand` crate, we've specified a version. With the `termion` crate, there is a wildcard operator, which would pull whatever the most recent version available is. This, as you'd expect, relies on Cargo to do the work of pulling the right crate version and getting it ready to be used. It also takes care of doing all the linking that would be necessary to add the functionality to the final executable.

> **NOTE** If you want to install crates separately, without having them installed with `cargo build`, you could use `cargo install` followed by the name of the crate. This will pull and install the most recent version of that crate.

This is not to say that these are the only libraries we'll be adding; they're just the only *external* libraries we'll be using. We'll use a number of modules that come with Rust. In the following code, you can see the complete list of modules that we're pulling in for this program. As before, we're declaring an external crate named `rand`, which has to be configured in `cargo.toml` to be used. We've added the `termion` crate, which is also external. The first version of Life used `thread` and `time` from the `std` library. We are adding `env` this time around, because we want to grab environment data. This is necessary to get command-line variables, since they are passed in as part of the environment.

```
extern crate rand;
extern crate termion;
use std::{env, thread, time};
use std::fs::File;
use std::io::{BufRead, BufReader};
use termion::clear;
use termion::color;
```

> **NOTE** *Each program inherits an environment from the user running the program, and this includes environment variables. Depending on the platform you're using, you may be familiar with the* PATH *environment variable, which tells the shell you're in where to find any program you try to run indirectly. This means you haven't specified the complete path to the program but expect the shell (the interface you're using) to figure out where the program is stored in order to run it. There are many other variables that are provided to the program when it starts running. This includes everything that was on the command line. If you're running a program from a GUI, there's a shortcut that provides this "command line," which may include parameters that are passed into the program. This would be the same as if you had typed the whole thing into a terminal or command prompt window.*

This program will also include some file I/O, so we need to bring in functionality to read from and write to files. This is going to be different from reading or writing from the terminal since we must map to the memory structure that stores the file information. Additionally, we're reading entire lines from a file rather than characters at a time. Because of that, it's beneficial to use a buffered reader. These are not limited to using with files, though we're going to be using them with files for this program. The buffered readers take care of a lot of I/O management for us and just present the data that we need. The lines that bring in the functionality for the file handling as well as the buffered reader are shown here:

```
use std::fs::File;
use std::io::{BufRead, BufReader};
```

Finally, we're using more than just plain print statements to output our generations. This is because we want to be able to use colors when we write data out, just so it's clear what we're looking at. We also want to be able to clear the screen rather than continuing to just scroll the lines from one generation to the next. The following lines bring in what we need from the termion module. This could have been done on a single line, just as was done earlier with env, thread, and time from std. Whether it's on individual lines or all on the same line, the effect is the same. The reason for one over another may be readability. You may feel it's more readable and clearer to have them on individual lines rather than having to parse a single line with modules separated by commas. On the other hand, you may feel like you want to be efficient and just use a single line. Either approach is acceptable as far as the language is concerned.

```
use termion::clear;
use termion::color;
```

One thing to keep in mind as we talk about bringing in these other modules is that we are effectively importing their namespaces so we can use them directly. Once we import all of this functionality, we can just call functions from the modules by calling them directly rather than having to use something like std::io::BufRead, which is an explicit call to something out of the std::io library. As before, if you think it's more readable and explicit to refer to functions and properties using their fully qualified names, you can do that. You don't have to once you have pulled in the namespaces, but you can.

Working with Command-Line Arguments

If you are mostly familiar with double-clicking icons to run programs, this whole thing may be foreign to you. It's possible to run a program by sending a number of parameters into the program on the command line. The program takes those parameters and hopefully does something useful with them. Parameters passed into a program allow you to control the behavior of the program.

In the following code, you can see an example of some command-line parameters used to change the behavior of a program. In the first case, you will see command-line switches, used to tell the rm program what type of removal to perform. This is a recursive removal of files, used to delete everything in a directory and then delete the directory. The switches here are prefaced with a - (though on Windows systems, the switches may more commonly be indicated with a /).

```
kilroy@opus:~$ rm -Rf junkdir
kilroy@opus:~$ dd if=/dev/urandom of=sparsefile bs=1M count=100
100+0 records in
100+0 records out
104857600 bytes (105 MB, 100 MiB) copied, 1.46983 s, 71.3 MB/s
```

The second example shows named parameters. You can see the names of the parameters and their values. This is a disk dump command with an input file (if) and an output file (of) as well as the block size and the count of blocks.

For this program, we'll do something simple for the purposes of demonstrating taking in command-line parameters. We're going to accept a single parameter, which is a filename. The filename will be a set of coordinates where a cell should be alive. Later on, we'll address how to read in that file and populate the grid with living cells. For now, all we're worried about is being able to identify the filename from the command line. We'll read the parameters into a vector of strings, as shown here:

```
let args: Vec<String> = env::args().collect();
```

A vector is a collection of a single datatype. In this case, it's a collection of strings. To populate the vector, we'll use the args() function. This function returns all the arguments from the command line. What we get as a return type from that function is an iterator. An iterator is a datatype that is essentially a pointer to a batch of related chunks of data. Figure 2.4 shows what may be a vector of a datatype like an integer or even a string. If you allocate the entire vector at once, you will have consecutive memory addresses, sort of what it looks like in Figure 2.4.

The iterator points to a memory location, initially starting at the top of the collection. The iterator knows the size of the datatype it refers to, so we can tell the iterator to go to the next item, and the iterator will refer to the correct memory location for the next value in the vector. In our case, we have a collection of all the individual

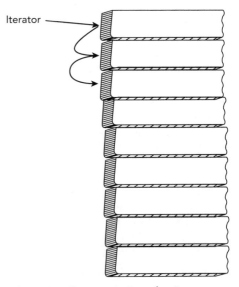

Iterator

FIGURE 2.4: Demonstration of an iterator

strings on the command line. Let's say we call our program using the command line `./life filename`. We use the `./` on a Unix-like operating system (Linux or macOS) to indicate we're running a program in the current directory. The vector from the command line will look like this:

```
./life
filename
```

The first value in the vector is the program name itself, as it's been entered on the command line. The second value is the name of the file we're passing into our Life program. Of course, if we'd typed additional values, those would be subsequent entries in the vector. If you wanted to pass in a multi-word string, you could quote it, and the parser would add those multiple words as a single value in the vector. Let's go back to the parser we're using, the `args()` function. This is going to return an iterator that we could use to get the arguments one at a time. To make use of them more easily, though, we use the `collect()` function. This places all the values into a collection, like the vector we're using.

The `collect()` function comes in the standard library and can be used to turn any iterator into a collection. This is a useful little function, as it turns out. You can call `collect()` on any iterator and get a collection back. This may allow you to chain a number of functions together to perform some transformation. You get an iterator from a collection, use that iterator to perform a transformation, and then call `collect()` at the end to get a collection back. We'll return to this idea in subsequent chapters, but in the meantime, just remember that an iterator is used to be able to easily move through a collection of values, like a `Vector`.

The last thing you need to know when working with command-line values is determining whether you've been passed any command-line parameters. In our case, we need to know whether we've had a filename passed in. If so, we can use the filename to populate the Life grid for us. If there is no filename, we can just go ahead with the usual process of filling in the grid randomly. Since the command-line values are in a vector, we can simply see whether the length of the vector is longer than 1. The `Vector` of command-line values is always going to have a length of at least one, since the program name is always the first parameter. Here, you can see the check for the length of the `Vector`:

```
if args.len() < 2 {
    for i in 0..74 {
        for j in 0..74 {
            if rand::random() {
                world[i][j] = 1;
            } else {
                world[i][j] = 0;
            }
        }
    }
}
```

Inside the `if` check is the code we'd used previously to populate the grid using random numbers. This is just two nested `if` loops for the x- and y-axes of our two-dimensional grid. The `if` check looks to see the value of `args.len()`, which is the function used to return the length of the vector. We could just as easily have checked whether the value is 1, since the argument list should always be at least 1. From a personal perspective, it seems like checking for equal to a specific value opens the door to missing out on a possible value. In this case, we wouldn't be missing a condition since we're just looking to see if there is anything on the command line aside from the program name. However, it's a bit of a habit to check less than on something like this, so you can make an adjustment to this code if you like, and it should work exactly the same.

```
    } else {
        let filename = env::args().nth(1).unwrap();
        world = populate_from_file(filename);
    }
```

Inside the block after the `else`, we need to take the name of the file. There are two functions that are important to look at here. First is the `nth()` function, which returns the *n*th value from the collection. You are telling the iterator to move to a position you have indicated in the value you pass to the `nth()` function. Keep in mind here that vectors are 0-based. The first value in the vector is `nth(0)` and not `nth(1)`. Since we know there's more than a single entry in the vector, we're safe trying to refer to `nth(1)` here. If we hadn't done the check to ensure there was a second value, trying to pull it back would have generated an error that we were asking for a value that didn't exist. The error would look like this:

```
thread 'main' panicked at 'called `Option::unwrap()` on a `None` value',
src/libcore/option.rs:378:21
```

The reason we get that error is because the `nth()` function returned a `None` value. That's because `nth()` is actually returning an `Option` rather than a `String`. Since it's an `Option`, we need to do something to extract the `String` value. `Option` is a complex type, a data structure rather than a single value. To get the real value we're looking for, we need help from another function. In this case, we use the `unwrap()` function, which will extract the `String` from the `Option` type and return it to us. Once we have the `String` back, we can pass it into another function that's going to populate the world from the file full of values. We'll take a look at the function that does that a little later in this chapter.

Option Types

The `Option` type is an `enum`, or an enumeration. The `enum` is a way of predefining a set of values. This allows you to let the compiler enforce what gets assigned to a variable. If you were to declare a variable with the type of an `enum` you had created, you would only be able to assign values defined in the `enum` to that variable. As an example, let's say we had created an `enum` called `MovieStar`, as shown next. You'll see the definition of the `enum` at the top, followed by a declaration of a variable and an assignment of a value from the `enum`. You have to ensure you are indicating the scope when you assign the value (`MovieStar::Audrey`). Without including the scope indication ahead, you'll get a scope error.

```
enum MovieStar {
    Audrey,
    Katharine,
    Bette,
    Ingrid,
}
let idol: MovieStar = MovieStar::Audrey;
```

The scope error is just one of the benefits of using an enum. If we'd written `let idol: MovieStar = Audrey`, the compiler would tell us it had no idea what `Audrey` meant—there is no `Audrey` in the scope. That's because `Audrey` exists only within the scope of the enum. Once we've defined the variable with the enum type we've created, the only values we can assign are those that are within the `enum` definition. As an example, let's say we tried `let idol: MovieStar =55`. The compiler would then generate the following error:

```
8 |        let idol: MovieStar = 55;
  |                             ^^ expected enum `main::MovieStar`, found integer
  |
  = note: expected type `main::MovieStar`
            found type `{integer}`

error: aborting due to previous error
```

Back to the reason we started talking about the `enum`—explaining the `Option` type. `Option` has two values. The first is `None`. This seems self-explanatory, and in our case, having a function return a value, `None` means there was nothing to return. This is a better result than generating a runtime error because you tried to access an element in a vector that didn't exist. The other possible value in the `Option` type is `Some`. However, `Some` expects a type to be defined. This is done by telling Rust that the type will be passed in. You can see the definition of the `Option` enum shown next. You'll see `<T>` in the definition of the `enum`. This indicates that the type for the `Some` value should be part of the declaration when you create a new identifier using `Option` as the type.

```
pub enum Option<T> {
    None,
    Some(T),
}
```

When we create a new identifier that is of the `Option` type, we have to specify the underlying type that will be carried in `Some`. We can do that during the declaration of the identifier, as you can see in the declaration of the identifier `mystr` that follows. When you declare and initialize the variable, in order to set a value you have to pass that value into the `Some` function, which sets the `Some` value in the `enum`.

```
let mystr: Option<String> = None;
```

In the following code, you can see an example of that. We declare an `Option` variable, with a string underlying it. `String` itself, in Rust, is a datatype that you may think of as an object because there is more to it than just the value of the string. This means in order to place a `String` into our `Option`, we need to create what is essentially a `String` object, or an instance of a `String` datatype if you prefer. That means we need to call the `from()` function in `String` in order to get a `String` datatype back. You can't just pass a bare literal (`"Some value here"`) in without creating an instance of `String`.

```
let response: Option<String> = Some(String::from("Some value here"));
println!("{}", response.unwrap());
```

You can again see the use of the `unwrap()` function here. That's because we need to get the underlying value out of the `Option` enum. `Some` itself isn't a value. Instead, `Some` is the access mechanism to get to the underlying value. To retrieve that value, determined by the datatype passed in when the `Option` was created to begin with, we need to use the `unwrap()` function. This gives us a `String`, and our `println()` function knows what to do with a `String` value.

> **NOTE** We've been using `println!` so far in this book instead of `println`. There is a `println` function, but when we add the `!` to the end of that function name, we call the macro named `println!` instead of the function. The reason for this is Rust doesn't have the ability to support a variable number of arguments. Whereas C and other languages will take a variable number of arguments, as in the `printf` argument that follows, Rust functions take a defined number of variables. This is safer, of course, but not helpful for things like printing, where you may want to format a string that includes a number of values from variables.
>
> ```
> int var1 = 55; int var2 = 42;
> printf("%d, %d\n", var1, var2);
> ```
>
> *The macro is able to handle the variable number of arguments and call the underlying* `println` *function to get the expected result. Macros are useful to extend the functionality of the program by extending the capabilities of the functions without having to introduce bad behavior into the language. What you see in the* `printf` *example here is a format string followed by a variable number of arguments. In C, this introduces the possibility for format string vulnerabilities where a format string can be passed into a* `printf` *statement from a user in order to extract the contents of memory. Rust avoids this by ensuring* `println` *doesn't take a variable number of arguments but supporting them by wrapping the function inside a macro.*

Keep in mind the `Option` enum as well as the `unwrap()` function. Because Rust is dedicated to safe programming, you'll find a lot of values that are wrapped into more complex datatypes. This allows the use of offensive programming techniques more easily. *Offensive programming* is a technique of developing software that doesn't expose the software to exploits by providing too many avenues into the inner workings of the program. Using offensive programming, the goal is to not create errors in the wrong place. As in our example with the `Option` enum, the actual value is wrapped inside a datatype. This means we can use the `Option` datatype to move values around without exposing the program to generating errors because of trying to access something that doesn't exist. All you need to do is check `is_none()` against your variable before unwrapping the value. You can see that here:

```
let response: Option<String> = Some(String::from("Some value here"));
if response.is_none() {
    println!("There is no value");
}
```

Similarly, there is a function you can use called `is_some()` to determine whether there is a value in the `enum`. With these checks, it's easy to make sure something is available before you try to do something that might generate an error. The word that keeps coming up when it comes to Rust programming is *explicit*. The way Rust has been created, it expects explicit programming. You have to do something explicitly to get a result rather than exposing your program to unintended side effects. Although it can be cumbersome and maybe a little harder to wrap your head around, it's a far safer way to program than with other programming languages that don't expect you to be explicit in what you're doing. You end up with unintended consequences if you take things for granted rather than putting them into the code. The advantage to Rust is that it includes functionality like `Option` to make that explicit programming easier.

READING FROM FILES

At this point, we can move on to the function that we called a few pages back that populates the game grid from a file. First, we should talk about what our file will look like. The only thing we need in our file is coordinate pairs that tell our Life program where the living cells are. You could adapt it to something like a binary string where every single cell is represented by either a 1 or a 0 to indicate whether it's turned on or off when the simulation begins. That requires a bit for every position in the game grid. If we have a grid that's 75×75, we need 5625 bits to maintain all the positions. Additionally, if you store that as the character 1 or 0, that's a single byte (at least) per position. We can store in binary, of course, but the problem with that is it's harder to read the file to know where everything is. Ultimately, a file that only contains coordinates of cells that are alive is easier to deal with. As a result, we're going to go with that.

```rust
fn populate_from_file(filename: String) -> [[u8; 75]; 75]
{
    let mut newworld = [[0u8; 75]; 75];
    let file = File::open(filename).unwrap();
    let reader = BufReader::new(file);
    let mut pairs: Vec<(usize, usize)> = Vec::new();
    for (index, line) in reader.lines().enumerate() {
        let l = line.unwrap();
        let mut words = l.split_whitespace();
        let left = words.next().unwrap();
        let right = words.next().unwrap();
        pairs.push((left.parse::<usize>().unwrap(),
right.parse::<usize>().unwrap()));
    }

    for i in 0..74 {
        for j in 0..74 {
            newworld[i][j] = 0;
        }
    }

    for (x,y) in pairs {
        newworld[x][y] = 1;
    }
    newworld
}
```

The function `populate_from_file()` is shown here. We pass in the filename as a parameter and the function is going to return a populated grid. The file itself is formatted as pairs of values on a single line. Each line, in other words, would have the coordinates for a single cell that should be considered to be alive. A portion of the file is shown next as an example of what that would look like. As you create your own file, you should keep in mind what the rules of Life are. If you just drop a handful of cells randomly on the game board, it's unlikely that anything will survive to a second generation. Any cell that has no neighbors is going to die off. Since your board may look very sparsely populated unless you put some time into it, none of the cells are likely to have enough neighbors to generate life either. That means the approach of populating from a file is a lot harder work, unless you had programmatic help to generate the file.

```
1 5
1 10
1 18
1 19
1 20
1 25
1 26
2 1
2 2
2 3
2 4
2 6
2 7
2 8
3 60
3 61
3 62
3 63
3 70
```

Once we've declared the new world that we'll be working in, there are two lines that are important. We need to open the file and get a file handle back that we can use. The following two lines are needed to get not only a file handle that the program can refer to but also a declaration of another handle that will take care of doing the reading for us so that we aren't doing any low-level programming and having to manage character by character or even line by line, necessarily.

```
let file = File::open(filename).unwrap();
let reader = BufReader::new(file);
```

You may notice right away that we're back to using unwrap() after we've opened the file. The reason for this is that we are not getting back a file handle from the open() call. Instead, we get another wrapped value. This time, the file handle comes back wrapped up in a Result datatype. Result is another enum, like Option. There are two potential values in the Result enum, and they are used for error handling and management. The first value is Err. If Err is populated, there was an error in the function that was called. The other potential selection is Ok. Ok contains a value. As you can see in the definition, the value is a type that has to be defined when you declare a result, similar to the Option enum.

```
enum Result<T, E> {
    Ok(T),
    Err(E),
}
```

Since the response to open() on the file is a result, we need to unwrap the handle to the file that is included in Ok. Otherwise, we just have a result that isn't of much use when we are trying to do something with the open file. What we'll do is pass it into a constructor for a `BufReader` instance. Out of that, we have what is essentially an object that we can use to interface with the file to read values. We're going to place the values into a vector, just as we used with the command-line arguments earlier, because it will be easier to use the vector when we want to populate our grid. We'll call the vector `pairs`, and it's going to be a vector of two integers. Each entry in the vector is going to be a paired set of integers.

```
for (index, line) in reader.lines().enumerate() {
        let l = line.unwrap();
        let mut words = l.split_whitespace();
        let left = words.next().unwrap();
        let right = words.next().unwrap();
        pairs.push((left.parse::<usize>().unwrap(),
right.parse::<usize>().unwrap()));
    }
```

This code fragment is where we read the pairs in. However, since the pairs are on individual lines, we need to do a little manipulation to separate the pairs into discrete values that we can then stick into our vector. First, though, we need to read the values. This is done using the function `lines()` from `BufReader`. This function will return two values. The first is `index`, which is effectively the line number. The second, which we will actually use, is `line`. Since we're getting two values back, we use a tuple construct to indicate the return values should be stored as a tuple. In this case, the tuple is just an ordered pair of values—index and `line`. We get these two values by using `enumerate()` on the result of the `lines()` function.

Let's take a closer look at this, because we're chaining functions together. It's probably helpful to look at what the result of each is, since it will be the input to the next. The `lines()` function returns a `Lines` value, which is an iterator. It iterates over all the lines in a file. We then pass the iterator into the `enumerate()` function. This function just iterates through the lines and returns values for us. So, we have a reader from which we collect lines and those lines are enumerated, meaning the values and metadata (the line number) are returned to us. Since the `for` loop expects a collection to iterate over, we are in good shape.

Extracting Values

Now, we can take a look at how we extract the integer pairs from each line. First, you need to recognize that the line variable isn't just a string—it's a result. Since it's a result, we need to perform an `unwrap()` on the result, so we get the string out that we need. The string we retrieve, however, is the entire line, complete with two integers and the whitespace in between. This means we need to split the complete line into two separate values. Fortunately, there is a function that will do that. We call `split_whitespace()` to get an iterator to the values that were on the line. Since we have an iterator, we need to use the function `next()` to get each value. The `next()` function in an iterator gets us the next value in the collection. We should have only two values, so we need to call it twice, as you can see here, extracted from the larger block shown previously.

```
let left = words.next().unwrap();
let right = words.next().unwrap();
```

Again, we get a result back, so we need to call `unwrap()` on it to get the string out. Once we have the two strings with the two values, we still have a problem. The problem is that they are strings. Of characters. That doesn't help us a lot, unfortunately, since we can't use a string to index to an array. We need to be able to convert the strings we have, which are just collections of characters, to integers. To that end, we have the fairly convoluted line here. That line is going to perform multiple functions in order to add the pair of integers to the vector we have:

```
pairs.push((left.parse::<usize>().unwrap(), right.parse::<usize>().unwrap()));
```

First, let's work from the inside out. Remember, we have two variables named `left` and `right`. These are the left and right values on the line, and since there are two values (assuming a correctly formatted file), one will be on the left side of the line and the other will be on the right side of the line—thus, the naming. It's far more descriptive than, say, `var1` and `var2`, and more interesting as well. We perform two tasks on the inside, but they are mirror images of each other, since the tasks have to be performed on both `left` and `right`. This is the conversion from string to integer. To perform that conversion, we can use the `parse()` function that comes with a string. Let's take a look at just that conversion, away from the rest of the line. We'll pull it out as though we were going to store the value in a separate variable:

```
let left_int: usize = left.parse::<usize>.unwrap();
```

We are using `usize` as the datatype to convert to here. This is the size of an unsigned integer, without specifying the number of bits to use. This means the size of the integer will be bound to the architecture of the system. If you are on a 64-bit system, `usize` would be a 64-bit integer. This is far more than we need, but the difference in memory utilization considering the number of values we'll be creating would be negligible. So, we create an unsigned integer variable, which would be dependent on the system architecture for size; then we need to perform the parse of the string to the integer. This requires that we call the `parse()` function on the `left` variable, indicating what we are converting to. Just as with other instances we have looked at, we will get a result back from that, so it needs to be unwrapped to get the actual integer out. So, to summarize, we have a string that will be converted to an unsigned integer using the `parse()` function, indicating the datatype. Then we need to unwrap the unsigned integer from the result that will come back.

We now have two unsigned integers, one from the left and one from the right. It may be hard to see, but going back to the original line where we push a value onto the vector of all the coordinate pairs, there are two sets of parentheses. The outside set is because it's a function, so we use parentheses to indicate that we are passing parameters. The inside set is because we need to pass a tuple into the `push()` function. The vector is of a pair of integers, so we have to push a pair on as a pair rather than as a pair of individual integers. From the perspective of the vector, or more accurately, the compiler, two separate integers are not the same as a pair of integers. Thus, we have to use `()` to create the tuple that needs to be added.

Populating from the Vector

The final piece of the function to populate from a file is to actually populate the grid. When we created the vector, it was uninitialized. This means we don't really know what values would be in it if we tried to look at them. Remember that we expect 1s and 0s for each cell so that we can do the right thing when it comes to determining when a cell contains a living entity. Since we are populating from a file that contains only living cells, we can start with the assumption that all cells are dead. Any cell that is then specified as being alive from the file can be switched to alive when we get there.

It's easiest to just initialize everything as though it were dead since there is no guarantee that we have an ordered list from the file, which means determining where the cells that are dead should be is difficult. It's a little brute force, but trying to determine what cells should be dead from the ones that are alive may be interesting but not worth the processing time to have the program figure it out. One way to do it, for instance, is to run through the game grid after we've set everything to 1 for living cells and just set the ones that aren't 1 to a 0. A single set is faster than a comparison for every cell followed by a set, as necessary. There's no need to complicate the program with something that may seem clever. To that end, we use a simple double loop to initialize the grid.

```
for i in 0..74 {
    for j in 0..74 {
        newworld[i][j] = 0;
    }
}
```

Once we have the grid initialized, we can use the vector of integers to turn on the living cells. This is a simple for loop, though not in the sense of a range of values as we have been using. Instead, we'll iterate through the vector, pulling out a tuple of values for each vector entry. We'll name the two integer values x and y for simplicity. Since we're using a vector to iterate through, we don't need the double loop we've been using until now. Here, you can see the loop used to initialize the grid with all the living cells:

```
for (x,y) in pairs {
    newworld[x][y] = 1;
}
```

Anywhere we have a pair of values, we just assign a 1 to that coordinate location. There is no check here to ensure that the value of x and y don't exceed the size of our array. We are expecting that whoever has created the file of values knows the size of the game grid and that none of those values in the file are larger than they should be.

Finally, at the end of the function, we have to pass back the resulting grid, so the variable named newworld is placed on a line by itself. This is the expression-oriented programming. The variable newworld becomes an expression that is evaluated to a value that is returned to the calling function. We now have a fully populated game grid, whether we are populating it randomly or populating it from a file.

OUTPUTTING TO THE TERMINAL

We can now move on to the final new function in our extended Life program. This is where we output the entire grid to a console (screen/terminal window). One thing to keep in mind here is the size of the game grid. If your terminal window or screen isn't large enough to accommodate the entire game grid, you're going to miss some cells. Here, you can see the function that displays the world:

```
fn displayworld(world: [[u8; 75]; 75])
{
    for i in 0..74 {
        for j in 0..74 {
            if world[i][j] == 1
            {
```

continues

(continued)
```
                print!("{red}*", red = color::Fg(color::Red));
            }
            else
            {
                print!(" ");
            }
        }
        println!("");
    }
}
```

First, we'll use a double loop again. This is to work through the entire game grid, just as we have done in the past. This is the easiest way to ensure we have looked at all the values. If a cell is alive, we'll write out a value that is visible. If the cell is dead, we'll write out a space to indicate that the cell is effectively empty. We don't want to use println() here. A println() call will add a new line (carriage return/line feed) at the end of the output. We can't do that until we are actually at the end of the line. Instead, we'll use the print() function. Again, we're using the macro version of the function, which will manage the parameters being passed in.

Using Colors

This is where we'll use the termion crate as well. To make things stand out a little, and be more interesting, we'll use the functions and properties in the termion crate to get some color. You'll notice that the print() statement includes a variable named red in the format string, as shown here. The variable red then gets assigned a color, which would be an escape string to tell the terminal to print anything that followed it in the color specified.

```
    print!("{red}*", red = color::Fg(color::Red));
```

Looking more closely, the variable red gets the value that results from calling color::Fg. This sets the foreground color of the output. If you wanted to set the background color, you would use color::Bg. We need something to pass into that function, though. Rather than trying to construct something from scratch, we'll just use the colors that have already been defined in the color module. You may notice here that the scope is specified, since we are pulling functionality from an external crate. We need to make sure the compiler knows what function or property is being referred to and, more importantly, where it can be found.

Once we have the color indicated, we just print out an * to indicate that the cell is alive. Since we'll use a space to indicate a dead cell, there's no reason to reset the terminal to the standard color. If you wanted to, you could use something other than a space for a dead cell. You may want to do something like a period, colored white for contrast, or whatever color you wanted to use, of course. Once you've run the entire program a few times, you may feel like you want to change it.

Printing Generations

Going back to the main function, we have one loop that we haven't looked at yet, which calls the generation() function and then the displayworld() function, which we've just looked at. The code for this loop is shown next. The program is set to use 100 generations, so we have a loop. You'll notice the variable _gens with the underscore in front of it. You don't have to use the underscore if you don't want, though the compiler will suggest that you do since the variable isn't used anywhere.

We never use it, because we have a counter we're using to count generations. The reason for this is there is a print statement just outside of this loop to indicate the initial population before we do anything other than load the initial grid. There are other ways to do this, of course, but it was the way that I wanted it to work.

```
for _gens in 0..100 {
        let temp = generation(world);
        world = temp;
        generations += 1;
        println!("{}", clear::All);
        displayworld(world);
        println!("{blue}Population at generation {g} is {c}", blue =
color::Fg(color::Blue), g = generations, c = census(world));
        thread::sleep(time::Duration::from_secs(2));
    }
```

Much of the loop is straightforward. We create a new variable called temp where we store the results of the generation. Once the generation is complete, we can set the world variable to the memory location of the new array created in the function generation(). Once that happens, remember, the temp variable no longer points to that memory location and is no longer valuable. This is okay, because we're going to start all over again on the next pass through the loop.

Rather than continuing to just scroll every generation, one after the other, which would look a little sloppy and hard to follow, it's easier to clear the screen. This can be done using clear out of the ter-mion crate. We want to clear the entire screen, so we need to call clear::All. This wipes the screen and resets the cursor at the top left of the screen or terminal window. Since this is essentially an escape character sequence that needs to be sent to the screen or terminal, it has to be sent in a print statement. We're going to use the println! macro to send the clear sequence.

Once the screen is clear, we can run displayworld(), which will write out the entire game grid, as you've seen previously. Because it's interesting to not only look at the output from generation calculation to see what is still alive and what is newly alive and also newly dead, but also look at the statistics, like the total number of living cells as well as the generation, we're going to print those values out. Since we've already headed down the path of colors in our output, this statement of the census data is written in blue. Again, you can use whatever color you like. You could also use different colors for different parts of the output.

Finally, we'll want to look at the generation rather than blanking the screen right away and starting all over again. We do this using sleep() from the thread module. The sleep() function takes Duration as a parameter. This means we need to create Duration. This is in the time crate, so again we're going to specify the entire scope—time::Duration::from_secs(2). We're going to call the from_secs() function out of the time crate and the Duration type. This results in a value with the datatype Dura-tion. This value, from our perspective, is 2 seconds, regardless how it is represented in memory for the program.

This is another good example of everything being abstracted in Rust. We don't just call sleep and pass in a bare value. Instead, we create a duration using the function from_secs(). This removes any potential confusion from just passing in an integer like 2. If you want to use milliseconds, you use from_milli(). If you want to use nanoseconds, you use from_nano(). With other languages, you may call a sleep function and pass in a value. You'd have to look at the documentation to determine what the value you're passing in is expected to mean.

Now that we have a working Life program, we can build it using `cargo build` and then run it. Running it will generate the output shown in Figure 2.5. You can see the different cells that are alive, as well as the statistics indicating the number of cells that are alive. The value you see here is down considerably from the initial population.

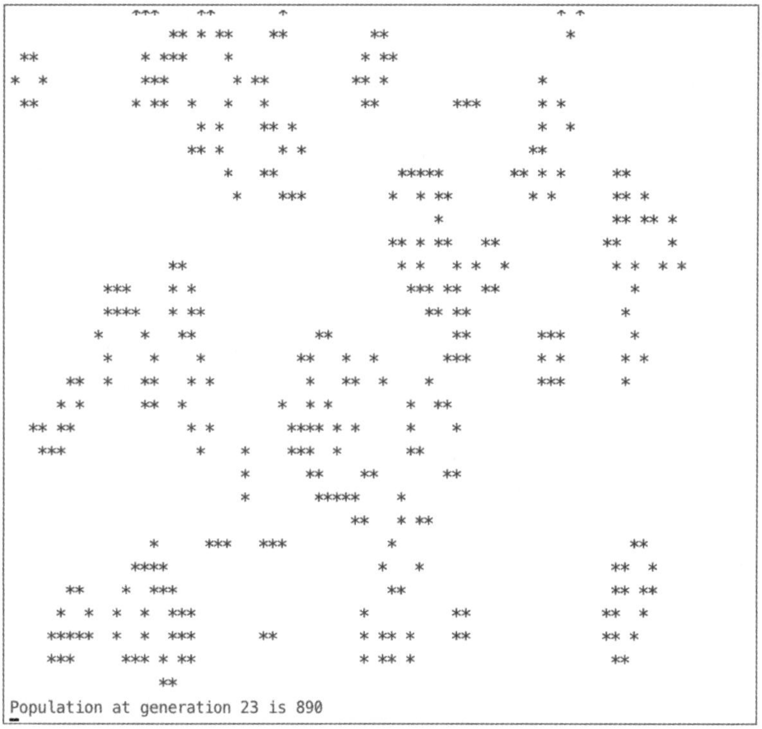

FIGURE 2.5: Life generation output

What you see here is only a portion of the output. Keep in mind that the game grid is 75×75 and there aren't 75 lines here. Perhaps about a third of the entire game grid is shown. Based on the size of the window you have available for display, you may want to adjust the program so that you can see the entire game grid.

SUMMARY

The most important topic from this chapter is ownership in the sense that it's an essential design aspect of Rust and, as such, will have continuing impacts on your programming. Every variable name is a pointer to a memory location. Only one variable name at a time can point to any memory location. This restriction changes programming practices because it affects how you pass variables around from one function to another, but it also removes the problems that can come with garbage collection and reference counting, which are memory management practices to prevent memory leaks or memory misuse that can lead to vulnerabilities.

Adding in modules is always going to be an important aspect of developing programs. The standard library, in any language, is going to be useful but not nearly enough to do really interesting things. This means we will have to import additional libraries. This can be managed automatically using `cargo` as a build manager. It also means you need to refer to any external functionality so that it can be linked in from the proper location. Anything that comes in a third-party crate needs to be flagged as an `extern crate` so that the functionality gets pulled in during the build and you don't receive any compiler errors because functions couldn't be found.

Reading from the command line is an important feature. This is something that is done in C-like languages as parameters to the main function. In Rust, we pull in the command-line parameters through the `env` module. They come in from a vector, which means we need to know how to work with vectors. A vector is a collection, sort of a cross between an array and a linked list where there is the data but also metadata that knows how to move from one element in the vector to another. Vectors come with iterators, which are datatypes that are used to move from one element to another by knowing where all the memory locations in the vector are.

Working with files is another important function, which we'll be using more of as we keep building on our experiences with Rust. You need to be able to not only open the file but also manage reading from one part of the file to another. This can be done using a `BufReader`. This provides us with iterators to move from line to line. Once we have those, we can easily read through the file.

One important concept to remember from this chapter is that values are often wrapped. This may be in a `Result` or an `Option` enum. These enums allow us to perform offensive programming by better managing errors. Providing an easy way to determine whether values exist without generating exceptions makes programming safer. Exception handling is good, but if it's not handled well, a lot of information can leak out to attackers to be used against the program. To get values out of these enums, we need to use the `unwrap()` function a lot. Often, when you call a function that is a part of the Rust library, you will get a response back in a `Result` enum, so getting used to handling those datatypes is a good idea.

Finally, we use a lot of the `println!` macro. Rust requires that you use this macro. Trying to call `println` directly will generate a compiler error telling you to use the macro instead. You indicate you are using a macro by appending the `!` symbol to a function name. One reason for using a macro in Rust, especially with respect to the `println()` function, is because Rust doesn't support a variable number of parameters being passed to a function.

Using the built-in printing functions, including `print()` and `println()`, even the macro versions, is insufficient for what we are doing. We used the `termion` crate and its support for easily passing escape sequences for colors. Additionally, we can use these sequences to clear the screen.

With all of that, we now have a fully working implementation of *Conway's Game of Life*—unless, of course, you want to take a pass at making some adjustments, which you can find in the following exercises.

EXERCISES

1. Add in boundary checking to the `populate_from_file()` function to ensure none of the values exceed the size of the array in the grid.

2. Create a function that saves out the game grid to a file when all the generations have completed running.

3. Take a second parameter on the command line and use it to indicate the number of generations the program should run.

ADDITIONAL RESOURCES

C - Command Line Arguments - `www.tutorialspoint.com/cprogramming/c_command_line_arguments.htm`

3

Building a Library

IN THIS CHAPTER, YOU WILL LEARN THE FOLLOWING:

➤ How to write to files

➤ How to work with JavaScript Object Notation (JSON)

➤ How to use and extend the struct

➤ How to specify lifetimes

In this chapter, we'll take two passes at a program. In part, this is because of the two different crates we can use for the JavaScript Object Notation (JSON) work. On top of that, some foundational issues need to be addressed. Consequently, we'll take a simple approach on our first pass so that we can spend some time on the foundational ideas that we'll use later and build on top of. The first pass, because it's simple, won't really be all that useful in the form you see it in. The second pass will be more useful, and it will be easier to talk about the second pass because of what we'll talk about in the first program.

That may sound arcane, so let's get practical. We'll take two passes at writing a program that stores a DVD library and manages the data in JSON format. This strategy lets us tackle several useful practices or techniques. The first is just working with JSON, since JSON is a data format used for storing and transmitting data. JSON is often used in web applications, but it may also be used as an underlying data format for applications that have structured or semi-structured data. One reason it's useful is that it's self-documenting, as you will see when we start writing the program. Each JSON record includes not only the data for that record but the name for that value as well. If you think about it in a tabular format like a traditional database, you not only get the row value in JSON, you also get the column name associated with each row value.

Another important concept we'll address in both iterations of our program is using a *struct*. A struct is a complex data type that allows a programmer to create their own datatype with multiple, related values that will be used together in the program. A struct is such a funda-mental element that we'll spend a decent amount of time on it. It will be the language feature that the programs in this chapter are built on. The struct underlies the binding of data and programmatic elements that act on that data. You'll learn more about that later in this chapter, since it is also an important part of Rust programming.

As discussed in the previous two chapters, Rust is focused heavily on memory safety. So far, we've talked about ownership. Ownership is important, but it also provides restrictions that require some additional thought when it comes to writing programs in Rust. It's fairly common to pass data from one function to another. Having that data no longer accessible once it passes into a new function is simply unworkable. This means we need a way of safely passing that data without losing access to it once a function has been called that needs it—which is why we need to start by talking about references in Rust.

REFERENCES

You may remember that when we passed a game grid into a function, we passed a new game grid back out, replacing the original one. This is, in part, because of the complication of passing data into a function and trying to change it so that the changes are intact to the function passing the data in. Because of the rules of ownership, that's not possible. You pass data into a function, and that memory gets released once the function ends since it has gone out of scope.

What if you want to pass data in just to be used by the function to perform something that was necessary, but you really need that data back at the end? It's not practical to be returning data and having to create a new variable to store it, as we did in the Life program in Chapter 1, "Game of Life: The Basics." As a result, we need a way to pass data into a function without losing it or having to do something weird like creating a new variable in which to store the data when the function returns.

Rust offers references, an option that is actually a little counterintuitive if you are familiar with the two common approaches to passing values, especially if you come from the world of C. In fact, even syntactically, it's a little backward. In most languages that give you the ability to uncover the memory location using a datatype called a pointer, where the contents of the datatype are the memory address, you can pass by reference or pass by value. This means that the value that gets placed on the stack for the called function to consume is either an actual value that can be used directly or a memory location that can be read from in order to get the value indirectly.

Let's take a look at this concept in C. First, we have a function that takes a parameter by value, which means the actual value of the variable will be placed on the stack. Second, we have a function that takes a parameter by reference, which means that the actual value passed to the function is an address to a location in memory where the value is stored, or the location where the value is to be stored. A common reason to pass by reference to a function in a language like C is because you want the value to be changed, which means the function needs to know the memory location to write a value to it.

```c
#include <stdio.h>

int twice(int x) {
    return x*2;
}

void readin(int *x) {
    printf("Enter a value");
    scanf("%d", x);
}
```

```
int main () {
    int x = 10;
    printf("%d\n", twice(x));
    readin(&x);
    return 0;
}
```

In the main function, the variable x is declared as an integer. No problem, because the first function, called twice, takes an integer as a parameter. The second function, though, takes an address (a pointer). This is clear because the variable has the prefix *, which indicates that what's coming is an address, not a value. Back to the main function, you can see that we are still using the variable x, but since the function expects an address, we have to prefix the variable x with an &, which tells the compiler to get the address of the variable and use that. Since we do the address retrieval in the parameters of the function call, that address is what is sent into the function. If you wanted to get the value back out from that address, you would do something called *dereferencing* by prepending your variable name with the *. That tells the compiler to take what's in the address contained in the variable and retrieve that value, using it instead of the address.

In Rust, it's backward, or at least the other way around. When we want to pass just a value in and not the actual address—which is what would normally be referred to by calling a variable name/ alias—we pass a reference to the variable. This is done using the & operator prepended to the variable name. Here, you can see essentially the same program in Rust as the previous C program:

```
use std::io;

fn twice(x: &u8) -> u8 {
    x * 2
}

fn readin() -> u8 {
    let mut input = String::new();
    io::stdin().read_line(&mut input);
    input = input.trim().to_string();
    let x: u8 = input.parse::<u8>().unwrap();
    x
}

fn main() {
    let mut x: u8 = 10;
    println!("{}", twice(&x));
    x = readin();
    println!("{}", twice(&x));
}
```

Honestly, there's an awful lot more here than in the C program, but let's start by focusing on the borrowing parts. You'll notice that we were able to pass the variable x into the twice() function and then still are able to use it afterward to take the return value from the function readin(). In fairness, this would work even if we hadn't used the borrowing notation because integers are specified Copy, which means the data can be copied (or passed by value if you prefer). This is because data stored in integer values can be known at compile time. Anything that requires allocation at runtime cannot be marked Copy.

So, let's look at something that can't be marked Copy and try to pass it into a function and then use it again. Since a `String` has to be allocated when it is created—meaning the memory is set aside dynamically when it is requested during the program's run—it can't be set to Copy. So, we can take a look at how to write the same program using a `String` instead of an integer. Here, you'll see that program with the necessary alterations made:

```
use std::io;

fn twice(x: &String) -> String {
    format!("{} {}", x, x)
}

fn readin() -> String {
    let mut input = String::new();
    io::stdin().read_line(&mut input);
    input = input.trim().to_string();
    input
}

fn main() {
    let mut x: String = String::from("bogus");
    println!("{}", twice(&x));
    x = readin();
    println!("{}", twice(&x));
}
```

We create a `String` and make it mutable so we can assign a new value to it later on. Then, we pass the reference into the `twice()` function. One thing about this version of the program is that the `twice()` function has a new function call we haven't dealt with before. This is `format!()`, and technically it's a macro for the same reason as the `println!()` macro we've been dealing with. We need to pass multiple values into the function without knowing how many values there will be. The macro takes care of the uncertainty of the number of parameters. Where we can pass in a format and variables into `println!()`, we can do the same with `format!()` and get a formatted `String` out, passing in a single `String` twice to double it up. This is a simple implementation, but you can see how it would work.

In both versions of this program, we are also taking in user-generated input. This is also something new, but it will be something you'll use later on. Interestingly, rather than the function `read_line()` passing the result out to assign to a variable, you have to create a mutable variable and then pass it into that function.

Adding a couple of statements, we can also see what happens when we call `readin()`, assigning the value that returns to the mutable variable x. If we add in the statement `println!("{:p}", x.as_ptr())`, we can see what the address of the variable x is at any given time. Adding one of these statements after the variable is created and another one after `readin()` is called yields the following output, showing you something interesting. Remember, based on the code earlier, what you're looking at is the address of the first identifier, followed by doubling that value. Then, the user enters **wubble**, which is doubled, and we see the new address based on having replaced the value stored in the identifier.

```
kilroy@milobloom:~/Documents$ ./test
0x7f9a8dc01990
bogus bogus
wubble
wubble wubble
0x7f9a8dd00010
```

This code shows us the relationship of variables to their data. The address is stored in the variable, and that address can be changed. When you assign a new string, there has to be a new memory allocation since the new string could be a completely different size. When the initial string is allocated, it is five characters long. Taking input from a user may be, and in this case is, larger. We can't take a five-character buffer and stuff six characters into it, which would be what would have to happen here because the input is six characters long. This means we need to allocate a new chunk of memory. Once that happens, the alias for that memory, the variable name, has to be reset to point to the new location.

The use of references (because of the ownership idea) and how variables are managed are concepts so fundamental to how Rust is constructed as a language that you need to get used to how they work. If you don't need to adjust a value, and you need to get to that value after a function is called, you can use a reference to pass the value into a function. That means the variable won't become owned by the called function, meaning that memory will be freed because the variable will go out of scope when the function concludes.

FIRST PASS

If you are familiar with C++ as an object-oriented language, you may know that it derives from the C programming language. In fact, C++ started as a preprocessor that runs before the C compiler runs when you are compiling an executable. C++ was initially implemented in a preprocessor that converted the C++ source code into C so it could be fed into the C compiler. All the object-oriented features need to be collapsed into standard C. This means the foundation for C++ becomes the `struct`. C includes the ability to create complex datatypes with the struct, which is short for data structure. You can combine multiple, related pieces of data into your own datatype.

Actually, a `struct` in C looks essentially like a `struct` in Rust. The following is an example in C. When we get to the first pass at the program, you'll see how much this `struct` looks like the one we'll use.

```
struct Dvd {
    char name[50];
    int year;
    char cast[100];
    int length;
};
```

The struct type in C is the foundation of the class in C++. In fact, in C++, a struct type is essentially a public class without any functions associated with it. Or, put another way, you can think of a class as a struct with functions or methods as part of the data structure. The class is a foundational idea of object-oriented programming, but even more than that, it is a foundational element of data encapsulation. Although data encapsulation is foundational to object-oriented design, it is not only associated with that approach to language design. In fact, the programming language Modula-2, designed by Niklaus Wirth (who also developed Pascal, which used to be a common teaching language), uses data encapsulation without being an object-oriented language.

The idea behind data encapsulation in language design and program design is to keep together the data and all the programmatic methods that act on that data. This protects the data from being acted on by other methods. One feature we get with common object-oriented languages like C++ and Java is the ability to ensure that the data within an object remains private, only accessible by the methods in that object. This ability to make properties private comes with the concept of public and private designations for the data.

Why mention all of this? In Rust, the `struct` is also foundational. As a modern language, Rust recognizes that data is not isolated. It is commonly associated with other pieces of data. Additionally, the Rust language developers recognize that once you have a complex datatype, you'll want to do things to it. This means you can attach a function to a `struct` using a `trait`—which gives you a way to act directly on the data from inside the data structure.

Now that we have all that out of the way, we can take a look at the initial version of the program, shown next. The first thing you'll see is that we're pulling in a new crate that we'll use to generate JSON out of the data structure we'll use.

```rust
extern crate rustc_serialize;
use rustc_serialize::json::{self,ToJson, Json};

#[derive(RustcEncodable)]
struct Dvd {
    name: String,
    year: u16,
    cast: String,
    length: u16
}

impl ToJson for Dvd {
    fn to_json(&self) -> Json {
        Json::String(format!("{}+{}+{}+{}i", self.name, self.year, self.cast,
self.length))
    }
}

fn converttojson (advd: &Dvd) -> String {

    json::encode(advd).unwrap()

}

fn main() {

    let a = Dvd {
        name: String::from("Four Weddings and a Funeral"),
        year: 1994,
```

```
        cast: String::from("Hugh Grant"),
        length: 117,
    };

    let encoded = converttojson(&a);

    println!("{}", encoded);

}
```

You may have noticed that the crate is called `rustc_serialize`. It doesn't specifically say JSON, because it is more general purpose than that. Serializing data is a common concept, especially when it comes to complex datatypes and data representation languages like JSON. Data serialization is just taking the data within the data structure and writing it out as a continuous stream, whether that's to a file, to a stream, or to a network connection. The reverse process, where you take input from a file or a network connection, typically, and put the data into the data structure correctly, is called *deserialization*. This process can be challenging and also introduces vulnerabilities into programs when not done correctly. For this program, though, we won't worry about deserialization; we'll just serialize a data structure. However, the JSON functionality we need is included in the serialization crate.

Let's talk now about the `struct` that is being used to store the data for this program. We're collecting all the related information associated with a DVD together into a single data structure, called `Dvd`. This information includes the name, the year it was released, the cast list, and the length, in minutes, so that we can store it as an integer in case we need to perform calculations on it later on. Another approach would be to store it as a `String`, as in `1:47` (one hour and 47 minutes). If we ever wanted to do something like add up the running times of a number of movies, we'd have to convert that string into an integer, so it makes sense to just store it as an integer to begin with. Here's the `struct` we're going to be working with:

```
struct Dvd {
    name: String,
    year: u16,
    cast: String,
    length: u16
}
```

As you will note, this looks a lot like the `struct` we had worked with in C previously. There are a couple of differences. First of all, the declaration of a variable in C is different from that in Rust. Additionally, each declaration in C is considered a separate declaration, which means that each line has to be terminated using a semicolon. In Rust, the entire `struct` is declared as one complete entity. As a result, we use commas to separate one element from another. What you will see here is that the final element in the struct is left on a line by itself without a comma. This is a stylistic decision, since you can add a comma to make it symmetric. This means all the lines in the `struct` look the same.

Adding a comma to the last line also allows you to easily add another element later on, without having to go back and remember to add the comma. It's not a complex thing, but you might be surprised at how easy it is to forget that comma and then get a compiler error later. Getting in the habit of putting the comma on all lines, since the compiler allows it, can be a good practice that saves you some hassle later on.

The other difference between this and a C `struct` declaration is that C requires that you terminate the declaration with a semicolon, just as you would with any other statement. This is not considered a statement that needs to be terminated in Rust, so you can leave the semicolon off.

Traits and Implementations

At the top of the `struct` declaration was a line that is related to adding functionality to the `struct`, meaning programmatic content that can act on the data in the `struct`. Before we get to that, let's talk about these programmatic implementations. In Rust, you define traits. These are actionable features that a struct may have. A trait in Rust is similar to an interface in C++ in the sense that an interface in C++ is an abstraction technique, just as a trait is an abstraction technique in Rust. You define a trait, including the way it is called as a function, without worrying about the implementation. That gets handled separately.

A trait allows you to indicate how you expect something to behave, without needing to worry about what that something is. That's where the abstraction comes in. You define traits and, in essence, you create contracts. Any implementation of a trait is expected to behave in a particular way, defined by the functions that are specified in the trait. Let's take a look at a trait—specifically, the trait referred to before the struct definition in the code we're looking at.

```
pub trait Encodable {
    fn encode<S: Encoder>(&self, s: &mut S) -> Result<(), S::Error>;
}
```

This trait defines a function called `encode`. This is just an interface definition, however. This is a trait that is expected to be assigned to a datatype. You're looking at a generic function. The reason it's called generic is because the types aren't specified. In fact, the type is a parameter that is passed to the function. Since no types are specified, it's generic, meaning it can be used without regard to the type. A generic function is a way of implementing code reuse and is called *polymorphism*. With a generic function, you create a function that applies to any datatype. That way, you avoid having to write separate functions for each datatype.

The process of creating a function implementation for every different datatype is called *overloading*, which means you have overloaded the name with multiple potential matches. Let's say, for instance, that we wanted to do something like doubling a value. The following examples, shown in Rust, have overloaded the function name `double()`. In some languages, this is possible because the signature for the function is different for every one of these, in spite of the name being the same. Since the passed parameters as well as the return value are different, that changes the signature of the function, so to the compiler they are different functions altogether. It's just for us that it's overloaded because it looks the same. Rust does not support this directly. In order to overload a function name, you would have to make it a trait that was implemented on a data structure.

```
fn double(x: u8) -> u8 {
    x + x
}

fn double(x: u16) -> u16 {
    x + x
}
```

```
fn double(x: f32) -> f32 {
    x + x
}

fn double(x: f64) -> f64 {
    x + x
}

fn double(x: String) -> String {
    format!("{}{}", x, x)
}
```

You may notice that in almost all those cases, the body of the function is identical. The only thing that's different is the datatype of the parameter as well as the datatype of the return value. Because of the minimal differences, the easiest way to implement this would be to use the following generic function. However, the generic function shown next doesn't work for all datatypes. In some languages, we can double a string by returning string + string, but that doesn't work in Rust. We have to create a format and pass the string in twice. Because of that, we would need to overload the generic with a specific implementation for the `String` type. For all numeric types, though, the following generic implementation works just fine.

> **NOTE** The generic implementation here avoids the potential problem of trying to multiply by 2. You can't multiply a floating-point number by 2, since that's not a floating-point representation. To double a floating point with multiplication, you would need to multiply it by 2.0. That means we can't have a generic function using multiplication between integers and floating points.
>
> ```
> fn double<T>(x: T) -> T {
>     x + x
> }
> ```

In brackets after the function name, you indicate the type is being passed into the function with the value T. That T can then be used in place of any datatype. In the parameter, we indicate that the variable named x has the value of the datatype being passed into the function. Additionally, we can indicate that the value being returned also has the datatype being passed in. In essence, this means that the datatype is a variable—something that isn't known when the function is written. It is known at compile time, however, which means the function can be built properly into the executable.

This process of knowing what function that needs to be called—meaning what address is going to be referred to when the function is called—is referred to as *binding*. From the standpoint of the language and the compiler (and for our purposes here, since this is a complex subject when you really dig into it), there is early binding and late binding. Early binding is where the compiler knows what is being referred to and it can be built into the program by the compiler. This would speed up the program, of course, since the address is known before it is run. If the address can't be identified until runtime, it's called *late binding*.

OBJECT ORIENTATION

Object-oriented programming was developed as a way to mimic real-world paradigms in a programming language construct. Object-oriented languages, or at least the idea of object-oriented languages, go back decades, but for quite a while, imperative languages were the thing. If you think about the imperative mood in English as a way of getting your head around the idea of imperative languages, we can consider the example Go! In English, as in other languages, the imperative mood is where a command is issued. This is commonly a verb, and you are indicating an action you want or expect to be followed. This would result in something being different after the command was followed. Taking the previous example, it may result in you leaving the room, so there would be one less person in the room. The same is true in imperative languages—we issue a command or a statement, and it results in something changing in the program.

There is much disagreement about what constitutes an object-oriented language. However, for the sake of argument, let's say that a language has to implement three elements in order to be considered object-oriented. The first is encapsulation. This means that the data within a program is contained with the code that will act on that data. In its purest form, anything outside of the object where the data is stored can't access the data. The only way to get access to the data is through the methods or functions that are stored with it. The data and the methods together create an object at runtime. You may be familiar with class languages like C++ or Java. Class languages are where the data and methods are put together into a class in the source code. It's only when the class is instantiated (called into being at runtime) that we have an object.

The second element of object-oriented languages is *polymorphism*. This is where any one thing can take multiple forms. Take the example of the generic function. We create a single generic function, and depending on the datatype the function is being called with, we have a different implementation of that function. You may also take a class that includes interfaces, which are generic in nature, and then create specific implementations of those interfaces. We end up with multiple things that are defined the same way but are implemented differently.

Finally, and this is the sticking point with Rust, which means it's not actually an object-oriented language, is *inheritance*. As there are no classes defined, there is nothing to actually inherit. The base definitions that relate to this in Rust are structs and traits. Both can stand on their own, but together, you can get polymorphism of a sort. Short of creating an instance of a struct, there is nothing else we can do. As a result, there is no way to get inheritance in Rust.

Beyond inheritance, Rust doesn't really implement encapsulation either. Methods or functions are tacked onto a data structure rather than being wrapped around the data, protecting the data from ill-advised direct access. However, just because Rust isn't an object-oriented language doesn't mean it's not powerful. The data protection comes in other forms in Rust, without needing explicit access rights and interfaces.

Back to our regularly scheduled program. We have the `Encodable` trait, which is a generic function, meaning that the definition takes in a type and then the function just deals with the variable being passed in no matter what the type happens to be. When a trait is specified, all you have is an interface that indicates what the call to that function should look like. Thus, we have the calling parameters and the return type. We are lacking an implementation. If a module specifies a type without creating the implementation, it is up to us as programmers to do the implementation. Fortunately, this is another place Rust has our backs.

In the case we're looking at, we have a `struct` and want to be able to make that `struct` serializable using the `rustc-serialize` module. This module can't possibly know about the struct that we have created, which means there are traits that have to be implemented. This involves writing code that implements the functions based on the data that is in the `struct`. In some cases, the Rust compiler can take care of that for us. That's what's happening in the following line:

```
#[derive(RustcEncodable)]
```

That line tells the compiler to take a pass at implementing the `RustcEncodable` trait. The module contains implementations for the common or built-in datatypes, but the compiler guesses what the implementation should look like and so it will do the implementation for us without us having to write any code.

In some cases, we have to do the code ourselves. This is true when it comes to converting the data structure we have to the JSON format. Fortunately, doing so is a simple process. In JSON, we use a self-describing format. You essentially have a key/value pair, or rather multiple key/value pairs, all wrapped in curly brackets and separated by commas. The following is an example of what JSON would look like with a single record:

```
{name:"Four Weddings and a Funeral",
year:1994,
cast:"Hugh Grant",
length:117}
```

The key/value pairs are listed on a single line. We have the key name, which would be the name of the column in a traditional database, followed by a colon (:), and then the value. This would be the row entry that aligned with the column in a traditional database represented in a table. After each key/value pair is a comma (,) to indicate there are more entries, and we work through the rest of the columns using the column name, and then the value that would go in the row associated with that column.

What we need to do is create a function that will format a string in such a way that we have key/value pairs so that the key/value pairs can be converted to JSON. So, we need to implement a trait that comes with the `rustc-serialize` module. We have to implement `ToJson` for our `Dvd` struct. The implementation is shown next. This is the same thing as we saw before, just pulled out for clarity:

```
impl ToJson for Dvd {
    fn to_json(&self) -> Json {
        Json::String(format!("{}+{}+{}+{}i", self.name, self.year, self.cast,
self.length))
    }
}
```

This code is reasonably straightforward. We are implementing the `ToJson` trait for the `Dvd struct` we have in this program. We have to do this since there is no predefined function for a data structure we have created. In implementing the trait, there is one function we need to create: `to_json()`. This will return a JSON object when it has finished.

Self-Identification

One thing you will notice in `fn to_json(&self)` is the parameter that is sent into the function. First, `&self` is a reference, meaning we are getting a copy of the data rather than the location of the memory where the data is being stored. Second, and more important, we are getting something called `self`, suggesting we are getting ourself passed to ourself. That seems confusing.

Imagine that we have our data structure in memory, and to help you with the imagining, you can take a look at Figure 3.1. You have a block of memory that has the name, year, cast, and length all stored contiguously. As an adjunct to that block of memory, though not stored in the same place, is the `to_json()` function. In essence, they go together. The function is a trait of the data, after all. It's like any trait you may have—hair color, eye color, height, weight, etc.—which is part of who you are. The `to_json()` function is simply part of the data structure. As a result, when the function refers to `self`, it refers to the particular instance of the data structure that the function is expected to act on.

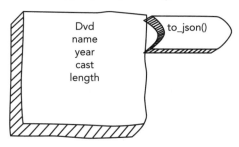

FIGURE 3.1: Representation of a Dvd structure

Perhaps something more concrete would help. Let's take a look at the previous representation again, but rather than just a generic definition with the 'column' or key names, we'll use a specific instance. We have defined a variable with the type `Dvd` and initialized it with the values you can see in Figure 3.2. The `self` variable gives the function `to_json()` (in this case) the ability to access all those values. As you can see in the function implementation shown previously, it does so by referring to `self.name`, `self.year`, `self.cast`, and `self.length`. The variable name is `self`, and each member of the data structure is accessed using the dot notation, meaning variable name dot member (i.e., `self.name` or `mydvd.name`).

FIGURE 3.2: Instance of a Dvd

For this instance of `Dvd`, the value of `self.name` would be `Hitchhiker's Guide to the Galaxy`. All the other member variables would be what they are in Figure 3.2. The year is 2005, cast is Zooey Deschanel, and the length is 109 minutes. Any time you need to refer to the data from inside a trait, you would use `self`, because the data structure is a parameter to the function.

The Rest

There isn't much left to this program, so we can talk through the last couple of functions. The first one to talk about is a single line, which means it could easily be called directly. Sometimes wrapping a function call from a module inside a function call written into your program is a good practice.

The reason is, down the road, you may want to do something else either before or after you call the module's function. It's easier to make the change inside a single function that may be called multiple times through a program than to have to make a change in many places in a larger program. For this program, it doesn't matter as much because we're going to call the function only once, but keeping with good programming practices is just a good idea. Think of it as muscle memory. You program in a way that can be maintained and updated, and you don't get bit later on if the program grows a lot more than you expected it to.

The function in question is shown next. This function takes in our Dvd struct and returns a string. You may notice that the Dvd being passed in is a reference. This is because we aren't going to do anything destructive with the data. All we need is a copy of the data because we'll format that data and return the formatted data in a string, which will be returned from the function. As far as the return goes, again we have an expression on a line by itself. The encode() function returns a Result, just as we've seen before, which means we need to unwrap that data structure in order to retrieve the String value in the Result.

```
fn converttojson (advd: &Dvd) -> String {

    json::encode(advd).unwrap()

}
```

Finally, we have the main function. This simple function is shown next. The first thing that happens is creating an instance of the Dvd struct we're calling. To create that instance, we have to pass in the initial values. Since we aren't creating this as a mutable variable, we'll set these values once, and they will remain for the lifetime of that variable. What you will see here is effectively a tuple with named parameters. This means that rather than positional parameters, where the position in the list determines how the values are assigned, the value gets assigned to the member with the specified name. The trailing comma in the initialization is a style thing and isn't necessary, just as with the definition of the struct.

```
fn main() {

    let a = Dvd {
        name: String::from("Four Weddings and a Funeral"),
        year: 1994,
        cast: String::from("Hugh Grant"),
        length: 117,
    };

    let encoded = converttojson(&a);

    println!("{}", encoded);

}
```

By comparison with another language, C, the initialization of a struct looks like the following code. It looks similar to the way we initialize a struct in Rust. We use named parameters here, though the names are treated essentially as member names by using the dot in front of each one. One thing to note is that we can't take a look at how a language like Java handles initializing a struct, because it doesn't have them. Instead, it uses the class, and you initialize a class by passing parameters into a new() function, which is the initializer for classes.

```
typedef struct Dvd {
    char title[50];
    int year;
    char cast[250];
    int length;
} DVD;

int main () {
    DVD a = { .title = "The Avengers", .year = 2012, .cast = "Robert Downey, Jr.",
.length = 143 };

    return 0;
}
```

Finally, we create a variable called encoded to catch the string that returns from the converttojson() function. As expected, we are passing a reference to the Dvd instance into that function. The encoded variable isn't strictly necessary since it just carries a string, which is the same type as the return from the function, so the function call could be inserted directly to the println!() function. The same thinking applies here as applied to wrapping our own function around the json::encode() function. Who knows what this may evolve into as more functionality gets added and as more consideration goes into the existing code. I may want to do something with that value, so it's best to hold the value in a variable that can be used rather than needing to call the function again. Calling the function multiple times costs processing time whereas retrieving a value from memory is probably far less costly. With modern processors, it's not a big deal, but we may as well be efficient if we can.

SECOND PASS

Now that we have our first pass complete, we can take a look at the preferred way of handling JSON. Instead of the rustc_serialize module, we'll use the serde module. This is a framework used for serializing and deserializing data in Rust. We'll do something a little more than just the usual dependencies list. As usual, we need to edit the Cargo.toml file. The dependencies section looks as follows:

```
[dependencies]
serde = { version = "*", features = ["derive"] }
serde_json = "*"
serde_derive = "*"
```

As noted, we are using the serde library, so no problem there. We are using specific elements of the serde library, so the different entries are not especially surprising either. You may be looking with a little curiosity at the first dependency entry, though. Rather than just the version (or wildcard since we want whatever is the latest version at the time of build), we now have a tuple of properties that we are going to flag that particular crate with. Any time we are creating a tuple, we surround it with curly brackets ({}). In addition to the version, which we indicate with the name version as well as its value, we need a particular feature. As a result, we have a list of features. Well, in this case, it's a list of one, but we have to put it in square brackets ([]) because there may be more than one. The feature we want to specifically enable when this crate is built on our system is derive, which we will use fairly early on in the program.

Speaking of the program, let's get to it. In the following code listing, you can see the bulk of the program. Later, we'll look at the main function separately, but since it's just a driver function used to test the other functions, it's not hugely interesting, other than we'll introduce a new way to create a string value. So, buckle your seat belt and get prepared for that a little later.

```
extern crate serde_derive;
extern crate serde;
extern crate serde_json;

use serde::{Deserialize, Serialize};
use serde_json::Result;
use std::fs::File;
use std::fs::OpenOptions;

#[derive(Serialize, Deserialize)]
struct Dvd {
    name: String,
    year: u16,
    cast: String,
    length: u16
}

fn json_from_str(raw: &str) -> Dvd {
    serde_json::from_str(raw).unwrap()
}

fn str_from_json(dvd: &Dvd) -> String {
    serde_json::to_string(dvd).unwrap()
}

fn dvds_to_file(f: &String, d: Dvd) {
    let file = OpenOptions::new().append(true).open(f).unwrap();
    serde_json::to_writer(file, &d);
}

fn dvds_from_file(f: &String) -> Dvd {
    let file = File::open(f).unwrap();
    let deserialized_json: Dvd = serde_json::from_reader(file).unwrap();
    deserialized_json
}
```

As usual, we start the with the externalities. First, we have to refer to the serde crates. These are in no particular order, since there doesn't have to be any order. Some of this is a style preference thing. You may want to order them in alphabetical order. You might also order them so that they look better visually, starting with the shortest and ending up at the longest. Since the compiler doesn't care at all—you're just indicating that you're using external crates and providing the names—you can order them as you see fit.

Then, of course, we move to the use statements. We are using both Serialize and Deserialize from the serde crate. We are also using Result from the serde_json library. We'll be reading in from and writing out to files, so we need a couple of modules from the standard library related to file I/O. This includes introducing the idea of options, which we will be using when we open the file where we're storing our JSON entries. More about that shortly.

First, let's take another look at the `Dvd` structure. This is the same one we used earlier. As before, we'll tack on a couple of traits. This time, we'll let the compiler generate both the `Serialize` and `Deserialize` trait implementations for us. You may remember (since it was just a couple of pages back now) the whole feature thing we had to do in the `Cargo.toml` file. This is exactly why we had to do that. If you don't enable that feature in the `Cargo.toml` file when you add your dependencies, the compiler won't have any idea how to generate these traits, so you'll end up with a whole bunch of errors related to serialization and deserialization of our `struct` during compilation. So, this is our `struct` with the relevant `derive` attribute added to automatically create the traits:

```
#[derive(Serialize, Deserialize)]
struct Dvd {
    name: String,
    year: u16,
    cast: String,
    length: u16
}
```

Now that we have the ability to serialize and deserialize (using JSON no less) our data structure, we can start looking at manipulating the data structure. As we did in the last pass on the program, we have a couple of functions that just wrap the functions from the `serde` crate. You can see the two functions here. The first one returns a `Dvd` `struct` from a string. The second takes a `Dvd` `struct` and returns a string from it. Neither of these would be possible without having the feature we enabled in our dependencies.

```
fn json_from_str(raw: &str) -> Dvd {
    serde_json::from_str(raw).unwrap()
}

fn str_from_json(dvd: &Dvd) -> String {
    serde_json::to_string(dvd).unwrap()
}
```

A couple of things to make note of here. The first is that we are again passing in references to the data, because we want to be able to make use of the data in the originating function after the function completes. (Yes, you're going to get sick of this being repeated over and over, but it is such an essential part of how Rust works, it bears repeating until it's completely part of how you think about writing the programs.) We're making use of the `serde_json` crate, using the `from_str()` function to create our data structure from a string and then the `to_string()` function to create a string from the data structure we have. These require the serialization and deserialization traits of the structure to have been generated. Certainly you can create your own if you like, but the compiler will do it for you, as noted previously.

Now that we have the ability to create a string from a data structure and a data structure from a string, we can go about writing out data to a file and then reading it back in. Because there are some important ideas in each of these functions, we'll take a look at them one at a time. The first one, the shorter of the two, is `dvds_to_file()`. This function takes not only a string with the filename to be written to, but also the data structure that will be written out to the file.

```
fn dvds_to_file(f: &String, d: Dvd) {
    let file = OpenOptions::new().append(true).open(f).unwrap();
    serde_json::to_writer(file, &d);
}
```

As we did in the Life game, we'll open a file. This time around, though, we're tacking a new function on to the chain used to open the file. Actually, it even starts with a completely different namespace. We'll create a new instance of the OpenOptions struct. This allows us to create a new file using the append(true) trait. That lets us add to the existing file without writing over anything that may already be in place. Once we have the append() trait, we can call the open() trait (function). Finally, we have to call unwrap() on the Result so that we get just the file handle and not the rest of the Result struct.

Finally, we have a file handle that we can use to pass to the serialization function that is going to handle writing JSON out to a file. One thing to note here is this assumes there is no problem opening the file. Ideally, we should be doing something with the Result struct to ensure we got an Ok and not an Err. We will assume that there isn't a problem opening this file. If anything does happen, a module will throw an exception, and the program will crash. The result may be the same in the end anyway—the program coming to a halt. It's just that we'd rather control how the program ends rather than letting it blow up. One thing at a time, though. Let's move on to reading in a data structure from a file.

Rather than having two parameters, for this function we just have the one parameter. This time, we're just passing in the filename that will be for the function. We'll take in JSON and convert it to our Dvd data structure. As a result, the function is a single line longer. Theoretically, it doesn't have to be, but again, we may want to do something with the value in this function rather than just returning it to the calling function. The complete function looks like this:

```
fn dvds_from_file(f: &String) -> Dvd {
    let file = File::open(f).unwrap();
    let deserialized_json: Dvd = serde_json::from_reader(file).unwrap();
    deserialized_json
}
```

Since we aren't writing, we don't need anything related to Append. As a result, we can just use the File struct as it is. We call the open() trait on that struct and then unwrap it, so all we have is the file handle. The file handle is the parameter needed by the from_reader() function from the serde_json library. This function takes the file handle, reads data from it, and converts the record that it finds there into the Dvd data structure. This is stored into the variable deserialized_json. Finally, we leave the expression deserialized_json on a line by itself. One thing to note here is that the file handle called file is a local variable. That means it goes out of scope at the end of the function, causing it to be deleted. The same is true for the previous function, of course. Once the file handle has been deleted, the underlying file gets closed because the file handle has been released.

The Driver

We have all the building blocks we need to develop a program that handles DVD records. We can serialize and deserialize, convert to and from strings, and do all the file handling that is useful for persistence. Let's take a look at a simple driver function that makes use of the functions we just created. Along the way, we'll take another look at how to create a String instance from raw data. This is not a driver in the traditional sense of a piece of software that talks to or manages hardware. Instead, it's a chunk of software that makes use of functions just to demonstrate that they behave the way we expect them to. So, enough about what a driver is—let's take a look at the main function that we're using.

```
fn main() {
    let rawdata = r#"
        {
            "name": "La La Land",
            "year": 2016,
            "cast": "Emma Stone, Ryan Gosling",
            "length": 128
        }"#;

    let mut d: Dvd = json_from_str(rawdata);

    let encoded = str_from_json(&d);

    println!("{}", encoded);

    let filename = String::from("file.json");
    dvds_to_file(&filename, d);

    d = dvds_from_file(&filename);
    println!("{}", str_from_json(&d));

}
```

The first thing to talk about is creating a `String` instance, especially since it's the very first line in the function. Well, multiple lines, really, but in the end we are creating a single string. What we are doing is creating a `String` instance from a raw string literal, meaning it's a static value consisting of UTF-8 characters. As a result, we indicate that by using the letter `r`. Since we're going to need to use double quotes (") in our raw string, we have to add the octothorpe (also known as a pound or hash symbol, #). So, raw string literal starts with an `r"`, but if you want to include quotes, you need to essentially escape it. A raw string literal that includes quotes starts with `r#"`. As with any string, you close both with the double quote, `"`.

What you can also notice here is the string carries over multiple lines. We don't have to escape the line breaks at the end of each line. You can think of it as a *here* string, which is a shorter version of a *here* document. If you aren't familiar with what a *here* document is, it is a string literal that starts and ends at pre-identified locations and includes everything between the two endpoints. In Unix, you might see a *here* document indicated in a script. An example follows:

```
kilroy@milobloom:~/Documents$ cat << EOF > test.txt
> This is a here document. All the text up to the point where the shell
> receives an EOF on a line by itself will be included in the file test.txt
> because that's the file that has been indicated as the output.
> EOF
kilroy@milobloom:~/Documents$
```

You can see the similarity here with what we are doing in Rust. We're essentially creating *here* strings indicating the start with either `r"` or `r#"` and then closing the *here string* with the `"`, which is the same as using EOF in the example from earlier. Now, we don't have to use the `String` constructor like we have been. We can just create a `String` instance from a string literal using these approaches.

Using that raw string value in JSON form, we can convert it to the data structure using the `json_from_str()` function. We pass in the `String` we created, and we get the data structure back.

We'll store that into a mutable variable called d. Making it mutable saves us from having to create another variable later on when we want to create a new data structure instance to store data in.

Once we have the data structure, we can return it to the JSON format using the `str_from_json()` function. When we get JSON, keep in mind that JSON is a text-based format. When we get JSON, we have a string where the contents of the string are formatted with keys and values, surrounded by curly brackets. This string allows us to write all the data out to a file without worrying about how it's formatted in the file and trying to get it deserialized correctly once we are trying to read it back in from that file.

Speaking of files, the next section of our driver takes those file-related functions for a spin. First, we need to create a string that contains the filename we are going to work with. This filename will be set statically since we're just testing functions. A better approach would be to take a parameter with a filename or to use a configuration setting in a file. For this purpose, it's fine that we're hard-coding a filename.

One thing to note about the filename string is we haven't specified a datatype for the variable. The Rust compiler infers this from the initialization. Since we're using the `String::from()` constructor, it's obvious that the contents of the variable will be a `String`. Additionally, because it's immutable there is no chance of trying to put any other datatype, like an integer, into the memory location where our `String` is stored. That memory location is effectively read-only. In general, though, it's best practice to specify the datatype, because being explicit is good for readability and clarity in how the program works.

The two function calls look just as you'd expect them to. We set the filename variable and then pass it and the data structure into `dvds_to_filename()`. After that, we reuse the `Dvd` instance declared earlier to store the contents of whatever is in the file we had previously used. This may be what we just wrote out if the file was empty when we did the write. So, we'll return the same data into our d variable that was already there. This is a single call to read, so we'll read only one record in.

Finally, just to validate that we got some data back and it looks okay, we call `println!()` again. Instead of creating a new variable instance to store the results from `str_from_json()`, we'll just send the result from that function into the `println!()` function since it will take a `String` as a parameter, and that's the return value we get back.

And now we're done with our little driver function to test out the functions we had created to demonstrate serialization and deserialization using the `serde` module.

SUMMARY

We started the chapter with a conversation about references. References are how we maintain our sanity when writing in a language that takes memory safety very seriously. Functions take in parameters that then belong to the function. This is the idea of ownership. We pass data into a function, and that function then owns the data. Once the function completes, the memory where the data was located gets released. Often, we don't want that—thus, references and borrowing. We can borrow data without losing it by sending references into the function. This is the difference between passing by reference and passing by value in other languages. Rust does a pass by reference by default, meaning it passes in the memory location, so the data is directly accessible.

In most languages, this means we can alter the memory directly rather than having to return values and replacing variable contents. In Rust, the data belongs to the called function. If we don't want that to happen, we need to pass by value. This is a reference. When we pass a reference, we use the & character, both in the function definition as well as with the parameter when we call the function.

Since we'll often be dealing with complex data structures, the core of that is the `struct`. In C++, you might think of the `struct` as the foundation of the class because a class has a collection of data, as well as a number of methods that act on that data. In Rust, we just have the `struct`, and if we want to do something with that programmatically, we use traits. You attach a trait to a `struct`, and then you can act on the data without having to pass the data into the function. You call the function from the `struct` itself.

These are different from a class in many ways. First, you can get polymorphism without having to inherit from another class. You implement a trait for your data structure. You can then implement a number of other traits so that you can attach functionality from anywhere a trait has been defined. Pull in functionality from a library and implement the trait for your data structure. This does not mean you have inheritance, though, which is what differentiates Rust from object-oriented languages. We can get some of the same end results without actually using inheritance. Inheritance means you take one thing and then define something else that includes all the same features, plus some others that you want to add.

Because we can apply traits to a data structure and then call that trait on that data structure, it alleviates the need to pass the data structure into the function, as noted before. Instead, the function is aware of the data structure. We use the `self` identifier to refer to the data that is attached to the function or trait. This gives us direct access to all the members of the `struct` without having to worry about any calling parameters. Since we are working on ourselves, in effect, we aren't passing anything to a function, which would kick in the rules of ownership and would cause the data to disappear when the function concluded.

We can handle serialization and deserialization in different ways. This is the process of taking a data structure and writing it out to storage or a communication channel and then reading it on the other side. Serializing is writing out, deserializing is reading in. Deserialization is challenging because you need to take data in and put it into a data structure in memory. You may not always know exactly what the data looks like, which means you have the potential of causing memory errors. Fortunately, we can use libraries. One of them is `serde`, which includes interfaces for traits that can be applied to your data structures. If you add the right feature, some of the traits can be created automatically by the compiler using the `derive` directive.

There are times the compiler will do the work for you, but it's not always the case. So, you may need to create the trait implementations on your own. For the programs we looked at in this chapter, we used JavaScript Object Notation (JSON), which is a self-describing data language and very helpful for transmission and storage. The `serde` library includes implementations of JSON for serialization and deserialization, fortunately, and you don't have to write the code yourself.

EXERCISES

1. Add some additional fields to the Dvd data structure and then update the first program to serialize and deserialize the new data structure.

2. Create a vector of Dvds and update the second program to read and write multiple Dvds from a file.

ADDITIONAL RESOURCES

Data Serialization - devopedia.org/data-serialization

Serialization and Deserialization - medium.com/better-programming/serialization-and-deserialization-ba12fc3fbe23

What is Object Oriented Programming - www.educative.io/blog/object-oriented-programming

What is an Object? - docs.oracle.com/javase/tutorial/java/concepts/object.html

Go and Rust - Objects without Class - lwn.net/Articles/548560/

Hangman

IN THIS CHAPTER, YOU WILL LEARN THE FOLLOWING:

➤ How to create traits for structs

➤ How to use the `match` statement

➤ How to generate random numbers

➤ How to set up initial error handling

➤ How to take user input

Although we won't be doing any graphical interfaces, we can still do the basics of a hangman game. Ultimately, the objective of hangman is to guess a word, one letter at a time. The whole drawing of a body hanging from a noose is nice if we're doing this on paper and can be highly entertaining if you want to take it a little further than the basics with a lot of flourishes to what you are sketching. The guessing game is what is at the core of hangman, though. As a result, that's what we'll start with. That also makes a good foundation for introducing additional concepts in Rust.

Along the way, we'll take a closer look at adding traits to structs, which we started exploring in the previous chapter. Adding traits to the data structure we'll use keeps a lot of the interaction with the data in the structure inside the structure itself rather than allowing the rest of the program to go directly to the contents of the structure. This is the data encapsulation idea we were talking about in the previous chapter. You keep access to the data to a minimum. Everything should be accessed through an interface to maintain the integrity of the data. This rule can't be enforced in Rust, but that doesn't mean we can't do our best to follow that approach in our programming practices.

We'll address some other new concepts in this chapter as well. One of these is the `match` statement. The `match` statement allows you to do pattern matching, directing program functionality based on how the pattern matching goes. This means you can have multiple outcomes from a match statement as compared with only one or two if you were using an if..then..else statement. This is especially useful in error handling, which is where we'll use the match statement.

We'll end up doing rudimentary error handling, building on some of the work we've done previously. Since error handling is such an important element of programming, we'll keep building on our error handling as we go, though taking complex concepts in stages is probably easier. You can always go back and enhance previous programs with more and better error handling. So, before we jump into the explanation of the program, let's take a look at the complete program, as shown here:

```
extern crate rand;

use std::fs::File;
use std::io::{self, BufRead};
use std::path::Path;
use rand::Rng;

struct Word {
    answer: String,
    length: usize,
    correct_count: usize,
    representation: String
}

trait CheckLetter {
    fn check_for_letter(&mut self, c: char) -> bool;
}

trait CheckComplete {
    fn check_complete(&self) -> bool;
}

impl CheckComplete for Word {
    fn check_complete(&self) -> bool {
        self.correct_count == self.length
    }
}

impl CheckLetter for Word {
    fn check_for_letter(&mut self, c: char) -> bool {
        let mut count: usize = 0;
        let mut found: bool = false;
        let mut response = String::with_capacity(self.length);
        let mut index = 0;
        for letter in self.answer.chars() {
            if letter == c {
                found = true;
                count += 1;
                response.push(c);
            }
            else {
                if self.representation.chars().nth(index) != Some('_') {
                    response.push(self.representation.chars().nth(index).unwrap());
                }
                else {
```

```
                        response.push('_');
                    }
                }
                index += 1;
            }
        if found {
            println!("Found a ")
        }
        self.representation = response;
        self.correct_count += count;
        count > 0
    }
}

fn read_lines<P>(filename: P) -> io::Result<io::Lines<io::BufReader<File>>>
where P: AsRef<Path>, {
    let file = File::open(filename)?;
    Ok(io::BufReader::new(file).lines())
}

fn read_list(filename: String) -> Vec::<String> {
    let mut v = Vec::<String>::new();
    if let Ok(lines) = read_lines(filename) {
        for w in lines {
            let word:String = w.unwrap();
            if word.len() > 4 {
                v.push(word);
            }
        }
    }
    v
}

fn select_word() -> String {
    let mut rng = rand::thread_rng();
    let filename:String = "words.txt".to_string();
    let words:Vec<String> = read_list(filename);
    let word_count = words.len();
    let selection = rng.gen_range(1, word_count);
    let select: String = words[selection].clone();
    select
}

fn main() {

    let body = vec!["noose".to_string(), "head".to_string(), "neck".to_string(),
"torso".to_string(), "left arm".to_string(),
    "right arm".to_string(), "right leg".to_string(), "left leg".to_string(), "left
foot".to_string(), "right foot".to_string()];
    let mut body_iter = body.iter();
    let mut result = select_word();
    let mut answer = Word {
        length: result.len(),
        representation: String::from_utf8(vec![b'_'; result.len()]).unwrap(),
        answer: result,
```

continues

(continued)

```
            correct_count: 0
        };

    let mut letter: char;
    let mut body_complete: bool = false;
    while !answer.check_complete() && !body_complete {
        println!("Provide a letter to guess ");
        let mut input = String::new();
        match io::stdin().read_line(&mut input) {
            Ok(n) => {
                letter = input.chars().nth(0).unwrap();
                if answer.check_for_letter(letter) {
                    println!("There is at least one {}, so the word is {}", letter,
answer.representation);
                }
                else {
                    let next_part = body_iter.next().unwrap();
                    println!("Incorrect! You are at {}", next_part);
                    if next_part == "right foot" {
                        body_complete = true;
                    }
                }
            }
            Err(error) => {
                println!("Didn't get any input");
            }
        }
    }
    if body_complete {
        println!("You were unsuccessful at guessing {}", &answer.answer)
    }
    else {
        println!("Yes! The word was {}", &answer.answer);
    }
}
```

OUR DATA

Let's begin by taking a look at the data structure, explaining the various data elements that are necessary. We're starting a little bit backward, though. We're talking about the data we need rather than talking about how to get to those data elements. Let's start by discussing program design rather than just the mechanics of how the language works. When you get to programs with a lot of moving pieces, it's useful to begin by breaking out the individual elements, including all the data you need and maybe even a rough flow of actions. Although some programs can be written on the fly, others require some thought up front. You may want to keep a pad close at hand for taking notes so that you aren't trying to keep everything in your head. Figure 4.1 shows an image of notes about this program in a notebook.

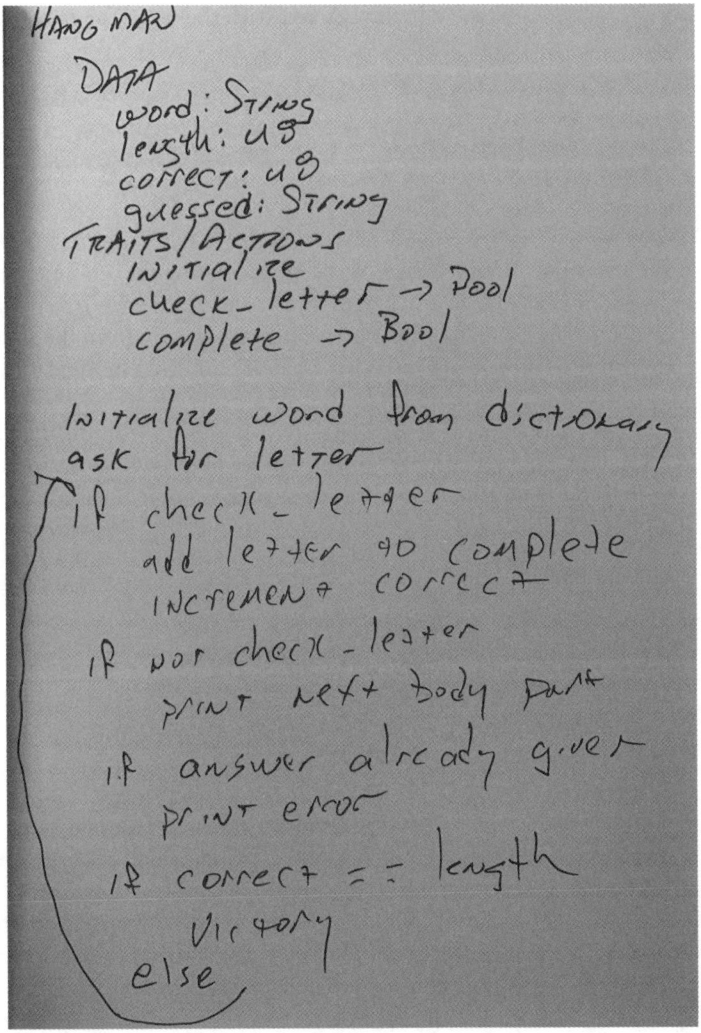

FIGURE 4.1: Notes on program design

You'll see at the top of the page some notes on the data that is necessary. You may think that all we need is the String used to keep our selected word, but it makes some sense to maintain other related information as well. In part, this is to keep from having to calculate it every time. Additionally, we may need to use it in different parts of the program, so it's better to store some of it so it can be used rather than having to be derived or calculated every time it's needed. As a result, we'll keep track of some different pieces of data. The first is the selected word itself. That's a simple decision—if we don't store it, we can't see whether someone has selected letters that are in that word.

The other data we'll make use of is perhaps debatable. You may decide you'd rather do it in a different way, but we can go over the rationale for each piece of data. Here's the data structure we'll use.

We'll call the data structure `Word` because it contains the data associated with the word the player will need to guess.

```
struct Word {
    answer: String,
    length: usize,
    correct_count: usize,
    representation: String
}
```

We'll store two integers. The first is the length, so we don't have to keep calculating it each time we refer to it. Of course, you could create a trait that returns the length and calculates it each time, but it's cheaper from a computational perspective to calculate it just once and pull it back from the data structure each time we need to use it. Both this integer and the other one we're storing in the data structure are defined as `usize`. This is one of the built-in datatypes, like the other types we're talking about here. The reason for this is because calls that are made later return a value with this type. It's easier to store it like this so that we can assign and compare as needed without having to do any conversions. In Rust, the `usize` datatype is the number of bits it takes to refer to a memory address. In most cases, this will be the same as a `u64`.

> **NOTE** *Given the amount of memory most systems have today, what size of integer or floating-point datatype you use is probably a matter of personal taste where it isn't dictated, as it is here, by the needs of the modules you're using.*

The second integer we'll store is the number of characters that the user has guessed. This helps us easily determine when the word has been guessed. Rather than checking a string, which can be expensive from a computational perspective, we can just keep track of the number of correct characters. When the number of correct characters is the same as the length, we assume that the word has been guessed correctly. This requires us to correctly identify all the characters in the word as they are being guessed and then accurately keep track of the number of correct letters as they are found. We'll get to that a little later.

Finally, we need to be able to give the user the representation of the word with the guessed letters in the correct place. If we don't do that, it's difficult for the player to be able to get the correct word. Even knowing the right letters doesn't help. If you know that the letters r, e, a, and g are in the word and the word contains four letters, what do you think the correct word is? You may guess *gear*, which might be correct. You may also guess *rage*, which may be correct. Without knowing the order of the letters, you may have no idea as a player when you have the right word and what letters to guess based on the letters that are in place.

This `string` will get initialized with the _ character in all the positions. As we find correct characters, we replace the _ characters with the right letter so that we can print the partial word, complete with underscores in the places where the letters aren't known yet. This gives the player a visual representation of the word.

We have the data we need at this point. What we need on top of that is a collection of functions that will be used to interact directly with the data in our data structure. These functions are called *traits*, and they need to be defined separately from the structure itself.

The Traits

As before, we'll start by talking through our needs when it comes to interacting with the data. First is probability initializing the record, but we must keep in mind that this is not object-oriented in the same sense that you may be used to from other languages. We don't have an object, so there is no initializer that we can use to put all the data into the right place, including performing some calculations. If, for instance, we were doing this in Java, we could create the class and add a constructor, as you can see here. This constructor allows us to set everything automatically by just passing the selected word into the constructor when we create an instance of the Word class.

```
public class Word {
    String answer;
    int length;
    int correct_count;
    String representation;

    public Word(String s) {
        this.answer = s;
        this.length = s.length();
        this.correct_count=0;
        char[] chars = new char[s.length()];
        Arrays.fill(chars, '_');
        this.representation = new String(chars);
    }
}
```

We don't have objects, so we don't have constructors automatically, though you could create one by creating a new() trait. We'll get to how to initialize the data structure later on when we create an instance of the data structure. For now, we can forego the constructor or initializer. We'll move on to the other functions we need to have access to. First, we must determine whether or not we have a correct letter. This task is going to be a pretty heavy lift because of all the things that need to be done to check to see whether we have a correct letter that has been guessed by the player. We'll pass in the guessed letter to that function.

The next thing we must do is determine whether the user has guessed the word. We need this trait because of all the essential data stored in the data structure. You can see the two traits defined here. Remember that a trait is just the definition of an interface. There is nothing in the trait definition aside from the function signatures that need to be implemented. We have two traits that will need to be implemented against our data structure. Nothing fancy, and there are probably other traits that we could implement, but if everything gets done here, there isn't as much for you to do on your own as an exercise, building on top of what we have.

```
trait CheckLetter {
    fn check_for_letter(&mut self, c: char) -> bool;
}
```

continues

(continued)
```
trait CheckComplete {
    fn check_complete(&self) -> bool;
}
```

> **NOTE** *The datatype for a character is* char. *In some languages, this single character may be represented internally as a byte, but Rust uses Unicode for underlying representations, so a character would likely be multiple bytes.*

When we define a trait, the trait gets a name, which you can think of as an identifier. The trait includes functionality, which means we define a function that the trait performs. The interesting thing about traits in Rust is that you can have multiple traits that all include the same method, and you can implement all those traits on the same data structure. For instance, let's take our Word structure and think about implementing it for another word game. We have a pair of traits that we'll implement for our Word: Double and Triple. Both include functions called increment. Here, you can see the implementations of these traits as well as how you call them:

```
struct Word {
    answer: String,
    length: usize,
    correct_count: usize,
    representation: String
}

trait Double {
    fn increment(&self) -> usize;
}

trait Triple {
    fn increment(&self) -> usize;
}

impl Double {
    fn increment(&self) -> usize {
        self.correct * 2
    }
}
impl Triple for Word {
    fn increment(&self) -> usize {
        self.correct * 3
    }
}

fn main() {
    let w = Word;
    Double::increment(&w);
    Triple::increment(&w);
}
```

If you implement two traits that have the same method on a single `struct`, you need to call those traits differently. In normal circumstances, you'd call the method from the trait, as in `w.increment()`. Since that would be ambiguous, we need to indicate clearly which `implement` method we're meaning to call. To do that, we call the trait identifier (`Double` or `Triple`) followed by the method, as in `Double::increment(&w)`, passing in the `struct` instance as a reference. Rust then knows which method you are meaning to call from which trait. This involves two traits with the same method name, but you can implement many traits with the same method. You just need to make sure you are clear which method you mean to call by indicating the trait first.

Implementations

Once the traits have been defined, we need to be able to implement them. Remember that the traits are just interfaces, which means they are only definitions of what the call to the function that underlies the trait is going to be. This obscures the actual implementation, so the calling program or function doesn't have to know anything about that. All it needs to know is what is getting passed into the function and what is going to be returned from the function. We can start with the simpler of the two traits. Here, you'll see the trait checking to see whether or not we have a completed word:

```
impl CheckComplete for Word {
    fn check_complete(&self) -> bool {
        self.correct_count == self.length
    }
}
```

One reason for having a trait separate from an implementation is because the implementation can know about the internals of the `struct` the trait is being applied to. You can see here that `check_complete()` is implemented by checking to see whether the `correct_count` member is equal to the length of the word being stored.

Our second trait is the longer, more complex one. Here, you can see the implementation of the `CheckLetter` trait—more specifically, the `check_for_letter()` method. This is how we'll determine whether a guessed letter is in the word that's stored. As a result, we take in two parameters. The first parameter, `&mut self`, is a reference to the specific `struct` instance the method is being called on. This is essential since we can have multiple instances of any `struct` definition. Each instance will have a different identifier to indicate the chunk of memory the data inhabits. This variable, `self`, is the reference to that piece of memory. In the previous implementation, it's a straight reference, meaning we're only looking at the data. In this implementation, we need to be able to make adjustments to the data, which means we have to pass it in as mutable; thus we have `&mut self`.

```
impl CheckLetter for Word {
    fn check_for_letter(&mut self, c: char) -> bool {
        let mut count: usize = 0;
        let mut found: bool = false;
        let mut response = String::with_capacity(self.length);
        let mut index = 0;
        for letter in self.answer.chars() {
            if letter == c {
                found = true;
```

continues

(continued)

```
                    count += 1;
                    response.push(c);
                }
            else {
                if self.representation.chars().nth(index) != Some('_') {
                    response.push(self.representation.chars().nth(index).unwrap());
                }
                else {
                response.push('_');
                }
            }
            index += 1;
        }
        if found {
            println!("Found a ")
        }
        self.representation = response;
        self.correct_count += count;
        count > 0
    }
}
```

In addition to the self variable, we pass in the character that the player is guessing. The return value is true/false using the bool type. Although it's not necessarily required any longer with modern languages, my habit of declaring variables at the top of a function comes from years of writing in languages where it was required. This also makes it easier to see all the data pieces in the same place rather than seeing a variable referenced in a function and then trying to figure out where it's declared so that you can understand what it is—what datatype, for instance.

Let's take a look at the variables that are being declared here. First, we'll keep track of all the correct letters in the word. This is the count variable, defined as a usize because we'll use it in places where a usize is required. So rather than doing a conversion between one datatype and another, we'll just declare it from the start as a usize. Because memory is inexpensive, it doesn't much matter how many bits we end up using to store a small number of variables, so a usize is as good as a u8.

Next is the found variable, which is a Boolean that lets us know whether or not we have found a letter. Ultimately, this is going to be the value that is returned from this function. Because we haven't found anything when the function starts, we initialize it with a value of false. We'll also need a string to store the representation of the word in progress, including the blank letters as well as the letters that have been guessed.

The primary reason for needing this additional variable is because Rust doesn't allow for direct access to each individual character in a String. In other languages, we could index directly into the string and replace a character. You can see an example of how this would work in C here. One reason this is the case is because in C, a character string is just an array. It's easy to index into an array and replace a value. From the perspective of the C compiler, a character array, what we call a string, is no different from an array of integers. That's why we can do what you see here:

```c
#include <stdio.h>

int main(int argc, char **argv)
{
```

```
    char word[25] = "This is a test";
    printf("%s\n", word);
    word[2] = 'u';
    printf("%s\n", word);

    return 0;
}
```

In Rust, the `String` isn't just an array. Additionally, characters in a `String` in Rust are represented in UTF-8, which is a Unicode representation. Unicode is a text encoding standard, developed because of the recognition that not all alphabets can be comfortably represented in the 7 bits that ASCII originally supported. Extended ASCII was 8 bits, but even that is insufficient for some character sets. Because of potential inconsistencies in the number of bits/bytes used to represent a character, it is felt that indexing into an array of characters leads to potential inconsistencies. If the character set is 16 bits, for instance, and you try to get to index 2, does that mean the second byte or the second character? If you really mean the second character, that changes the implementation based on the character set in use, which means a more complex implementation.

We'll delve into how we get around this apparent limitation later. Part of that workaround is the `index` variable, which keeps track of where we are in the string so that we can retrieve the correct character out of the current representational value and put it into the new string we're creating. Again, because of the way Rust handles memory management, we're doing a create and replace rather than making adjustments to the existing one.

Let's take a look at the guts of this function now, which is the loop where we go searching through the string. In the next code section, you'll see it pulled out of the rest of the function so we can take a closer look at it.

```
for letter in self.answer.chars() {
        if letter == c {
            found = true;
            count += 1;
            response.push(c);
        }
        else {
            if self.representation.chars().nth(index) != Some('_') {
                response.push(self.representation.chars().nth(index).unwrap());
            }
            else {
                response.push('_');
            }
        }
        index += 1;
    }
```

Because we have a `String` and we need to look at individual characters out of that `String`, we need an iterator. The function `chars()` is what's going to get us an iterator over the characters in the `String`. Each character in the `String` will be placed, one at a time, in the identifier `letter`. The `for` loop takes care of getting us through the entire string, a character at a time. For every letter in the string, we check to see whether it matches (is equal to) the character that was passed into this function in the identifier `c`, which should be the character that the user entered.

If the two characters are equal to one another, we indicate that we found a character by setting the found variable to true. We need this later to be able to pass back to the calling function so that the function can do the right thing by indicating to the user that they were correct in their guess. We also increase the count of correct letters we have found. Finally, we need to create the representation of the letter with all the guesses intact. Since we're going a letter at a time, we can push the correctly guessed character into the String and it will be in the right position when we're all done. That push() is called on the response string, passing in the guessed character.

If the letter guessed is not the same as the letter at that position, we have some figuring to do. First, just because it doesn't match this current guess doesn't mean there wasn't a previously guessed correct character at that position. Because of that, we can't just push an underscore onto the string serving as our ongoing guesses. Instead, we need to determine whether there was a previously correct guess there. If the existing character is correct, we'll push that onto the new string. Otherwise, we'll push an underscore character to indicate that position still doesn't have a correct guess.

Using the *Option Enum*

Most of that sequence of code shown previously is straightforward, since we're just pulling a single character out at the index position where we're using the nth() function on the string. The one thing that may be a little harder to understand in that statement is the call to Some(). Remember that values are not generally straightforward in Rust; they're usually wrapped in a complex datatype. This is another example. The nth() function returns an Option. Option is an enum, meaning there are previously defined values that can be held within the Option. In this case, there are two. The first is None, meaning there is no value.

Whereas many languages include the concept of null/nil or undefined, Rust doesn't have that. Instead, it provides other mechanisms to achieve the same purpose since Rust isn't allowing you direct access to memory like other languages do. In C, for instance, you might use the following code to see whether there is anything to check. You can see an example of that next. If you aren't aware, C uses the idea of pointers, which means an identifier or variable contains a memory address rather than a value. The memory address contained in the identifier contains the value itself. To get access to the value, you have to dereference the identifier to indicate that you want the value and not the contents of the identifier itself. In this small sample of code, you'll see a pointer variable get defined. The problem with this is there's no memory allocated for the value, so there's no memory location to be stored in the pointer.

```
#include <stdio.h>

int main(int argc, char **argv)
{
    int *i;

    if (i) {
            printf("We have a value!");
    } else {
        printf("There is no value!");
    }

    return 0;
}
```

This can be problematic and introduce unexpected or undefined behavior. Although there are ways to mitigate those problems if the programmer knows appropriate techniques to deal with memory management and error handling, the language itself was never designed to address these situations itself. It was always the expectation that the programmer would do the right thing. Rust takes a different approach. The expectation is not that the programmer handles all memory management and then appropriate error handling in case something goes wrong. You may notice that in C, we aren't even checking to see whether the value is null or nil or undefined. Instead, we're just checking to see whether there's a value at all.

So, we have an Option and we've talked about the case where there's no value, which would return a None as the contents of the enum response or identifier. This may be a slightly bumpy ride to explain thoroughly, so hold on. In Rust, an enum is a tagged union. In essence, the enum is a datatype with a fixed number of values. In the case of the Option, we have two possible values, Some or None. However, it's slightly more complex than that. Figure 4.2 shows a visual representation of our Option. We have both Some and None, and within Some, you can see that there is a T, indicating that Some is a generic, which can hold any datatype you like.

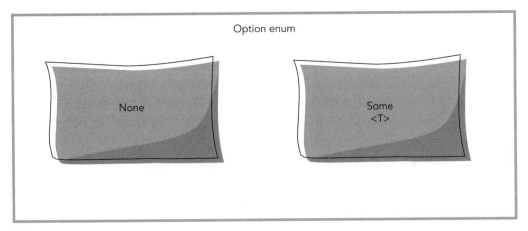

FIGURE 4.2: Option enum

If the function returning our Option has a value to return, it returns Some, including the value inside it. In our case, nth() returns an Option, so we have to match that same Option when we do the comparison. If the location we're checking contains an underscore, what's going to be returned is Some with an underscore inside. This, for our purposes, will be represented as Some('_'). As a result, that's what we need to compare against. We're looking for any case where this isn't true, and we'll push whatever character happens to be there onto the existing String. If there's an underscore, we push the underscore. Remember that this is only the case if we don't find a match from the character the player has provided.

Finishing Up the Implementation

We've gotten through the hard part, so we just need to wrap up what's left. It's all straightforward but worth going through, at least for completeness. In the following example, you'll see the last section of code from the implementation of the `CheckLetter` trait. It may look strange out of context, lacking the opening curly braces, but it's easy to explain with enough additional context, so let's take a look at what we have.

```
        index += 1;
    }
    self.representation = response;
    self.correct_count += count;
    count > 0
  }
}
```

First, we need to increment the index value so that on the next pass, we're looking at the right place in the existing representation string. This could easily be represented as `index = index + 1`, but C introduced various shorthand methods for doing arithmetic for concise statements and many succeeding languages have adopted the same syntax. All the line says is we'll increment the index value by 1.

We need to do some work on the values stored in our data structure now that we have completely gone through the word looking for matching characters. First, we need to set the `representation` value to the `String` we have been working on, putting any correct characters into the right place and leaving underscores in places where there haven't been any correct guesses as yet. This is one of the reasons we had to set the `self` value being passed in as mutable. We are changing some of the stored values. Again, because of ownership rules and no copy trait for the `String` datatype, we have to do a build and replace on any string value we are making any changes to.

While we replaced the `String` value, because it's a string, we can simply increment the `correct_count` value since it's an integer and it's mutable. We need to make sure we are adding all the correctly guessed characters, meaning we might have found multiple positions where the character was located, so we don't just do an increment of 1. We need to add in the `count` value because that's where we've been keeping track of all the correctly found letters.

Finally, we need to return a Boolean value. This indicates whether or not a letter was actually found. Remember that when we return a value, it's an expression rather than a statement, so it's a single value on a line that is not terminated by a semicolon. If we have found a correct character, no matter how many of them, we want to return `true`. Because of that, the expression is `count > 0`. If count is equal to 0, it means no letters were found in the answer we are storing. If that is the case, we return `false`. If even one letter is found, the return value will be `true`.

READING FILES AND SELECTING WORDS

We have our data structure and our traits that work on the data structure. What we need to do now is select a random word from a word list so we can let the user start guessing letters. We have two functions that will take care of that here, but those two functions, as short as they may be, include some important concepts. One is another case where generics are useful but provide some additional bounds on the generics using a new keyword. The other is a way of handling errors that result from your code in a clean and simple fashion. Because Rust wraps values in data structures, errors can be easily conveyed. In most languages, you have to write a number of lines to handle errors, even in cases where exceptions are supported, or perhaps *especially* in cases where exceptions are supported. Rust uses a different approach.

Handling Errors Concisely

Exception handling is common in modern languages. Exceptions actually make life much easier for a programmer than languages that don't use some form of error control or exception handling directly in the language. An exception is a case where something bad has happened in the program that can't be or explicitly isn't handled. This is a very common thing in library functions, for instance. The library function runs across a case that it wasn't designed to handle and rather than providing a lot of additional code to take any potential response or situation into account, the function simply throws an exception and expects the calling function to correctly handle the situation.

Since this may be harder to understand without an example, let's take a look at one. In the following example, you'll see a short Java program that attempts to open a file. Of course, Java is entirely object-oriented, so all we need to do to open a file is to create a `File` object with the name of the file passed as a parameter. The object constructor will take care of opening the file. There are a lot of cases where a problem can arise in opening a file, though. Let's say the user running the program doesn't have permission to open the file. Opening the file will fail in that case. Another situation is where the file doesn't exist and the `File` object is only trying to open the file rather than creating a new file in the case the file doesn't exist. If you're opening a file only for reading, for instance, you don't want a new file created since there won't be anything to read.

```
import java.io.*;

public class openfile {
    public static void main(String[] args)
    {
        try {
            File file1 = new File("thisfile.txt");
        }
        catch (FileNotFoundException e) {
            System.out.println("Couldn't find the file");
        }
    }
}
```

Java uses a `try/catch` construction to handle exceptions. You set up the possibility that an exception will occur by putting the code that may throw an exception inside a `try` block. In our case, it's just creating a new `File` instance with a filename passed into the constructor method. Since there may be many problems with interactions with the filesystem, we can take precautions and tell Java to be aware that an exception may need to be caught. This is done in the `catch` block. There may be multiple `catch` blocks after a `try` block because you can have a number of very specific exceptions. The one being caught here is for a `FileNotFoundException`. There may be others, in which case those exceptions are not being handled, and they will cause the program to fail.

The purpose of handling exceptions is to allow the program to either clean up from an error and continue with an alternate plan or exit gracefully. In the case of a file not existing in the filesystem, we only sort of have a way to clean up here. This would be a problem if the program continued on and tried to make use of the `file1` object, since we're not doing anything to redirect the program or try something else. We just print a message (not even an error message, since that's a different method altogether) and forget it. At least the program won't just die here because the exception is caught by the program. Any other exception than the specific one caught will cause the program to fail with an unhandled exception.

Other programming languages have other ways of dealing with exceptions. C++, for instance, also uses `try/catch` to handle exceptions. Exception handling has the potential to introduce badness into programs, as it turns out. On Windows systems, C++ programs use something called structured exception handling (SEH). This is a data structure that wraps up the error condition and includes other data. This data structure can be misused by attackers to subvert the normal flow of the program.

In Rust, we aren't going to use exception handling in the same way that other languages use it, but there is a way of handling error conditions cleanly. First, let's take a look at some code to open a file in Rust using a long-winded way of handling errors that may come up.

```
let file = File::open(filename);

let mut file = match file {
    Ok(file) => file,
    Err(e) => return Err(e),
};
```

First, we create a `File` using the `open` trait, which takes a filename as a parameter. Since this is a rewrite of the actual function in our program, we're using the identifier `filename` here just as we did in the actual program—it's a clear indicator of what's inside. The error handling comes in the next line. As we've done before, if you're familiar with the C programming language and languages that have inherited from it, you may be familiar with `match` if we talk about it as `switch`. In C, `switch` is a keyword used to perform multiple comparisons cleanly. We could write the previous code in a block of `if` statements, like the following:

```
if file == Ok(File) {
    file = file;
} else if file = Err(e) {
    return Err(e);
}
```

This rapidly gets unwieldy with a lot of different comparison points. So, in C, we'd use the following as a way to do this comparison of one value against multiple possibilities. You can think of the `switch`, or even the `match` in Rust, as a multiway branch. Depending on the contents of the variable we're checking, the program can go one of multiple directions.

```
switch(file) {
    case Ok(file):
        file = file;
        break;
    case Err(e):
        return (Err(e));
}
```

So, back to Rust, and you'll forgive the muddling of some Rust constructs in the C examples shown previously. In our `match` statement, we're comparing the contents of the file identifier with two possibilities. If we got an `Ok` that included a file handle, which is the first case we're checking, we set the `file` identifier to the file handle and continue on our merry way. If, on the other hand, we receive an `Err` with an error message as a result of the attempt to open the file, we'll return from the function passing the resulting error back to the calling function. The `return` keyword is a way to quickly dump out of a function in cases like this.

Now, in the case of the function we'll use, we use a shorthand rather than the `match` statement. The following code shows the function, and we'll get to the signature in a minute since it looks pretty complex, but for now let's just look at the call to open the file. You'll notice that at the end of the line where we open the file, there is a `?` (question mark). This is the shorthand. It tells the compiler to effectively use the same `match` setup we had earlier. If there's an error, return from the function, passing the error back. If we get a clean result from the open call, just put the resulting file handle into the `file` identifier.

```
fn read_lines<P>(filename: P) -> io::Result<io::Lines<io::BufReader<File>>>
where P: AsRef<Path>, {
    let file = File::open(filename)?;
    Ok(io::BufReader::new(file).lines())
}
```

The expression at the end of the function does a number of things for us. First, we'll return an `enum` of our own from this function, so we need to wrap the result of what we're doing inside an `Ok`. You may remember that `Ok` is one of the potential values for a `Result`. The other potential value is `Err`. Since the `?` is taking care of the case where we get an `Err`, we need to handle the `Ok`. More than just passing back an `Ok`, though, we'll pass back an iterator for all the lines in the file. This iterator is part of the `BufReader` data structure. So, inside the `Ok` line, we create a new `BufReader`, passing it all the lines from the `File` structure. So, now we have a `Result` that is being passed back, containing an `Ok`, indicating everything was fine, and the iterator over all the lines from the `BufReader`.

Generics and Bounds

Let's back up a bit, though. We've taken care of the inside of the function. Let's look again at the function signature:

```
fn read_lines<P>(filename: P) -> io::Result<io::Lines<io::BufReader<File>>>
where P: AsRef<Path>,
```

Reading this left to right, you can see the name of the function is `read_lines`, because we're just going to read all the lines in a file. This is a generic function, to a degree. Remember that a generic function is one that can take multiple datatypes as parameters. Normally, you would see that indicated by a `<T>`, which suggests that the datatype itself will be referred to with a T. That datatype gets passed to the function. For our purposes, we'll refer to the datatype in the function with a `<P>`. The reason for that is that it's not really a type we're working with. It's a path, meaning a path to a file. That path has the identifier filename, which is passed into the function.

The return value is where it starts to look complicated, but as you start to pull it apart, particularly knowing what's being returned from the function, it becomes easier to follow. Remember that ultimately, we're returning a `Result` that contains the `BufReader` structure so that later on we can make use of all the lines in the file. Working from the outside to the inside, you can see that we're first returning an `io::Result` from this function.

A `Result` on its own doesn't mean anything, though. The `Result` is a structure that contains some other value. One way of looking at the complicated return value is visually, as seen in Figure 4.3. On the very inside of this structure is a `File`. This gets used to create a `BufReader`, which is a structure providing the ability to get access to the contents of the `File` easily. From the `BufReader`, we can create an iterator to easily get through all of the lines (every string of characters in the file terminated by a carriage return and line feed). This iterator is returned inside a `Result`.

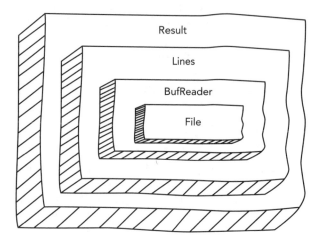

FIGURE 4.3: Embedded values

In the code, all these individual structures are referred to by indicating which crate they're associated with. We could've included the right use statements at the top of the file that would've let us skip including the `io::` portion of each of these structures, but `io::` clarifies what's being referred to, even if it makes the line longer and potentially more confusing because of how dense it looks.

Finally, we get to the `where` keyword. This is a way of providing bounds to a generic. Remember at the beginning of this function definition, we were using `<P>` as a datatype. The `where` keyword provides some specificity around what this means. We could leave it alone and just let the datatype be included when the generic is called. We need to do a little more to the value being passed in, though.

We'll pass in a `String` to this particular function. However, what we need is a `Path` value. The `AsRef` trait performs the conversion for us. `AsRef` is a trait that gets implemented for the `String` type, and it returns a `Path` value. You may be wondering how we got here when we started talking about `where`. The `where` keyword provides context for the `<P>` type. It tells us that in reality, `<P>` is going to be a `Path`, and no matter what datatype gets passed in, the `AsRef` trait will take care of the conversion to the `Path`, since that's necessary for the function we'll be using.

A Vector of Lines

We have one more function to look at, associated with reading in our word list. This function makes use of the one we have just been pulling apart in great detail and creates a `Vector` of `Strings` out of the iterator of lines. Let's take a look at the function to start off:

```
fn read_list(filename: String) -> Vec::<String> {
    let mut v = Vec::<String>::new();
    if let Ok(lines) = read_lines(filename) {
```

```
        for w in lines {
            let word:String = w.unwrap();
            if word.len() > 4 {
                v.push(word);
            }
        }
    }
    v
}
```

First, we have a function called `read_list` that takes in a `filename` as a `String`. We get back a Vector of type `String` from this function. It's not hard to recognize that what will be passed into this function is the name of the file that contains the word list we're using. Remember that this will eventually be converted to a `Path` type that the `File` data structure can make use of. The `Path` type makes sure that the string contains something that looks like a file path or just a filename. We aren't going to do anything with this value other than pass it along to the function we've already looked at.

The first thing we do is create a `Vector` identifier, named `v`. Single-letter identifier names aren't always ideal because they can get lost when you're trying to read the code, but it works here, and it's not a very long function. You just need to make sure you have your reading glasses on so you can see the `v` in places where it's referred to. This variable needs to be mutable because we're going to keep adding to it—therefore, we use the `mut` keyword.

The next line isn't as complicated as it may seem to be, but it does look awkward, in part because the place where we assign the return value to a variable isn't set aside in parentheses to make it clear we're checking a Boolean at the same time we're doing an assignment. Let's examine this line, broken out from the rest of the function so that we can see what's happening:

```
    if let Ok(lines) = read_lines(filename) {
```

Okay, take a breath, and let's take a careful look here. First, we are using a conditional, indicated by the keyword `if`. This means we'll do something based on the result of some true/false result. Simultaneously, we're creating a new variable with the identifier `lines`. This is done in `let Ok(lines)`. We use the `Ok` because the function being called next returns a `Result` and not a `Vector` or even an iterator. That means if we want to match what comes back from `read_lines`, we need to put what we have in the context of a `Result`. `Ok()` provides us that same `Result` context that can be matched correctly.

To handle the case where `read_lines()` returns an `Err`, there should be an `else` statement to match the `if`. Just using the `if` without the `else` doesn't prepare for the case where there's a problem reading from the file and isn't good error handling practice. However, that little problem aside, we can continue looking at the remainder of this function to see how we're placing all the individual words, each on its own line, into the vector.

Remember that what we get back from `read_lines()` is an iterator. This means we effectively have a list and an accessor to that list. The iterator provides us with the means to get to the first item in the list and then traits, which move us through the list one item at a time. As we've done in the past with iterators, we'll use a `for` loop to get individual items out of the list. Because what we're pulling from this list is words, we're going to call the individual item identifier `w`. As before, you can use a longer identifier that's easier to recognize as you're reading through the code.

What we get in w is not a `String` but a `Result`. This means we need to unwrap that result to get the `String` so that we can add the word to our vector. Although we could do this in a single step, there's one other action we want to take before just adding the word to the `Vector`. As a result, we'll create a variable to house the unwrapped `String` and call it *word*. This gets assigned the result from the call to w.`unwrap()`, which would be the `String` component of the `Result` data structure.

Short words aren't a lot of fun when you play hangman, so before adding a word to the `Vector` of possible words, we'll make sure it's of sufficient length. So, we do a quick check of the length of the `String`, making sure it's at least five characters in length, before we accept it as a possible word to present to the player. Once we know it is of sufficient length, we use v.`push(word)` to push the word variable onto the v `Vector`. `push` is a trait of the `Vector` type that just adds whatever the parameter is to the end of the list of values being compiled.

Finally, we need to return the vector. As always, we leave a value on a line by itself, and this is where having short identifier names can be problematic. If you didn't know any better and didn't know Rust very well, you might almost think someone was trying to paste something in and left off the Ctrl key when hitting the v key. Instead, we're just leaving the variable v on a line by itself as an expression that gets returned to the calling function.

THE REST OF THE STORY

One more function, then the main left to discuss here, which ain't nothin'. There are still some issues to consider, including some design decisions. One of the first design decisions comes in the one function we have left to consider. Let's take a look at that function and pull it apart:

```
fn select_word() -> String {
    let mut rng = rand::thread_rng();
    let filename:String = "words.txt".to_string();
    let words:Vec<String> = read_list(filename);
    let word_count = words.len();
    let selection = rng.gen_range(1, word_count);
    let select: String = words[selection].clone();
    select
}
```

This is the function where we select a word to use in our game. This function returns a `String` value but doesn't take any parameters. It drives the entire process of reading in the file and adding the lines to a `Vector` by calling the function `read_list()` that we already went over. Before we get there, though, we must create an instance of a random number generator. Once we have all the words read in, we select one at random. This requires the `rand` crate and specifically the `thread_rng()` function, which initializes the random number generator.

For simplicity, the next line sets the filename statically. It's not the best place to set the filename, which is where a design decision came in. This was done strictly out of simplicity and could certainly be done much better. It also assumes that the file `words.txt` is in the directory that the program is running out of since no path has been assigned. There's no search path for files in the operating system or in the Rust I/O functions, so it has to be where you're located for this to work. You'll notice here that we're creating a `String`, which means we can't use a collection of bytes, which is effectively what we have between the set of double quotes. As a result, we need to use the `to_string()` trait on that collection of bytes to create a `String` type from it so that it can be assigned to the identifier we've created.

Next, we call the function we spent a lot of time looking at that returns a `Vector` of `Strings`. As a result, we have to define a `Vector` of `Strings` to hold what comes back from the function. That identifier is named `words`. So far, so good, right?

When you're generating a random number, you need to know what the bounds are. Many random number generators work by generating a value between 0 and 1, and then you have to perform the math to get a useful value from that, since you probably don't want a floating-point value that's less than 1 but non-negative. Fortunately, we have a function that can generate a value within a range that comes with the `rand` crate. However, we need to know the upper bound so that we can pass that value into the function giving us the random number. The upper bound will be the length of the `Vector` of words. When we know how big the `Vector` is, we know the number of words. The lower boundary will be 1, which is the first word in the `Vector`.

Once we have the random number, we need to pull the word at that location out of the `Vector`. Well, technically we can't just pull the word out of the `Vector`. That's why we're using the `clone()` trait. There's no copy trait to make a copy of a `String` if we were to just assign the `String` at the selection position to the new `String` identifier `select`. We also can't just turn ownership of that memory location over to the new identifier, because that memory belongs to the `Vector`, and we can't just pull a piece out of the entire allocation. We can, though, create a copy of the `String` value by using `clone()`. This returns a completely new memory allocation that can be assigned to the identifier `select`. This is the expression that gets returned from the function, so, as always, it's left on a line by itself.

Initialization

The first thing we need to do in the main function is generate our word. Remember that this is a data structure, so it's not as simple as just asking for a word from the function we just looked at. Instead, we have to do a `struct` initialization. That comes by assigning all the values to all the members in the `struct`. You can see that done as the first part of the main function here:

```
    let body = vec!["noose".to_string(), "head".to_string(), "neck".to_string(),
"torso".to_string(), "left arm".to_string(),
    "right arm".to_string(), "right leg".to_string(), "left leg".to_string(), "left
foot".to_string(), "right foot".to_string()];
    let mut body_iter = body.iter();
    let mut result = select_word();
    let mut answer = Word {
        length: result.len(),
        representation: String::from_utf8(vec![b'_'; result.len()]).unwrap(),
        answer: result,
        correct_count: 0
    };
```

Before we get there, though, remember that in hangman, you have a sequence of body parts that start showing up to indicate the progress toward failure. A good way to keep track of where we are in a list is to use an iterator, and we can get an iterator to a `Vector`, so we'll create a `Vector` of `String` values. As before, we need to actually create a `String` datatype, which means we have to use the to_string() trait on each of our string literals. This particular collection uses the values noose, head, neck, torso, left arm, right arm, right leg, left leg, right foot, and left foot as all of the body parts.

Once we have the Vector, named with the identifier body, we can create our iterator, which will be named body_iter. We retrieve the iterator from the Vector by using the iter() trait on our Vector identifier. The iterator will be initialized starting at the first value in the Vector, which is why all the body parts were placed in the order they need to be in. Actually for our purposes, the one that matters the most is right foot, since that's the value we'll be looking for later on.

At this point, we can move on with creating our data structure containing the answer. First, we use select_word() to get a random value out of the word list. Then, we initialize the identifier answer using Word { }; with all of the members initialized using their names inside. This initialization happens in a particular order. You may notice that we don't assign the answer member until late in the initialization. The reason is that once you've assigned result to answer, result is no longer available for checking the length. You could check the length of answer, but that becomes ambiguous since you aren't really acting inside the struct as yet, since it hasn't been initialized. Consequently, it's easy to call result.len() a couple of times and then just assign result to the identifier answer inside the struct.

There is one line in the initialization that's worth taking a closer look at. Remember that we want to be able to print a number of underscores based on the length of the word selected to indicate where unguessed letters are. To create that initial representation, we create a String with a particular length that contains the same character in all the positions. Here's the line so that it's clear:

```
representation: String::from_utf8(vec![b'_'; result.len()]).unwrap(),
```

We're creating a String from a UTF-8 byte slice, which is different from a String in internal representation, even if it looks the same to us when it's displayed. We create a UTF-8 byte slice by creating a Vector of characters. The b'_' is used to indicate to Rust that _ is a byte. We want to make the Vector result.len() long. Of course, from_utf8 will return a Result, which means we must unwrap it to get the String out so that we can assign it to the representation identifier.

Playing the Game

We are now at the point in the program where we are actually going to play the game. This is essentially a small loop where we take input, check to see whether the input is correct, and then respond accordingly. There is a little more to it than that, but that's the essence of the rest of the main function, which you can see here:

```
let mut letter: char;
let mut body_complete: bool = false;
while !answer.check_complete() && !body_complete {
    println!("Provide a letter to guess ");
    let mut input = String::new();
    match io::stdin().read_line(&mut input) {
        Ok(n) => {
            letter = input.chars().nth(0).unwrap();
            if answer.check_for_letter(letter) {
                println!("There is at least one {}, so the word is {}", letter,
answer.representation);
```

```
            }
            else {
                let next_part = body_iter.next().unwrap();
                println!("Incorrect! You are at {}", next_part);
                if next_part == "right foot" {
                    body_complete = true;
                }
            }
        }
        Err(error) => {
            println!("Didn't get any input");
        }
    }
}
if body_complete {
    println!("You were unsuccessful at guessing {}", &answer.answer)
}
else {
    println!("Yes! The word was {}", &answer.answer);
}
```

First, we define a character identifier to take the input from the player. This is going to keep changing, so we have to define it as mutable. We'll also need to determine whether we've reached the end of the body so that we'll know when to terminate the game. Once we have those two variables in place, we can start the game loop.

We're using a `while` loop here because we need to check for a pair of Boolean conditions at the top of the loop. The `while` loop says to run the enclosed group of statements as long as these conditions remain true. As soon as they're no longer true, drop out of the loop. For our purposes, we're checking a pair of negatives. First, we want to make sure that the answer is not complete by using the `check_complete()` trait on our `word` data structure. You could do it the other way around and use `check_not_complete`, which would mean you weren't negating the result using the `!` operator. Either way is fine. Again, it's a design decision. You could decide to use the two `!` operators, negating two values to get a true so that the loop continues, which means you reverse the way you check things.

Inside the loop, we ask for a letter to be provided using the `println!` macro. Then, we create a mutable `String` value to take the input into. This is because there is no read character function with Rust I/O. So, we read an entire line using `io::stdin().read_line()`. It may look strange to call a function on a function, but what's actually happening is that `io::stdin()` is returning an `Stdin` data structure. That data structure has a trait called `read_line()`, which is used to read a line of data from standard input.

As always, we get a `Result` back, so we'll use `match` again to check the value of `Result`. If we get an `Ok` back, we go through the process of checking to see whether the letter is correct. First, that means pulling a character out of the `String`. This is going to be the `nth(0)` character in the `String`. The player can enter a complete sentence for all we care. We'll take only the first letter. If the letter is part of the word, we tell the player that there was at least one instance of that letter in the answer and print out the new representation with all the right letters in place. If the letter isn't in the answer, we get the next `String` in the `Vector`. Once we've bumped the iterator, we tell the player they got it wrong. This is where we need to check to see whether the new value matches `right foot`, and if it does, we set the Boolean value `body_complete` to `true`. This will drop us out of the loop on the next pass through the check.

At this point, we get to the other part of the `match` statement. There are two possible values for a `Result`. The first is an `Ok`, and we've already dealt with that. The other possible value is an `Err`. The `Err` in this case has to be that we didn't get any input, because that's the only way we'd get an empty value back from `Result`. As a result, we tell the player that there is no input. This should be a hint to enter something on the next pass through.

We now have two potential ways to drop out of the loop. We'll check those again in the `while` statement. If all the letters have been found, the call to the trait `check_complete()` will drop out of the `while` condition. If we've completed the body hanging from the gallows, that will also drop out of the loop. That means when we drop out of the loop, we need to know which condition was met. If the `body_complete` Boolean is `true`, that means they were unsuccessful, so we tell the player they were unsuccessful and put them out of their misery by giving them the answer. If the body isn't complete, that must mean they were successful, so we tell them they were successful and print the word out that they already know.

SUMMARY

We covered a lot of ground in this chapter. First, we looked more closely at how to add traits to our data structures. This is different from just making use of traits as we have in the past. This time, we showed you how to create and implement them. When creating a trait, you first have to define the interface. That means you give it a name and then provide a definition for a function that the trait will perform. You name the function, provide the parameters including types, and then you provide any return datatype.

One important idea that comes along with traits is the idea of `self`. This is an identifier that allows a trait to get access to the member variables from inside the trait. After all, the trait is just a function that gets attached to a type. You could have multiple instances of the same type that the trait is attached to, so the trait needs a way to get access to the exact data for that instance. That's where `self` comes in. It's an identifier that gives you access to the contents of the instance. If you want to assign a value to a member variable, you need to use `self.`*member*, replacing *member* with the identifier name.

Traits are ways to implement generics. A generic is a function, for instance, that can make use of multiple datatypes. That's what makes it generic. The trait is the generic part. The implementation is the specific part, where you provide code that relates to the datatype you're implementing the trait for. When you create a generic, the datatype is one of the things that get passed into the trait. That's what allows the specific implementation to be selected since the compiler knows what datatype the trait is being called against so that it can put the right implementation into the executable when it's created.

We can provide more specific binding, and we may need to provide more specific binding in some cases. This can be done with the `where` keyword. This keyword allows you to take a generic and make it more specific, as we did when we took a `String` and converted it to a `Path`. This was done using the `AsRef()` trait, which converts from one datatype to another if a reference is provided. The trait takes one reference in and provides another reference on the other side.

The `match` keyword is another valuable one to know. We can do error checking with it because any time we get a `Result` back, we get an `Ok` and an `Err`. We can use `match` to check for either condition.

This is like other multiple condition keywords in other languages, like `switch` in C/C++. `Result` provides only two potential values, but `match` has the potential to check against far more than just two values.

We don't have to use `match` to perform error handling, though. If you have a statement that returns a `Result`, you can append a `?` to the statement and Rust will automatically take care of the `Result` value. Since there's an actual value wrapped inside the result, we need to unwrap it. If the `Result` contains an `Ok`, Rust will unwrap the value inside and assign it to the left-hand side of an assignment. If the `Result` contains an `Err`, Rust will drop out of the function currently being executed, returning an error to the calling function.

We looked at how to take input, both from files as well as from the console. In files, we can create a `BufReader` from a `File` structure and that gives us a way to read data from the file using traits on the `BufReader` data structure. In the case of console input, we have a similar data structure called `Stdin`. This data structure has traits for reading input from the console. We can read lines and place the result into a `String`.

This is not the best way to write the hangman program. In some cases, we made easy choices at the expense of good programming practices. However, you have a chance to make the program better by making changes indicated in the following exercises.

EXERCISES

1. Add appropriate error handling conditions. The first case is in the read_list() function, where you should handle the case where an Err is returned instead of an Ok. Do something productive here. Add in any other error handling you can find where a positive return is assumed and the negative case isn't addressed.

2. Accept a command-line parameter with an alternate word list. Retain the default word list in the case where a command-line parameter is not provided.

3. Add the capability for longer (and presumably harder) words.

4. Add the capability for the player to guess the word at any time.

ADDITIONAL RESOURCES

What is an Enum in Programming Languages - `www.thoughtco.com/what-is-an-enum-958326`

Beginner's Guide to Error Handling in Rust - `www.sheshbabu.com/posts/rust-error-handling/`

Rust Error Handling - `medium.com/better-programming/rust-error-handling-84e7bd169e47`

5

In Concurrence

IN THIS CHAPTER, YOU WILL LEARN THE FOLLOWING:

➤ How to write concurrent programming and its challenges

➤ Using interprocess communication

➤ Including encryption in programs

➤ Reading directories

➤ Using return values from programs

As we are working in an age when every computer you buy has multiple processor units in it, it generally makes sense to consider how to write programs that can take advantage of that fact. This means breaking up our programs into units that can be executed simultaneously. What you will have is different execution paths that can be assigned to unique processor units. Writing parallel processing programs does not come without some challenges, however. In this chapter, we're going to cover some of the challenges associated with concurrent or parallel processing. Along the way, we'll talk about some fundamental and philosophical underpinnings—partly because it's helpful, but partly because it's just interesting.

A central processing unit (CPU) is actually a collection of pieces. Typically, a CPU has an arithmetic logic unit (ALU) that performs all the arithmetic and logic operations, meaning much of the program execution that doesn't relate to memory movement. The CPU also has registers, which are small chunks of memory used for fast storage and retrieval and containing essential data related to program execution. Finally, there is a control unit, which helps direct the traffic flow within the CPU, making sure the program is executed in the right order, and all the program elements (executable code and data) are where they need to be when they need to be there.

There are many advantages to having multiple processors. First, you can run multiple programs at the same time if you have multiple processors. However, it's not as straightforward as that. Just adding more people to do the work doesn't help if you don't have someone who can make sure the work is assigned in a reasonable way across all the people. Without that one person managing all the workers, you end up with a lot of people standing around doing nothing. This is where the operating system comes in. The operating system needs to be able to allocate tasks to different processors that are available.

This is great. We have an operating system that understands multiple processors and can shift work between them. That means more work gets done all at the same time. How does this help us as programmers of one application? We have one application, so why do we care that a multiprocessing system can run multiple applications at once? After all, one application has a single execution path through the program, right? Not necessarily. We can write programs that may be efficient, taking multiple simultaneous execution paths. This does require thinking, in much the same way the operating system has to, about how to distribute the workload. Not all programs can be written that way, however. It requires someone who can efficiently consider how best to handle a complete task using multiple workers.

This is where we run into a problem, though. Let's say you have 20 windows in your house. Having a single person wash the outside of your windows is time-consuming. The answer is hiring more people, right? Well, to a point. You give each worker a bucket of soapy water and a sponge as well as a ladder. All should be in good order. Well, you'll want to rinse the windows after washing them, and unfortunately, there is a single hose to rinse the windows with. This means you need to make sure your workers are synchronized in a way that ensures there isn't a fight for the hose because all your window washers want to use it at the same time.

We have a similar problem when it comes to our processors. So, consider having a system that has several of these little collections of electronic components, all within a very small space. Let's say you have four of these CPUs. Each CPU can handle the execution of a program all on its own since it has the control unit, access to input/output, and an ALU to handle the actual execution of operations. This is similar to our window washers. Our window washers have a control unit, access to input/output, and an ALU, just as they had a bucket of soapy water, a sponge, and a ladder. The problem comes with the water, which is similar to access to memory on the system.

And that's part of where we have a problem. Memory for a program exists in just one place unless you have a really special-purpose computer where each processor has its own main memory, but even that still raises the issue we're going to spend some time talking about. Let's say you have a program that you have broken into two separate execution units. Those units need ways to communicate so they can coordinate their actions. Additionally, and perhaps more importantly, these different execution units are going to have to read from and write to variables stored in memory. This is where the dining philosophers come in.

THE DINING PHILOSOPHERS

Immanuel Kant, René Descartes, David Hume, John Stuart Mill, and Friedrich Nietzsche walk into a bar. No, wait, not a bar. They walk into an Italian restaurant. Because there are five of them, they won't fit nicely in a booth or at one of the rectangular tables. This means they need to be seated at a round table. As you'd expect, they each get a beautiful silverware setup wrapped in a very nice cloth napkin. This is a fancy restaurant, after all. No paper here. All cloth. Being well-behaved philosophers, they take the napkins and tuck them into their collars since they all plan to have spaghetti, and we all know how sloppy that has the potential to be as sauce goes flying off the individual strands of pasta while you're slurping them up. What they discover is that each silverware setup has a fork and a knife. This means we have a setup that looks like what you see in Figure 5.1.

After the breadsticks have been consumed, including the one that had to be split because six breadsticks for five philosophers leaves one left over, the bowls of spaghetti come out. Here's the problem we have: consuming spaghetti requires two forks, one to wrap the pasta around the second, so you don't just have long strands of spaghetti dripping tomato sauce all over the places not covered by the napkins. This requires a little bit of sharing. If Hume wants to eat, he needs his fork plus the fork of Mill, who is sitting to his right. He picks up his fork in his left hand and reaches for the fork on his right, except that Mill has picked that up. In fact, all of the philosophers have their own fork in their left hand.

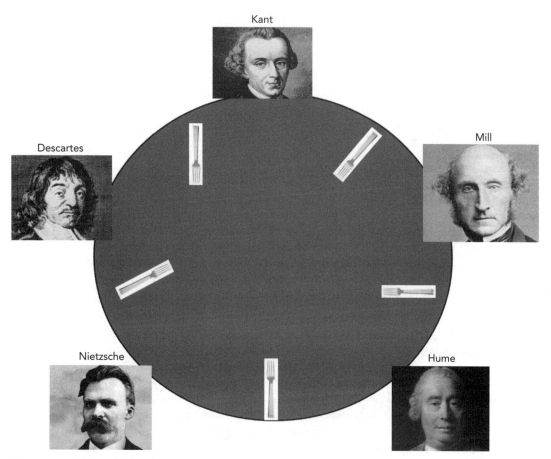

FIGURE 5.1: Dining philosophers

If no one puts down a fork, no one can eat. If this continues over a long period of time, the spaghetti gets cold and isn't nearly as much fun to eat. Worse, though, if it continues for a really long time, the philosophers start to collapse from starvation. We can't have that, since none of them have written their signature papers as yet, leaving the rest of us unenlightened. We need a solution to this problem.

This is a problem that was proposed in the mid-1960s by Edsger Dijkstra, a famous computer scientist who is also responsible for one of the essential algorithms used to get data across the Internet as well as to get you from your home to the dentist's office you've never been to. The idea behind this particular scenario is to demonstrate the issues of concurrency and synchronization. If the philosophers can't figure out how to coordinate their activities, they will all starve. That means this is also a demonstration of issues with resource contention. Multiple actors/devices trying to get access to a single resource at the same time is a problem that needs to be solved.

> **NOTE** *Dijkstra's algorithm is a way of getting information from one place to another in the most efficient manner. It is used in global positioning system (GPS) devices you use to get directions from your house to the dentist. It is also used in shortest-path-first routing algorithms to get from one place on the Internet to another.*

Of course, when it comes to such issues as making sure a process gets adequate time in the processor, which is one of the scenarios this problem is meant to highlight, that's up to the operating system and not us as lowly programmers. However, it can be our job to make sure we design algorithms in such a way that we aren't encouraging starvation—the case where a process doesn't get the resources it needs to complete processing.

Let's say that rather than a fork, and rather than Kant and Hume, we have thread A and thread B, which you can think of as thread Kant and thread Hume if it's more amusing to you. Thread Kant takes possession of (locks) a memory location with the identifier of Reason. It maintains that lock even while it is doing processing on other things and has no need for Reason while it continues to chug along. Hume, on the other hand, really needs Reason; but since Kant has it locked up, Hume can't access it. This isn't so much the ownership issue with Rust but one of the issues with concurrent processing. You can't, or at least you shouldn't, allow two separate threads read/write access to any memory location at the same time, so each thread locks the memory location so no one else gets it, since any other access could cause corruption to either of the accessing threads.

It's bad etiquette to hoard a resource, of course, and that's even more true if others are waiting to use it or if at least there is an expectation that there may be another thread or process that may use the resource. This is where we come back to the issue of everyone with a fork in their left hand and no fork for their right hand so they can twirl up the spaghetti in order to eat. One way to address this state of affairs is with communication. There are different ways this communication can be addressed. We're going to take a look at mutexes, semaphores, and interprocess communication. In some cases, we have the application needing to manage the memory access, since the operating system may not know to protect against access from one process thread to another. These different mechanisms are how the application will manage access.

> **NOTE** There is a difference between threads and processes. A process is a running instance of a program, which is an inert executable on disk. When you run any program, you end up with a process in memory. This process can also spawn other processes. Any process that spawns another process becomes a parent, and the processes spawned become children. Commonly, whether it's a Unix-like operating system (e.g., Linux or macOS) or Windows, if you kill a parent process, you also kill all the children. Each process gets its own memory space, even if they are related in a parent/child way. A thread, on the other hand, is a separate path of execution within the same process. It behaves like a process in that it will also be in the processor queue waiting for time. However, it shares the same memory space with all the other threads that are part of the process. Multiprocessing, regardless of the language, can be beneficial because if you can break up an algorithm so different tasks can be executed simultaneously, the overall task can be completed faster.

Mutexes and Semaphores

Two ways of addressing the problem of accessing the same memory location at the same time are mutexes and semaphores. A *mutex* is a data type or data structure used to protect a memory location. The term is short for *mutual exclusion* or *mutually exclusive*. The point is that as long as one thread is accessing a memory location, no other thread can get access. You might think about a mutex as being a lock on a piece of data. Before any thread attempts to gain access to a memory location, it applies the lock. You might visualize it as placing a piece of data inside a box that has a lock on it. You can see a representation of this box with the lock in Figure 5.2. Just imagine the mutex being the key that locks and unlocks the box where the data is located.

The problem with a mutex is that it is done within the program rather than being enforced outside of the program. This means that all of the threads have to cooperate and agree to use these mutexes or locks. In its simplest form, you have a variable that is checked to see if there is a value. A very simple implementation is shown next, written in C because it's usually clear and straightforward to see what is happening in C, as it's a reasonably stripped-down language without much of anything that is taken care of for you, the programmer. In the following snippet, we have a value, `mutex`, that is checked to see if there is a value. If there isn't, or rather, if the value is 0, we set a non-zero value and then go off and do something before setting the variable back to 0 so some other piece of code can get access to a variable that is being protected:

```
if (mutex == 0) {
    mutex = 1;
}
// do something
mutex = 0;
```

FIGURE 5.2: Visual representation of a mutex

Technically, what we've just seen is a semaphore. A *semaphore* is nothing more than a variable that sets a flag that another portion of the code can check. Semaphores are binary in nature. Either they are set, or they are not. A semaphore, especially in this case, can be used as a mutex since the purpose of this variable is simply to indicate that work is going on, and some data shouldn't be touched while the value is non-zero. You could also implement this as a Boolean value since all we care about is whether the value is set, true, or not set, false.

A more robust implementation of a mutex is shown next, using the mutex library in C. This also uses a variable to determine whether the lock is in place or not. Rather than setting it directly, we use the pthread_mutex_lock() function, passing a reference (meaning the address of the variable) to that function so it can make the change. You may also note that the lock we are creating isn't just an integer or a Boolean. There is a datatype that comes defined in pthread.h that has an underlying representation we don't know about. We just create a variable of the pthread_mutex_t type and pass it to the right functions so the lock is set. This means code that is executing and also trying to set the lock so it can perform work will have to wait. Only one thread of execution can take place at any given point in time.

```
#include <pthread.h>
#include <stdio.h>
#include <stdlib.h>

int main(void)
{
    pthread_mutex_t lock;
    int counter = 0;

    if (pthread_mutex_init(&lock, NULL) != 0) {
        printf("error\n");
        return -1;
    }

    pthread_mutex_lock(&lock);
    counter +=1;
    pthread_mutex_unlock(&lock);

    return 0;
}
```

To use the mutex, we have to initialize it using the pthread_mutex_init() function. This sets up the variable we are using as the lock. If we don't get a 0 returned from that function, something went wrong. On Unix-like operating systems, it's common for 0 to be the return value from any program that has succeeded. Any non-zero value is considered an error. This function follows that convention, returning a 0 when the lock initialization succeeded. You will also see return –1 in the block of code that follows. This is the return value from the program itself, with –1 indicating that there was a failure in the code somewhere.

Rust has mutexes, as you'd expect, since Rust enables concurrent programming. Rust is all about safety in programming, after all, so of course Rust would implement a way to protect memory from being clobbered. In the following code, you will see an example of how Rust implements a mutex. First, you will see the included modules. We'll skip by those for the moment, except to say that these are what you need to include if you want to use a mutex and a thread in Rust. The first thing we do is to create the data we want to lock by creating a mutex inside of a reference counter. The ARC in this case stands for atomically reference counted. We create a new reference counter and stick a mutex inside of it, initializing the data the mutex watches over to 0.

```
use std::sync::{Arc, Mutex};
use std::thread;

fn main() {
    let data = Arc::new(Mutex::new(0));

    for _ in 0..15 {
        let data = Arc::clone(&data);
        thread::spawn(move || {
            let mut data = data.lock().unwrap();
            *data += 1;
            if *data == 15 {
                return
            }
        });
    }
}
```

We'll get more into the elements of threads later in the chapter, so we're going to pass those by and focus on the mutex. In order to make any change to the data, we have to lock the mutex. We also pass the value from inside the mutex to an identifier that we can modify. The code data.lock(). unwrap() gives us a reference to the data. To do anything with that data, we need to dereference, which is what the * does for us. We don't have to worry about releasing the mutex because it goes out of scope once the thread has completed.

While semaphores and mutexes provide important data to programs, especially those that are multi-threaded and so share the same memory space, they are of limited value in programs. Their purpose is to prevent something from happening while something else is going on. You can think of them as the flag person at a road construction site. The flag person has a sign that flips back and forth, depending on the condition of the construction or of the traffic coming the other way. Either way, the sign is an indication of whether you can proceed or not proceed. It's either Stop (false) or Slow (true). If the flag person needs to send a signal to the other end of the construction site, where there is another flag person, they need something other than binary communications, such as the color and model of the last vehicle that has been let through.

Interprocess Communications

As soon as we have multiple threads, we have multiple execution paths. When that happens, we need a way to pass data from one point in the execution path to another point in the execution path. Since they are separate execution paths, we can't just call a function and pass data into that function as a parameter. Think of it this way: if we are in the same house, we can easily communicate, even if it requires shouting from one floor or room to another. Once one of us is no longer in the same house, we need another way of communicating. We could use tin cans with a length of string connecting them, where one of us is talking into one of the cans while the other one of us has the other can held up to their ear.

The same sort of thing applies to multiple threads or even multiple programs, since the moment we have the ability to communicate between threads, that functionality can allow us to communicate between programs as well. Let's say, though, for simplicity, that we are just talking about a single program and two separate execution paths, which you can see in Figure 5.3. We start off our program, and it forks into two separate threads. These two threads are based on the same executable code but are no longer connected from the perspective of the processor. They are, in effect, separate programs that won't return to the main program at any time. When they terminate, they have terminated just like a program would terminate—they come out of memory and cease execution.

> **NOTE** When it comes to concurrent processing, there are two terms you will run across that are related but don't mean exactly the same thing. Without getting into all the operating system aspects, you may see spawn and fork come up with regard to starting up new processing units. When a process gets spawned, the process that initiates the spawn is the parent process, and the spawned process is the child. The child process is its own thing. It shares no memory or code with the parent. When you fork a process, however, the forked process is a clone of the parent, although it's still considered to be a child of the parent. The forked process has the memory and executable segments of the parent. In either case, when a parent is killed or comes to an end naturally, the child will be killed.

Even though they are separate processes, there is often a need for related processes to communicate. In Figure 5.4, you can see where there is a place for data to be dropped so it could be picked up by the other process. This place sits in between the two threads. In practice, this is sometimes implemented in something that acts a bit like a pipe rather than a file where data is dropped. In reality, it's a bit more like a document. On Unix-like systems, for instance, you would use a Unix socket, which is a file in the filesystem that two processes communicate through. Of course, on Unix-like systems, everything is a file in the filesystem, so this is nothing particularly new. Since data is written out while not necessarily being listened to, a file seems to be a better metaphor or implementation lookalike than a pipe.

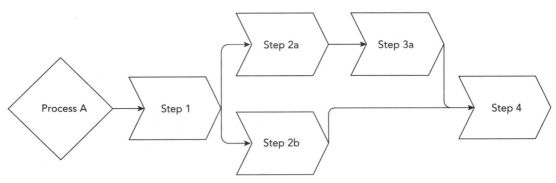

FIGURE 5.3: Multithreaded program

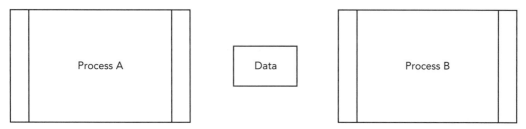

FIGURE 5.4: Process memory sharing

In Rust, there are different ways to achieve interprocess communication. One factor to consider when you are looking at interprocess communication (IPC) is whether you need to be bidirectional. Some of the ways IPC is implemented, regardless of the language, are unidirectional, which means if you need to go both ways, as it were, you need two of these implementations: one where one side is the server (receiver), while the other is the client (sender), and another where the roles are reversed.

One type of messaging available in Rust is something called a *channel*. Rust uses multi-producer, single-consumer (MPSC) channels, meaning you can have multiple threads or functions that are writing to a channel but only a single thread or function that is receiving what is on the channel. The following is an example of implementing channels in Rust, though only using a single producer rather than multiple producers. We include the MPSC functionality. To create a channel, we call `mpsc::channel()`, which returns a tuple with the two ends of the channel. With one side, we can use `send()`, sending any data that we need. In this case, it's a string of characters. Once the send has happened, we can issue a `recv()` to get the data out of the channel.

```
use std::sync::mpsc;

fn main() {
    let (snd, rcv) = mpsc::channel();
    snd.send("Wubble wubble foo").unwrap();
    println!("Message is: {}", rcv.recv().unwrap());
}
```

One thing you will notice is that both `send()` and `recv()` have `unwrap()` called on them. You can skip that part if you like, but the compiler will issue a warning that there is a result that isn't being processed. All we need to do is call `unwrap()`, and the compiler will be satisfied. In a more robust implementation, you would check the result to make sure there wasn't a problem either sending or receiving. For our purposes here, we're just going to make the compiler happy so we can demonstrate the use of channels.

Other types of IPC will vary from operating system to operating system, since it's up to the operating system (the kernel) to support the means for threads or processes to message one another. One reason for this is that the kernel handles things like file and memory access, which are common ways for IPC to be implemented. In the case of shared memory, the kernel needs to be able to allow multiple processes to access the same memory segment without allowing every process on the system to get access to that memory. Some implementations are based around files, which are also managed by the kernel and also require permission settings to restrict access to the information being passed from one process to another.

Interprocess communication features have been in operating systems since the 1960s, when multi-processing systems (systems that were capable of running multiple programs at the same time) were being developed. However, many of the current capabilities for interprocess communication began life on Unix-like systems. One of these is Unix domain sockets, which are commonly implemented using files. The communication happens by reading and writing to something that looks like a normal file on the filesystem.

Later on in this chapter, we'll take a look at another type of interprocess communication. One of the challenges we will face is that some implementations only work on Unix-like systems, while others only work on Windows. On Windows, for instance, we would use a feature called *named pipes*. This is similar to something called *Unix domain sockets* on Unix-like systems. Sometimes these are just called *Unix sockets* or even just *sockets*. To use this implementation, you will need to be on Linux, macOS, or some other Unix-like operating system. This includes, by the way, Windows Subsystem for Linux (WSL).

THE MAIN EVENT

The program we will look at is going to use the directory listing from the current directory and calculate cryptographic hashes on each of the files. This will require that we take on the functionality to compute those cryptographic hashes. In addition, we're going to let separate threads take on the hash calculation for each file. Finally, we'll use an IPC mechanism to pass the hash off to a function that takes care of displaying the value once it has been calculated. In the following code, you can see the entire program before we start dissecting it. The first thing you will notice is the large number of use statements. It's always easier to reuse functionality that already exists rather than having to create functionality from scratch. This keeps our code smaller, which ideally means less testing.

```
extern crate sha2;

use std::thread;
use std::{env, fs};
use std::fs::{ReadDir,DirEntry};
use sha2::{Sha256, Digest};
use std::os::unix::net::{UnixStream, UnixListener};
use std::io::Read;
use std::io::Write;
use std::path::Path;
use std::process;

fn sock_server(mut listener: UnixStream) {
    loop {
        let mut response = String::new();
        let _length = listener.read_to_string(&mut response).unwrap();
        println!("{}", response);
    }
}

fn get_files(path: &String) -> ReadDir {
    fs::read_dir(&path).unwrap()
}
```

```
fn read_file(filename: &fs::DirEntry) -> Result<String, ()> {
    if !filename.path().is_dir() {
        let contents = match fs::read_to_string(filename.path()) {
            Ok(contents) => contents,
            Err(why) => panic!("{:?}", filename.path())
        };
        Ok(contents)
    }
    else {
        Err(())
    }
}

fn main() -> Result<(),()> {
    let current_dir = String::from(env::current_dir().unwrap().to_str().unwrap());
    let (mut side1, mut side2) = match UnixStream::pair() {
        Ok((side1, side2)) => (side1, side2),
        Err(e) => {
            println!("Couldn't create a pair of sockets: {:?}", e);
            std::process::exit(-1);
        }
    };
    let serv_handle = thread::spawn( || { sock_server(side1) });
    for file in get_files(&current_dir) {
        let entry = file.unwrap();
        if let Ok(file) = read_file(&entry) {
            let msg = format!("{} : {:x}", entry.path().to_str().unwrap(),
Sha256::digest(file.as_bytes()));
            side2.write_all(&msg.into_bytes());
        }
    }

    Ok(())
}
```

Of course, before we even get to the use statements, we are using an external crate. This is for the cryptographic hash. We'll be using the Secure Hash Algorithm (SHA) that calculates a value that is 256 bits in length, which is commonly called SHA-256. In Cargo.toml, you need to add the line sha2 = "0.8.1" in order to get the right package built. That will use the package that was current at the time of this writing. Of course, you can also just use * instead of the specific version number. If you ever want to know what version is current when you are writing code, you can find the crate you are looking for at crates.io. Each crate's page should give you the requirements line that needs to go into your Cargo.toml file.

Unix Sockets

We're going to bounce around a little bit as we work through the program, so we can talk about all the relevant pieces of related functionality at the same time rather than going function by function and having to talk about different elements separately. We'll start with the Unix sockets function, in part because the server end of that communication stream is handled in the first function we hit starting at the top of the file. There is some functionality we need out of the standard libraries. In the following code, you will see those lines that pull in that functionality from those standard libraries. You may find it strange that `io::Read` and `io::Write` are necessary here, but you will generate errors trying to implement the Read and Write parts of the sockets without those lines. Fortunately, the Rust compiler is very helpful, and it will tell you those crates are missing.

```
use std::os::unix::net::{UnixStream, UnixListener};
use std::io::Read;
use std::io::Write;
```

> **NOTE** It may go without saying, but just to be clear, it's worth mentioning that as we are using Unix domain sockets, you can't run this program directly on Windows. It won't compile, because the necessary library doesn't exist on Windows. This does not mean that if you are on a Windows system, you are completely out of luck. What you can do is install the Windows Subsystem for Linux and a Linux distribution on top of that. These distributions are available in the Windows Store. One recommendation would be to use Cmder for your command-line access program since it will support the Windows Command Processor (cmd.exe) as well as PowerShell and Windows Subsystem for Linux.

Let's take a look at the function that will serve as a listener for us. This will be started in a thread of its own, waiting for connections with data that will be printed out to the console. The following is the function we're going to use. The `Unixstreams` we are going to be using to communicate through are similar, at least in how we use them, to the MPSC functionality we used previously:

```
fn sock_server(mut listener: UnixStream) {
    loop {
        let mut response = String::new();
        let _length = listener.read_to_string(&mut response).unwrap();
        println!("{}", response);
    }
}
```

The socket is going to be initialized in a different function, so an identifier will be passed into this function. This needs to be mutable because it's a stream, which means there are elements within the data structure used to keep track of where in the stream the communication is. This is similar to using the `BufReader`, as we have in previous chapters. The `Unixstream` will take care of managing getting data from the sending side, including all of the underlying communications mechanisms to manage the connection between the two parties.

Since we have no idea how long we are going to be taking data, the easiest way to keep listening and reading is to just create a loop. Previous loops we've looked at have had conditions that allowed the loop to terminate naturally. This may have been when a condition occurred, as in a `while` loop, or it may have been once a certain number of iterations had been reached, as in a `for` loop. Neither of those is going to help us here, because we don't know when the last message will be received, although technically we could write a `while true` loop, and it would serve the same function as what we are using. For this function, we just use `loop {}`. This is effectively an infinite loop that will keep going unless there is something inside the loop that performs a break to terminate the loop. In our case, we are just going to wait until the thread is terminated, which will terminate the loop from the outside.

Inside the loop, we perform a `read_to_string()` on the `Unixstream` that was passed into the function. This is going to return a length that won't be used. A convention in Rust is to prefix any unused variable with an underscore (_). So, you will see the length get placed into the identifier named `_length`. This tells the compiler that the variable isn't going to be used beyond storing the return value, so it shouldn't generate any warnings to indicate that the identifier isn't used. The thing we care about is passed into the `read_to_string()` function. Since we expect it to be altered by the function, it is passed in as mutable. As usual, what comes back from this function is a `Result`, which means it needs to be unwrapped. Even though we aren't going to use the result, it's just a good habit to remain in.

Finally, we just write out the data we receive. This is done using a conventional `println!()` call. Since we are getting a string back from the read function, there is nothing fancy that needs to happen. We're just going to print out what we get from the sending function.

File and Directory Handling

Before we get started here, we should talk about what will be happening in this next section. We're going to be getting a cryptographic hash from what we find in the current directory. There is no use in generating a cryptographic hash from a directory, although we'll get into some reasons for this later on. As a result, we need to make sure that we are only looking at files and not directories. So, let's take a look at the code for the functions we will be reviewing in this section:

```
fn get_files(path: &String) -> ReadDir {
    fs::read_dir(&path).unwrap()
}

fn read_file(filename: &fs::DirEntry) -> Result<String, ()> {
    if !filename.path().is_dir() {
        let contents = match fs::read_to_string(filename.path()) {
            Ok(contents) => contents,
            Err(why) => panic!("{:?}", filename.path())
        };
        Ok(contents)
    }
    else {
        Err(())
    }
}
```

The first function looks very simple, but in fact, there is a lot going on with it. First, we are taking in a `String` value that should be the full path to the current directory. This means whatever directory the user is in when executing the program is going to be the directory we will be getting a complete directory listing on. Once we have the listing, we will then be performing work on the files that we find there. As a result, what we will be passing back from this function is an iterator. This iterator is a pointer into a list of all of the entries in the directory. Later on, we will make use of this iterator. As with other iterators, what `ReadDir` actually is, in terms of implementation, is a struct. This means it not only has data associated with it but also has traits. We'll get to some of those traits later on, but as with so much of Rust, be aware that data isn't ever just data. Much of what you get back from libraries in Rust is data structures that can have actions taken on them.

The one line in the `get_files()` function is `fs::read_dir(&path).unwrap()`. You will notice, as usual, there is no semicolon at the end of this line. This means it's not a statement but an expression. The `read_dir()` function takes a `String` as a parameter. This should be a directory path. If it's not, this function will generate an exception. As we are in control of all of the code in this program, it's not a big deal, but it's also not good practice to assume you are getting what you expect without doing a check. It would be simple to add this check by making sure we have a clean result and not an error.

When we call `read_dir()`, we pass a reference to the path identifier since the called function has no need to own the memory where that information is located. All the function needs to do is be able to read the directory. In cases where only the data is needed, we can use a reference. That's a good tip to remember when you are developing software and writing functions. If there is no need to own the information being passed into the function, you should make the passed-in identifier/variable a reference rather than letting your function own the data. Not owning the data makes life a little easier from the perspective of writing functions and especially when it comes to calling functions. If you are going to be writing any function or module that someone else will use, keep this in mind so you aren't making life more difficult for the programmer down the road. Programming can be challenging enough sometimes without adding additional issues that need to be surmounted. Of course, when you control all the code, you can do whatever you want. As mentioned in previous chapters, though, getting into good habits and sticking with them means you don't have to keep changing the way you are writing.

> **TIP** Getting into good programming practices early makes it a lot easier to succeed in a programming job. Lots of things will vary from position to position, which is why there are style guides—things like ways to name identifiers as well as where to put curly braces (on the same line as the statement or on a separate line by itself). If you develop good programming practices that follow good hygiene and makes code more readable, you'll be better thought of in any programming position.

In the next function, `read_file()`, we take in the name of a file that we are going to read the contents of. We're going to return a `Result` for a change. This is because we need to handle the case where what's passed in isn't a file but is a directory (or something else) instead. Passing back an error allows the calling function to handle the error, effectively ignoring directories in the case of the implementation we'll look at in a little bit.

The very first thing we do in the function is to determine whether what has been passed in is a directory or not. Remember that if it's a directory, we're just going to ignore it and return an error from our function. In the following code, you will see the check to see whether we have been given a file rather than a directory. What you will see is this is a function that will return true if the file name is a directory. We negate the response because we want to do something if it's not a directory.

```
if !filename.path().is_dir() {
```

There are actually a few things to consider here. The reason for negating the is_dir() result is that the actual code is in the case where it isn't a directory. If it's a directory, there isn't much of anything we are doing. We are essentially just returning an error. To be perfectly honest, one reason the code was written this way was that initially, there wasn't an error being returned. It wasn't until I'd been playing with it for a while that I realized I needed to return an error to be able to ignore the case where there was a directory. Had I realized that sooner, I might have written it without the negation (!) and placed the error in the first clause and the code in the second.

There is something that is a little more explicit about doing it this way. Sometimes code is expressive: you write it in a way that the meaning is clear, and you don't have to parse it out. What this code says is that if the file name passed in isn't a directory, we perform some functions. The error return is just an ancillary thing that's necessary for the remainder of the code to work correctly, but the important thing in this function is what's in the block after the initial if.

Something else to consider here is, why not just check to see if we have a file on our hands? Again, some of it is about being expressive in a way that the intention is clear. However, some of it is a case of misreading the documentation. In reading through the is_file() trait documentation, it seemed as though there was a case where the is_file() call might fail to return false if the entity provided was a directory. The documentation says is_file() returns true in the case of a regular file. This says that anything that isn't a file and not a directory should return true. However, knowing a fair amount about filesystems, I know that in the case of Unix-like operating systems, a directory is a file. It's a special file, but it's still a file. Everything is a file on Unix-like systems. Because of this, my particular bias was not to entirely trust that we'd get a false on a directory if it were passed to is_file(), which meant I returned to is_dir() since it was clear that would always return true in the case of a directory. The check just needed to be negated so we could look for the case where the entity provided wasn't a directory.

> **NOTE** *These are the sorts of things you end up working through as you are writing programs. Ultimately, writing programs is not a science, in the sense of there being one way to write the program. Writing programs is a bit of an art because you need to think about things like readability. There are also a lot of different ways of putting together a program of any substance—perhaps as many different ways of writing a program as there are programmers.*

There's a little more in this function to unpack here:

```
let contents = match fs::read_to_string(filename.path()) {
    Ok(contents) => contents,
    Err(why) => panic!("{:?}", filename.path())
};
```

The first line should be familiar. We are going to use the match statement again because we want to quickly and easily compare results that come back from the read_to_string() function. This is a function that takes the contents of a file and places those contents into a String identifier. If the Result value that comes back from the function call is Ok, containing the string value, we place that value into the identifier contents. If what comes back is an Err, for whatever reason, we're going to do something a little different. Rather than just returning the error contents or even printing the error, we're going to call the panic!() macro.

The reason for using panic!—and you could debate whether it has value in this instance or not—is that you have reached a state where the program simply cannot or should not continue. The call to panic! is used to notify the user that something catastrophic has happened. The program itself, or at least the thread the panic! macro is called from, will terminate and provide any notification that is in the parameters sent to panic!. In this case, we are using a formatter and passing the name of the file that caused the problem so the user can better understand at least where the error occurred. While you can use this for troubleshooting your program, you should think about whether you want to leave these statements in the program. When it goes to a release state, do you want that to be the user experience?

So, formatting. This is not something that we've talked a lot about it, and you may have noticed there is something funny in this format string. Remember that the { } pieces in the format string indicate where parameters go. There is a lot more we can be doing with formatting. The thing about formatting, though, is that the data type needs to support that formatting. If data structures don't know how to be formatted, none of the output functions or macros will be able to handle them. One way around that, which is what we are doing here, is to use the debug output formatting. We indicate that by using :? inside the positional indicator, { }. This tells the output macro—panic!() in this case—to use the internal representation of the data. This means the pretty printing (making the data look nice on output) is bypassed. You'll see as close to what is stored in memory as is possible.

At the bottom of the function, we are doing another return from the function by using the Err result. However, we aren't giving the Err a name or even content, so we pass in an empty set of parentheses. This means the Err result is returned, but there is nothing contained within it.

Even though we've talked about match before, there is an important part of match that hasn't been covered. The match keyword expects something that is essentially a function. This is called a *closure*, and it's an important concept, so here comes a fresh section where we will talk about closures and what they mean to you.

Closures

Sometimes it's helpful to have a little dose of the whole computer science thing so you can understand how the different pieces fit together and can make your programs better and more efficient. This is a little bit where closures fit in. We get into the idea of language design and features that language designers need to consider. First, closures are implemented in languages that support first-class functions. To make use of first-class functions, you don't need to know what they are or even why they are called that. But knowledge is fun, right?

If you come out of the world of C/C++ programming, first-class functions may be a completely foreign thing, although there have been capabilities in C++ to support some of this in more recent versions of the language. Since closures are generally found in languages that support first-class functions, closures will be a strange thing to you as well. C has a tiered approach to different elements in the language. Essentially, not all memory structures are created equal in C. In the first-class bucket are variables. What this means is a variable/identifier can be passed into a function as well as returned from a function. You can assign one variable to another identifier.

If you think about it, a variable name is an identifier that refers to a location in memory where the contents of the variable are stored. The identifier itself is just an alias for a place in memory. A function name is the same thing. A function name is an alias for a place in memory that can be jumped to from the perspective of executable code. Passing parameters to or even returning information from a function is just a reference to a memory location. However, not all languages see it that way and make a differentiation between data identifiers and function identifiers. This is not to say you can't do things with functions in C, but it requires getting a memory address to the function location and passing that memory address. In essence, you can pass a function by reference in C, but you can't pass by value; so you don't have all the same capabilities with functions as you do with variables, which makes functions something less than first-class citizens in the language since they don't have all the same rights and privileges.

By comparison, if you look at a language like C#, which does allow you to pass functions as parameters, as well as return functions, you could get something like the following as a function. This function takes two parameters. The first is an integer. The second is a function. This allows a level of abstraction because you could have an interface that was called `Dbl` where the implementation was handled by a number of functions underneath. The `Dbl` interface was just a consistent way of performing a task that was reasonably explicit from a readability perspective. The function being passed in is the one doing the actual work:

```
public int Dbl(double i, Func<int> f) {

    return (f(i));
}
```

This brings us to closures, which allow us to have very narrowly scoped functions. In essence, it's a little like passing a function into a function. But instead of passing a function into a function, you just have a function inside of another function. This brings us back to the code we were looking at in the last section, repeated here so you don't have to flip back. You can look at this section a little differently now:

```
let contents = match fs::read_to_string(filename.path()) {
    Ok(contents) => contents,
    Err(why) => panic!("{:?}", filename.path())
};
```

What you will see is that what you have with the `match` keyword is really a function inside a function. We'll see this again later in this chapter, because this is a fairly limited implementation. What we get with this closure, or any closure, are very tightly scoped identifiers. Nothing that happens inside the `{};` is available outside of that scope, even in the rest of the function this happens in.

Closures are sometimes called *anonymous functions*, although there are some distinctions between the two. One reason a closure is called an anonymous function is that you get all of the scoping features (and some of the syntax) of a function without having to name it. Since it has no name (look at the code shown previously, and you will see no name associated with the brackets that denote the function/closure code—it is anonymous), we have the ability to write functions without defining them as functions and allow them to be very tightly controlled and scoped. This closure is only relevant to the `match` statement it goes with. There is no reason to create a larger function to send the `match` off to. We just create something that looks a little like a function and don't give it a name, and we're off to the races.

THREADING IN THE MAIN

Now that you understand a little about closures, we can take a look at the `main` function, where we are going to make use of them when we create threads. In the following code, you will see the complete code from the `main` function before we start to dissect it. There is a lot of work being done in the `main` function, which is something of a design decision as well as a convenience factor. The convenience is not having to either create global variables, which is generally a bad programming choice, or pass variables around between functions, which can be problematic at times. As a result, we have the case where we are getting the location of the current directory and then setting up streams for our threads to communicate with before we finally create threads to do the hashing:

```
fn main() -> Result<(),()> {
    let current_dir = String::from(env::current_dir().unwrap().to_str().unwrap());
    let (mut side1, mut side2) = match UnixStream::pair() {
        Ok((side1, side2)) => (side1, side2),
        Err(e) => {
            println!("Couldn't create a pair of sockets: {:?}", e);
            std::process::exit(-1);
        }
    };
    let serv_handle = thread::spawn( || { sock_server(side1) });
    for file in get_files(&current_dir) {
        let entry = file.unwrap();
        if let Ok(file) = read_file(&entry) {
            let msg = format!("{} : {:x}", entry.path().to_str().unwrap(),
Sha256::digest(file.as_bytes()));
            side2.write_all(&msg.into_bytes());
        }
    }

    Ok(())
}
```

Before we go any further, let's tease apart the very first line of this function, because there is a lot going on in it. We will need the name of the directory we are currently in so we can pass that value into another function later on. As a result, we need an identifier to store that value, which we are calling `current_dir`. We need this to be a string, so we are going to use a `String` data structure constructor named `from()`. This trait takes the value we'll get back from the call we'll be making in a moment and returns a `String` structure to be stored in `current_dir`.

You may notice that inside the call to `String::from()` there is a lot going on. First, we need to get the current directory, which we can pull from the `env` crate because it would be stored in the environment that is given to the program when it is executed. This includes things like the `PATH` variable, storing all the directories where executables might be found, as well as the current directory. The problem with the trait that returns the current directory to us is that it comes back as a data structure called `PathBuf`. On top of that, the `PathBuf` structure we get will be wrapped inside a `Result`. As always with a `Result`, we have to `unwrap()` it to get the goodies out.

Once unwrapped, we have this `PathBuf`, which is not a `String` or anything our `String` type can take as an input to be stored as a `String`. However, the `PathBuf` structure has a `to_str()` trait that we can call. This returns a `str`, which is still not a `String`, although the contents of the two—at least, the contents we care about (and not any overhead that may be stored inside the data structure)—will be roughly the same: an ordered collection of Unicode characters. Since the `to_str()` trait returns a `Result`, as you'd expect, we need to unwrap that `Result` to get the underlying `str` data.

So, we have a `PathBuf` that needs to be unwrapped, which then has `to_str()` called on it to return a `str` value that also has to be unwrapped. Fortunately, the resulting `str` is an acceptable data type to create a `String` from, so that is what is passed into our `String` constructor.

Creating Streams

Earlier, we talked about interprocess communication (IPC). We're going to take a different approach to IPC from the ones we looked at earlier. The following is the block of code that is being used to create the two ends of the conversation that the stream will be used for. We are using `UnixStream` for this, and setting it up is very simple. As we've done before, we are using a `match` statement because the return value from setting up the `UnixStream` is going to be a `Result`, and we need to know whether the setup was successful or if it generated an error. The method being used to create the stream is `UnixStream::pair()`, and it returns a `Result` with a tuple, which in this case is a pair of `UnixStream` structures:

```
let (mut side1, mut side2) = match UnixStream::pair() {
    Ok((side1, side2)) => (side1, side2),
    Err(e) => {
        println!("Couldn't create a pair of sockets: {:?}", e);
        std::process::exit(-1);
    }
};
```

We are going to need to make changes to these identifiers, so they have to be mutable. The reason for this is that they are data structures associated with a stream, which means they are being read from or written to, and the structure will have to keep track of where in the stream it is. There will be internal values to the structure that need to be altered, so the entire structure has to be mutable. Additionally, these structures will need to be passed into a function where they will be consumed.

As discussed in the last section, the `match` statement uses a closure, which is a self-contained and unnamed function. For that reason, everything that is associated with evaluating the `match` statement is inside a `{}` block. But the whole thing is a statement, so it needs to be terminated with a semicolon (`;`). The simple case here is if we get an `Ok` back. The pair of structures will be returned into the two identifiers in the `let` statement at the top of the block.

The one case that's going to be problematic is if, for some reason, the two `UnixStream` structures can't be set up. This is going to result in an `Err`, as we've seen before. It's the implications for the rest of the problem that are problematic. If the IPC streams aren't going to be available, there is no reason to continue with the rest of the program. This means we need to exit the program if this error condition ever occurs. We could just do the panic call as we did before, but this time, the program should just exit with an error code. Of course, rather than just dumping the program, it would be helpful to print an error so the user knows what has happened. The error is in the `println!` statement, and you'll see that the parameter that gets passed into `println!` is the identifier `e`. This is the error structure that results from the failed call. We want to print that out in its raw form, so again, we're going to use the debug formatting.

The exit is a call into the `std` crate. It's a simple call, and if you are familiar with writing C or even other similar languages, you may be familiar with it. We're going to follow the Unix convention of returning a non-zero value for an error. Since it's what I'm used to, I'm going to use a –1 because it makes a good error value, being negative. You can feel free to return any non-zero value you like. The non-zero part is important since some operating systems keep track of what the return value from the program is and will provide an indication of abnormal failure if the return value is non-zero.

Cryptographic Hashing

Part of what we are going to be doing in the next section is performing a cryptographic hash on the contents of a file. It's important to note that the hash is calculated on the contents of a file. This is always the case. You can change the name of the file, the date and time stamp, and permissions on it, and the hash value for the file will remain the same. This will be true of our program as well. The hash is going to be calculated on whatever data happens to be in the file. So, before we talk about generating the hash value, we should spend a short stretch here talking about what a cryptographic hash actually is and what it is valuable for.

The value is really easy to talk about. Depending on the depth we go to, what it is can be very detailed and complicated. So, we'll start with the hash value. As noted, it is based on the contents of a file or a string or basically any data you would like to toss into the hashing algorithm. No matter how many times you run that same data through the hashing algorithm, you will get the same fixed-length value. The length of that value is determined entirely by the algorithm used. Because the value never changes, you can use it for two purposes. The first is making sure one file has exactly the same contents as a second file. This is especially valuable with binary-based files like executables because it's otherwise, at a minimum, time-consuming to do that verification.

The thing about the algorithms used for these hashes is there is no direct correlation between the input data and the output hash, which means the input can't be reversed based on the hash value. Just to demonstrate that point, you can see two hash values shown next. The first is based on the two characters *H* and *i* together. In bytes, that would be the values 48 and 69 in hexadecimal. The second character pair is 48 and 68. You'll see there is a single bit of difference because we've subtracted 1 from the second byte in the first example to get the second byte in the second example. That single bit of difference generates an entirely different value in the hash:

```
kilroy@cutter:/mnt/c/Apps/Cmder$ echo 'Hi' | md5sum
31ebdfce8b77ac49d7f5506dd1495830  -
kilroy@cutter:/mnt/c/Apps/Cmder$ echo 'Hh' | md5sum
747991f32c850b279da5c1e0f68efb95  -
kilroy@cutter:/mnt/c/Apps/Cmder$
```

The second thing we can use a hash value for is to make sure something hasn't changed. You might use this if you were encrypting data and then transmitting it. If you wanted to verify the received value against the transmitted value, you could get a cryptographic hash before you sent and then verify the hash on receipt. This hash value is commonly called a *message authentication code* (MAC). We use the same hash algorithms, or at least we can, for both file hashing as well as message authentication codes.

There are a small number of cryptographic hash algorithms that are commonly used. These are complex mathematical formulas that we aren't going to go into here. You've already seen Message Digest 5 (MD5). A *digest* is another word for a hash value. The problem with MD5 is that it's short. There are only 128 bits in the output of an MD5 hash. While that seems like a lot, it's only

3.4 × 10^38 values. Sure, that may seem like a lot to you, but think about how many different data sets we'd want to generate hash values for. The moment we have two sets of data inputs that generate the same output, we have something called a *collision*, and the more collisions we can generate, the more potential there is for manipulating data that looks like it's valid when it's actually not.

> **NOTE** *The collision problem is generally referred to as the Birthday Paradox. This is a mathematical puzzle of sorts, and it refers to the peculiarities of probability. In order for there to be a 50% chance of getting 2 people with the same birthday (month and day) into a room, all you need is 23 people. At 70 people, there is a 99.9% chance that 2 of them will have the same birthday. We don't hit 100%, though, until there are 367 people in the room, because there are 366 potential birthdays, including February 29. This case where there are 2 people with the same birthday is a collision, and what it says is that you have a 50% chance of a collision at a very small number.*

The Secure Hash Algorithm 1 (SHA-1) is a replacement algorithm for MD5. It uses 160 bits rather than 128. While this is only 32 more bits, which might not seem like a lot, remember that with bits, we are talking about powers of 2—so 32 additional bits is actually several orders of magnitude more potential values over MD5. However, what we will be using shortly is SHA-256, meaning we'll be using 256 bits for the result of our hashing. That may be only twice as many bits, but the number of potential values we get is far more than two times the MD5 values. We end up with 1.15 × 10^77 potential values.

Creating Threads

We're in the final stretch here, so we're going to take a look at the last part of the program; but we're going to start by taking a quick look at the last part first because it's the easiest to deal with. Remember that when we declared the main function, we indicated it was going to return a Result. This means at some point we need to return an Ok result in the case that the program is successful. We've already taken care of the case of returning from the program with an error, although we will have the potential for an additional error coming up in a moment. The very last line in our main function is going to be Ok, so we return the Result the way we are supposed to. This is not a requirement for all programs, but you'll be able to do this at any point you like. Remember that Ok contains a value. We don't need a value, so we're just going to pass in a null set.

```
    let serv_handle = thread::spawn( || { sock_server(side1) });
    for file in get_files(&current_dir) {
        let entry = file.unwrap();
        if let Ok(file) = read_file(&entry) {
            let msg = format!("{} : {:x}", entry.path().to_str().unwrap(),
Sha256::digest(file.as_bytes()));
            side2.write_all(&msg.into_bytes());
        }
    }

    Ok(())
}
```

Now we can get into the important bits that we're here to talk about. The first line looks a little like a `match` statement, except that we're passing a function as a parameter into the `thread::spawn()` method. Remember the closures we were talking about earlier? This is a closure. What we didn't talk about earlier was passing values into our anonymous functions, so let's take a look at the specific part of the first line that has the closure. The `||` part is where you would include the parameters being passed into the function. If you wanted to pass the identifier (and its value) x, for instance, you'd use `|x|`. Remember that in part, closures are all about scoping. If you want to use x without doing anything to it, you can pass x into the closure in this way, and anything done to it inside the closure remains in the closure.

```
thread::spawn( || { sock_server(side1) })
```

In this case, we're going to use the `UnixStream` data stream as it is, so we pass it into the function called `sock_server()`, which we defined and discussed earlier. This is the server side of the `UnixStream`. Our closure only contains the call to this method, which is what's going to be run as a separate thread. That single function does not have to be it. We have a function, after all, and can add in as much code as necessary, but all we need here is to create a thread for our IPC listener.

Once the thread has been spawned, the primary thread continues by dropping to the next line of code. This is a `for` loop used to get a file name out of the `get_files()` function. With the `file` identifier, first we have to unwrap the value from the `Result`. With the value, we can read the contents of the file into the identifier `file`. With the contents, we can move on to generating the hash value. This is done all at once alongside generating the message, including the name of the file and the hash value. The line this all happens in is shown here:

```
let msg = format!("{} : {:x}", entry.path().to_str().unwrap(), Sha256::digest(file.
as_bytes()));
```

Rather than using an output method, we're just going to create a string using the `format!` macro, which will take a format string and return a `String` value from it. This allows us to take multiple values and create a single `String` value from them. In some languages, you can do something like concatenating a bunch of strings together, and we could get our message that way. In Rust, that's problematic, because it requires decisions about copying or moving and a lot of memory movement. The approach used here allows a single memory allocation based on what the contents will be inside the format string.

We're using a new formatting type here. Because we are getting a very long, 256-bit value from the hashing function that doesn't make much sense as a decimal representation, because it would be potentially more than 70 characters long, we're going to print out the value in hexadecimal. This is done by using the `:x` format specification inside the positional indicator. The result from this line of code is going to be something that looks like *filename : hashvalue*. Because we're using a separate thread to do our printing so we can continue along with hashing files, we are just creating the `String` value and sending that to the client side of the `UnixStream`. This is done using the `write_all()` method. This sends the `String` to the server end of the stream, where it will be received and printed.

SUMMARY

Concurrent programming creates a number of challenges, only some of which we have looked at here. The first is simply how to create multiple threads inside a single process. This is done using the `std::thread` crate, which shows that Rust has threading capabilities built into it as standard functionality. Once we have multiple threads in a process, we need a way for them to communicate with each other. This is done with interprocess communication (IPC), which can be used to communicate between threads or between entirely separate processes. There are many different ways to handle IPC. In Rust, one way is to use `UnixStream`, which creates two ends of a communication channel. These are buffered I/O channels, so they take care of all the communication mechanisms and where they are in the stream. All you need to do is read from and write to the channel.

Another important concept covered in this chapter was closures. These are essentially functions inside of functions, and they don't have names, which makes them anonymous. You can pass values into these functions. Because one purpose for closures is to contain a scope, anything that happens within the closure remains in the closure. This is something we used as part of creating a thread, because the thread creation method requires a function to be passed to it. This can be done easily by passing an anonymous function using a closure.

We also used cryptographic hashing in this chapter. This is a useful capability because it can not only be used on file contents, as we did here, but also as message authentication codes when encrypting messages between two parties. There are a few different ways to do hashing using Rust, but using the `sha2` crate is the easiest and, to be honest with you, the best because this crate has the largest space to generate values in, which means there are far fewer opportunities for collisions.

As part of generating the cryptographic hashes, we needed to get directory listings. This is done with the `ReadDir` data structure, which provides an iterator to the list of entries in any directory. The iterator lets us use a loop to work through all of those files. For our purposes, all we needed to do was determine whether a file was a regular file or a directory and read the contents of any of the files into a `String` identifier.

EXERCISES

1. Add in the capability to pass a directory into the program, and use that instead of the current directory.

2. Create a separate thread to do the hashing and pass the file name to that thread, which would then send the result to the output thread.

ADDITIONAL RESOURCES

Dining Philosophers Problem Using Semaphores - www.geeksforgeeks.org/dining-philosopher-problem-using-semaphores/

Dining Philosophers Problem - www.tutorialspoint.com/dining-philosophers-problem-dpp

Semaphores in Process Synchronization - www.geeksforgeeks.org/semaphores-in-process-synchronization/

Mutex vs Semaphore - www.geeksforgeeks.org/mutex-vs-semaphore/

Clients and Servers

IN THIS CHAPTER, YOU WILL LEARN THE FOLLOWING:

➤ How to write network programs

➤ How to implement a server using TCP

➤ How to call operating system tasks from your program

Okay, in this chapter, we're going to do something a little naughty. It's entirely in service of learning, though, so it's fine. And it makes complete sense in the context of the subject matter for this chapter. In the spirit of only doing programs that are at least somewhat useful or are at least fun, we're going to write a remote access client/server.

In case you're old enough, it will be similar to Back Orifice or Sub7. If you are unfamiliar with those two programs, they were called remote access Trojans (RATs). We aren't going to be doing anything with the Trojan part, which only suggested that they appeared to be something other than what they really were. In many cases, these programs could be installed on your system, and you might think they were something else. For example, you may think the program was some helpful utility to keep track of time or appointments. It could have appeared to be anything that would get you to run it or install it on your system. One thing to keep in mind about Back Orifice and Sub7 is they are both more than 20 years old at this point. The sophistication required to get people to install things was minimal back then.

Back Orifice was written by a programmer going by the name Sir Dystic with Cult of the Dead Cow (cDc). It was written to be a way of remotely administering systems. This was back in the days when there weren't a lot of ways to administer Windows systems remotely. As a result, Back Orifice was a tool that not only had legitimate uses but also could be used for less legitimate purposes, including gaining remote control of anyone's computer without them being aware of it. It used a client/server architecture. You installed a small server app onto someone's system or (ideally) your own Windows server. Then you could use the client to connect to the server and issue commands to the server.

> **NOTE** It's possible you have seen Cult of the Dead Cow in the news in recent years, even if you knew nothing of them before. Beto O'Rourke, a presidential candidate in the 2020 race, was previously a member of cDc, calling himself Psychedelic Warlord. This was sometimes mentioned in reference to the candidate in news articles. cDc were well known in security communities around 2000 and have had several high-profile members.

In the case of Back Orifice (BO) and Back Orifice 2000 (BO2K), the client was a graphical user interface (GUI). We're going to keep things simple and just focus on the client/server aspect of it and leave the interface with the user at the command line. The name Back Orifice, by the way, is a bit of a joke. At the time, Microsoft had a product called BackOffice Server, bundling several common server applications together into a single package. It later became Small Business Server. So, if we want to manage a Windows system, we may as well use a Back Orifice server. Of course, there is also the pun of *back orifice* as in *backdoor*, which BO certainly provided.

The purpose of this exercise is to demonstrate client/server activity. More specifically, this is about introducing you to network programming on both sides of the equation—the sending as well as the receiving side, since the development looks different based on what we're doing. On the receiving side, we have to set up a listener, which requires more work than just setting up an input/output channel and writing to it to get a message to another system.

Because just sending traffic back and forth from one system to another isn't particularly interesting in and of itself, we want something to send and receive that has some substance or is meaningful in some way. In our case, this means sending a command to a remote system, getting the response to that command, and sending the response back to the sending system. These will be some version of operating system commands, although we will probably make them system-agnostic so it doesn't matter what the remote server is as long as it's running the server we have written.

One of the problems we see a lot in programming, especially web programming, is a lack of validating input to make sure it's what we expect to see. Rather than just taking any old command and passing it without looking into the operating system, we're going to make sure we are taking an approved command that we understand. Another problem is that programmers sometimes assume what they are getting from a different part of the program is going to be clean. If we were really lazy, we could assume that what we get from the client is going to be valid input because it had been vetted. However, there is nothing in particular to stop someone sending in a bogus command to our application. This means we are going to do the validation on both ends—at both the client and the server.

Ideally, we would use encryption between the client and the server. But to keep everything simple and so you can see the process from just the network programming perspective, we're going to start without any encryption between the client and server. Also, we're going to limit ourselves to talking about the server in this chapter. There is more than enough to fill the chapter with just the server. We can take a look at writing the client in the next chapter.

PLANNING

As we are talking about two different programs here that need to communicate back and forth, we are adding a little complexity. As soon as we start getting a little complex, it's really helpful to sketch out what the program is going to do. The sketch or plan doesn't have to be as complex as a complete design document that is dozens of pages with a lot of detail, but documentation is helpful. This is especially true when it comes to any program that has some heft to it and may eventually be looked at by someone else—meaning someone other than you, the original programmer, may want to do some bug fixing or extend its capabilities.

There are a number of ways of doing this planning. The first thing to do is jot down (on paper or in a text document or some Office-like document with formatting and a lot of bells and whistles) the requirements. In our case, we have fairly simple requirements. We can list at least some of them here:

Client

➤   Take input from user

➤   Assess input for valid command

➤   Initiate communication channel with server

➤   Send communication

➤   Receive response

➤   Print out response for user

➤   Lather, rinse, repeat

Server

➤   Start listener

➤   Wait for input from client

➤   Receive input

➤   Validate command

➤   Send command to operating system

➤   Receive response from operating system

➤   Transmit response to client

➤   Return to waiting for input from client

There is a bit of a flow to these requirements, meaning you could almost create a flow chart from them and show how the program operates by just looking at the requirements. We get a lot of useful information out of these requirements. First, we need a way to take input from the user. This isn't specified in detail, meaning we could accept a command on the command line, or we could just prompt the user for a command to send. We also need the ability for the server to initiate a listening network port that the client can communicate with.

Another way of writing up documents like this is to use a visual language. One such language is the Universal Modeling Language (UML). This is a way of visualizing the design of a system or piece of software so it can be seen easily. Sometimes systems are so complex that diagrams are easier than just plain text for communicating the functionality. Of course, the text helps with additional details, because you aren't going to see everything in a diagram, but the diagram helps you make connections more easily than trying to visualize dozens or hundreds of functions all communicating with one another without a diagram.

UML can be used for a lot of different purposes, including generating a class diagram for object-oriented systems with all the class definitions and their interfaces. It can also be used for activity or communication diagrams. We're going to create what is essentially an activity diagram, showing what the program is going to do for us. In Figure 6.1, you can see a UML diagram of the client portion of our system. It shows a flow of the program, including a decision point. We need to know when we are going to exit the client program since we're going to assume that the user wants to send multiple commands, one after the other. As a result, we need a way for the user to indicate that they are done sending commands and want to quit. We could force the user to send a Ctrl-C into our program, which would terminate it, although not cleanly. However, that's impolite and not good programming practice.

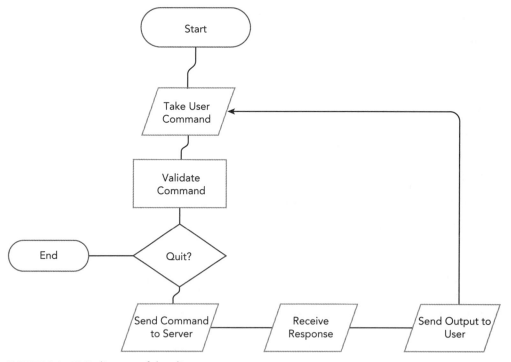

FIGURE 6.1: UML diagram of the client program

You can do the same thing for the server side if you like. Using UML may not work well for you, depending on how you like to visualize. You may prefer to use pencil or pen and paper, and that's perfectly fine. One tool you can use, although there are a lot of others, is Visio. The diagram seen in Figure 6.1 was initially done as a rough idea using Creately. You can use a free version of this web-based application to create your diagrams, although doing anything useful like exporting the finished diagram will cost you for a subscription. Depending on your preferences, you may find either an online tool or a native application to use if you decide you like using UML to visualize what the interactions of your program are going to look like.

NETWORK PROGRAMMING

Before we get started with writing any code—and I apologize for going on since I'm sure your fingers are just itching to type at this point—we should talk about networking at a conceptual level. No reason to assume people who are writing programs know a lot about networking, but at least some level of understanding is helpful, so you know what you are using and why you are using it. As a result, we're going to look at a common network stack and what the different layers do. Once we have the common network stack, we can talk about protocols that may be in use. While the Open Systems Interconnect (OSI) model is commonly used and discussed when analyzing or parsing communications stacks, it has seven layers and is probably far more than we need. Instead, we're going to use the four-layer Transmission Control Protocol/Internet Protocol (TCP/IP) stack.

The idea behind using a stack to visually represent a communications process is that data travels vertically through the stack, passing through each layer, both up and down, as it is either created or read. Figure 6.2 shows a representation of the TCP/IP stack. At the bottom of the diagram is the Network Access layer. This is where the system is physically connected to the network, as well as the drivers that are necessary to make that physical connection possible. This is also where any media access happens. Commonly, in local area networks, Ethernet is the protocol at this layer since Ethernet takes care of all local network access and communication.

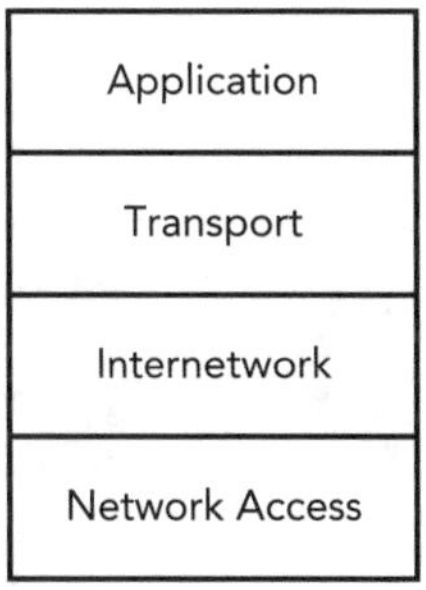

FIGURE 6.2: TCP/IP layers

Above the Network Access layer is the Internetwork layer, sometimes called the Internet layer. It's called the Internet layer because this is the layer that takes care of getting messages between (inter) one network and another network. We need a way to get off our local network and onto someone else's local network. The Internet layer handles all of the addressing and message passing necessary to make that happen. The protocol you will commonly see at this layer is the Internet Protocol (IP). IP provides a two-part address for every system on a network that is going to communicate using TCP/IP. The first part of an IP address is the network part, which indicates the network identifier so all the devices know whether an address is on another network and determinations can be made about how to get to that other network. The second part of an IP address is the host. This is a much smaller portion of the overall address and uniquely identifies the host on the network.

For the most part, this ends the pieces that you don't have to worry too much about. IP addresses are assigned by whoever runs the network, which may be done dynamically by some device like your home router as systems come onto the network. As long as you are plugged in or have a WiFi signal, you don't worry about the Network Access layer. When it comes to writing programs, though, we have to start being concerned at the Transport layer. Each layer of the network stack has some way of addressing components at that layer. At the Network Access layer, it's the Media Access Control (MAC) address, which uniquely identifies every device on the network. At the Internetwork layer, it's commonly the IP address, since we live in a predominantly TCP/IP world. When it comes to the Transport layer, we need a way to differentiate one application listening for network connections from another. This is done using ports.

There are two Transport layer protocols to be concerned with. Mostly, you'll end up using one more than the other, but it's useful to know about both so you can make smart decisions based on what your application needs. The first and most common is the Transmission Control Protocol (TCP). This is a protocol that guarantees not only delivery but also delivery in the correct order. Imagine a network that looks like what you see in Figure 6.3. You are the client, and you want to get to the server. There are two paths to get there. One path goes through Router B, and the other goes through Router C. Both paths will allow traffic to arrive at the server, but one path may be slower than the other. Usually, Router A will know which path is going to be better, but maybe a bunch of data was sent to Router B before Router A became aware there was a problem with that path that was going to slow the transmission. This means data sent later through Router C might arrive before the earlier data sent through Router B.

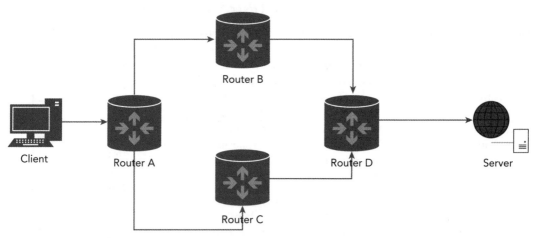

FIGURE 6.3: Network transmission

If we didn't have a lower-layer protocol taking care of reordering the messages being sent, we, as programmers, would have to figure out how to deal with that. Fortunately, this is where TCP comes in. TCP keeps track of all the segments, which are the units that TCP breaks information into if necessary, effectively numbering them so the receiving end knows how to put everything back together again. TCP will also know when a segment goes missing because the segments are numbered. If a segment goes missing, TCP will call back to the sending system to let it know there was a segment missing. In practice, what happens is the receiving system says Got 1, Got 2, Got 3, and so on, back to the sending system. If the sending system doesn't receive Got 2, it knows that segment 2 went missing and it needs to resend. All of this is what makes TCP a guaranteed delivery (or reliable) protocol. This is quite different from the User Datagram Protocol (UDP).

> **DEFINITION** *Each layer of our network stack has a name for the chunk of data that is encapsulated by (meaning includes the headers for) that layer. These data chunks are called* protocol data units (PDUs). *At the Network Access layer, they are called* frames. *The Internetworking layer refers to its PDUs as* packets. *When it comes to the Transport layer, it depends on the protocol being used. TCP calls the PDUs* segments, *while UDP uses* datagrams.

One disadvantage of TCP is that it is very chatty, constantly sending back acknowledgments of data received and all the control messages necessary to guarantee delivery. As already noted, TCP also waits until everything is received and in order before delivering the data to the application. If data goes missing in the network, the application just has to wait until the missing data is found. This can be an enormous pain if timeliness is a factor. Imagine you are on a video conference. If the video stream is using TCP for transmission, the application has to wait until all of the video has been received for some given period of time (probably microseconds) before displaying it. If there is a delay, you get a video freeze and a very choppy experience.

Fortunately, we don't have to let our Transport layer protocol do all that extra work for us if we don't need it. Real-time protocols like streaming video or streaming audio commonly use UDP because there is almost no overhead to UDP. It does no checking to make sure datagrams are received. If they get there, they get there. UDP doesn't care. This means video received out of order can be tossed. A few microseconds of missing video won't even be noticed. This does require that the application know the order of the video or audio, since you wouldn't want to insert video or audio out of order. It would look and sound weird to get something from a few microseconds ago inserted into the stream. That means the application needs to be able to identify the correct order and just discard something that's late in arriving. This results in a better user experience overall.

So, why do we start to care when we get to the Transport layer? Because the programmer is responsible for deciding on the port that the application is going to listen on. This becomes the effective address of the application. The Transport layer multiplexes network communications to allow many applications to listen all at the same time. Without the Transport layer and the ports used at that layer, you'd only be able to listen with one application at a time because the only addressing you'd have would be for the Internetwork layer. That's a bit like sending a letter to a city and expecting the city to figure out where it goes from there. With TCP and UDP, we can provide an address directly to the house rather than expecting the post office to figure it out by city and name.

Fortunately, there are things called *well-known ports*. This is a list of numbers that is maintained by the Internet Assigned Numbers Authority (IANA). Common Application layer protocols and their associated port numbers have to be registered with the IANA so everyone knows what port number to connect to when they want to use a particular Application layer protocol. For instance, if you wanted to initiate a request to a web server, you would use TCP port 80. This is changing since most web servers are encrypting all their communications. Rather than the Hypertext Transfer Protocol (HTTP), the protocol for encrypted web communication is Hypertext Transfer Protocol Secure (HTTPS). This protocol uses port 443. Anytime you apply Transport Layer Security (TLS) to an application protocol, you are effectively creating a new Application layer protocol, which requires a new port number. This prevents the listening application from suddenly getting encrypted messages and not knowing they are encrypted.

Fortunately, on the sending side, it's quite a bit easier. We initiate a request, which has the destination port for the application we are trying to connect to. The request does require a source port because the source port on the sending side will become the destination port on the response. Think about a letter you need to address, such as what you see in Figure 6.4. You write the destination address in the lower-right (or middle) of the envelope. How does the person who receives the letter know how to get a response to you? When they reply, they would take the address in the upper-left, which is the sender's address, and put it in the lower-right (or middle) on the envelope that's going back. In our case, the operating system takes care of the address that would go in the upper-left of the envelope. It knows our IP address, and it assigns an ephemeral port, which means the port will only be available as long as the application is communicating with the server.

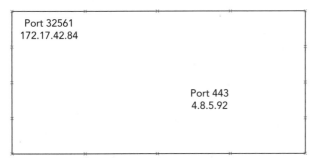

Port 32561
172.17.42.84

Port 443
4.8.5.92

FIGURE 6.4: Network envelope

So, now you understand the network bits at a conceptual level. Let's take a look at how that might work in practice.

Programming Sockets

Socket programming is a term commonly used for network programming. It comes from Berkeley sockets, which was an application programming interface (API) developed to add network programming capability to the Berkeley Systems Distribution (BSD) of Unix. As it was one of the first APIs to allow network programming under Unix, it was widely adopted, and the API remains in use even outside of Unix-like operating systems. The Berkeley approach used the standard Unix philosophy of treating everything as a file. This means you open up a connection to a system, and you get a data structure back that behaves as though it were a file handle. You can treat the connection (through it's data structure) just as you would a file, meaning you can open, read, write, and close a network connection, just as you could a file.

However, on the server side, where the application listens, there are other steps that need to be taken. To get a sense of what this would look like as a native inhabitant of the world where sockets were first developed, we are going to take a look at a very short program that would make use of the BSD sockets libraries. Because this is Unix, everything would have been written in C, which is how we are going to get an introduction to the steps necessary. A little later on, we'll take a look at one other programming language and how socket programming is done, but looking at it in C helps us to see all the steps that go into the program. We'll be using the server program written in C, which you can see here:

```c
#include <stdio.h>
#include <netdb.h>
#include <netinet/in.h>
#include <stdlib.h>
#include <string.h>
#include <sys/socket.h>
#include <sys/types.h>

int main(int argc, char **argv) {
  int sock_filed;
  struct sockaddr_in serverside;

  sock_filed = socket(AF_INET, SOCK_STREAM, 0);
  serverside.sin_family = AF_INET;
  serverside.sin_addr.s_addr = htonl(INADDR_ANY);
  serverside.sin_port = htons(800);

  bind(sock_filed, (struct sockaddr*)&serverside, sizeof(serverside));
  listen(sock_filed, 1);

  close(sock_filed);

}
```

As with any C program, we need to import all of the needed functionality from the libraries we are going to be using. We need to include the header files for those libraries so all the necessary functions have been defined when we make use of them. If they aren't defined, we'll generate compiler errors. All of the #include lines you see there are needed to pull in the functions as well as the data structures needed to make this program work. This is the same as Rust, although the keyword is different. In Rust, the keyword is use. From a practical standpoint, #include is a preprocessor directive, meaning the preprocessor takes the contents of the file indicated and adds them into this file so everything needed is declared where it needs to be declared.

The first thing we do is create a file descriptor variable. This is the place where the program is going to store the reference to the socket once we create it so it can be accessed later on. You will notice this is an integer, because that's how file descriptors are stored in C. Once we have the file descriptor defined, we need to create the data structure where all the information about our socket is going to be stored. This is a reasonably detailed data structure, as you will see shortly. In the meantime, just know that the data type is struct sockaddr_in.

Once we have our variable declarations, we can start using them. First, we need to create our file descriptor for the socket. This is done with the socket() call. Passed into that call are two constants that indicate two things. First, we are using the Internet family; and second, we are using a stream socket. What these two facts tell the library is that we want to use IP as our network protocol and TCP as our transport protocol. The return from this call is a numeric value that will be used later on when we want to interact with the socket. At this point, all we have is a file descriptor. We still have a lot of work to do.

We need to start populating the different fields in the data structure now. The first thing we are going to do is indicate that we are using IP for our addressing. This entire data structure is going to contain all the essential elements of an address because that address will need to be used when we actually start up the socket operation. The two most important components of the address are the actual IP address that we want to listen for connections on and the port number. Systems may have multiple IP addresses. In fact, any system that speaks TCP/IP will have at least two IP addresses. Any network interface, including the loopback interface used to communicate back to the system the interface is on, will have its own IP address. Your primary network interface and the loopback interface will both have IP addresses, as will any other interface (let's say you are running wireless and wired at the same time, for instance, which may mean you have three IP addresses).

What you can do, and what is being done in this example, is say you want to listen on all the available interfaces. We do this here by using INADDR_ANY as the address set in the data structure. You will notice a call to htonl() here. That is all about byte order. It is short for "host to network long." Not all systems order their bytes the same way, so for consistent communication to happen, the bytes need to be put into network order. Network order is big-endian, meaning the most significant values are written first. This is how you are used to seeing numbers written, if you think about it for a moment. When you want to write one thousand two hundred thirty-four numerically, you don't write 4321; you write 1234. The 1 is the most significant value because it is the largest of all the values (one thousand). Intel processors, which you are probably most used to, are little-endian, so the previous value would be written 4321. This means the value would need to be reversed to be put into network order.

In the next line, we set the port. This also has to have the bytes reversed because a port consists of two bytes when it is represented in memory. This allows us to have values from 0–65535, where a single byte would only allow us to have 0–255, which isn't a lot of port values when you consider the number of protocols that are in use in the world. This also raises an important point. The port value here is 800. By convention, all ports from 0–1023 are considered administrative ports, which means listening on any of those ports requires administrative privileges. Regular users can't start a program that listens on ports 0–1023. You have to be an administrator or, in Unix parlance, a root user.

Finally, once we have the address configured, we can bind to the port and address we have specified. This process ensures that no other application is already using that port. It also registers our application as the user of the port so no other application can come along and use it. What we are doing is creating a mapping inside the operating system so any connection and communication that comes into port 800 will be sent off to our application. Remember, it's really the operating system that's doing the listening for network connections and network traffic. Everything that happens with networking passes through the operating system.

Once we have done the port binding and have the operating system on notice to send communications on our port to us, we have to listen for these communications. It's not enough to bind to the port, which is just a registration process. It's like creating a curbside lemonade stand. It's not enough to put up a table with a sign saying *LEMONADE*; you need to have someone sitting at the table to serve anyone coming up, desperately in need of something to wet their parched throat. Of course, you should also have lemonade, too, or you'll have unhappy customers, but we can take care of that part later on (actually serving customers).

There are some additional steps that need to happen to have a fully functional server application. Just because we are accepting connections from clients doesn't mean we are doing anything with them. To do something with them, we need to `accept()` them. Even that's not enough, though. The call to `accept()` just completes the connection with the client, providing us a handle to the communications channel. Once we have the channel open, we can read from it and write to it.

As you can see, creating a server application is not a completely simple process, in that it requires several steps. You'll also see the same setup in a Python script that creates a socket, binds the socket to a port, and then listens on that port. Finally, here, we `accept()` connections. Since we probably want to keep taking client connections rather than be one and done, we stick the `accept()` into an endless `while` loop. As long as `True` remains true, this one line of code will continue to run. As far as I know, `True` has no plans of not being true any time in the near future, but then that's either an existential or a deeply philosophical question and far beyond the scope of this book.

```python
import socket
import sys

sock = socket.socket(socket.AF_INET, socket.SOCK_STREAM)
servAddr = ('localhost', 5000)
sock.bind(servAddr)
sock.listen()
while True:
    conn, clientAddr = sock.accept()
```

Of course, once we accept the connection that has been made, we need to do something about it. Just accepting the connection isn't hugely helpful. We need to either write something to the `conn` connection or maybe read from it. This is a variable that represents the handle for the channel we will be performing any input/output on.

This is a low-level approach to writing network programs in Python. There are libraries available that make it considerably easier. One of these is Twisted, which provides implementations of a number of different network protocols. Similarly, when it comes to writing network programs in Rust, there are some libraries that take care of all the protocol and connection specifics. We will take a look at some of those later on in the book, but for now, we're going to stick with the low-level networking functions.

RUST TCP SERVER

We're going to start with a simple server that implements a couple of commands. What you see next is the complete program as it stands, with two commands that have been implemented. The two commands we are going to start with are simple and deal with the file system. The first is just getting a list of the files in the working directory where the program is running. The second command is one to make a directory on the server. This will assume, of course, that the user has rights to the directory the program is currently in. Otherwise, the call to make the directory will fail. This may be of more concern on a Linux (or other Unix-like) system than it is on a Windows system. However, it will mostly depend on whether a "change-directory command" has been implemented. Before we get to worrying about that, however, we should take a look at the program:

```rust
use std::io::prelude::*;
use std::net::{TcpListener, TcpStream};
```

continues

(continued)

```rust
use bufstream::BufStream;
use std::fs;

fn make_directory(param: &str)  -> String {
    match fs::create_dir_all(param) {
        Ok(_) => String::from("Success"),
        Err(err) => err.to_string()
    }
}

fn get_file_list() -> String {
    let mut listing = String::with_capacity(8192);

    for file in fs::read_dir(".").unwrap() {
        let entry = file.unwrap().path().display().to_string();
        listing.push_str(entry.as_str());
    }
    listing
}

fn handle_req(conn: TcpStream) {
    let mut req = String::with_capacity(512);
    let mut response = String::with_capacity(4096);
    let mut reader = BufStream::new(&conn);
    match reader.write(b"> ")  {
        Ok(_) => (),
        Err(err) => println!("Received an error on write! {}", err)
    };
    let size = reader.read_line(&mut req);
    if size.unwrap() > 0 {
        let mut params = req.split_whitespace();
        let command = params.next().unwrap();
        match command {
            "flist" => response = get_file_list(),
            "md" => response = make_directory(params.next().unwrap()),
            _ => response = "Unacceptable command"
        }
        match reader.write(&response.into_bytes()) {
            Ok(_) => (),
            Err(err) => println!("Received an error on write! {}", err)
        };
    }
}

fn main() -> std::io::Result<()> {
    let listener = TcpListener::bind("0.0.0.0:3333")?;

    for stream in listener.incoming() {
        handle_req(stream?);
    }

    Ok(())
}
```

As usual, we're going to break this program apart piece by piece. We can start with the `main` function, since that is reasonably straightforward, and we've already seen pieces of this in other languages. So, let's pull the `main` function out of the rest and see how it works:

```
fn main() -> std::io::Result<()> {
    let listener = TcpListener::bind("0.0.0.0:3333")?;

    for stream in listener.incoming() {
        handle_req(stream?);
    }

    Ok(())
}
```

To start with, we're going to return a value from the program. This is going to be a `std::io::Result` because if we generate an error from different pieces of the function, that error will be returned from the `main` function, which means it will be returned from the program itself. The first place we can generate an error is in the very first line. We are creating our listener, as we did before. Where before, in C, we had to set a lot of values before we could create the socket, we take care of that by simply using the `TcpListener` struct. This, by definition, assumes that we are using an Internet stream socket. In C, this would have been the same as setting the values `AF_INET` and `SOCK_STREAM`.

The important values when we bind in Rust are going to be the IP address of the interface we want to listen on as well as the port. In this case, we are going to listen on 0.0.0.0. This tells the operating system that the program wants to listen on all IP addresses, which means we are going to listen on all interfaces. A system can't listen on any IP address it doesn't own (have an interface configured with), so 0.0.0.0 doesn't actually mean every IP address, just every IP address the system has configured. We're also going to listen on port 3333. A quick search indicates this is a port known to be used by the game *Rainbox Six: Lockdown*. Additionally, it's used by some malicious software. It's unlikely to be used on the systems we're going to be running it on, so it's safe to use.

Once we bind to the port, we can start listening for connections. This is something the `TcpListener` takes care of for us. As a result, all we need to do is wait for the connections. Once a connection comes in, we pass the resulting handle off to the function `handle_req()` to process. This keeps the `main()` function simple because the number of commands could get large, so we want to make sure our entry function is going to be simple and easy to follow rather than cluttering it with a lot of extra work. For us, the purpose of the `main` function is to establish the server and accept connections that get handed off to another function to take care of. It's best not to try to do too many different things in any single function, although you certainly could. Simplicity leads to clarity, which means better maintainability and understanding of what's going on. As mentioned before, even if you were the one to write a program, returning to it and trying to remember what it was you were doing and why you were doing it isn't always as straightforward as you might think.

One last note here before we leave this function. You will notice that our `stream` identifier gets a `?` inside the call to `handle_req()`. The `?` takes care of the whole issue of getting a data structure back that indicates success or failure, wrapping the value that you are looking for. What the `?` is shorthand for is "unwrap on Ok but panic on Err." This means if we did happen to get an `Err` back from the call to `incoming()`, the `main` function would generate an error and exit. Since it's the `main` function, it would mean the entire program would also exit since nothing works if there is a failure in `main()`. This is not to say that failures in other functions won't or can't cause a program to fail. The `main` function drives the entire program, though, so it's not like you can even say, "Well, this function failed, but we'll just fall back to the calling function to return to a sense of sanity." When the `main` function fails, there is nothing to fall back to.

> **WARNING** The whole `?` thing can be confusing, and it's an area where I find documentation can be misleading. There are methods that return a `Result` where the `?` should be useful, except that taking the example straight out of the documentation can lead to compilation errors. If you look at the Rust documentation, you will see a chunk of code in isolation. It may use the `?` to automatically unwrap values. What you don't see, because it's lacking from the documentation, is the function definition, which indicates that there is a return value. To use `?`, you need to define the function in a way that you can return an error that your function calls are going to return. In other words, align the error that may need to be handled by `?` with the error that is defined to be returned from the function you are writing. The error may need to be passed through from the called function, then returned by your function.

Handling Requests

We have a connection that has come in, but we haven't taken anything from the other side as yet. All we have is a connection that is bound inside of a stream data structure. This stream data structure will take care of all the overhead of the I/O so we can focus on the interaction with the other end of the conversation—sending, receiving, and processing anything that we get. Let's take a look at the function that is going to handle our requests for us. This is a framework, as noted before, that can be extended with additional commands. The reason for specifying commands rather than just blindly handing down commands to the operating system, getting the result, and sending it back to the client is that we have no idea what the user on the client end may be doing or trying to do. We want to protect the system where our server is running, so we are going to only expose what we allow the user to do. The function that handles our requests is here:

```
fn handle_req(conn: TcpStream) {
    let mut req = String::with_capacity(512);
    let mut response = String::with_capacity(4096);
    let mut reader = BufStream::new(&conn);
    match reader.write(b"> ") {
        Ok(_) => (),
        Err(err) => println!("Received an error on write! {}", err)
    };
    let size = reader.read_line(&mut req);
    if size.unwrap() > 0 {
        let mut params = req.split_whitespace();
        let command = params.next().unwrap();
        match command {
            "flist" => response = get_file_list(),
            "md" => response = make_directory(params.next().unwrap()),
```

```
            _ => response = "Unacceptable command"
        }
        match reader.write(&response.into_bytes()) {
            Ok(_) => (),
            Err(err) => println!("Received an error on write! {}", err)
        };
    }
}
```

As we'd expect, because we have already looked at the call to this function, the function receives the connection that has already been accepted from the client. This uses the identifier conn, which is just a convenience to keep from having to type *connection* all the time. Additionally, from my perspective, I'm not always sure off the top of my head whether a word like *connection* may be used by some module I am using, so it's safer to use a shortened version like conn rather than *connection*. Of course, any identifier name that makes sense and is readable would work. And, as already noted, conn is just four characters, so it's easy to type.

There are some additional identifiers we are going to need for this function. You can see them at the top of the function. The first is the string we are going to use to extract the request into. This could be a long command line, depending on the different commands we are going to allow and the parameters that may be needed, so we'll just allocate 512 characters for the string. For a command, this should be more than adequate. In most cases, the command will be a handful of characters, even with the parameter. We also need a place to store the response we get when we execute the command at the operating system. This could be really large, especially when you are thinking of things like directory listings. If we get to the point where we allow file contents to be displayed, we may want to consider a string that is even larger than the 4096 (4k) bytes being allocated.

We have the TcpStream that was passed into us, called conn, but that doesn't allow us to do any I/O, so we need to derive an I/O structure to communicate with the other end. We are going to use a BufStream for our I/O device, which will provide us with the traits for reading and writing that we will need. We need this to be mutable, because the data is going to continue to be altered as we make use of it. Any I/O structure will be changed when you perform I/O because the data structure needs to keep track of where you are in the flow. The underlying data in the structure is going to be altered. That means we can't have an immutable variable. We pass in our conn identifier, and the BufStream structure gets created with the TcpStream at its heart.

The first thing we are going to do is send a prompt to our client. This indicates that we are alive and waiting to accept commands. The client can do whatever it likes with this prompt, including discard it if it likes. We present it so the client knows the server is functioning and also that the client has connected to this particular server that is expecting commands to be sent rather than, say, a web or e-mail server. Even though we are writing, we still get a Result back, because the function is going to let us know whether it's successful or not. Anytime you are doing an I/O operation, there is a chance of failure, so it's best to check to ensure that the I/O succeeded. Even if you don't care much about it, it's still helpful to check the result.

In our case, the only thing we are really going to care about is an Err condition, since it will indicate that we are having communication issues. If we get an Err, we are going to let the server side know that there was an error on write and print out the complete error. We don't really care whether the write was successful, though. Or, rather, we don't have to do anything if it's successful. However, because there are two potential values coming back in the `Result`, we need to be able to catch both, or the Rust compiler will complain at us. The way we handle that is by using the _ character inside the `Ok()`, indicating we aren't going to do anything with the value. Then, a blank pair of parentheses indicates what is essentially a noop (no operation). We've handled the `Ok()` result, but we aren't going to do anything about it.

We will want to get the command back from the client side, so we have to call a read. In this case, we want to read everything that is coming in, so we're going to use `read_line()` on our `BufStream` structure. We are going to need to pass in the `req` identifier as mutable so the results from the read will be placed into it. This is one of those cases where we are actually getting multiple values from the function call. This could have been sent back as a tuple, certainly, but in this case the function takes a mutable identifier and returns the length. This doesn't mean we need to do anything with the length, but we do need to collect it. What we will do is check to see that we are getting a result that is a useful length. As a placeholder, this is set at anything longer than 0. However, what is probably more useful is to get the length of the shortest command and make sure we are at least getting that. Anything shorter than the length of the shortest command isn't going to be a valid command.

One problem we have, or will have, is that some of our commands will take parameters. That means before we can do anything about the command, we need to extract the command from its parameters. The best way to do that is to break the entire line at the whitespace. What we will get out of that is an iterator that will let us get each of the words one at a time. The relevant lines are shown next. We call the `split_whitespace()` trait on the `req` identifier, which is a `String`. The command is going to be (or at least should be, if the user sent something useful) the first word out of that line. As a result, we are going to assign the first word to the identifier command:

```
let mut params = req.split_whitespace();
let command = params.next().unwrap();
```

We need to next make sure the command is one that we recognize. In order to do that, we are going to use the `match` statement in Rust. The following is the `match` statement, which is small at the moment because we have only implemented two of the commands for this server application. We are using case-sensitive commands because it's easier and it seems like the right thing to do. Tell people to turn Caps Lock off to fix any problems with sending commands. Because we are using case-sensitive commands, we are just matching string for string. This works like any other `match` clause we have looked at except that we aren't matching a data structure. We are matching one string to another.

```
match command {
    "flist" => response = get_file_list(),
    "md" => response = make_directory(params.next().unwrap()),
    _ => response = "Unacceptable command"
}
```

> **NOTE** *You may note that we regularly use* `unwrap()` *in order to get values back. This isn't always the right thing to do, since some traits/functions also return errors. If you might get an error back, you can't just call* `unwrap()`. *You would need to be able to handle the error as well as the* `Ok()`. *As you are writing programs, it's helpful to refer to the documentation to identify the return type from a function's definition. In the case of the* `next()` *iterator, the return is an* `Option` *rather than a* `Result`. *The* `Option` *enum returns either* `Some()` *or* `None()`. *If we get a* `Some()` *back, there is a value. You could write the code to match on* `Some()` *or* `None()` *and unwrap if a value was returned. Using* `unwrap()` *is cleaner than doing that, but you need to be aware that if there was a* `None`, *there is no value, so there is potentially a case where you try to use a value that doesn't exist. This will likely cause the program to crash.*

What you will see inside the `match` statement is a call to the correct function based on the command received. For the command `flist`, we are calling the function `get_file_list()`. There are no parameters required for that. However, we are going to get a string back, which will be stored in the `response` identifier. You'll notice that every command (well, the two implemented here) will catch the return string in the `response` identifier. Since whatever is in response is going to be what gets sent to the client, we can also use it for error messages. At the bottom of the `match` block, you will see _, which is a catchall for the case where we didn't get a valid command from the user. In that instance, we populate `response` with a message indicating it's not a valid command.

In the case of the function call to make a new directory, we expect a parameter. As a result, we are going to pass two parameters into `make_directory()`. The first will be our command that we extracted from the vector of strings. The second is going to be the next string off the vector. We don't need to pass in anything more than that since there are no other parameters needed to make a directory. Everything else will be discarded. We have what we need, so there's no reason to make a fuss about anything extra that was provided.

Operating System Calls

In previous chapters, we've looked at making operating system calls, so we don't need to spend a lot of time discussing that practice. However, we do still have a pair of functions here that we haven't discussed yet. These are the two functions that do the work in the operating system to perform the requested tasks. Let's take a look at the first one, which is not only the first in the program listing but also the shorter of the two. You can see it here:

```
fn make_directory(param: &str)  -> String {
    match fs::create_dir_all(param) {
        Ok(_) => String::from("Success"),
        Err(err) => err.to_string()
    }
}
```

We are making a directory, and we need a parameter. What we are getting is a str, as opposed to a String. This is effectively just an array of characters without all of the traits and metadata that come with the String. Additionally, we are borrowing the param rather than actually consuming it. One thing worth remembering from earlier, when we called next() on the iterator to pass this value into this function, is that the iterator moved to the next position. We didn't pop the value off. We just moved the piece of data pointing to where we were in memory. Since we aren't popping it off, we have to do the borrow thing because the actual value remains in the data structure that we had the iterator to point to.

This is a simple function that consists of a single call from the fs crate to create_dir_all(). However, that gives us a Result that we need to handle. As a result, rather than just calling create_dir_all() and calling it done, we need to make sure the call was successful. Remember that we are expected to pass a String back from this function, which will be sent back to the client. In the case of an error, it's simple. We just pass back the text of the error message, and that will get sent back to the client. We don't get anything back from the operating system with any sort of message when we succeed in creating the directory. As a result, we need to create a message. The word *Success* seems like a reasonable response when the command is successful since we have nothing else to go with.

When it comes to the other function, we will have plenty of text to be sending back. The problem is going to be sizing the string correctly so we have enough space to get all the data we might get from a directory listing stored. The other problem is making sure what we pass back isn't too much for the string on the other end. There may be some value in creating a constant here so the two ends are in sync and the String in the calling function is going to be large enough to take the return from this function. To get started, though, we'll just use a hard-coded integer value (hard-coded meaning the number is written directly into the code where it's used rather than using a constant or variable, which would be easier to change once). The function, to refresh your memory, is here:

```
fn get_file_list() -> String {
    let mut listing = String::with_capacity(8192);

    for file in fs::read_dir(".").unwrap() {
        let entry = file.unwrap().path().display().to_string();
        listing.push_str(entry.as_str());
    }
    listing
}
```

We've seen at least pieces of this before. We used a similar mechanism when we were doing the hashing of all the files in a directory. We're going to use the same fs::read_dir() call as we did there. In this case, though, we don't need to walk through all the entries to determine which ones are files. We're just going to get a listing of the files and put them into a big string to send back to the client. This means we are returning a String from this function.

The first thing we need to do is create an identifier that can hold the contents of our directory listing. This will be a String since it will just be the text of the file names. We're going to have to do a little conversion from what we get back from read_dir() to turn it into a String value, but first things first. We have our identifier called listing, which has a capacity of 8192 characters. Again, this would be better written as a constant that could be changed in one place if it needed to be altered, so that everywhere in the code that the constant was used would pick it up rather than trying to find it everywhere it's used as a bare value. We'll keep that as an exercise for you to do at the end of the chapter, however.

Remember that when we call `read_dir()`, we get back an iterator to all the directory entries. As a result, we need to do some work to get `String` values from that iterator. First, we store each `DirEntry` structure in an identifier called `file`. To get the character representation, we first need to `unwrap()` the `DirEntry` from the `Result`. Then we call `path()` on the `DirEntry` value to get the pathname, including the file name. Then we need to get a displayable value of the path value by calling `display()`. Even this is not enough, though. We need to convert that result to a `String` using `to_string()`. The whole chained sequence can be seen here:

```
let entry = file.unwrap().path().display().to_string();
```

Remember that we have a `String` value for our directory listing. We can't just concatenate to a `String` in Rust because that gets into the problem of copying and memory issues. As a result, what we need to do is just push our current `String` value onto the existing `String`. The problem is that pushing doesn't expect a `String`. It expects the less structured `str` data type, instead. That means we need to convert our `String` to a `str` using the `as_str()` trait. So, to summarize, we have our entry identifier, which carries a `String`. We call `as_str()` on entry to get a `str` value, which we then push onto the listing identifier using `push_str()`.

The iterator we get back from `read_dir()` will run through all the entries in the directory, both files and directories. By the time the iterator gets to the end of all the listings, we will have one very long string that contains all the directory entries. This will be returned by leaving the identifier on a line by itself. Again, this is because Rust expects an expression for a return rather than a return statement and a value. We use the identifier on the line by itself without a semicolon, and the value will be automatically returned from the function. This, in the case of this program, will be sent back to the client and displayed there. Assuming the client gets written that way—and that's how we're going to be writing the client in the next chapter.

SUMMARY

Network programming doesn't have to be scary or complicated. It does require some decisions, though. First, do you care about the data you are sending, so you want to see all of it on the other end? If so, you probably want to use TCP for your Transport layer protocol. If, on the other hand, you are more concerned with speed and real-time data transmission and don't care about the odd dropped packet or two, you probably want to use UDP. TCP is a more commonly used protocol because most applications care whether the data gets to the other end intact and in sequence. UDP is really useful for audio and video. It may also be useful in protocols where there is redundancy built in or there may be multiple answers coming back. One other consideration is that TCP requires overhead to establish connections (it is considered connection-oriented, while UDP is connectionless). This takes a little bit of time to set up. If we are sending very short transmissions, TCP may simply have too much overhead. This is the case in domain name system (DNS) queries where there may be a lot of them, but they are very short. The application handles this by sending out multiple requests so that if it doesn't get one of the answers back, it's not terribly bothered by that fact. One answer is sufficient.

Once you have your transport protocol—and we're going to assume you'll want to use IP as your Internetwork layer protocol rather than something like Internet Packet Exchange (IPX), which wouldn't work with TCP anyway—you can start writing your server. You need to set some parameters, like what interface you are going to be listening on. This is usually done by specifying the IP address, since the IP address is bound to the interface. If you want to listen on every interface on your system, you just specify 0.0.0.0 for the address. If you only want to listen on your local system, you specify 127.0.0.1 for your address.

In Rust, you specify the address family as well as the Internetwork protocol by using the `TcpListener` structure. When you create a new `TcpListener`, you need to indicate a port. When you are determining what port to use, there are a couple of factors. First, any port value below 1024 is going to be an administrative port, meaning it requires administrative privileges. If you don't have administrative privileges, you need to select a port value that is 1024 or above. You should also consider what other applications may already be using the port number you want to use. There is a registration for well-known port numbers associated with protocols or applications. While most of them are below 1024, there are still a fair number you will run across that use higher-number ports. The Internet Relay Chat (IRC) protocol, for instance, uses port number 6667.

To get your server running, you need to bind to the port, which you have done by creating an instance of `TcpListener`. Once you have bound to the port, meaning you have registered your application as the place to send messages that come in on that port, you need to start listening. This tells the operating system you are ready for business, and it can start sending data your way. Finally, you need to start accepting client connections. You can listen all day long, but if you don't accept the client connections, your application won't be doing anything.

In Rust, it's best to use a structure that is capable of handling a lot of the I/O overhead for you. We used `BufStream`, which gave us the read and write traits we needed to communicate with the client. It's easier to let a higher-order module like `BufStream` take care of the communication rather than trying to deal with low-level issues. For a start, it makes error handling considerably easier.

EXERCISES

1. Add a constant (e.g. `const STRSIZE: i32 = 10;`) for a string size, and make use of that constant wherever the result is used.

2. Add the command for erasing a file. For simplicity, you could assume that there are no wild-cards and you will only get a single file rather than a list of files.

3. Add some indication that a request has come in. This should be written out to the console where the server is running and is probably best implemented in the `main()` function.

4. Add in an indication of what command is being executed, by printing to the console.

ADDITIONAL RESOURCES

Unix Socket - Client Examples - `www.tutorialspoint.com/unix_sockets/socket_client_example.htm`

Understanding socket for client server application - `medium.com/coding-rust/understanding-socket-for-client-server-application-d030fa58a896`

7

Client-Side Applications

IN THIS CHAPTER, YOU WILL LEARN THE FOLLOWING:

➤ How to network client applications

➤ How to encrypt network communications

➤ How to use regular expressions

We need to write a client to go along with the server from the last chapter. The thing about client programming is, it is tied to what the server does—unless you are writing a bare client that just initiates the connection to the server and expects the user to do all the work with talking to the server. You may be familiar with netcat, called the TCP/IP Swiss Army knife because it's useful in so many places. Once you have picked up how to write the networking pieces for both Transmission Control Protocol (TCP) and User Datagram Protocol (UDP), writing your own implementation of netcat in Rust should be a piece of cake. Take input from user, send to server. Receive response from server, output to user, rinse and repeat, so to speak.

One aspect of network programming that we didn't take on with the server was handling encryption. This was not an oversight, though so much network communication today is done using Transport Layer Security (TLS) for encryption. It's easier to understand how network communication happens without muddling it all up by adding encryption into the mix. Ultimately, we're going to be doing the same things once we add in encryption. We will, though, need to make sure we have encryption providers layered in on top.

Once we add in the ability to perform encryption—which is basically essential if you are going to communicate at all with web servers, since most web servers today are using TLS to communicate with clients—we need to make adjustments to our server. There is almost no overhead with modern encryption and modern processors, so there isn't much of a reason not to use encryption, even if it seems like everything you are transmitting isn't sensitive. It's just easier to configure the web server to use encryption out of the box rather than decide later on that you need to add it in. By then, you not only need to do the configuration but probably also need to make a lot of adjustments to the pages on the web server so the links refer to the encrypted connection rather than the plaintext connection.

Going back to the client/server we've been working on, we need to develop a client for the server from the last chapter. We're going to build it as plaintext, simply to match the existing server. However, once you've seen how the encrypted communication works, you can go back and retrofit the existing server easily enough to accommodate a client that has encryption included as a capability. In fact, you could make it something that could be toggled so you could send plaintext as well as encrypted messages, all between the same client and server.

One thing to note here is that both client and server need to know whether the messages are going to be encrypted. One reason for this is that there is a handshake process that happens to exchange keys needed to encrypt and decrypt messages. The handshake won't work if one side is trying to send plaintext messages, and the other is trying to start a key exchange process. Think of it as both sides needing to be speaking the same language. A plaintext message is not the same language as an encrypted message. Just as an example, *wubble wubble* is not the same as *U2FsdGVkX18nTbRagcE Rt6ew1yqKvQEI5csU+2TMv3Q=*. The first is plaintext (although a gibberish word written twice). The second is the American Standard Code for Information Interchange (ASCII) representation of the encryption of *wubble wubble*. To most people, the second doesn't look like anything that could be read, so essentially it is another language.

A major hallmark of Rust as a language—and it's hard to come up with another language that approaches language design like this—is its focus on protecting itself and other applications from misuse. You may think of it as a focus on security, but *security* is an ambiguous term that's often misused. Certainly, this is a point that has been made before in previous chapters, but it's worth repeating. Plus, it's hard to know how much of the earlier chapters you've actually read. The thing about security and application protection is, it's as much in the application design and controls built into the code as it is about the work the language puts in. As a result, when we are putting the client application together, we are going to spend some time making sure the user input is what we expect it to look like. This means commands are what we expect since they will eventually be passed to the operating system on the server side.

When we finish, we will have a client that is capable of taking input from a user, ensuring that at least the command is correct, and then passing it along to the server using a TCP connection. We'll take a pass at some sanitization using regular expressions along the way to make sure we aren't getting anything like a command delimiter that could potentially be used to issue another command. As we are calling commands specifically rather than just passing whatever we get to the operating system, this is far less likely, but it doesn't hurt to check for potential application misuse with invalid input.

ENCRYPTION

Encryption is taking something that's readable and converting it to something that isn't readable without some additional information. A very simple encryption cipher, meaning an algorithm to perform the transformation, is the rotation cipher. This is where you take an alphabet and then put the same alphabet after it, shifted by some number of letters. The key, meaning the piece of information that unlocks the decryption process, is the number of letters the bottom alphabet is shifted by. Take a look at the following two alphabets, and you will understand what a rotation cipher looks like:

```
abcdefghijklmnopqrstuvwxyz
defghijklmnopqrstuvwxyzabc
```

> **NOTE** This type of encryption is sometimes called a Caesar cipher *because Julius Caesar is said to have used this as a way of sending notes to his troops in the field, in case the notes were intercepted by the enemy. Without knowing the key (and the messenger wouldn't have had it), it would have been difficult to decrypt the message. You may also hear of something called rot13, which means you rotate the alphabet by 13. It was a common cipher to use to obscure information in messages posted to public forums on the Usenet, which was a collection of groups similar to e-mail lists. It wasn't impossible to read the message, but it took effort, in case there were people who didn't want to read it. This could be used for potentially offensive messages or spoilers.*

If we take the word *wubble*, for instance, we find a letter on the top row and then find its corresponding letter in the bottom row. This becomes the *ciphertext*, meaning the message after it has been through the transformation process. In our case, that would be *zxeeoh*. And you thought the plaintext was a nonsense word. To return it to its original state, if you had received the ciphertext, you'd need to know the key, meaning the number of letters you are shifting. Our key is 3, because we have shifted over three characters (a->b, b->c, c->d). Once you have your two alphabets laid out, you can use the bottom alphabet to find the letter in the ciphertext, and then find the plaintext letter in the alphabet shown previously.

There is a problem with this approach, though. First, there are no symbols. This means no punctuation. You could, of course, add punctuation if you wanted. You'd have to agree on the order of all the symbols you wanted to include ahead of time. Without punctuation, you're limited to short communications where it would be obvious what the meaning is without any punctuation. The other issue is that there is no way in the scheme presented here to handle spaces. You might think that all you'd need to do would be to leave a space exactly where it is, and all the text would be replaced. What you end up with is a way to start guessing what the key is. If every message started with five characters where two identical letters were in the third and fourth positions in the word, you might guess the word was *hello*. From there, you would know what the conversion to get from the ciphertext to *h*, *e*, *l*, and *o* would be. The rest might be easy enough to handle.

> **NOTE** One way to break simple ciphers is something called frequency analysis. *No matter what language you are writing in, different letters in the alphabet will be used a different number of times because of the occurrence of these letters in words that are commonly used. The most commonly used letters in the English language (and this will vary a little from one source to another depending on the set of input used) are E followed by T, and then A, I, N, O, and S all used roughly the same. If you look for the most used letter in your ciphertext, you can start to replace that with E. Next, you can substitute your T for the second-most used letter. Once you have these letters, you may be able to start guessing words and learning other letters. It's an iterative process, but frequency analysis can be used effectively against simple ciphers.*

This raises an issue for us. Actually, a couple of issues, if you think about it. First, if you are concerned about sensitivity, don't use something as unsophisticated like the Caesar cipher. It's too easily broken with simple techniques. More important, though, is the value of the key. No matter what type of encryption you are going to use, you will be using a key of some sort. That key needs to be protected. You can't very well send the key along with the message. That would allow almost anyone to be able to get the plaintext back from your ciphertext. Even if they didn't know the encryption algorithm used, they could try multiple decryptions with the key until they got something that made some sense.

Encryption Algorithms

There are a lot of encryption algorithms available for use. Some are better than others, and some have different purposes than others do. For example, one way we categorize encryption algorithms is to talk about whether they are symmetric or asymmetric. This means, is the same key used for encryption and decryption or not? If the same key is used, it's a symmetric encryption algorithm since there is symmetry over both sides of the process—the encryption key is the same as the decryption key. If you need separate keys for encryption and decryption, you are working with asymmetric encryption.

This is where usage comes in, as well as the difference in keys. First, most asymmetric algorithms use large keys. Currently, the Rivest-Shamir-Adleman (RSA) algorithm is very common when asymmetric encryption is needed. While you may still see 1024-bit keys, it's more common to see 2048- or 4096-bit keys used. By comparison, the Advanced Encryption Standard (AES) is a symmetric algorithm that often uses 256-bit keys today, although you may still see 128-bit keys in use.

This is not to say that RSA and other asymmetric encryption algorithms are better than symmetric algorithms like AES. They are simply different ways of achieving a similar end; and because they are entirely different processes, they use a different data set as input. Because they are very different processes, they are actually used for different things. Asymmetric algorithms tend to use more processor to achieve the end state, while symmetric algorithms can be lighter weight. As a result, you probably wouldn't want to use asymmetric encryption to handle anything that's real-time, because it wouldn't be real-time when you were done. At least that was the case when we really started using these algorithms consistently on computers. Today's processors are far more capable than those even a handful of years ago.

No matter which type of encryption you are doing, you have the problem with keys. With asymmetric algorithms, it's a little easier. You have a repository that anyone can use to store the public half of the key. Since the two halves of the key are sometimes called *public* and *private*, this method of doing encryption is sometimes called *public key cryptography*. If your public key is stored in this repository, I could grab your key and encrypt a message to you. Your private key, the other half of the public key, would be the only key that could be used to decrypt the message that was encrypted with the public key.

This method requires that everyone have access to the repository. On top of that, everyone would need to know where the repository was. Even if you have a public key and I can encrypt messages to you, that doesn't mean I have a public key or that I have put it into the repository, so you may not be able to respond to me with an encrypted message. However, that may not matter, as long as I can get the secret plans for a killer peanut butter chip cookie to you. No need to do anything in response other than to say thank you. Then make the cookies, which couldn't be sent to me (were you feeling so inclined as to send samples) in an encrypted way, so no need for any key.

One of the issues with these repositories is they are not always public. You might have a certificate repository where these keys were stored. You would need to have access to the same certificate repository as other people who want to make use of your keys. In some cases, as in the case of Pretty Good Privacy (PGP), there is just a website where keys can be searched and retrieved. This raises another issue. If, for instance, you were to go looking for my keys in the public PGP repository, you would find several keys all associated with the same e-mail address/identity. This is because I didn't hold on to the private key, which meant I needed to keep recreating key pairs. You would now have to guess which one of the key pairs was associated with my current private key (none of the ones you find are current). As noted previously, key management is an important concept.

With symmetric-key encryption, we have a different problem. We have the case where the same key is going to be used by both sides. When I send you a message, I'm going to use key Z, but you will also use key Z. Figure 7.1 shows the use of key Z to take plaintext and create ciphertext out of it. This process works backward, as well. I can take the ciphertext on the right and apply the key along with the decryption algorithm, and I will get the plaintext message back. So, where's the problem? Well, if I encrypt a message to you using key Z, how do I get key Z to you? We can certainly create key Z between us, and both of us have a copy of it to send messages back and forth. This is called a *pre-shared key*. We share the key before either of us do any encryption with it. However, one problem with this approach is that over time, the key becomes vulnerable to attack.

There are a lot of ways to attack cryptography, and the more ways we find to do better cryptography, the more attacks there are against these systems that make use of cryptography (*cryptosystems*). One way to attack them is to continue to collect ciphertext. Over time, enough ciphertext may be accumulated that the key might be derived. In most cases, if this is even possible, it takes an enormous volume of ciphertext to work with. The longer you use a key, the more chance there is of accumulating that large amount of ciphertext.

Going Hybrid

Fortunately, there are solutions to the problems that come with using either asymmetric or symmetric encryption. The first is to just use symmetric key encryption but have a way for both ends of the conversation to derive the same key at the same time. This was a process that was first described in the public realm by two mathematicians named Whitfield Diffie and Martin Hellman. This is not to say they discovered the process before anyone else. Those who had gotten there first were doing it for military or intelligence agencies. They were prohibited from writing about and certainly from publishing their work in any public fashion.

The method of key derivation that Diffie and Hellman documented is perhaps best described through the analogy of color mixing. You can see in Figure 7.2 how two different people might arrive at the

Plaintext   Ciphertext

FIGURE 7.1: Creating ciphertext with a key

exact same color without ever sharing the actual color. The process starts with the assumption that both parties, commonly called Bob and Alice, are starting with the same base color. In terms of creating a key, both Bob and Alice have the same base number they are starting with. You can see this, in the paint analogy, at the very top of Figure 7.2. While both know the base color, neither transmits this base color. If anyone were to intercept the base color, they might be able to derive the key, just like Alice and Bob.

With the base color, both Bob and Alice add a color of their own choosing. In terms of key creation, this should be a random value that gets applied to the base value using a known algorithm. This isn't simply adding two numbers together. Once Bob and Alice have their results, they each have a new color. These new colors can be safely transmitted to the other person. The base color may be known, but the colors that Bob and Alice selected to add to the base color are not known and can't be derived with just the color (numeric value) that each sends to the other.

Once each person has the color that the other has created (the numeric value), all each needs to do is add in the color they added to their own creation.

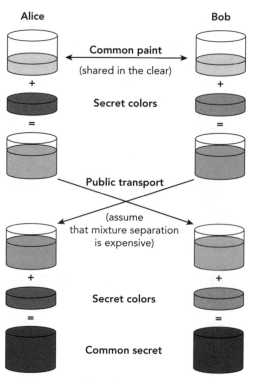

FIGURE 7.2: Diffie-Hellman key derivation

This results in final color = base color + Alice color + Bob color as well as final color = base color + Bob color + Alice color. No matter which order we add the colors together, we are going to get the same result. The same is true of deriving a key. It doesn't matter which order the values are applied to the algorithms being used. This is the commutative property of mathematics. No matter what order you are using, as long as the operations are the same, you are going to get the same value in the end.

This is a simple process. However, there is another way we could actually exchange keys. We could still use the Diffie-Hellman process but add another layer of protection on top of it if we wish. This is where we can use public key cryptography to exchange sensitive data. Messages that are encrypted with Bob's public key by Alice can be decrypted by Bob using his private key. Alice, similarly, may have a public key and a private key. Bob could use the public key to send data, like the initial derived color, to Alice so she could then apply her transformation to get the final key that will be used by both parties for encrypting and decrypting communication going forward.

> **NOTE** The key that is used to perform the encryption/decryption on an ongoing basis is usually called the session key. It is commonly a symmetric key since we probably want the speed of symmetric encryption for real-time or near-real-time communications.

Encryption Algorithms

We are not limited in the encryption algorithms we use, other than deciding whether to use symmetric or asymmetric algorithms. You can't just pick an algorithm and decide which type of key you want to use later. The algorithm determines whether it's symmetric or asymmetric. Or, if you want to think about it the other way, you decide whether you need symmetric or asymmetric, and then you determine the algorithm that uses the right type of key mechanism.

Back in the old days, there was the Data Encryption Standard (DES). This was based on an encryption algorithm developed by IBM called Lucifer. DES used a key length of 56 bits, and it was developed in the 1970s. The United States government, through the National Bureau of Standards (NBS), requested an encryption cipher that could be used as a standard. DES isn't an encryption algorithm, per se. It's actually a standard that refers to an algorithm. DES lasted the better part of three decades. Unfortunately, electronic commerce got in the way: more people started using DES, which led to more people looking at DES and finding weaknesses.

The interim replacement, while a longer-term replacement was identified and published, was 3DES. 3DES uses the same encryption algorithm as DES, but it uses three rounds of that algorithm. Where DES used a 56-bit key, it was said that 3DES used a 168-bit key. In actuality, it used 3 different 56-bit keys, each of which was applied in a different round of the application of the algorithm. You may notice I've been careful not to say a different *encryption*, saying a different round of the *algorithm*, instead. That's because we don't do encryption on each round. Instead, say we name the three keys A, B, and C. We do a round of encryption using key A. Then we do a round of decryption using key B. Remember that encryption and decryption are just transformations using mathematical algorithms. Since we aren't doing the decryption with the key used for encryption, we just end up with transformed data. Finally, key C is applied with a round of encryption.

The current standard is called the Advanced Encryption Standard (AES). This is a standard based on the algorithm Rijndael (roughly pronounced "rain doll"), which was selected because of its speed and flexibility. AES supports multiple key lengths. That means when 128 bits—the initial length of the key—becomes insufficient to withstand attacks, we can use a longer key, like 256 bits.

There are other encryption algorithms different from the ones selected by the US government for its own use. These include some of the algorithms that didn't get selected for AES. Today, you will commonly see AES used for encryption of data between a web client and server. You may also see algorithms like Salsa20, ChaCha20, or the International Data Encryption Standard (IDEA) used, especially if you are communicating with international systems or systems that are used to communicating with international systems. There are other algorithms like Blowfish, Twofish, and RC4, which are probably less common but still symmetric encryption algorithms.

Transport Layer Security (TLS)

Once upon a time, there was a browser (of the web variety) called Mosaic. It was developed by students at the University of Illinois at Urbana-Champaign (UIUC). One of those students, along with some other people, including venture capitalists, took Mosaic and created another browser out of it, called Netscape. The thought was that the browser market was going to be huge, and Netscape would own the biggest and best browser available. Netscape became a company, in addition to being a product. Netscape, in the mid-1990s, recognized the eventual rise of electronic commerce (e-commerce) and realized the need to encrypt data between client and server. This was not a capability of any of the existing protocols in use by web-based communication.

> **NOTE** *Of course, another company called Spyglass had licensed Mosaic to be used as the foundation of Spyglass's own browser. That browser then found its way to Microsoft as Internet Explorer. Eventually, Microsoft (and every other operating system vendor) began shipping browsers with the operating environment, meaning there really wasn't any commercial market for standalone browsers. Today, Netscape lives on in the Firefox browser. This is because Netscape went open source in 1998, spawning Mozilla. Mozilla begat Firefox as a separate development project. One could say that Firefox is a reasonably direct descendent of the first widely popular Internet browser.*

The first web encryption was called Secure Sockets Layer (SSL). Over time, it went through three versions before finally being abandoned because of all the problems in its conception and implementation. It was superseded by Transport Layer Security (TLS). Even TLS went through a few iterations because as soon as you introduce encryption, you may attract the interest of people who really want to see what is inside those encrypted communications. If it's important enough to be encrypted, it must be interesting, so you'll have people wanting to decrypt it. Both SSL and TLS went through iterations in versions because people who were trying to decrypt found that they could, with effort, decrypt the encrypted messages of each successive version. That's the back-of-the-napkin history of how we are at TLS version 1.3.

TLS is a set of protocols used to establish an encrypted communication channel between a client and a server. It is capable of handling a lot of different means of creating that channel, including different ways of exchanging keys as well as multiple encryption algorithms. With TLS, you aren't locked into, say, Triple DES (don't use Triple DES—I am just using it as an example). TLS can support any symmetric encryption algorithm that both sides can support. Ultimately, TLS is a way to negotiate how the encryption is going to be accomplished. TLS itself is there to handle the handshake and subsequent negotiation, as well as passing certificates if needed. It also handles managing capabilities between the client and server ends so the right (and best) encryption can be selected that both parties can handle.

So, we can take a look at some code (I know; finally!) now that implements TLS on the client side. This is Rust that just initiates a conversation with a hard-coded website (www.wrox.com, in this case). Once it has the conversation started, it issues a Hypertext Transfer Protocol (HTTP) request, gets the response, and then prints the response to the console. Nothing very fancy, but it's worth taking a look at how we need to create the TLS connection with the remote server. First, we are going to use the `native-tls` crate for TLS communications, so that needs to be added to the `Cargo.toml` file. Then, we indicate that we are using the `native_tls` module (note the difference in the symbol used—the crate uses a hyphen because we don't use underscores in crate names, while the module uses the underscore).

```
use native_tls::TlsConnector;
use std::io::{Read, Write};
use std::net::TcpStream;

fn main() {
    let tlsconn = TlsConnector::builder().unwrap().build().unwrap();

    let tcpstream = TcpStream::connect("www.wrox.com:443").unwrap();
    let mut tlsstream = tlsconn.connect("www.wrox.com", tcpstream).unwrap();

    tlsstream.write_all(b"GET / HTTP/1.1\nHost: www.wrox.com\r\n\r\n").unwrap();
    let mut response = vec![];
    tlsstream.read_to_end(&mut response).unwrap();
    println!("{}", String::from_utf8_lossy(&response));

}
```

First, we need to create a `TlsConnector` data structure. We need to create a builder. We do this by calling `builder()` on our `TlsConnector`. This returns a struct called `TlsConnectorBuilder` (once we have unwrapped it from the `Result`). We don't need to store this anywhere since we're just going to call `build()` on that struct to get the `TlsConnector` struct back. This may seem a little circular, calling a trait on a `TlsConnector` in order to get a `TlsConnectorBuilder` struct back in order to call another trait just to get a `TlsConnector` struct back. However, this is what it takes to do all the initialization necessary.

The `builder()` trait is a little like a factory in an object-oriented language. We use factories in object-oriented languages to create objects for us without having to worry about the details of the objects. The factory is what is called a *design pattern* because it's a common programming tactic. You create an interface that can be abstract in nature that returns an instance of the object. This is similar in that we have a trait called `builder()` that abstracts a lot of the work being done. What we have at the end is a struct that is capable of negotiating the TLS connection and storing all the details needed to maintain that connection.

The next two lines look a little like they are repetitive. In fact, this is the way Rust handles TLS connections. First, we need to create a `TcpStream` struct and use it to connect to the website on port 443, which is the port for HTTP connections that use TLS. Once we have the `TcpStream`, we use that to initialize the TLS connection. This means we call `connect()` on the `TcpStream` and then use the resulting struct as a parameter to the `connect()` trait on the `TlsConnector`. We will be using the resulting `TlsStream` to handle the reading and writing for us. This is like any other stream structure in that it takes care of managing the stream, knowing where we are, and taking care of reads and writes, returning data as needed on reads.

Most of the rest of this will look like similar reads and writes we have done, especially in the previous chapter when we constructed the server. One difference may be what we are sending to the server. What you see is a single line of HTTP—or rather, multiple lines of HTTP that have been put into a single line to send to the server in one shot. The line breaks come from the characters that have been escaped. Different operating systems may require different characters for a line break, but what you are seeing is a carriage return (\r) and a line feed, or newline (\n).

> **NOTE** *The terms carriage return and line feed originate with typewriters. When you have a physical device that is putting characters on a page, that physical element needs to track to the right horizontal space on the page. This means it travels across so the next character typed will appear to the right of the last character and not have all the characters just pile up on top of each other. When you are done with a line of text, you need to get the element back to the first position on the line. This is a carriage return. Again, though, we run into the situation of typing over letters if we just go back to the beginning of the line. This is why we also need a line feed, meaning the paper needs to advance vertically in the platen, which is the roller that holds the paper and can move the paper up and down. In programming languages, the newline character (\n) has often been used to represent both a carriage return and a line feed, but that's not always the case.*

In practice, the \r\n is not needed. You can use just the \n, but putting in \r\n also works and allows us to have the conversation we just had. What is important is that you need a newline (carriage return + line feed) at the end of each line of the header (i.e. GET /, etc. or Host:, etc.). You also need a bare line at the end of all the headers to let the server know you are done sending your request. An example of what this sort of request would look like is next. You should be able to get away with \n\n to do that on most platforms. The \r\n\r\n you saw previously doesn't prevent it from working, but it's unnecessary to send that many carriage return/line feed combinations. In the example that follows, there would be a newline at the end of the GET line. There would then be a newline at the end of the Host: line followed by a blank line to indicate to the server that the request was complete, and it should send back the response, which you can see follows.

```
GET / HTTP/1.1
Host: 192.168.4.1

HTTP/1.1 302 Found
Server: TornadoServer/4.5.1
Content-Type: text/html; charset=UTF-8
Date: Mon, 14 Sep 2020 00:49:34 GMT
Location: https://blocked.eero.com/?url=192.168.4.1&reason=local_blacklist
Content-Length: 0
```

By comparison with the TLS client program in Rust, we can take a look at how the same program would be written in another language. Because it's easier than some other languages, we can look at how Python would handle the same tasks. Doing the same thing in C, for instance, would take a lot more setup than we're going to do in Python, so it's a little more analogous to what we are doing in Rust:

```
import ssl
import socket

context = ssl.create_default_context()
with socket.create_connection(("www.wrox.com", 443)) as sock:
    with context.wrap_socket(sock, server_hostname=";www.wrox.com") as conn:
        conn.write(b'GET / HTTP/1.1\rHost: www.wrox.com\r\n')
        print(conn.recv().decode())
```

We need two modules to make this program work. The first is the `ssl` module, which includes both SSL as well as TLS functionality, although SSL has been deprecated for years. As the initialism has been in wide use for so long, it's generally considered easier to keep referring to it as SSL, even though we've moved beyond SSL to TLS. The other module we need is the socket module, which is going to handle the lower-level connection for us.

We need to create a default context for our connection. This can be more complicated if there are certificates necessary for authentication on the client side. However, we don't need that, so we are just going to use the default SSL context. Next, we need to create a socket that will handle the connection. This is done with `socket.create_connection()`, feeding in a tuple containing the hostname and the port number. On the next line, we're going to take the resulting variable `sock` and wrap it inside of the SSL context we already have. We do this using the context variable we already have in place that has the SSL context, calling `wrap_socket()` on it. We have to pass in the `sock` variable created in the previous line, as well as the server name. This is done to validate the server during the hand-shake, making sure the common name in the server's certificate matches the name we have provided, meaning we are connecting to the server we expect to be connecting to.

> **TIP** Encryption offers a security control to ensure confidentiality. Checking the name of the server in the certificate to be sure it's the same as the server being visited is another control. If the two names don't match, you may not be sending data to the server you are expecting to be sending data to. This violates confidentiality because suddenly a third party may be in the middle. This might be the case legitimately if there really were a third party in the middle for monitoring, although there are usually considerations for such situations, preventing errors on every visit to a website. If an attacker is sitting in the middle of the connection, though, they may not be able to provide a legitimate certificate, and the names certainly won't match. Because misconfigurations have caused issues with name mismatches and other encryption errors, users may have gotten used to accepting such errors without recognizing what may be going on.

TLS Server

You've seen what the client side looks like when it comes to doing encryption using TLS. We can wrap this conversation up by looking at the server side since there is much more involved with creating a server in general than a client, and that's at least as true when it comes to TLS. This is in part because of one aspect of asymmetric key encryption we haven't discussed. When you have two keys, you need a way to store and manage those keys. The owner of the key, meaning the person who gets to use the private key, typically has a certificate. The certificate manages the identity of the entity that holds the certificate. This entity can be a person, meaning the person would be identified by an e-mail address as well as a name. The entity can also be a system. In that case, the system is identified by its fully qualified domain name (FQDN), which is a compound value that includes the hostname as well as the domain name. You may get, for instance, `host1.wubble.com` as an FQDN. The hostname is host1, while the domain name is `wubble.com`. The FQDN can also support subdomains, so you could do `host1.labs.wubble.com`, for instance. Anything that includes the hostname as well as the domain name, whether that includes subdomains or just the domain itself, would be an FQDN.

Certificates are especially important when it comes to creating a TLS server. The certificate is the foundation of the connection and is used to validate the server. Your browser, in the case of web-based communications, will make sure the FQDN you are visiting matches the name on the certificate (called the *common name* or CN in the parlance of the protocol used to manage the certificates). If it doesn't, your browser will generate an error suggesting you may be on a rogue website. This means when we write a program using TLS, we have to have a certificate to feed the initialization with. Let's create a certificate using OpenSSL. The commands needed to create the right kind of file follow. It requires creating the certificate, which isn't verified by any authority, so it wouldn't work well in the larger world but is good for our purposes. Next, we need to export to a file our Rust program can ingest:

```
$ openssl req -x509 -newkey rsa:4096 -keyout key.pem -out cert.pem -days 365
-- snip --
writing new private key to 'key.pem'
Enter PEM pass phrase:
Verifying - Enter PEM pass phrase:
-----
You are about to be asked to enter information that will be incorporated
into your certificate request.
What you are about to enter is what is called a Distinguished Name or a DN.
There are quite a few fields but you can leave some blank
For some fields there will be a default value,
If you enter '.', the field will be left blank.
-----
Country Name (2 letter code) [AU]:US
State or Province Name (full name) [Some-State]:Colorado
Locality Name (eg, city) []:Parker
Organization Name (eg, company) [Internet Widgits Pty Ltd]:WasHere Unlimited
Organizational Unit Name (eg, section) []:
Common Name (e.g. server FQDN or YOUR name) []:foo.wubble.com
E-mail Address []:root@wubble.com
$ openssl pkcs12 -export -out certificate.pfx -inkey key.pem -in cert.pem
Enter pass phrase for key.pem:
Enter Export Password:
Verifying - Enter Export Password:
```

We have a certificate, meaning we have the keys we need to establish encrypted communications with any clients who initiate connections to us. That means we can move on to writing the code that makes it all work. The bare bones of a TLS server are shown next. Most of the modules that will be needed are ones we are familiar with. In addition, we need the `Identity` and `TlsAcceptor` from `native_tls` for the server. These will provide us some new functionality that we'll look at shortly. We are also going to use `std::sync::Arc` for a reference counter so we know when the threads we are going to be creating are done. We have used this module before but only very briefly when looking at parallel processing. We're going to make the server multithreaded so we can take in multiple connections at the same time:

```
use native_tls::{Identity, TlsAcceptor, TlsStream};
use std::fs::File;
use std::io::Read;
use std::net::{TcpListener, TcpStream};
use std::sync::Arc;
use std::thread;
```

```
fn main() {
    let mut cert = File::open("certificate.pfx").unwrap();
    let mut myidentity = vec![];
    cert.read_to_end(&mut myidentity).unwrap();
    let certidentity = Identity::from_pkcs12(&myidentity, "passphrase").unwrap();

    let tcplistener = TcpListener::bind("0.0.0.0:7999").unwrap();
    let acceptor = TlsAcceptor::new(certidentity).unwrap();
    let acceptor = Arc::new(acceptor);

    for clientstream in tcplistener.incoming() {
        match clientstream {
            Ok(clientstream) => {
                let acceptor = acceptor.clone();
                thread::spawn(move || {
                    let clientstream = acceptor.accept(clientstream).unwrap();
                    /* do something here using clientstream */
                });
            }
            Err(e) => { /* connection failed */ }
        }
    }
}
```

Skimming through the code, we'll take a look at the unique pieces that we haven't looked at before. The first is loading up the certificate file that we created earlier. This is done initially by just reading in the contents of the file. First we open it, and then we read the entire contents of the file into an identifier named `myidentity`, which is a vector. Now that we have the contents of the file, we need to make use of it. We're going to create an identifier named `certidentity`, which will hold the contents of that file once it has been parsed into a certificate by `Identity::from_pkcs12()`. There are two values we need to pass into that function. The first is the vector holding our certificate file. The second, though, is the passphrase needed to unlock the certificate. A passphrase keeps the certificate from being used by anyone other than the person or system to whom the certificate belongs, assuming the passphrase is kept protected.

> **NOTE** When we created the certificate, we converted it to the PKCS #12 file format. This is the Public Key Cryptography Standard #12. There are a number of other standards that can be used for storing and managing public keys and certificates. This is the one that happens to work with the Rust certificate implementation. Another common one is PKCS #8.

Much like we did with the TLS client earlier, we create the TCP component first, and then we add on the TLS part. This means we create the `TcpListener` using the binding information—IP address and port to bind to—and then we can create the `TlsAcceptor`. When we create the `TlsAcceptor`, we have to pass in the `Identity`, `certidentity`, that was created earlier. This allows our `TlsAcceptor` to initiate the encrypted communication using the certificate. We also need to create a reference counter based on the `TlsAcceptor` because we are going to be passing off client connections out of that

`TlsAcceptor`. Here you can see the three relevant lines that give us the TCP listener, the TLS acceptor, and then the reference counter:

```
let tcplistener = TcpListener::bind("0.0.0.0:7999").unwrap();
let acceptor = TlsAcceptor::new(certidentity).unwrap();
let acceptor = Arc::new(acceptor);
```

One thing you will see in the Rust code here, as discussed in previous chapters, is the explicitness of the functionality. This is clear in the loop that accepts new connections. You will see in the `for` loop, pulled out here so you can see it clearly without having to flip back and look, that we are accepting a TCP connection. This is because while it's a port that is commonly used for TLS, all of the TLS bits come after we have initiated the TCP connection:

```
for clientstream in tcplistener.incoming() {
```

This means we have a TCP client connection that needs to be handled. This client connection needs to be passed over to the TLS functions, which will handle doing all the decryption as well as all the negotiation that goes along with decryption—determining encryption cipher, key size, and key exchange mechanism. What we need to do is create the TLS connection based on the `TcpListener` identifier named `clientstream`. We do that with the following line of code, which is nestled inside all of the pieces needed to make sure we had a valid client connection and not an error. Once all that is taken care of and we start spawning threads to handle the client, we use this to manage the TLS connection based on the TCP connection we have with the client:

```
let clientstream = acceptor.accept(clientstream).unwrap();
```

You now have the bones of creating a TLS-based server that can take connections from clients. You would still need to write all the code that did something with the client connection, but at least you have a framework for taking on the TLS elements, including creating an identity from a certificate file.

REMOTE ACCESS CLIENT

We can go back to developing the remote access client to talk to the server from the last chapter. As discussed earlier, we will not only take input from the user of this program but also make sure the commands we accept are valid. While this makes the process a simple one, there is a lot to go into it. At a high level, we are going to initiate a connection to the server based on a connection string provided on the command line. Once the connection has been created, we take commands from the user, validate those commands, and then send the commands off to the server if they are valid. The client program needs to know when the user is done talking to the server, so we need to also accept `exit` as an additional command. We're going to do that one command using regex just to demonstrate regex as a way to check data against expected patterns. Next, you can see the entire program before we start to pull it apart:

```
use std::io::prelude::*;
use std::net::TcpStream;
use std::env;
use std::io;
use regex::Regex;
```

```rust
    fn validate_input(input: &String) -> bool {
        let mut valid: bool = false;
        let mut params = input.split_whitespace();
        let command = params.next().unwrap();
        match command {
            "flist" =>  valid = true,
            "md" => valid = true,
            _ => valid = false
        }
        valid
    }

    fn handle_input(mut serverstream: TcpStream) {
        let mut recvstring = [0; 4096];

        let mut keepgoing: bool = true;
        let re = Regex::new(r"^[eE][xX][iI][tT]$").unwrap();

        let mut size = serverstream.read(&mut recvstring);
        println!("{}", String::from_utf8_lossy(&recvstring));

        while keepgoing {
            let mut input = String::new();
            match io::stdin().read_line(&mut input) {
                Ok(_n) => {
                    input = input.trim().to_string();
                    if re.is_match(input.as_str()) {
                        keepgoing = false;
                    }
                    else {
                        if validate_input(&input) {
                            match serverstream.write(&input.as_bytes()) {
                                Ok(_n) => { () },
                                Err(_e) => {
                                    panic!("Unable to write to server");
                                }
                            }
                        }
                        else {
                            println!("Not a valid command");
                        }
                        size = serverstream.read(&mut recvstring);
                        println!("{}", String::from_utf8_lossy(&recvstring));
                    }
                }
                Err(error) => println!("error: {}", error),
            }
        }
    }

fn main() {
    let args: Vec<String> = env::args().collect();
    let serverstring = &args[1];

    match TcpStream::connect(serverstring) {
```

continues

(continued)

```
        Ok(mut serverstream) => {
            println!("Successfully connected to {}", serverstring);
            handle_input(serverstream);
        },
        Err(e) => {
            panic!("Unable to connect to {}", serverstring);
        }
    }


}
```

Creating the Connection

We're going to start at the bottom of the program listing since that's the entry point of the program. For me, putting the main() function at the bottom of the program listing is a matter of habit, having worked for too many years in languages (including C) where the functions needed to be defined before they could be used. As a result, you top load all the non-main functions and stick the main function at the bottom. That way, everything has been declared before it's called.

We are going to pull the connection string off the command line in the form of *hostname:port*. As a result, we need to pull the arguments from the command line into a vector of strings. This is going to be stored in the identifier args. The only thing we need is the parameter that includes the host and port. This is the second parameter on the command line since the first is always the program that was executed. We get that using the reference args[1] and store the value in the identifier serverstring.

When we make the connection, we use TcpStream::connect(), passing in the string value we took off the command line. As this is going to be a Result we get back, we need to perform a match on it or some similar mechanism (you could use an if statement if you preferred, for instance) in order to determine what we get. If it's an Ok(), we need to take the wrapped value, which will be a TcpStream struct, and place it into the identifier serverstream, which will be the data structure we use to communicate with the server. This struct needs to be mutable because the data inside the structure will be changing. Remember that we enclose the identifier in the Ok() check inside the match block. That's where the identifier gets named (think of it as being declared), so it's where we need to declare it as being mutable. With a successful connection, we call handle_input() and pass that function the serverstream struct since that's the function where we are going to manage the connection.

As we've done before, we need to handle error conditions. If we get an error from the connection, we need to exit the program. This error could come from a number of conditions, including a poorly formed connection string or a server that isn't listening on the specified port. In either of those cases, we can't easily recover gracefully. Rather than calling println!(), which may end up falling through to some other code that expects a working connection, we call panic!() since it will print out the error message we specify but also exit the program without trying to execute any other code.

Validating Input

Let's hop back up to the top of the program listing again. We're going to take a look at a short function used to validate input from the user. This is going to look much like the function used to validate input on the server side. The difference here is that we aren't doing anything with the input. That means we are going to just determine whether it's valid or not. This is a binary result—yes or no. As a result, we will need a return value that is going to be yes or no—or, for our purposes, true or false, which will be the same thing in this context. You can see the `validate_input()` function next. We pass in a `String` value, which is the command string provided by the user:

```
fn validate_input(input: &String) -> bool {
    let mut valid: bool = false;
    let mut params = input.split_whitespace();
    let command = params.next().unwrap();
    match command {
        "flist" =>  valid = true,
        "md" => valid = true,
        _ => valid = false
    }
    valid
}
```

The first thing we do is to create the identifier that contains the Boolean value we need to keep track of. We're going to be safe and initialize this to `false`. The only way to get `true` back from this function should be if we do specifically find a command that we're looking for. Any other case should result in a `false`, making this the default case. There is a problem we have with our input, though. We are going to get a complete command string, which may include parameters necessary for the command to function. We need to extract the command portion out. We do that with these two lines:

```
    let mut params = input.split_whitespace();
    let command = params.next().unwrap();
```

The first thing we need to do is get a vector of strings split on whitespace. This should be any number of spaces between the words in the command string. The vector will contain individual strings, but we only need the first one. As a result, we are going to just pull the next entry in the vector. In the identifier `command`, we store the first word, which should be the command portion of the command string. Once we have the command, we can pass it through the `match` statement. If we have a match between the command and the commands we are accepting, we will set the `valid` identifier to be `true`.

One principle to remember is that of memory safety. In cases where values are passed by reference into a function, the memory location the reference points to can be altered. We don't want this to happen, because we are still going to need the unaltered string from the user to send intact to the server. Fortunately, we have borrowed the value, meaning we have sent the value into the function rather than the location of the identifier. In the calling function, the identifier remains intact. To return to the calling function, we just hand back the value stored in the identifier `valid`.

Regular Expressions

We interrupt the analysis of this program to dig into a big concept that we'll be implementing in the last function we will take a look at. Rather than a large sidebar or diversion in the middle of talking about the program, we're going to take a break from the program here between functions to talk about regular expressions, commonly abbreviated *regex*. Regular expressions as an idea originated in 1951 with a mathematician named Stephen Kleene, who was talking about regular languages that are expressed using a mathematical notation called *regular events*. Since then, some languages have implemented these regular expressions, and it is a foundational idea beneath the way different shells and utilities in Unix-like operating systems work. A regular expression, for our purposes, without going down the mathematical route, is a way of expressing a pattern of characters in order to locate text within a document or data stream. It's also a good way of identifying patterns within text. If you were looking to determine whether someone had provided a phone number or IP address, for instance, you could do that with regex. One way of searching for an IP address is with the regular expression pattern

```
/\d{1,3}\.\d{1,3}\.\d{1,3}\.\d{1,3}/
```

This is not a perfect example since it captures a number of patterns that are not valid IPv4 addresses. However, it does provide an example that we can discuss. The entire regular expression is captured within the forward slashes (/.../) because those may be used in some places where you'd use regex. The first pattern we are looking for is a digit, expressed with a backslash *d* (\d). We need between one and three digits to be considered a regular expression. This rules out anything bigger than a four-digit number but also rules out the case where no digits are found. After we have the first octet, we need a dot (.). This is expressed using another backslash because the dot is a special character in regex, being a wildcard for any single character. If we want the literal dot or period, we have to escape it, which is what the backslash does—it tells the interpreter that we really mean to use what comes after the backslash as it is rather than it standing in for something else. Four of these dotted decimal values, and we have an approximation of an IP address.

Another way of doing this would be to insist on every place in the IP address having a value, even if that value was a 0. Then we could do the following: [0-2][0-9][0-9]\. [0-2][0-9][0-9]\. [0-2][0-9][0-9]\. [0-2][0-9][0-9]. What this says is that for each decimal value, we have three digits. The first digit has to have a value between 0 and 2. The value of the first digit in an IP address will never be higher than 2 since each portion of the address can have a maximum value of 255. After we have a three-digit number, taking into consideration that the first two values may be 0s, we need a dot, so we have to use the backslash to escape the dot. This regular expression could also be used to identify an IPv4 address, assuming all the positions were filled with values (i.e. 004.002.002.001 for 4.2.2.1).

This brings up an issue, actually. There are different forms of regular expressions, depending on the platform you are using. For instance, the first example where we used \d to indicate a digit is valid only if you are using Perl Compatible Regular Expressions (PCRE) or if you are using the editor vim. Similarly, using PCRE, you could use \w to indicate any alphanumeric character. If you wanted to indicate multiple alphanumeric characters, you would use \w+. Using \W would indicate any non-alphanumeric character (non-word character). This might include space characters, for instance.

If you wanted to look for alphanumeric characters, you would use a pattern like [a-zA-Z0-9]. The brackets indicate that any value inside would match that position. It doesn't mean you have to have exactly that pattern. If you wanted to look for multiple alphanumeric characters using this notation, you would use [a-zA-Z0-9]* because the * is a wildcard. This pattern says, "Match the preceding character 0 or more times." If I were to look for the string /wub*le/, for instance, the pattern provided would match the following words: *wule, wuble, wubble, wubbble,* and so forth.

In the old days, there was one form of regex because other people hadn't come along and made the syntax easier to use and more expressive at the same time. There was one form of regex, and that was what you used. Today, a regex pattern may work on one platform without working on another. Basic regex does not support the ? character, for instance, although extended regex does. Not all utilities or programming languages support extended regex, so it's worth keeping in mind some of the differences. An example of the ? wildcard would be /[bh]?ear/. Again, the forward slashes are used strictly as delimiters indicating the start and end of the expression. What this expression says is, "Look for any word that has either a *b* or an *h* followed by *ear*." However, the word may not even include the *b* or the *h*. This means the expression would successfully match *ear*, *bear*, and *hear*.

This is where wildcards can get tricky. Another way wildcards can get tricky, in particular, is the * character. This is because the * character is greedy. If you were to use [a-zA-Z0-9]*, for instance, it would match as many alphanumeric characters as it could get its hands on. This may not be what you want. For instance, if you were looking for alphanumeric characters that include the four letters *wrox*, the regex /[a-z]*wrox[a-z]*/ wouldn't do you a lot of good because the [a-z]* would consume the *wrox* in any pattern that might include strictly lowercase letters. Always keep in mind the wildcard you are using and what the pattern might look like using easier delimiters.

Another special character, called a *metacharacter*, is the | character, which is used for options. If you were looking for different names where any one of several would be acceptable, you could use something like /[Ric|Franny|Mandy]/ to find places where the names Ric, Franny, or Mandy were found. Think of it as an *or* character, which is the same usage as in languages that have inherited some design characteristics from C.

You can start to see all the uses for regex, especially in your programming. It's a better way to do complex matches, especially in instances where you don't know whether someone is going to use the same case you expect (they may use uppercase where your program is looking for lowercase, for instance). You can use a regex pattern that will match no matter what the case of the input is. Regex becomes a valuable tool when you are doing any sort of data validation because you can use it to match expected input as well as patterns for data. As noted, we can look for IP addresses, and by extension, we can use it for hostnames. We could use it for validating a complete phone number as well. Any data where there is a well-defined pattern can be validated using regex. Fortunately, Rust has a crate for regex, which means we can take advantage of it for pattern matching.

This is just a brief overview of regex, of course. It is deceptively simple because there are just a handful of characters you need to pay attention to. However, it's the kind of topic that entire books are written about because of how dense and detailed you can get using regex. Unless you are using them on a regular basis, regex can be difficult to decipher. Once you start using it on a regular basis, it becomes easier to read.

The Final Function

We are into the final function of our client program. The reason for stopping to talk about regex is that we are using regex to do some pattern matching for us. There is a lot going on in this function because we take in input; then make sure the input is one of our acceptable commands, using the function we looked at earlier; and then send the command to the server, receive the response, and provide the response to the user. You can see the entire function here before we start pulling it apart to explain the different pieces:

```
fn handle_input(mut serverstream: TcpStream) {
    let mut recvstring = [0; 4096];

    let mut keepgoing: bool = true;
    let re = Regex::new(r"^[eE][xX][iI][tT]$").unwrap();

    let mut size = serverstream.read(&mut recvstring);
    println!("{}", String::from_utf8_lossy(&recvstring));

    while keepgoing {
        let mut input = String::new();
        match io::stdin().read_line(&mut input) {
            Ok(_n) => {
                input = input.trim().to_string();
                if re.is_match(input.as_str()) {
                    keepgoing = false;
                }
                else {
                    if validate_input(&input) {
                        match serverstream.write(&input.as_bytes()) {
                            Ok(_n) => {
                                size = serverstream.read(&mut recvstring);
                                println!("{}", String::from_utf8_lossy(&recvstring));
                            },
                            Err(_e) => {
                                panic!("Unable to write to server");
                            }
                        }
                    }
                    else {
                        println!("Not a valid command");
                    }
                }
            },
            Err(error) => println!("error: {}", error),
        }
    }
}
```

First, there are some identifiers we need to establish. We need a byte array to take data back from the server we are communicating with. We also need a Boolean value to determine whether we should keep looping to ask the user for the command they want to execute. Finally, we need to establish a regex structure that contains the pattern we are going to match on. The pattern we will be looking for is "^[eE][xX][iI][tT]$", which will indicate to us whether the user wants to exit the program. This takes into consideration all different possibilities for cases of letters. We could write it as *eXiT*, for instance, and this pattern would match. The two characters we didn't talk about earlier are ^ and $. They indicate the start and end of the line, respectively. That means we wouldn't be able to type *Brexiting* and have it match because the *exit* is not at the beginning nor the end of the line.

The first thing we want to do in the following two lines is to accept data from the server. You may remember that the first thing we did on the server side was to essentially provide a prompt to the user. These two lines accept the prompt from the server side and then print it out to the user:

```
let mut size = serverstream.read(&mut recvstring);
println!("{}", String::from_utf8_lossy(&recvstring));
```

Once we print the prompt from the server, we are ready to start the loop where we accept data from the user. Since we want to run this loop at least once, we can use a `while` loop using the Boolean value `keepgoing` that was set to `true` initially to ensure the loop would execute at least once. Inside the loop, we create an identifier to accept the command from the user as a `String`. We do this inside the loop because we want a clean copy each time, and the scope of this identifier only needs to be inside the loop. There is no reason to have it available outside the loop. Each time we pass through the loop, we create a new `String` value to accept the command string from the user.

Once we have the `String` identifier created to put our user's input into, we can get the input using `io::stdin()::read_line()`, which takes a mutable `String` value as a parameter. This is where the user's input is placed; but on the other end, we still have a `Result` to contend with because the trait may generate an error. Otherwise, it will return an `Ok()` that contains the number of characters in the input string. You will note the _ prefix on the identifier in the `Ok()` match. This indicates that we have an identifier we are going to capture but not use. It's a convention in the language, and the compiler will remind you that if you create an identifier and then don't use it, you should use the _ prefix for the identifier. Assuming we have good input and not an error, we can use the following code to perform two essential tasks:

```
input = input.trim().to_string();
if re.is_match(input.as_str()) {
    keepgoing = false;
}
```

The first task is to strip all whitespace off the end of the string. We are going to call the `trim()` trait on our `input` string. This removes all whitespace from the end of the string value. We need to do this because the newline character was accepted and is stored in the string along with everything else. When we get around to doing the match to determine whether it's good input, any extra characters will cause the match to fail. Next, we need to determine whether the user entered some variation on *exit* using the regex structure we had created the `re` identifier for earlier. We call the `is_match()` trait on the struct, passing in the input identifier. Just as in the previous line, we have to do some conversions to make everything the data type expected. If the user has entered some version of *exit*, we set the Boolean value to `false`. This ensures we won't continue asking the user for input.

If the user has entered something other than a variation on *exit*, we continue going. The following code is how we determine whether the user has provided a valid command string. Remember that we are using a Boolean value to determine whether the input is valid or not. If it is valid, we are going to send the entire command string, including the command and any necessary parameters, to the server.

This is done using the `serverstream` identifier, which contains the data structure for our server connection. We use the trait `write()`, making sure to pass our `String` value as bytes rather than as a `String`:

```
if validate_input(&input) {
    match serverstream.write(&input.as_bytes()) {
        Ok(_n) => {
            size = serverstream.read(&mut recvstring);
            println!("{}", String::from_utf8_lossy(&recvstring));
        },
        Err(_e) => {
            panic!("Unable to write to server");
        }
    }
}
```

As with so much else of Rust, we get a `Result` back, which we need to handle. If we get an `Ok()`, again getting back the number of bytes that were successfully sent, we need to read the result from the server side. This is done using the same `read` trait we used earlier when we were getting the prompt from the server side. Once we have the data back from the server, we need to do some conversion of the data again because we've received bytes from the server side, and `println!()` doesn't know what to do with raw bytes. We need to convert to a `String` value using the `from_utf8_lossy()` trait. This takes UTF8-encoded bytes and converts them to a Rust `String` data structure that `println!()` knows how to format for output.

In the case of an `Err()`, however, we need to do something. If we can't write to the server, we're going to assume something catastrophic happened. We will use the `panic!()` call to print an error and exit the program. If we can't write to the server, there is probably something wrong with the connection, meaning there isn't much reason to go ask the user for something else to do if we couldn't even do the first thing.

If we didn't happen to get a valid command, we need to deal with that. Since we're done with what happens if we do have a valid command, we need to look at what happens if the earlier `if validate_input()` clause wasn't true. In this case, we just print that it's not a valid command, and we'll fall through the loop to start over, where we try again by accepting the user input and making another attempt to validate a command.

Just to clean all the way up, once we have dealt with the other end of the earlier `match` clause, we can move on to the rest of the function. If an `Ok()` is returned from the user input, we run through the process of validating it, getting it to the server, getting results, and dealing with any errors. We still have the case where we got an error from reading user input. Presumably something weird happened since we're just asking for the user to type something in at the console or command prompt. However, in a `match` statement, you have to handle all possibilities, and `Err()` is a possibility from a `Result`, so we need to handle the error case. We're just going to take the error and print it out so the user can see that something happened.

At this point, you have a working client that can communicate with the server from the last chapter. There is still a lot of additional work to do, including potentially adding encryption as well as a lot of additional commands, but you have the framework of a client/server application in place.

SUMMARY

Encryption has become such an important programming concept because so much of what we send over the open Internet today is encrypted. This means programmers have to be able to handle encrypted communication on both the client and server sides. It doesn't mean you have to have a deep understanding of encryption and all the algorithms that are used, but having a conversational understanding of important ideas is useful to be effective. First, you need to know that encryption is the process of transmuting data so it can't be read by someone who doesn't have the key, which is necessary to unlock the encrypted data. The key is the most important aspect of any encryption scheme. If you aren't protecting the key, there isn't a lot of use doing the encryption to begin with.

There are a couple of types of encryption algorithms—symmetric and asymmetric. The first uses the same key for encryption and decryption. The second uses a pair of related keys: one for encryption, one for decryption. The encryption key is the one that should be given out to everyone, and it's called the public key. Without the public key, no one can encrypt messages to you in an asymmetric encryption scheme. Any data encrypted with the public key can only be decrypted using the private key, which only you should have and have access to use. Keys are commonly protected with a passphrase, so even if they do happen to get out into the wild, they shouldn't be usable.

Since the key is the most important aspect of encryption, we have a problem making sure both parties have a key. This is especially true if you are using symmetric encryption where both parties have to have the same key. One way to protect the key is for both parties to use Diffie-Hellman key exchange, which is a process where both parties mutually derive the same key without ever letting anyone listening in on the process also be able to derive the key.

In many cases, hybrid cryptosystems are used where asymmetric encryption may be used to initiate the connection and pass the keys while symmetric encryption is used for the actual session data. This is because symmetric encryption is commonly faster. Transport Layer Security (TLS) is a hybrid cryptosystem, meaning it is a set of protocols that support multiple encryption algorithms and key exchange mechanisms. It is capable of using asymmetric or symmetric encryption, depending on what the two parties agree to. TLS is all about making it possible for two endpoints to agree on how they are going to encrypt messages to one another.

Regular expressions are a very common way of implementing patterns that can be used to search for data. Once you have this way of searching in place, you can use the same techniques for data validation since you are looking for patterns in chunks of data. Regex is perhaps most commonly used on Unix-like systems, but there are languages, including Rust, that support the use of regular expressions. This requires understanding how to create a pattern and then feeding it to a regular expression structure. This structure includes traits that can be used to match strings against the pattern, providing a yes/no answer as to whether the match was successful.

When it comes to our client program, we need to use a `TcpStream` structure to take care of the connection for us. This structure includes read and write traits for communicating with the server side once the connection is up. If we wanted to implement TLS on top of a TCP connection, we would use `TlsConnector` or `TlsAcceptor` structures, depending on whether we wanted to write a client or a server. These structures wrap the TCP connection, letting the `TcpStream` handle the lower-level communication while the TLS wrappers take care of the encryption and decryption.

EXERCISES

1. Add a help function so if the user enters `-h` instead of a `hostname:port` connection string, you print out help text indicating how the program is to be used.

2. Change the program so you construct the connection string (`format!` would be helpful for this) once you have validated the two parameters—say, IP address and port number. You could use regex for this validation.

3. Add a function that takes care of interacting with the user to accept input. Change the `handle_input()` function so it doesn't get input from the user but instead calls the new function.

4. Implement another command on the client side that matches one you have implemented on the server side.

5. Add encryption capabilities to both the server and the client.

ADDITIONAL RESOURCES

Transport Layer Security - `developer.mozilla.org/en-US/docs/Web/Security/Transport_Layer_Security`

Networking 101, Transport Layer Security - `hpbn.co/transport-layer-security-tls/`

What is TLS and How Does it Work? - `www.internetsociety.org/deploy360/tls/basics/`

Crate regex - `docs.rs/regex/1.4.2/regex/`

Regular Expressions - `developer.mozilla.org/en-US/docs/Web/JavaScript/Guide/Regular_Expressions`

What is Regular Expression - `www.regexbuddy.com/regex.html`

Using TLS with Rust Authentication - `ayende.com/blog/185764-A/using-tls-with-rust-authentication`

8

Going Relational

IN THIS CHAPTER, YOU WILL LEARN THE FOLLOWING:

➤ About different types of database platforms

➤ How to manage databases in Rust

➤ How to use multiple source files

➤ About application architectures

Doing basic input/output (I/O) operations is nice, but at some point, you want what you are doing to be persistent. Once you start to persist information you are working with, it's helpful for it to be found again. Chances are you may not be working with a single data set over and over. Modern applications are more likely to deal with complex data structures, and once you start talking about complex data structures, you need a structured way to store and retrieve them. Ideally, you'd also be able to search through all the data you have in an efficient manner, rather than reading every single record you have to determine whether it's the right record. Think of flipping through every page in a cookbook in order to find the one recipe you are desperate for. You're hungry, after all, and the longer it takes to find the recipe, the worse off you're going to be when you get around to eating.

You may get lucky, and it may be one of the first dozen recipes. Imagine, though, that you are looking through *The Joy of Cooking*, with thousands of recipes. It seems like it would be far easier to find what you were looking for if there were a way to categorize or index the recipes. Fortunately, a book like that would have an index, making recipes easier to find. There may also be a categorization scheme that would help you get to what you were looking for faster. This is what a database does for us. A database allows us to store data in a structured way as well as providing us the ability to quickly retrieve data records without having to serially read through all the records to find what we're looking for.

Once we start talking about persistent data storage, we should also think about structuring our applications differently. This requires thinking about application architectures. So far, we've been dealing with small applications, but as we start talking about managing data, the applications are going to get bigger—and even if they remain small, you want to think about how you are going to allow the different components of your programs to communicate with one another. An application architecture will help you with that by providing some structure to the application.

Along with the smaller, simpler programs has been the way we have organized all our functions. None of the programs we have written so far have been especially large, so it's easy enough to keep all the code in a single file. It makes it easier to find what you are looking for. At some point, though, having too many functions makes it harder to maintain the program. You're always scrolling up and down through your source to compare one thing against another. It would be easier to split functions out into different files. This may be especially true when it comes to developing our own struct types along with associated traits. Having those separate can be more helpful. With a modern editor, having multiple tabs open makes it easier to refer to different functions and data without having to scroll up and down.

In this chapter, we're going to talk about using databases; specifically, we'll be going through the use of a traditional relational database using two different database systems. We're also going to split out our source code into multiple files and look at how Rust handles referring to different files in the same project, since, unlike C, we don't use #include to indicate that there is another file that should be considered a part of the one the pre-processor or compiler is working on. Instead, there's a simpler way with Rust. Finally, we're going to take a look at a couple of different application architecture types that may help you consider how you are constructing your application. Once you have a design or architecture in mind, it helps determine where you should be putting different elements.

APPLICATION ARCHITECTURES

Application architectures are useful in part because they can create nice boundaries around where functionality goes. This is how you get modularity, which allows you to swap out components more easily if you decide you want to make changes later on. If you are, for example, interacting with the screen and the keyboard all over the place through your application, you can't switch to a different paradigm for I/O. As always, the ability to reuse code saves you work with your programming and, hopefully, a lot of bugs since you aren't starting from scratch all the time but instead are using code that has already been developed and tested, at least to some degree.

We're going to talk about three different application architectures to give you an idea of how to think about application development from multiple perspectives. First is a classic approach to large-scale application design, commonly called *n-tier*. This is especially relevant when we talk about working with databases, since it's a common approach to web application architecture. However, not all modern web applications use n-tier. Some have moved or are moving to a service-oriented architecture, often called *microservices* today. We'll talk about microservices and how they relate to application design. Finally, though not least, we will talk about Model-View-Controller (MVC), which is a design philosophy especially used in applications written for Apple platforms like iOS and iPadOS.

n-Tier Applications

While you can use n-tier design in any application, it may be easiest to think of when talking about a web application. Think about an e-commerce site, for example, that has an interface you communicate with, where you search for products, get information about them, and then, ultimately, purchase them. For an application like this, you need someplace to store the information about the products, like a database. You also need some element that is going to handle all the business logic, meaning all the programmatic elements. Finally, you need something that is going to communicate with the user. This would be a three-tier design. If you add in the browser where you are going to view the site, you can think of it as a four-tier design. Figure 8.1 shows an example of a traditional web application design.

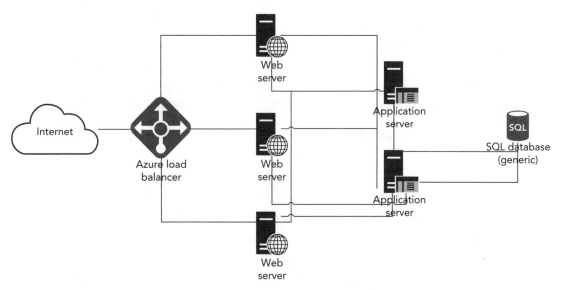

FIGURE 8.1: Traditional web application design

You see an additional layer in this figure since larger sites may need the ability to scale across a number of servers. Let's start with the left-hand side of the diagram. Across the vast, uncharted Internet somewhere is someone sitting at their computer trying to visit your website. This is the presentation layer, where the pages are rendered for viewing and interacting with. When this person, let's say her name is Suzanne, clicks on a link leading her to your site, she first hits a load balancer. The load balancer is used to spread requests across a number of servers that are behind the load balancer. Processing requests at layer 4 (TCP) of the Open Systems Interconnect (OSI) model is cheap as far as requests go. We can allow a single system (or perhaps a pair of systems that look like one system) to handle those requests, shunting them off to a set of servers that sit behind the load balancer.

When Suzanne's browser sends its request, it will be in Hypertext Transfer Protocol (HTTP), so we need an element that will be able to handle those HTTP requests. HTTP is handled, commonly, by a web server. Application software like Apache HTTP Server (httpd), Nginx, or Microsoft's Internet

Information Server (IIS) would be commonly used at this tier of our application design. The web server is just going to handle the HTTP request to determine what is being requested. If the request is for a static page of Hypertext Markup Language (HTML) with no parameters to process programmatically, the web server may just find the requested page on its filesystem, sending the response back with the contents of the file. Suzanne's browser can handle the HTML and display it. If Suzanne has sent data to the server, though, as in the case where she is searching for a product, the web server alone can't handle it. It will need to bring in another piece of software.

The application server, which handles running programs or functions, can sit alongside the web server on the same machine, as may be the case with PHP, a scripting language that may be handled with a module within the web server. The application server may also be on its own system entirely or at least within its own application space. This may be common with something like a Java application server like JBoss or Tomcat. The request is sent on from the web server to the application server. The application server itself may need to handle HTTP requests since the web server may just forward on the request to it. In addition to handling HTTP requests, the application server will take parameters from the end user—Suzanne, in this case—and perform programmatic operations with them.

One operation, as previously mentioned, is looking up product information. This would commonly require a database server. Again, this database server is a piece of software that takes requests and provides responses. It may be a request to store a piece of information, or it may be a request for information that is already stored. In our example shown in Figure 8.1, the database is a separate physical server system. It doesn't have to be, but in our case, it is.

This gives us three primary tiers to our application model, four if you count the browser. Conceptually, you can think of the following if you like to apply generic labels to things:

➤ **Presentation layer:** This is the user interface, which would be the user's browser in our case.

➤ **Application layer:** This is the service layer and would be the web server for our example.

➤ **Business logic layer:** This is where application functionality occurs, called the business logic layer because it is where the business rules are applied and implemented (all the things that make the "business" of the application work).

➤ **Data access layer:** This is the place where data is sent to persist and be retrieved.

The problem with this way of conceptualizing the different layers, at least for me, is that the application layer seems confusing. It sounds like that's where the application lives, except the application logic is in the business logic layer. Perhaps an easier way to think of it is the following three tiers. Again, this is conceptual, so we're going to be bundling a couple of physical/actual layers together for our tiers:

➤ **Presentation layer:** This is the layer that takes care of presenting everything to the user, including taking any input back from the user. For us, this would include both the user's browser as well as the web server, or at least components of the web server, since the web server is responsible for providing the information that is presented in the user's browser.

➤ **Application layer:** This is where all the business logic takes place, meaning all the programmatic elements. The application layer may be responsible for formatting data in such a way that it can be passed back to the presentation layer for correct display.

➤ **Data tier:** This is again where persistence happens. This is commonly the database server, although there are other ways to achieve persistence.

You can easily see how this applies to web servers where you have different components, even if they are just applications rather than different servers. It may be less easy to see how to apply this to native application design. One way to think about this is to always have one element/module/function handling I/O. You shouldn't have all of your functions, wherever they happen to be in your application, communicating directly to the user. Make sure all of your I/O happens in one place. This allows you to do something else for your user interface without having to make changes to every function in your application.

The same goes for your data persistence. Every function shouldn't be allowed to talk directly to your database server. The best way to handle all of these things is through the use of interfaces. If you think about it, we've already spent a lot of time talking about a way of implementing this. The struct in Rust provides us with the ability to create an interface. You build a struct, for instance, that contains a reference to your output handle, whether it's the stdin/stdout that would be used for a console interface or whether it's a file handle. Attached to that struct, you create traits that can be used in a generic fashion. It doesn't matter which the underlying I/O handle or interface is; the piece you, as the programmer, call is always going to be the same.

Microservices

Many years ago, this idea came into being as something called service-oriented architecture (SOA). SOA was a way of taking all the modularization that was possible with object-oriented design and exploding it out. Perhaps imagine the scene from *Iron Man 2* where he takes the 3D molecule of his new element and blows it out so it's really large, allowing you to see all the individual atomic particles it consists of. The same thing is essentially true here. Before, even with object-oriented design, you had all these little elements that were compacted together to create this one thing—a molecule or atom, if you will. What if you blew it up, though, and thought about it at the proton, electron, and neutron level?

This is essentially the idea behind microservices. Where before you may have had a class, in object-oriented terms, that was providing a function that you could think of as a service, now you can actually start to think of it as a service. This service will be consumed by other services. Each microservice will have its own separate interface for others to communicate through and will also have what would essentially be contracts: I, state your name, do solemnly swear that as a service, I will provide the following to anyone who asks. Then each service fills in the blanks of what they will provide to the outside world. This is codified in the interface to the service—meaning the way the service gets called.

Figure 8.2 shows an example of an application that was designed using a microservices architecture. One common reason to use a microservices design is if you are using a mobile application. Some of the application logic is contained in the mobile application, but it may reach out to a web-based instance of the application backend to do a lot of the work. The app on the mobile device knows how to reach out to an application programming interface (API) gateway in a cloud environment. You can see that in Figure 8.2, where either a browser or a mobile application might make use of the API in the cloud. All of the microservices, some of which you can see in the diagram, would be endpoints in the API.

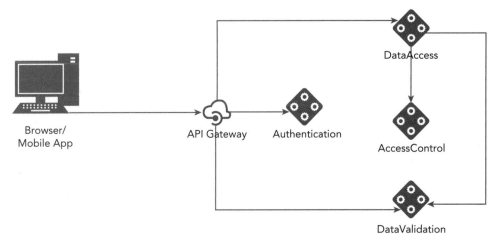

FIGURE 8.2: Microservices design

> **NOTE** Rust can be used for developing microservices applications. Microservices applications are often developed using containers, a way of virtualizing applications. There is a container in the Docker hub, a marketplace for Docker containers, for Rust development. You could create an application in this container and quickly deploy microservices (small applications).

The only thing the application knows is how to call the endpoints, similar to remote procedure calls, in the cloud-based application. All of the critical code is there, so it's under the control of the development team or the company offering the overall application. This makes updating it a lot easier. There is no need to wait for the end user to update the application on their end. The code running on the endpoint is mostly inconsequential. All updates can be done on the cloud-based instances as soon as code is ready to be deployed.

This is not to say that you have to be developing mobile or web-based applications to make use of a microservice model. If you have the ability to do interprocess communication, in whatever fashion, you can implement microservices in a native application like the ones we have been working on. You just need the ability for one component to be able to talk to another component, and there are many ways to accomplish that.

Model-View-Controller

A popular application design pattern is called Model-View-Controller (MVC). In fact, this is not incompatible with the other application design strategies we've talked about. With MVC, you just have very clear directions that messages can flow between the three primary elements of the application—the model, the view, and the controller. Figure 8.3 shows how you'd think about an MVC application and the different components. On the left, you have the model, which is where the data and its representation—as well as the code used to manipulate and access it—reside. In the view, you have the code that interfaces with the user interface. In between the two, you have the controller. It handles all of the primary business logic required to make the model connect to the view in a meaningful way.

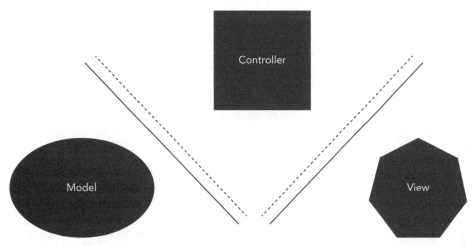

FIGURE 8.3: Model-View-Controller

What you can see in Figure 8.3 are a pair of semi-permeable membranes. They are represented by a dotted line and a solid line, similar to what you would see on a road where passing is allowed in one direction but not the other. Information is allowed to pass through the dotted line but not in the other direction. This means the model can't talk to the controller directly, nor can it talk to the view at all. Any communication that goes between the model and the view has to go through the controller. Another way to think about MVC is in Figure 8.4. This shows how information flows. The controller makes changes to the model, meaning states and data will change inside the model. Changes that are made in the model then get reflected to the view. The diagram may be misleading in this regard since it suggests the model talks to the view. The update has to go back through the controller.

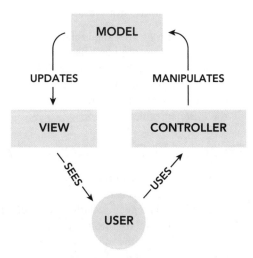

FIGURE 8.4: Model-View-Controller

This design pattern is decades old, going back to 1979 when it was introduced for Smalltalk, an early object-oriented language. As a result, it's been well-tested over the years. As noted earlier, Apple development is based on the MVC design pattern. One of the important aspects of MVC is containment and modularization, which is a good reason it's popular. Keeping some elements of your program isolated from others helps keep bugs out of your code as well as unexpected behavior when you have a component suddenly talking to another component that it's not supposed to talk to. Designing your program right up front is very beneficial for correct program behavior (meaning, nothing unexpected). This is why doing the design up front is so useful. You develop the interfaces and communication flows early and then make sure you follow them.

DATABASES

We need to store data. We can't assume the program is always going to be running, so data will always be in memory. Even were that the case, as with a server (pretend for a moment there is no downtime), at some point you may simply have too much data to store in memory. Plus, the idea that services are always going to be up and running forever (meaning never updated and never, ever a service outage) is just unrealistic. All of this is to say that we need persistent storage, meaning data is available no matter whether the application is running or not, and if you stop and start, the data will be available to the application. On top of availability, you really want to be able to look up data quickly and easily. Thus, a database server or the like is the way to go.

Not all databases are created equal, though. For many years, there was one predominant database type, and perhaps that's still true, although the situation is changing. The most common database type since the 1970s, when it was developed, is probably a relational database. Relational databases are structured around tables. A table is a way of organizing data into rows and columns. The column is the data type or specific property, while the row is the unique instance of the collection of properties. Each row in a table has a unique identifier to identify the record, meaning the entire collection of properties. The database software then builds an index based on those unique identifiers to make looking for information faster.

One reason they are called relational databases is that you can create relationships between different tables by linking the identifiers of one table with another table using something called a *foreign key*. What this says is that the two tables are linked by attributes (properties). This helps you simplify your overall database by creating these linkages rather than duplicating the data across multiple tables. Of course, this can make searching for data interesting since you need to make the connection between the different tables yourself.

Structured Query Language

Alongside the development of relational databases in the 1970s came a language used to interact with the databases. This is the Structured Query Language (SQL—both "S-Q-L" and "sequel" are considered appropriate pronunciations). It's designed to be able to extract data from a relational database as well as insert data into the database. Along the way, there are other features that you can use in the language; but for the most part, those are going to be the primary tasks you will be performing when interacting with a database, especially when it comes to writing Rust (or any other) programs. Rather than writing a complete SQL program, you will be inserting SQL statements into your Rust in order to perform the tasks mentioned.

Let's take a rapid pass over some of the essential pieces of SQL that you will need to know. This way, you'll better understand what's going on when we get to writing a Rust program that interacts with the database, since just connecting to a database isn't very interesting. You will want to know enough SQL to create statements, commonly called *queries*. We'll start by taking a look at a database. The first thing we need to do is create the database. For convenience, I'm using MySQL Workbench because I can design the database visually, and it will create the SQL statements for me. The following SQL code is used to create a table within a database, which is done using the statement `CREATE DATABASE stratapp`, where `stratapp` is the name of the database:

```
CREATE TABLE `stratapp`.`findings` (
  `findings_id` INT NOT NULL AUTO_INCREMENT,
  `title` VARCHAR(75) NOT NULL,
  `finding` VARCHAR(125) NOT NULL,
  `details` VARCHAR(4196) NOT NULL,
  `justification` VARCHAR(2048) NULL,
  `findingscol` VARCHAR(45) NULL,
  PRIMARY KEY (`findings_id`),
  UNIQUE INDEX `findings_id_UNIQUE` (`findings_id` ASC) VISIBLE);
```

What this SQL statement says (and it's a single statement, spread over multiple lines to make it easier to read) is that we are going to create a table in the `stratapp` database called `findings`. This is the `stratapp`.`findings` part: it says `stratapp` is the database, and `findings` is the table. This is about making sure we are creating the table in the right database. Inside the parentheses are all of the column, or attribute, definitions. The first attribute is `findings_id`, which is going to be the unique identifier. It will be an integer and isn't allowed to be null, meaning it can't be blank. It's also set to auto-increment, which means the database itself will take care of creating a new identification number for us. The rest of the columns are strings, which are identified as variable character arrays (`VARCHAR`) with the length specified in parentheses. Finally, we need to tell the database server what we are going to index on—which column is definitely the unique one that can be used to clearly identify a row. The last two lines tell the database server which column is the primary key for the index and also that the key is unique.

One problem with SQL is that different databases may support slightly different syntax for queries. This is perhaps especially true when it comes to performing administrative tasks like creating users and assigning permissions. Just because a database is relational and accepts SQL to perform queries doesn't mean every database is going to work the same as every other database.

Now that we have a table, we can start by putting some data into it. This is going to use the `INSERT` keyword. With `INSERT`, you have to tell the database what you are inserting. This means you aren't going to just give it a set of values. You need to assign the values to the attributes. The SQL statement that follows is used to insert a row into our table. You'll see the parts that are parameters, the column/attribute names, and the values are in parentheses. What the query says is that we are going to insert into the `findings` table the set of attributes in the first set of parentheses with values associated with each attribute in the second set of parentheses. In the case of the `VARCHAR` attributes, they are quoted so the database trying to interpret this query will understand it's a string/`VARCHAR` value—everything inside the quotes gets put into an attribute:

```
INSERT INTO findings (findings_id, title, finding, details, justification) VALUES (1, \
  "This is my title", "This is the finding", "Here are a bunch of details", "This is the \
  justification for why");
```

At the end of the line is a semicolon (;). This is a command delimiter and tells the SQL database the command is complete. The fact that there is a command delimiter suggests that you could put multiple statements on a single line. The other symbol to note is the backslash (\). This indicates that the SQL interpreter should ignore the next character, which is a carriage return/line feed (sometimes known as a newline). Using this, we can continue a query on a separate line for easier reading. This was done because to insert this line, I was using the `mysql` text-based interface rather than a graphical interface.

When we created the table, we indicated that the identification column should be non-null but also should be auto-increment, meaning the database server could take care of assigning a value to the identification if it wasn't provided as part of the insert. This means we can leave off that attribute, and the insert will still work just fine. You can see next an example of another insert without the `findings_id` attribute provided. This query works just fine:

```
INSERT INTO findings (title, findings, details, justification) \
VALUES ("This is a fresh title", "We have another set of findings here to \
discuss", "Here are some additional details that should be helpful", \
"And one more justification, in case just being told isn't enough");
```

Once we have some data in our table, we can issue another query to retrieve it. This one is going to be a SELECT query, meaning we are going to tell the database to select rows that match a set of criteria. The simplest query is to select all rows. In order to do this, we don't specify any criteria. We can also indicate which attributes we want to provide in the output. If we want everything, we just use a wildcard character (*). The following shows a query that provides all the columns back and has no criteria to match against, so all the rows in the table will be returned. In this case, because these are long string values, \G has been appended to the query, telling the program being used to interface with the database server that the output should be stacked vertically rather than horizontally in a table:

```
select * from findings \G;
*************************** 1. row ***************************
   findings_id: 1
         title: This is my title
       finding: This is the finding
       details: Here are a bunch of details
 justification: This is the justification for why
*************************** 2. row ***************************
   findings_id: 2
         title: This is a fresh title
       finding: We have another set of findings here to
discuss
       details: Here are some additional details that should be helpful
 justification: And one more justification, in case just being told isn't enough
2 rows in set (0.00 sec)
```

Normally, the output would be in a table with actual columns and rows, but in some cases, the rows wrap in an unwieldy fashion, making the output a lot harder to read unless you've really dragged open the terminal window you are using. Even if you are using a graphical interface, as can be seen in Figure 8.5, you can run into issues with the width of the columns. You'll see that in the second row, for instance, the value in some of the columns is truncated. That doesn't mean the value is lost. It just means the interface being used has a fixed width for the column, and the output is wider than that. You can fix it by dragging out the width of that column so it's wider.

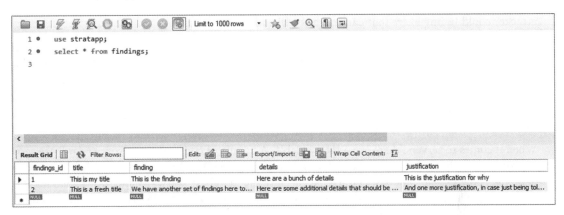

FIGURE 8.5: MySQL Workbench with the query

If we wanted to be more specific in the query, we could output only a couple of columns, for instance, or only rows where one of the columns had a value that we were looking for. An example of one of these queries is next, along with the output. We only want the findings_id and title columns as output from the query. Additionally, we only want rows where the title attribute contains the word *fresh*. This means we are going to use the keyword LIKE in the query and then provide a pattern for the server to look for. We are going to use a different wildcard character with this query. This character is going to be a % rather than a *:

```
SELECT findings_id,title FROM findings WHERE title LIKE "%fresh%";
+-------------+----------------------+
| findings_id | title                |
+-------------+----------------------+
|           2 | This is a fresh title |
+-------------+----------------------+
1 row in set (0.00 sec)
```

You'll notice the SQL keywords in all of the examples have been entered in capital letters. This is not essential, but for our purposes, it's easier to identify what is SQL and what is something from the database or table. You can feel free to capitalize the query string in any way you want when you are writing your own. The WHERE clause in SQL is very powerful, and it's where you will make essential selections rather than just getting every row in the table. Sometimes you want everything, but it's going to be more likely that you want a specific row or set of rows, so getting used to all of the different ways of writing a WHERE clause may be useful for you.

Server or Embedded

We've been communicating with a database server so far. This can sometimes be more than you may want to deal with since it requires the installation and management of not only a server application but also a system to put the server application on. Managing a database server is non-trivial. Once you start requiring a server, you also require a means to talk to the server. This can be done over the network if your application is going to be running on a different system. However, there are some problems with doing that. For instance, you now have a port open that others can get access to. That might mean your data could be accessed, especially if you don't have strong authentication for access to the database server. It could also mean the exploitation of an existing vulnerability where the attacker could be anywhere that can reach the IP address and port.

Another way of addressing the issues associated with a server is to use an embedded database. This means the application contains all of the code necessary to manage a file in a way that provides the same functionality as the database server. You can still use SQL to issue queries to the database. You can also search quickly and easily because the embedded database is maintaining indexes to the data. The application needs to have library functionality built into it that can handle all the needed functions for a database.

When it comes to servers, there are a lot available. A couple of common open source database servers are MySQL (including its fork called MariaDB) and PostgreSQL. On the commercial side, a common database is the Oracle Database. Oracle has been selling database software since 1979, making it one of the first commercial relational database management systems (RDBMS). Another common database on the commercial side is Microsoft's SQL Server.

> **NOTE** *MySQL was a long-time open source project offering free access to database management software. It was initially developed in 1995. In 2008, Sun Microsystems acquired MySQL AB, the company that was primarily responsible for developing MySQL. This company also had paid support for the database software. In 2010, Oracle acquired Sun Microsystems, meaning it owned its own commercial database server as well as the open source server MySQL. MariaDB was forked from MySQL because of concerns of the ownership of the open source software by Oracle. The original developers of MySQL are the current maintainers of MariaDB.*

On the embedded side, there are probably several that could be used, but the primary embedded relational database that supports SQL for interaction is SQLite. This is a software library that was developed in 2000 by General Dynamics under contract to the United States Navy. Currently, you may be using SQLite without even being aware of it. This is an underlying database used by Apple for many of its products. It's also the embedded database used by the Chrome browser to store a lot of information, including your browsing history.

Accessing Databases

Using Rust, it's easy to connect to databases. We can either connect to a server or use an embedded database. We can take a look at how to do both of these here. We're going to continue to use the MariaDB/MySQL server to connect to, although there is also a crate available for PostgreSQL if you prefer to use that for your database server. There are other crates for the commercial servers if you want to use those, but once you have the hang of how the connections work and the mechanics of creating the connection and sending queries to the server, you should be in good shape to swap out the different crates to connect to the different servers. First, we can create a connection to a MariaDB/MySQL server. To do that, we are going to use the `mysql` crate. As always, we need to make sure that's included in the requirements in the `Cargo.toml` file. A simple program to make a connection to a remote MySQL server is shown here:

```
use mysql::*;

fn main() {

    let connstr = "mysql://root:Passw0rd!@192.168.4.25:3306/stratapp";
    let sqlpool = Pool::new(connstr).unwrap();

    let connection = sqlpool.get_conn().unwrap();

    println!("{}", connection.connection_id());

}
```

The first thing we do is to create a connection string, formed as a universal resource locator (URL), which you'd use when connecting to a web server. Our string includes the username and password needed to connect to the server, followed by the server IP address and port. Finally, we need to indicate the database we want to use. A database server will contain multiple databases, even if the database is the only one you have created and it's your database server. There are system databases used to manage the server in addition to your single database. The `/stratapp` part of the URL tells the database server which database we want to make use of.

The `mysql` crate in Rust uses a pool of connections to the server, allowing for better parallel processing. This means we need to create a new `Pool` from the connection string. The `Pool::new()` trait is going to initiate the connection to the server, returning a `PooledConn` struct. From the resulting pool, we need to get a connection so we can interact with the server. This is done using the `get_conn()` trait on the `sqlpool` identifier, which gets a connection from the pool. This will return a `Conn` structure that we can call other methods like `connection_id()` on.

Once we have a connection identifier, we can print out the value since it will just be a numeric value. This indicates that we have created a successful connection to the server.

WRITING A DATABASE PROGRAM

We'll be extending what we've talked about with regard to accessing databases by using an embedded database to store information rather than a database server. This is going to be a little different from what we've done so far, since the embedded database is just going to use a file to store the information in. This does, however, require some additional software. We need some libraries from the sqlite3 project to make this work, in addition to telling Rust we will be using the Rust `sqlite` crate. As usual, we tell the Rust compiler we have a dependency in the `Cargo.toml` file. The crate name is `sqlite`, and you should be able to take the latest version, meaning you can use "`*`" for the version number.

BUILDING WITH SQLITE

SQLite requires some additional work, since we are pulling in functionality from a third-party source. This means we need libraries to build and run the program. The first thing you need to have is the `sqlite3.lib` file so you can build the program. The Windows version will be included in the root of the `ch8_dbapp` directory structure. To build your Rust program on Windows, you will need to put it into `target\debug\deps`. If you want to switch your build target to release, it will need to go into `target\release\deps`.

If you want to build the library yourself, you will need a copy of the source code and the precompiled library available from `https://www.sqlite.org/download.html`. Put the `sqlite3.def` and the `sqlite3.dll` files from the precompiled zip file into the decompressed source code directory. You will need to have Visual Studio installed in order to create the library. If you open a Developer Command Prompt, you will be able to run the following command and create your own `sqlite3.lib` file. Replace `x86` with `x64` if you are using a 32-bit system:

```
lib /DEF:sqlite3.def /OUT:sqlite3.lib /TARGET:x64
```

When you run your Rust program, `sqlite3.dll` has to be in a library path. Putting it into whatever directory you run the program out of will be sufficient. For example, I will often run the programs out of the root of the directory tree for this program. This means I will put the `sqlite3.dll` file there and run the program using `target\debug\ch8_dbapp.exe`.

On Linux, just make sure you have installed the `sqlite3-dev` package for your distribution. It should have the libraries needed to perform the build.

There is another SQLite crate for Rust called `rusqlite`, which you can try. It works a little differently than the one we are using but could be substituted if you found, after reading the documentation, that you had a preference for it. Opening the connection is the same. The way you handle query results is slightly different, but the way you interact with the database to execute queries is the same. One difference is that `rusqlite` defines a `NO_PARAMS` constant that would be used when your statement had no parameters. This might be the case if the statement was entirely self-contained. We won't be using the `NO_PARAMS` constant since it's not used in the `sqlite` crate.

Main and Modules

There are a couple of things we will be doing in the main part of the program that we haven't done before. First of all, we're going to be using a module that we have created. There is a keyword for that, which we will get to. Second, we are going to handle the case where the traits we call have different responses. We are going to let Rust take care of some of the more challenging aspects of handling results from calling traits. One of the problems with using results in Rust is that handling the result values costs a lot of lines of additional code that can make it harder to read. Additionally, in many (if not most) cases, you don't want to do anything special with the result, so it may be best to let the language take care of the result cases and just give you back the value you are really looking for. This shorthand is a little bit of syntactic sugar.

> **NOTE** Syntactic sugar *is a feature of a programming language that makes the language more expressive or easier to use/read. As a concept, it has been around since 1964. In object-oriented languages, calling methods on a class is considered syntactic sugar, and you could say the same thing about calling traits on a struct. If you use* `mystruct.trait(param1, param2)`, *it's effectively the same as calling* `trait(mystruct, param1, param2)`. *You are passing in the struct instance as a first parameter, which is how the trait knows what specific instance is being acted on—all the variables that belong to the individual instance you are calling the trait on.*

In order to talk about the syntactic sugar example in our code, we should take a look at the complete `main.rs` file. You will notice there are some functions missing from it. There is just the `main()` function. Don't be alarmed. This is by design, and we'll get to why that is very shortly. This, though, is the complete code that belongs to the source file we're working with:

```rust
use sqlite;
use sqlite::Connection;
use std::env;
use std::error::Error;

mod dbfuncs;

fn main() -> Result<(), Box<dyn Error>> {
    let conn = Connection::open("stratapp.db")?;

    conn.execute(
        "CREATE TABLE IF NOT EXISTS findings (
            findings_ID INTEGER PRIMARY KEY,
            title TEXT NOT NULL,
            finding TEXT NOT NULL,
            details TEXT,
            justification TEXT)")?;

        let args: Vec<String> = env::args().collect();
    if args.len() > 1 {
        let command: &str = &args[1];

        match command {
            "add" => dbfuncs::addrecord(&conn)?,
            "list" => dbfuncs::listrecords(&conn),
            _ => println!("Didn't send a valid command in")
        }
    }
    else {
        println!("Please specify add or list as a command line parameter");
    }

    Ok(())
}
```

First, as always, we need to include the crates we are using. The `Cargo.toml` file needs to include `sqlite` as a dependency so all the necessary components can be built when we build our executable. That allows us to use the different components from that crate. In this code, we are pulling in the different components we need individually. Instead of that, we could of course replace the two lines with a single line that read use `sqlite::{self, Connection}`. That would say the same thing as the two lines. There may be something a little more explicit about using two lines since it's clearer that you are using the two different elements. If it's on a single line, your eye may not immediately notice there are multiple elements. This is as much an individual preference as anything else, however. In my case, it's because I discovered what I needed as I was writing and just created a new line rather than adjusting an existing line.

The one new line you will see toward the top of this code listing is `mod dbfuncs`. This tells the compiler there is a module it needs to read in. There are different ways to structure this module, including creating a directory with the name of the module. The easiest way, and the way we are going to do it, is to create a file with the name of the module. This means in the source code directory, there is a file named `dbfuncs.rs`. As long as that file is there, the Rust compiler will be happy and just pull in all the code from that file, compiling it along with the code in the `main.rs` file.

The other new aspect of the program we are using is the way we are going to provide results. We will be returning a basic result from the main function; but, more importantly, we will be handling error cases. What you will see in the source code is the following line:

```
fn main() -> Result<(), Box<dyn Error>>
```

This line tells the compiler we are going to return a `Result` data type. Remember, `Result` is an enumeration, meaning it has predefined values. Those values can also contain associated data, which is generally the case. The primary reason for including the return type in this way is to be able to more easily handle errors that result from called functions. Errors are specific to the crate where the error is generated, and in some cases, they are specific to the trait where the error has been generated. This means getting specific can be problematic if we are calling several different traits that might generate errors. That's why we want to be as generic as possible. The way we declare the error in the return type allows us to take different error types and return them.

To handle multiple types in a consistent way, we need to be able to abstract them a little. When the Rust compiler is turning your source code into executable language, it does its best to create a tight, optimized executable file. This means being explicit in your code is helpful because the compiler will know exactly what code and references to include and where to include them. When we try to create a generic error, we run into the case of the compiler needing to do something called *dynamic dispatch*. With dynamic dispatch, the decision about what code to move to or what data structure to include has to be made at runtime. In other words, dynamically rather than statically. This causes a performance hit at runtime.

What we are going to use is a generic construct called `Box`, which allocates a container on the heap. The heap is where dynamic data is allocated, meaning data that isn't known at compile time. Anything known at compile time is allocated on the stack. `Box` is effectively a reference to a chunk of memory, which means you can put anything into a `Box` because `Box` is just a pointer to a location in memory. We need to tell the compiler what is going to go into the `Box`, though, so we tell it we are going to put an `Error` into the box. The construct `Box<dyn value>` is called a *trait object*. This is because we are taking something that would normally be specific and turning it generic. Rather than a specific implementation of a trait, we are indicating that we are going to use a generic version, and the specific version will be known at runtime. This can be confusing, so perhaps the diagram seen in Figure 8.6 can be helpful to sort it out.

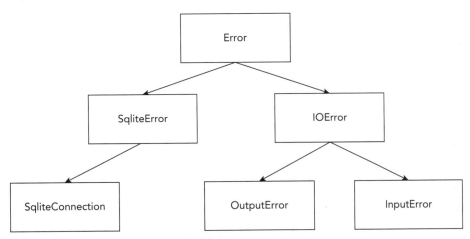

FIGURE 8.6: Error hierarchy

The generic error is just Error. You may also have several implementations that take on the characteristics of Error but also include their own specific characteristics, as in the case of SqliteError, for instance. Even beyond a specific Error with some additional characteristics, you may find something more specific. You may get an SqliteError and also an SqliteConnectionError. Each level of granularity gives us more details about what may have gone on. Rather than getting just an "Error occurred," we could get "Unable to connect to SQLite database." However, if we needed to support multiple error types, we would need to back up to the generic Error since all the specific ones have the characteristics of the generic Error. Since all of them have that in common, we can use the common characteristics to be able to support multiple errors that may return from any given function.

If you have a case where you need to be able to handle multiple specific types at the same time, you can use a trait object like Box<dyn value>. It's going to give us the ability to handle the different errors we could get from the main() function. This brings us to one of the reasons for handling the errors this way. In the past, we had used a match statement to catch whether the Result was an Ok() or an Err(). This gets to be complicated to put together; and while it's certainly more explicit, and being explicit is good, it takes away from the expression of the important parts of the function. That's just error handling, and while it's really important, it shouldn't take up so much space in the program that it's harder to read the primary path through the function. The following code is a different way of handling the error condition while simultaneously providing us the value we are looking for:

```
let conn = Connection::open("stratapp.db")?;
```

This statement uses the Sqlite::Connection struct to open a file that will be used for a database. This open() trait will create the file with the necessary management tables and other structures needed for the file to act like a SQLite database. The important part of this line, though, is the ? at the end. This is syntactic sugar that shorthands the entire match clause where we look for the Ok() and the Err(). The ? says that if we get an Ok(), just unwrap the value and place it into the identifier on the left-hand side of the equal sign. If there is an `Err()`, print out the error and drop out of the function, returning the error in the `Result`.

You can see how much easier this is than how we have done it before. However, there is a catch, as you might expect there would be when you go from complicated, or at least verbose, to simple. The catch is that the function you are in has to be able to handle the error being generated in the return value from the function. This requires knowing what error is being generated, meaning you have to know the specific instance of the error type. Not all documentation is going to provide that to you. One way of figuring out the specific error instance is to force the error to be generated so you can see what the type is. Even that's not necessarily straightforward since a trait call may end up being multiple error conditions. If you don't have permissions to open the file, for instance, you'll get one error. If you don't have write permissions to a directory and the file doesn't exist, you may get a different error since the `open()` call won't be able to create the file when it needs to.

As you can see, error handling is complex. It can take a lot of work and detailed documentation or at least a lot of experimentation to consider all the different use cases that could result in errors if you want to handle them all differently. In our case, the error conditions are fatal, so we really want the program to fail. If we can't open or create or do anything with the database file, we may as well terminate the program since nothing else we want to do is going to work.

Once we have opened the database file, we have a connection to the database stored in an instance of a `Connection` struct. With the handle to the database, we can start sending SQL commands to the database. One way of doing this—and there are several—is to use the `execute()` trait in the `Connection` struct. The complete command follows. The call to this trait performs a one-off execution of an SQL statement. We don't expect anything back from the database in terms of results. The only thing we would get is an `Ok()` result if everything performed as expected and an `Err()` if there was a problem. You'll see the `?` again at the end of this statement, and this is another reason why we are using the trait object for our return type. We are expecting potential error conditions from two separate traits. Even if we knew there was one error the other function might generate, we now have at least one other error that will be generated here, so we need to have a way of returning different error conditions:

```
conn.execute(
    "CREATE TABLE IF NOT EXISTS findings (
        findings_ID INTEGER PRIMARY KEY,
        title TEXT NOT NULL,
        finding TEXT NOT NULL,
        details TEXT,
        justification TEXT)")?;
```

The SQL statement is fairly straightforward and readable as it is. What it says is that we need to create a table called `findings`; however, we only need to create the table if it doesn't exist. If it does exist, the remainder of this statement will not run. We specify the columns, which are primarily text values except for the row identifier, called `findings_ID`; it is an `INTEGER` and also the primary key for the table, meaning the database software will create a way to identify the rows based on this one attribute. In some cases, we require a value to the attribute. This is where we use the `NOT NULL` specifier. It tells the database to generate an error if the values for these attributes are not provided when a row is being inserted into the table.

Once we have created the table, if it's needed, we move on to checking what the user wants to do. For this, we expect a command-line parameter. We've used all of this before, where we get the command-line arguments and then check the parameters to determine what the user wants to do, calling the right function as needed. The thing is, though, that we need to make sure the user has actually provided us with a command. If the user hasn't provided a command-line parameter, trying to pull that value will generate a program fault. Following is the code fragment where we determine if there are indeed command-line parameters. If so, we set an identifier to contain the first parameter past the program name. Then we perform the match clause that we've used before:

```
if args.len() > 1 {
    let command: &str = &args[1];

    match command {
        "add" => dbfuncs::addrecord(&conn)?,
        "list" => dbfuncs::listrecords(&conn),
        _ => println!("Didn't send a valid command in")
    }
}
```

One note here is that in the addrecord() function, we are going to receive an error condition. This is because there are traits that get called, which you will see later, which could generate an error. This is not required in the listrecords() function. For both functions, we are passing in the identifier for our instance of the Connection struct, conn. We need to borrow it, so we are going to use &conn rather than just conn. This allows us to handle opening the connection in the main() function and just pass the connection handle into the functions. Another way of handling this would be for each of the database functions to open the connection. That's not very efficient from a programming perspective since you are duplicating code, which is why we open the connection at a higher level than the database functions and just pass in the handle to the connection for the functions to consume.

Finally, if the user hasn't provided a command, we generate an error, telling them they need to tell us whether they want to *add* or *list*. If we have dropped to the end of the function, it must be that everything went okay, so we just return Ok(()), meaning we are returning an empty value contained in the Ok() enumeration for the Result.

Database Functions

This is a very simple program in that it only implements a pair of functions that the user can perform. First, we can add records to the database. Second, we can list all of the records in the one table in our database. There are probably other things we could do with the table we have and the data it includes, but this is a good start, and it demonstrates executing SQL statements as well as issuing a query that returns results from the table and what we do with those results. Following is the complete source code for the dbfuncs.rs file:

```
use sqlite;
use sqlite::State;
use sqlite::Connection;
use std::io;

pub fn addrecord(conn: &Connection) -> io::Result<()> {
    let mut title = String::new();
```

continues

(continued)

```
        let mut finding = String::new();
        let mut details = String::new();
        let mut justification = String::new();

        println!("Title");
        io::stdin().read_line(&mut title)?;
        println!("Finding text");
        io::stdin().read_line(&mut finding)?;
        println!("Details of the finding");
        io::stdin().read_line(&mut details)?;
        println!("Justification");
        io::stdin().read_line(&mut justification)?;

        let commandstring = format!("INSERT INTO findings (title, finding, details,
justification) VALUES (\"{}\",
            \"{}\", \"{}\", \"{}\")", title.trim(), finding.trim(), details.trim(),
justification.trim());
        let _statement = conn.execute(&commandstring).unwrap();

        Ok(())
    }

pub fn listrecords(conn: &Connection) {
    let mut statement = conn
        .prepare("SELECT * FROM findings")
        .unwrap();

        while let State::Row = statement.next().unwrap() {
            println!("---------------------------");
            println!("Title = {}", statement.read::<String>(1).unwrap());
            println!("Finding = {}", statement.read::<String>(2).unwrap());
            println!("Details = {}", statement.read::<String>(3).unwrap());
            println!("Justification = {}", statement.read::<String>(4).unwrap());

        }

    }
```

You'll see that the same crates are imported in this file, because it's a different source code file and is compiled separately. Since we refer to the data structures and traits in the code here, we need to make sure we pull in the right external references. The `Cargo.toml` file covers the entire project, though, so we only need to add the dependency once. For every source code file that makes use of the structures and traits from a crate, we need to use the appropriate crates so the Rust compiler knows what we are talking about when we refer to something outside of the statements in this file. You can think of it as adding additional namespaces so the compiler knows where to look for the different elements.

Adding Records

The `addrecord()` function is long but simple. Much of the length comes from taking input from the user since we have to create `String` identifiers for all of the different values. We need individual identifiers because we need to construct an SQL statement that includes them. It's easier to just create all the different identifiers than it is to keep appending String values onto an existing String with the full statement. Let's take a look at the function declaration as well as the section where we define all of the identifiers:

```
pub fn addrecord(conn: &Connection) -> io::Result<()> {
    let mut title = String::new();
    let mut finding = String::new();
    let mut details = String::new();
    let mut justification = String::new();
```

The first thing you may notice is we have a new keyword on the front of the function declaration. The pub is necessary to indicate that these are public functions, so anyone outside of this module can use the function. This is because we have a module we are creating. This is a separate file from the other code in this project. Because of that, we need to set some access control conditions. We only have two functions, and both of them need to be accessible from outside of the file they are contained in. That's why they need to be declared as pub. They need to be accessible publicly.

Our return value is dictated by the trait we are using to take input from the user. We'll get to that trait later on, when we call it, but you need to know that we have the potential to get input/output (I/O) errors. Because we have traits that might generate an I/O error, we need to pass back an io::Result<()> for the return value. This allows us to skip the use of a match statement and just lets us allow Rust to take care of the Result for us. The rest of the previous section of code is straightforward String definitions. We call the new() trait to make sure we get a new String value allocated, although we haven't initialized it or indicated how big it will be.

The next section of code, which follows here, is where we get input from the user. Good practice is to prompt the user in a useful way. The prompt used here is not especially verbose but gives a cue as to what needs to be provided. We assume the user knows the purpose of this program and will enter the appropriate value for each of the prompts. The reason we need the return value is this sequence of code. You will see that the lines where we call the read_line() trait on the io::stdin struct have a ? at the end. This indicates we get a Result from it. Even though the value we care about is passed in as a mutable parameter, meaning the input from the user is going to be placed into the identifier we hand in, the trait still returns a Result, which needs to be handled. It would be very unusual to get an error taking input from the console; but the read_line() trait is used for more than just this struct, so it is defined in a way that it just returns a Result in case we run into errors doing other I/O operations, like those involving files. The Ok() result is simply discarded after it's unwrapped, because there isn't anything in it we especially care about here. Since the ? triggers an immediate return from this function in the case of an error, either we need to handle the error ourselves to prevent the return from the function or we need to be able to return an error value:

```
println!("Title");
io::stdin().read_line(&mut title)?;
println!("Finding text");
io::stdin().read_line(&mut finding)?;
println!("Details of the finding");
io::stdin().read_line(&mut details)?;
println!("Justification");
io::stdin().read_line(&mut justification)?;
```

Finally, we have the code where we send the SQL statement to our database. The two statements that make that happen follow here, as well as the `Ok(())` we need because we have said we are returning a `Result`. The `Ok()` doesn't need to contain anything since it won't get consumed in our program; that's why we return an empty value, indicated by the `()`:

```
    let commandstring = format!("INSERT INTO findings (title, finding, details,
justification) VALUES (\"{}\",
        \"{}\", \"{}\", \"{}\")", title.trim(), finding.trim(), details.trim(),
justification.trim());
    let _statement = conn.execute(&commandstring).unwrap();

    Ok(())
}
```

First, we construct a `String` that contains the SQL statement. This looks a little ugly because we need to escape the special character `"`. In Rust, the `"` character indicates the beginning or ending of a character string value. Since we are in the middle of one of these character strings, another double quote would end it before we were finished. And the values we are providing need to be in quotes because they are string values. This is a potential problem. The solution to the problem, however, is simple. We just use a `\` character before the `"` character in the SQL statement to indicate to the compiler that we mean the `"` character literally rather than as a termination character for the character string parameter.

The actual SQL statement should look like this: `INSERT INTO findings (title, finding, details, justification) VALUES ("value 1", "value 2", "value 3", "value 4")`. You'll see that the parameters to the `format!()` trait are all the identifiers for the data we took from the user. The `read_line()` trait will include the newline character that comes from the user pressing the Enter key at the end of the line of input. We don't want that newline in the middle of the SQL statement, so we need to use the `trim()` trait to remove the newline character. This gives us just the input without the character we don't need.

Finally, we call `execute()` on the connection, passing in the command string. Since the `execute()` trait wants an `str` rather than a `String`, we use `&commandstring`, which passes the value in the right format for the trait. As before, we'll get a result back from this trait call, so we need to `unwrap()` the resulting value. As we aren't going to do anything with the value that comes back, we are using the identifier `_statement`, which indicates we won't use it, and the Rust compiler won't warn us that we've created an identifier that isn't ever used. The `_` character that is prepended on the identifier indicates that we know the value is never going to be used, and we're okay with that. The only other line left is the necessary `Ok(())` because we are returning a `Result` from this function.

Listing Records

This is another very simple function, but we'll handle the database interaction differently than we have before because we're going to get values back from the SQL query we send to the database. That's very different from the fire and forget that we've been doing until now. Following is the code for the function, which has two sections—handling the SQL query and then handling the results that come back from the SQL query:

```
    pub fn listrecords(conn: &Connection) {
        let mut statement = conn
```

```
            .prepare("SELECT * FROM findings")
            .unwrap();

    while let State::Row = statement.next().unwrap() {
        println!("----------------------------");
        println!("Title = {}", statement.read::<String>(1).unwrap());
        println!("Finding = {}", statement.read::<String>(2).unwrap());
        println!("Details = {}", statement.read::<String>(3).unwrap());
        println!("Justification = {}", statement.read::<String>(4).unwrap());

    }

}
```

The function definition is what we've seen before. We are borrowing the `Connection` from the `main()` function. We are not returning any value because nothing we do is going to generate an error that we absolutely have to handle. This means we can skip right ahead to where we create a query and send it to the SQL database. Instead of `execute()`, which is the fire-and-forget approach, we are going to use `prepare()`. This sets up the query without directly executing it. The SQL statement itself is `SELECT * FROM findings`. This means we want to take all rows and columns from the table named `findings`. Later on, we're going to have to skip the first column because we don't need to look at the row identifier value. In order to not have to skip a result, we could have used an SQL statement like `SELECT title,finding,details,justification FROM findings`. That would have returned just the attributes that we really care about seeing.

We are able to break up the complete Rust statement onto multiple lines, which makes it easier. This is because Rust, unlike other languages, including Python and Swift, uses a statement delimiter to indicate when the statement is complete. We can spread this out over as many lines as we need to make it more manageable or more readable. The Rust compiler will keep assuming it's the same statement until it encounters the `;` at the end indicating the statement is complete. When you are chaining a number of traits together, this approach has some value to keep you from wrapping a line, which can make readability more challenging.

The `prepare()` trait returns a `Result`, but we aren't forced to deal with the error condition, so all we need to do is `unwrap()` the `Statement` struct that will be returned from the call to that trait. Once we have the `Statement`, we can proceed to retrieve all the rows. This query has no restrictions on what comes back, so we will need a way to run through the entire table. This is going to require an iterator.

The iterator we are going to use is built into the `Statement` struct. The first line of the loop where we process all the rows is going to take a moment to explain, so let's extract it from the rest of the loop and take a look at it. Following is the top line of the `while` loop that handles the iterator. While it looks like a reasonably straightforward `while` loop, there is actually a lot going on:

```
    while let State::Row = statement.next().unwrap() {
```

The first thing to look at is `statement.next()`, which is the iterator through all the rows. It returns an enum called `State`. `State` has two possible values. The first value is `State::Row`. The other value is `State::Done`. The `while` line actually says while the result from `statement.next()` is `State::Row`, continue the loop. As soon as the result from that trait becomes `State::Done`, we will drop out of the loop. We don't need to store any value, but we do need to get rid of the `State` enum, so we call the `unwrap()` trait on the `next()` trait.

Let's wait a second to let all of that sink in, because there is a lot to process. Okay, now take a breath and let me write it a different way. As long as what we get back from the next possible value in the collection of values that came back from the query is a row, we can do something with that row. The moment we get a `done` back, meaning there are no more rows, we drop out of the loop and continue with the remainder of the function, such as there may be. Now, let's take a look at what we are doing with each individual row, making the assumption that we have a row to process. Following is what we are doing with the row, which is really just writing out each value on a line by itself; trying to do it in a tabular form with columns would quickly make it difficult to look at since each value could be hundreds of characters long and a single value might not fit on a line in our output, much less four of them:

```
println!("------------------------------");
println!("Title = {}", statement.read::<String>(1).unwrap());
println!("Finding = {}", statement.read::<String>(2).unwrap());
println!("Details = {}", statement.read::<String>(3).unwrap());
println!("Justification = {}", statement.read::<String>(4).unwrap());
```

The top line is just a break because we assume at some point there will be multiple rows, so we need to have a visual break between the blocks of values. You can move this visual break to the bottom if you prefer. It depends on whether you want the line to be on top of the block, meaning you will always start with this line, or on the bottom, meaning there will always be a line at the end of all of your output. There is no particular reason to go one way or the other beyond a matter of taste.

All the rest of the lines are the same except for the attribute they refer to. Let's take a look at this because there is a little trickery hidden in each line. First, we have our `statement` struct. During the first pass through the `while` loop, this struct is going to point to row 1. Inside of this row, we have a number of columns. To get each column out (the rows are managed by calling `next()` to get to the next row, but we're only dealing with a row at a time, so no need to think too much about the rows right now), we call the `read()` trait on the `statement` identifier. Since there are multiple columns or attributes, the `read()` trait needs to know which one we want. We tell it by passing in a positional identifier. Since we are going to skip the first column, which holds the index value, we start at 1. The next column is 2, and so on.

The tricky part comes because `read()` has no idea what the type of the value coming back is. This means we need to tell it. It may not be intuitive how we need to tell the call to the trait how to type the response. You indicate the type by calling `read::<String>(1)`. This calls the implementation of `read()` that is used for the `String` data type. The positional parameter is passed in after indicating clearly which data type we are calling `read()` for. As always, we need to call `unwrap()` because we get a `Result` back that contains the value we care about.

Let's recap that last part because it isn't necessarily intuitive and may require another pass to fully explain it. We need to `read()` the column value. However, the Rust compiler has no way of knowing at compile time what the data type in that column is. This is especially important in these lines because `println!()` needs to know how to format the data it is going to print. Therefore, we need to help the compiler along by telling it which implementation of `read()` to call. We need to make sure we call the one that is going to return a `String`, because `println!()` knows how to handle that data type. What we end up with is `read::<String>(1)` to get the right column, provided inside the parentheses, and the right data type. The 1 is there as an example. Of course, as you can see from the full code, that value changes based on the attribute or column we want to read.

As there is no return value, once the `while` loop completes, the function completes. With this, we have a complete program that is capable of storing values to a database and also retrieving the values.

SUMMARY

Databases are powerful tools for programmers. These days, it seems like a large number of programs use databases for storing information. This is made even easier when there are embedded databases like SQLite to use rather than relying on a database server. This has opened the door to programs like Google Chrome using embedded databases to store all of the information they use, including your browsing history, credentials, and other user-specific information.

Relational databases are commonly used and have been commonly used since they were developed in the 1970s. Relational databases are composed of tables. These tables are or can be related. The language used to interact with relational databases is the Structure Query Language (SQL). This is, or can be, a very complex language, but in most cases, you need to be able to create databases and tables, insert data into a table, and also retrieve data from the table. It's worth it to check the documentation for how a database server handles SQL. For instance, some database servers expect a command delimiter like a `;` to terminate each command. Other database servers are less picky about such things. Also, you can insert comments into a line of SQL, and different database implementations will use different characters to indicate a comment is coming.

There are different crates used to interact with database implementations. Communicating with database implementations like MySQL/MariaDB or PostgreSQL will require different crates. The same is true for interacting with an embedded database like SQLite. In fact, there is more than one crate that can be used to interact with a SQLite file. The one we chose for our program was just called `sqlite`, although you can also look into `rusqlite`. In either case, there are some traits you will commonly use, including `open()`, which opens the file containing the database. This opens a connection to the database, and that's reflected in the value that is stored in the identifier—a `Connection`.

Once you have the connection in place, you can start interacting with the server. If you have a fire-and-forget command like a `CREATE TABLE` or even an `INSERT INTO`, you can use the `execute()` trait on the `Connection` struct. This sends the SQL statement to the database, where it is executed. You would use this approach if you weren't expecting anything back from the database aside from an indication of success or failure.

If you want a response back, you are probably going to be executing a `SELECT` SQL statement. This means you will probably be creating a `Statement` struct, calling `prepare()` on the `Connection` to return the `Statement`. Once you have the `Statement`, you can iterate through all of the rows, doing whatever you need to do to the data you get back. In our case, we just printed out the results, but you may have other transformations you want to perform on the data you get back from the database.

If you have a large project, you don't have to put everything into a single source file. If you are going to use multiple source files, you need to make sure you include these other source files using the `mod` keyword along with the name of the module (the first part of the file name, dropping the `.rs` suffix). You will also need to be sure you make the functions you want to expose to other modules (or files) public by using the `pub` keyword at the front of your function definition.

Finally, you may want to spend a little time thinking about the best way to design your application. If you are using a client/server approach, you may want to use an n-tier application architecture. Many application development platforms use the Model-View-Controller design pattern. This is certainly true with all of the Apple devices and their associated application programming interfaces. You could also use a service-oriented architecture, sometimes called microservices. This breaks your application up into individual services that other components or services interact with.

In a native application, none of these may apply. So far, we've been designing simple applications that don't use any particular application architecture. They are designed to be simple and run directly on someone's computer, rather than on a web or application server.

EXERCISES

1. Implement a database struct that includes the traits `addrecord()` and `listrecords()` but also contains the code that opens the database. You would need an identifier to contain the `Connection` as well as a trait that opened the database using a file name passed in.

2. Make `listrecords()` act the same as `addrecord()`, meaning have it return a `Result`, so the calls to the two functions (or traits, if you have done exercise 1) act the same.

3. Change `listrecords()` so it returns a vector of strings that contain the entire collection of output, so the calling function could write out to the console or a file rather than having `listrecords()` write out to the console all the time.

4. Change `listrecords()` so it doesn't pull in the `findings_ID` attribute but only pulls in the attributes you will be displaying.

ADDITIONAL RESOURCES

SQL Tutorial - www.w3schools.com/sql/

SQL - Overview - www.tutorialspoint.com/sql/sql-overview.htm

Intro to SQL - www.khanacademy.org/computing/computer-programming/sql

MVC: Model-View-Controller - www.codecademy.com/articles/mvc

Understanding Model-View-Controller - blog.codinghorror.com/understanding-model-view-controller/

What is N-Tier Architecture? - dzone.com/articles/what-is-n-tier-architecture

About SQLite - www.sqlite.org/about.html

Investigating Rust with SQLite - tedspence.com/investigating-rust-with-sqlite-53d1f9a41112

No(SQL) Going

Relational databases are not the only way to go when it comes to storing data. In fact, the way application development is today, it may not even be the preferred way. When relational database technology was being developed several decades ago, data description languages weren't really available. This was a time where every bit cost a significant amount of money. Stored data required space on large, expensive disk drives, fractions of the size of what we can put onto a thumbnail today. In 1980, IBM released the first 1 GB disk drive at a cost of $40,000. Today, that would be over $125,000. A 256 GB secure digital (SD) card is about $50. On top of the price difference in acquisition, there is also the price difference in maintaining it. The IBM drive in 1980 weighed 550 pounds and required a lot of power to operate. An SD card, meanwhile, doesn't even weigh an ounce.

You can see that storage came at a premium back in the 1970s and 1980s when relational databases were initially being developed and enhanced. Why is this relevant? Data description languages are expensive from a storage perspective. A language like the eXtensible Markup Language (XML) has the possibility of more than doubling the number of characters being stored. If disk space is expensive, the number of characters you are storing matters. Similarly, a data description language like JavaScript Object Notation (JSON) adds a lot of additional bytes to what is being stored.

Today, though, storage is cheap, and data description languages like XML and JSON provide a lot of flexibility in terms of how data is stored, searched, and retrieved. In short, we can afford to use JSON or XML now because storage and bandwidth have such limited costs. This means we don't have to be as rigid about how we structure data repositories like databases. We can allow the creator of the data to determine how the data is going to be structured, and we can just store it in a flexible backend. This is why we are going to take a look at a trend away from relational databases called NoSQL.

To talk about NoSQL, we need to better understand data description languages since that's often how data is stored, in addition to transmitted. Additionally, saying NoSQL isn't the same as saying SQL, since NoSQL just means a database server that doesn't use SQL as the interface language. It says nothing at all about how the data is structured and formatted under the hood.

We've been trickling in some good programming practices throughout the book in order to expand your programming capabilities away from strictly the syntax for the Rust language. In this chapter, we are going to look at using assertions. Often, when you are programming, you need to know where a condition is set, but you don't want to have your code littered with a lot of extra if statements with associated prints; so you have some breadcrumbs through your code to remind you where you are and what is going on along the way. These may be hard to identify when it comes to getting a release version of your code.

One way to declutter your code is to use assertions. These are statements you put into your code to perform a task if the condition is true. If not, the code continues to execute as normal. The statement is still in the code, which means you still need to be careful about what you do if the assertion is true. The assertion statements will continue to execute in release versions of the executable. But assertions are not only valuable for debugging. They have other uses as well.

ASSERTIONS

Assertions are a common feature in many programming languages. There are many benefits to the use of assertions. At their core, assertions are used to validate a condition before continuing with the execution of the program. There are some important programming ideas where assertions can be valuable, but before getting to them, let's look at a simple and straightforward piece of code that uses assertions. This is in the C programming language. In the code you see next, we are checking whether a pointer (a reference to a location in memory, if you aren't familiar with pointers) has a value or not. If there is no value, meaning it's NULL, there isn't a point to trying to dereference the memory location, meaning trying to extract the value from that memory location. If we tried, we would generate a program crash:

```c
#include <stdio.h>
#include <assert.h>

int main(int argc, char **argv) {

    int *p = NULL;

    assert(p);

    if (*p == 5) {
        printf("The value is equal to 5");
    }

    return 0;
}
```

First, it's C, so we need to include functionality from external libraries. The first is the standard input/output library, and the second is the library that contains the assert() macro. This is a simple example just to demonstrate how it works, but imagine there is a lot of code here before we get to the assertion. You have a pointer, which is identified by *p. In C, the asterisk denotes a pointer variable. To see how the assertion works, we need that pointer to have an invalid value. NULL is the best approach here, although leaving the pointer unassigned may end up leaving it completely uninitialized, meaning the value in that memory location is whatever was written there the last time the physical memory was used. Think of it as a random value. This random value may be a memory location that doesn't exist in our program's memory space. When a program tries to access a chunk of memory that doesn't belong to it, you will get a segmentation fault, meaning the program is trying to access a memory segment that doesn't belong to it.

Keep in mind that this is one of the reasons Rust exists. These sorts of conditions can exist in programs—especially ones written in C, because C allows programmers to do very powerful but mostly dangerous things like directly accessing memory through pointers. Because Rust takes care of memory management in ways that help protect us, these sorts of segmentation faults are much harder to achieve in Rust programs. I'm reluctant to say *impossible*, because never say never, but the memory safety features in Rust make it pretty darned hard to get to a condition like a segmentation fault.

In this program, the very first line after the declaration is the assertion. Since we set the memory address to a null value, it is unreasonable to expect that it's changed between the declaration and the assertion, but it's clearer to see it without a lot of other code cluttering the idea. The assert(p) statement checks to see whether the variable p has a value (effectively, whether it is non-zero). If you aren't used to this way of expressing value-existence, a clearer way would be to use the line assert (p != NULL). This results in the same thing. If the variable p has no value, we can't possibly access a nonexistent memory address. Rather than trying to continue with the program, this check will cause the program to simply fail. The following shows what it looks like when we run the program as it's written:

```
C:\Users\kilro\Documents>atest.exe
Assertion failed!

Program: C:\Users\kilro\Documents\atest.exe
File: assert-test.c, Line 8

Expression: p != NULL
```

You can see the condition evaluated to false, so the program failed because the assertion failed. This isn't the cleanest way to do this, but it's a good way. This is especially useful if you are performing testing and you want the program to fail so you know whether a condition exists at a certain point in the code. This can keep you from setting breakpoints in your code and checking manually. You know what condition you want, so you write an assertion to make sure a condition you expect is true. If it's not true, the program will fail and tell you which source code file and which line the assertion failed on.

In Rust, the assertion is a little more complicated. Not in the sense of it being harder to write—instead, you get some additional flexibility in what happens. With C, all you need to do is declare the assertion. In Rust, you can declare the assertion while also providing a message that can be displayed. A very simple version of a Rust assertion follows. It's also very clear because we are using a Boolean for the identifier we are checking. This is the currency of the assertion. At some point, the statement being evaluated has to evaluate to either a true or a false. Otherwise, the assertion isn't an assertion:

```
fn main() {
    let x: bool = false;

    assert!(x, "Expected a non-null value");

}
```

We can write a slightly more complex version of an assertion in Rust to show you some of the additional capabilities. Following is the same program but with a different data type for the identifier and a more meaningful message to send if the assertion fails. The Boolean value comes from the comparison in the assertion rather than directly from the identifier:

```
fn main() {
    let x: i32 = 15;

    assert!(x == 30, "x is not 30 as expected, instead it is {}", x);

}
```

Since assert!() is a macro, we can have a variable number of parameters. Rather than just the Boolean condition and the text value that gets displayed, we can place a value into the text in the same way as when we are printing or formatting text data. In this case, we are indicating that we expected the value 30, but instead, another value was found, providing the value in the statement. When it comes to running the program, you will find you get a panic, similar to the result from the C assertion. This is the result of running the Rust program with the assertion of the value of the identifier x:

```
C:\Users\kilro\Documents>afunc.exe
thread 'main' panicked at 'x is not 30 as expected, instead it is 15', afunc.rs:4:5
note: run with `RUST_BACKTRACE=1` environment variable to display a backtrace
```

If you indicate that you want a backtrace by setting the RUST_BACKTRACE environment variable, you will get in your output something that other languages and environments called a *stack trace* or a *call stack*. When you are making function calls, the information about the function goes onto the stack in memory. A backtrace or stack trace shows the path through the program prior to the program panicking and stopping. This includes all the functions that were called, which is why it's called a call stack. Every function, when called, gets put on a stack. The backtrace just pops off all the functions from the stack, printing out the information about the function as it goes. On Windows systems, it's not as direct as on a Linux system. On a Linux system or even a macOS system, you could run the program using RUST_BACKTRACE=1 afunc. On a Windows system, you have to set the environment variable before you run the program, as you can see here:

```
C:\Users\kilro\Documents>set RUST_BACKTRACE=1

C:\Users\kilro\Documents>afunc.exe
thread 'main' panicked at 'x is not 30 as expected, instead it is 15',
afunc.rs:4:5
stack backtrace:
   0: backtrace::backtrace::trace_unsynchronized
             at C:\Users\VssAdministrator\.cargo\registry\src\github.com-
1ecc6299db9ec823\backtrace-0.3.40\src\backtrace\mod.rs:66
   1: std::sys_common::backtrace::_print_fmt
             at /rustc/b8cedc00407a4c56a3bda1ed605c6fc166655447\/src\libstd\
```

```
sys_common\backtrace.rs:77
   2: std::sys_common::backtrace::_print::{{impl}}::fmt
            at /rustc/b8cedc00407a4c56a3bda1ed605c6fc166655447\/src\libstd\
sys_common\backtrace.rs:59
   3: core::fmt::write
            at /rustc/b8cedc00407a4c56a3bda1ed605c6fc166655447\/src\libcore\
fmt\mod.rs:1052
   4: std::io::Write::write_fmt<std::sys::windows::stdio::Stderr>
            at /rustc/b8cedc00407a4c56a3bda1ed605c6fc166655447\/src\libstd\
io\mod.rs:1426
   5: std::sys_common::backtrace::_print
            at /rustc/b8cedc00407a4c56a3bda1ed605c6fc166655447\/src\libstd\
sys_common\backtrace.rs:62
   6: std::sys_common::backtrace::print
            at /rustc/b8cedc00407a4c56a3bda1ed605c6fc166655447\/src\libstd\
sys_common\backtrace.rs:49
   7: std::panicking::default_hook::{{closure}}
            at /rustc/b8cedc00407a4c56a3bda1ed605c6fc166655447\/src\libstd\
panicking.rs:204
```

What you will see here is a portion of the entire backtrace of the function calls prior to the panic from the assertion. You may notice that a lot of them come from the fact that you are doing a backtrace. You can't monitor without the monitor being part of the program. Monitoring can make it harder to determine the actual trail of the program without all of the overhead pieces. However, once you get used to knowing what to ignore, you can see the functions you care about. In our case, it's not all that important. There is only one function, so it was the only one that got called without the backtrace and printing functions.

Design by Contract

The Eiffel programming language is object-oriented, and a way of protecting code was described by the language's creator, Bertrand Meyer, in 1986. This was an idea called *design by contract*. With design by contract, you set conditions that have to be in place before making use of a function. Similarly, there are conditions that are guaranteed to be met once the use of the function completes. Figure 9.1 is a visual representation of how this would look. You send inputs into a function or method, but before the function or method is called, there are some conditions that have to be checked and validated. Similarly, the function or method will output values, and those values have to be checked and validated.

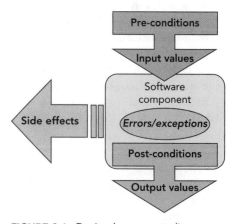

FIGURE 9.1: Design by contract diagram

One way to implement a design by contract is through assertions. You create an assertion that matches the condition you need to be in place before you do anything with the data being passed in. Similarly, once the function comes to an end, you can create assertions. If either the pre-condition or the post-condition is not met, you generate a panic, and the program doesn't complete. This may seem harsh, but if the contract conditions aren't met, you will have a failure one way or the other. In languages without assertions, or if you simply weren't aware that assertions existed in the language you primarily write in, another way of handling this would be to write a series of `if` statements. Using Java as the language for an example, this is how you might make sure you had the right data coming into the function:

```java
public class main {
    public void doSomething(final int x, final int y) throws Exception {
        if (x < 1) {
            throw new Exception("Didn't get the value we needed");
        } else {
            /// do something meaningful here
        }
    }
}
```

This is just a fragment of what might be a larger program, and with this one, you can see we are checking a single condition for the variable x. There are no checks on the variable y. Adding these additional checks would require additional conditional statements. This makes the resulting code clumsy and cumbersome. In Java, using this structure, the easiest way to dump out of the function is to throw an exception. This may be a little clumsy, just using generic exceptions, but it's simpler than creating a new exception class for these specific cases. The biggest issue with this approach is the cumbersome and ugly code that becomes problematic to keep errors out of and, especially, is difficult to read clearly.

This is the way all functions should be handling data coming in. Never assume the data is going to be clean coming into a function or match the parameters expected. Functions should be checking data before making use of it, especially in larger projects. This is why design by contract is so enticing, especially in languages that easily support it. If you could easily implement these data-validation checks, it would help prevent program failure by functions trying to make use of data that is invalid, or at least potentially invalid.

A good way to see design by contract is to take a look at an example out of the Eiffel documentation. The conditions are clear and explicit. The following Eiffel code clearly shows the pre-condition in the `require` clause. The post-condition is in the `ensure` clause. We have to make sure the parameter being passed in is a valid number that could express an hour, meaning it has to be 1 or greater but 12 or less. When the method concludes, it sets the `hour` variable to the parameter, h, passed into the method. The post-condition verifies that the value was actually set, meaning the two variables contain the same value:

```
set_hour (h: INTEGER)
    require
        valid_argument_for_second: 1 <= h and s <= 12
    do
        hour := h
    ensure
        hour_set: hour = h
    end
```

When you create a module in any language, like a crate in Rust or a class in Java, you are creating an interface specification. This includes the functions exposed by the module as well as the parameters the functions or methods expect. Using design by contract, you can formalize the interface specifications by providing not only parameters by type but also the expectation of the bounds for those parameters. Documenting these parameters is one thing, but enforcing them is something else altogether and has to be done on the side of the function, meaning it's up to the developer of the function to perform that enforcement.

Rust supports design by contract in a couple of different ways. The first is through the use of assertions. Second is a crate called `contracts`. This is a set of functionalities that provides you, the programmer, the ability to set pre- and post-conditions for the methods you are developing. These conditions are just assertions, but they are placed in specific locations in the program. A *pre-condition* is an assertion that goes before the function, while a *post-condition* is an assertion that goes after the function. The following program creates a `struct` and adds a trait to it called `doSomething()`. This trait carries a pre-condition. You can see this noted with attribute syntax. The pre-condition here says if the value passed in to the function, x, is not a positive value, the program should fail with the message indicating the value wasn't large enough:

```rust
use contracts::*;

struct BigValue {
    localval: i32

}

impl BigValue {
    #[pre(x > 0, "x was not sufficiently large")]
    fn doSomething(mut self, x: i32)
    {
        println!("{}", x);
        self.localval = x;
    }
}


fn main() {
    let y = BigValue{
        localval: 2
    };
    y.doSomething(-1);

}
```

> **CONCEPT** *An attribute is metadata associated with a program or a program's components. In Rust, it takes the format* `#[Attribute]`. *The attribute could be a command to the compiler to do something. It could also be a macro that is applied to the program. In Rust, there are inner and outer attributes. An inner attribute applies to the thing the attribute is contained within. An outer attribute applies to the thing that follows the attribute.*

As with assertions, using the contract form of verifying the data we are getting will result in a panic in the program if the contract isn't fulfilled. The error message, seen next, is effectively the same as when we looked at using `assert()` in Rust earlier:

```
PS C:\Users\kilro\Documents\design> .\target\debug\design.exe
thread 'main' panicked at 'Pre-condition of doSomething violated: x was not
sufficiently large: x > 0', src\main.rs:9:11
note: run with `RUST_BACKTRACE=1` environment variable to display a backtrace
```

The program shown previously only shows pre-conditions and makes use of a trait in a struct, which is not the only way to implement contracts in Rust. We can also have a very simple program with a `main` function and, perhaps, other functions. While all functions could have the pre- and post-conditions, we can take a look next at how we'd implement both in a small function in a small program. This program is similar to the last program, except the struct has been removed, and the function, previously a trait, is now just a plain function:

```
use contracts::*;

#[pre(x > 0, "x was not sufficiently large")]
#[post(x < 15, "x is too large")]
fn do_something(mut x: i32)
{
    println!("{}", x);
    x = 25;
}


fn main() {
    do_something(4);

}
```

The pre-condition is the same as the last time we looked at it. There is now a post-condition. This ensures the state of the program is controlled because any value that is returned falls within expected ranges. In addition to return values, there are side effects. Over the course of the function, additional functions may be called, although that's not the case in what we have here. When these other functions are called, there are side effects outside of the control of this function, which is only responsible for the data it directly controls. A post-condition doesn't have to only check values within the scope of this program. It could also call functions used to check values or states within the broader program to ensure that nothing bad has happened as a result of what this function did.

In practice, you may not want your program crashing in a production setting. As a result, panics are not the greatest things to have in your code. There is a way around that. The `contracts` crate contains not only `pre` and `post` attributes but also `debug_pre` and `debug_post` attributes. If you only want to verify correct functioning while you are developing the code, to make sure you catch places where bad things may happen, you can use the debug versions if you only want to catch the problem while you are using the debug profile. If you need to make sure nothing bad happens all the time, use the regular contract language.

Under the hood, of course, as you may have guessed, these attributes are effectively macros that use `assert()` as well as `debug_assert()`. Using the `contracts` crate rather than handling the assertions yourself makes the resulting code clearer. Rather than having to put the assertions into the function, you put the language before the function, making the contract explicit.

NOSQL

It is said that NoSQL is a misnomer. The reason is that *NoSQL* commonly refers to a collection of database types that are different from the relational databases discussed in the last chapter. Relational databases are collections of data represented as tables because they are collections of columns or attributes and rows, or instances of those attributes. More than just tables of data, though, relational databases make connections between the different tables. A database may have several tables, each with a set of attributes. These tables may be related in some way, so a relational database keeps track of those connections. If they aren't explicitly connected in the database, any query can make those connections.

Structured Query Language, the SQL referred to in NoSQL, is just a language used to interact with relational databases. However, some of the database implementations that fall under the NoSQL categorization can be queried using SQL. This is why it's a misnomer to call these database types NoSQL. In fact, they are just other means of storing data in structured forms (meaning, the data can be queried to get responses) that are non-relational in nature.

There are several types of NoSQL databases. The first is a key-value database. This kind of database, embodied in the Berkeley DB implementation, among others, stores exactly what it says: values that are retrieved from the database by way of a key. Effectively, you end up with something called a *hash table* or *dictionary*. If you are someone who has networking experience, especially with switches, you may be familiar with this in the content addressable memory (CAM) that is used in switches to look up a port number from a media access control (MAC) address. You may also commonly see key/value pairs in configuration files or even in the Windows Registry.

The key in a key-value pair is the name of the attribute. As an example, take a look at some settings from a Secure Shell (SSH) configuration file. The ones you see here are delimited by spaces. In some cases, you may see something like a colon (:) between the attribute name and the value. On the left side of the space is the attribute name, and on the right side is the value. The first attribute name is Port, and the value of that attribute is 22:

```
Port 22
AddressFamily any
ListenAddress 0.0.0.0
```

Another type is a graph database. This is a way to store highly connected data. Rather than rows and columns, graph databases store nodes that contain information. These nodes are connected via edges. Figure 9.2 shows an example of how you could visualize the data in a graph database. In a traditional relational database, you might have collections of data that all look roughly the same, meaning the same collection of attributes in each collection. In a graph database, all nodes are stored in the same place, regardless of the data stored in each node. If you want to connect a pair of nodes, you create an edge with a label indicating the relationship between the two nodes. Rather than creating definitive connections between entire tables, as in a relational database, you create connections between specific instances of data.

These are databases you are probably familiar with, even if you may not be aware of it. One of the most famous implementations of a graph database is the Facebook data store. Information about you, created in Facebook, is stored in a graph database. This way, every person may have a completely different set of data about them, but you can connect it all up without having to be concerned about whether you've fully populated a row in a database. The nodes may not be completely structured in the sense of having specific pieces of information required to be filled in. Once the data is in the database, you connect it up with other pieces of data. This allows you to easily connect different nodes by following the edges through paths in the database.

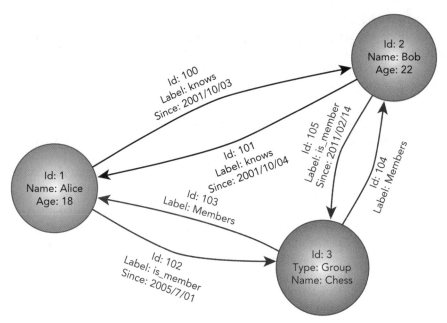

FIGURE 9.2: Graph database

The one type of NoSQL database we are going to focus on, though, is the document store. This is where you take what is essentially a complete row of a relational database, encode it in a way that you know what each attribute is, and store the complete collection as a document. Let's take an example from XML, seen next. This is a record of a person, collecting common information you would expect to keep track of for someone: name, address, phone number, date of birth, and interests. If you wanted to, you could make the phone number a complex piece of information and indicate the type of phone number provided. This would allow you to have multiple phone numbers, including home, work, and mobile. Or, more likely, mobile and work:

```
<person>
    <name>
        <first>Ric</first>
        <middle></middle>
        <surname>Messier</surname>
    </name>
    <address>
        <street>255 Elm Street</street>
        <city>Nowhere</city>
        <state>UT</state>
        <zip>90389</zip>
    </address>
    <phone>999-998-9987</phone>
    <dateofbirth>
        <month>June</month>
        <day>20</day>
        <year>1902</year>
    </dateofbirth>
    <interests>Rust</interests>
</person>
```

With a document store database, you take this chunk of XML and store it all together as a document. The great thing about this is you don't have to worry about creating the schema, meaning the definition of the database structure, ahead of time. Instead, each chunk of data is self-describing because you are using XML. The tags tell you what data is inside the tag. You can also clearly see where the data begins and where it ends. This allows you to be completely flexible about what you store and also provide additional information about the record without having to go in and redo the schema for the entire table or create a whole new table just to create associations in.

You don't have to use XML, of course. There are other types of documents that are also self-describing and could be used in a document-store database. JSON and the Yet Another Markup Language (YAML) format also come to mind. They are similarly self-describing collections of data, meaning they can be indexed easily inside a database because there is an attribute or property and the value associated with that attribute or property. This means everything is findable once it's inside the database store.

A common document-store database is MongoDB. It is a database system that has been around for over a dozen years now. It uses JSON-formatted information to store in the database. This brings up the notion of how to select a database system if you want to use a document-store database. To index data, the database system needs to understand the data format the document is in. If it doesn't understand the data format, it can't distinguish the metadata (the description or tag) from the data. This makes the data impossible to index because it's all just a large glob of information.

INSTALLING MONGODB IN DOCKER

To write a Rust program that uses a document-store database, we need a MongoDB instance. If you have a Linux system, you can just install MongoDB on that system and have a MongoDB service. MongoDB is open source and free to use, as well as being in most package repositories. However, another way is to use Docker, a system that manages containers—a way of virtualizing applications rather than entire machines. Docker is also free and generally available in Linux package repositories, regardless of the distribution. Getting a MongoDB instance up and running inside Docker is easy. First, install Docker on your system—Windows, Linux, or macOS. Once it's installed, you can pull the MongoDB image using the following command:

```
PS C:\Users\kilro> docker pull mongo
Using default tag: latest
latest: Pulling from library/mongo
f08d8e2a3ba1: Pull complete
3baa9cb2483b: Pull complete
94e5ff4c0b15: Pull complete
1860925334f9: Pull complete
9d42806c06e6: Pull complete
31a9fd218257: Pull complete
5bd6e3f73ab9: Pull complete
f6ae7a64936b: Pull complete
80fde2cb25c5: Pull complete
1bec62fe62fc: Pull complete
2cf4970a1653: Pull complete
39fac3226e16: Pull complete
```

continues

(continued)

```
86bca9c64faf: Pull complete
Digest: sha256:df9eca84736a666d5f7e7a09aeb8a6d8d073698d5b7349400f10
ee75812e0e95
Status: Downloaded newer image for mongo:latest
docker.io/library/mongo:latest
```

With the latest MongoDB container image installed, running the Docker image is also simple. The command is shown next. We are going run a Docker image but detach and run it in the background, which is why we use `-d` for the parameter. We also need to do some port forwarding. Using `-p 27017:27017` says that requests coming in on the IP address for our host should be forwarded to that port in the container. We also want to bind a volume to the container. The way we do that is to use `-v .\mongo`, which says the directory `mongo` in the working directory where we are should be bound as a volume inside the container. Finally, the last parameter is the name of the container:

```
PS C:\Users\kilro> docker run -d -p&#x00A0;27017:27017 -v .\
mongo mongo
```

Using Docker allows us to keep the application isolated from the rest of the operating system. We can also easily manage the installation of the application inside the container without worrying about installing or uninstalling the entire application.

WORKING WITH MONGODB

Where traditional, relational databases use tables to collect information, MongoDB uses collections. In MongoDB, you have a database, and inside the database, you have a collection. While there are a lot of ways to interact with the MongoDB server, one simple way is through the MongoDB Compass application, which you can get from the MongoDB website. It's freely available and makes interacting with the server a lot easier than either programmatically or through a graphical user interface (GUI). Figure 9.3 shows the dialog box used to create not only a new database but also a new collection to be stored within that database.

MongoDB Compass works well, no matter whether you are using a Docker image for your database or if you are using a service running without application virtualization. It's a good way to double-check that your insertions have worked once you have run the insert program. We're going to take two different approaches to working with the database. The first is to populate a database with JSON documents from a file. The second is to perform a search of our database, looking for data we have put into it.

Inserting Data

Inserting data into our database is a straightforward concept, as it is with working with relational databases. The difference with inserting into a document database is there is no query, as there would be with a relational database. There is also no indicating which columns you are going to insert into. You simply create the document, in our case a JSON object, and insert it. We can take a look at the

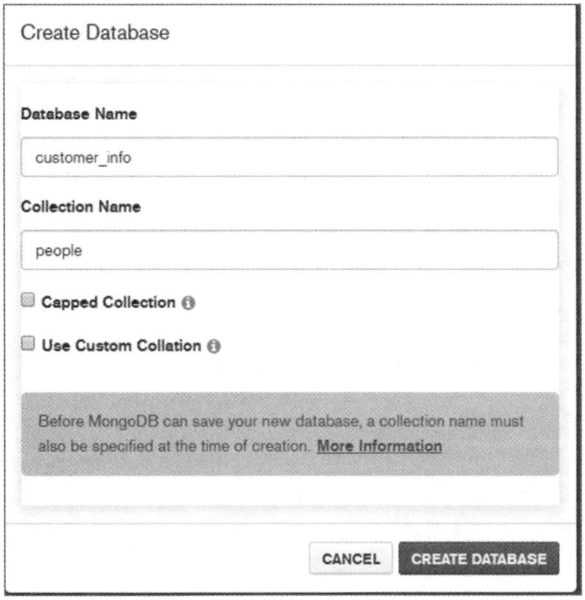

FIGURE 9.3: MongoDB database creation

entire program here, where we are reading a collection of JSON objects from a file and then writing them out one at a time into our database:

```rust
use mongodb::{sync::Client};
use mongodb::bson::doc;
use serde_json;
use serde::{Serialize, Deserialize};
use std::fs::File;
use std::io::BufReader;

#[derive(Serialize, Deserialize)]
struct Person {
    name: String,
    age: i32,
    occupation: String,
    location: String,
    phone: String
}

fn read_records(filename: &str)  {

    let file = File::open(filename).unwrap();
    let buf_reader = BufReader::new(file);

    let deserializer = serde_json::Deserializer::from_reader(buf_reader);
    let iterator = deserializer.into_iter::<serde_json::Value>();
    for item in iterator {
        let p: Person = serde_json::from_str(&item.unwrap().to_string()).unwrap();
        println!("Populating data");
```

continues

(continued)

```
            match db_populate(p) {
                Ok(_o) => (),
                Err(e) => println!("Unable to insert data because of {}", e)
            };
        }
    }

    fn db_populate(record: Person) -> mongodb::error::Result<()> {
        let client = Client::with_uri_str("mongodb://localhost:27017")?;
        let collection = client.database("customer_info").collection("people");

        let data = bson::to_bson(&record).unwrap();
        let document = data.as_document().unwrap();
        let insert_result = collection.insert_one(document.to_owned(), None)?;

        let data_insert_id = insert_result
            .inserted_id
            .as_object_id()
            .expect("Retrieved _id should have been of type ObjectId");
        println!("Inserted ID is {}", data_insert_id);

        Ok(())

    }

    fn main() {

        const FILENAME: &str = "people.json";

        read_records(FILENAME);

    }
```

As usual, at the top of the file, we have to indicate which crates we are going to use for additional functionality. We need two crates from MongoDB. The first is `sync::Client`, indicating that we are going to use synchronous communication with the database. This means we are going to send requests to the database and wait for responses, if they are coming. The other option is to use asynchronous communication. This means we would have to poll the database to see if there is a communication waiting after we have sent something in. For our purposes, we don't need to do asynchronous because we aren't connecting with a large cluster or sending a lot of requests in, so we wouldn't be able to wait for responses. This brings us to the `Cargo.toml` file, which you can see a portion of here:

```
[dependencies]
"bson" = "*"
"serde_json" = "*"
"serde" = "*"

[dependencies.mongodb]
version = "1.1.0"
default-features = false
features = ["sync"]
```

We are going to be using the `bson`, `serde_json`, and `serde` crates. As we've done before, we don't care which version we take in, so we just use the `*` to indicate whatever version is available. The difference here is the specific configuration settings for `mongodb`, seen in the `dependencies.mongodb` configuration block. This sets the version, although you can easily replace that with the wildcard as the others are set to. Since we want to override the default features, we indicate that by setting the `default-features` configuration parameter to `false`. Most importantly, we need to set the `features` parameter to `["sync"]` because we want to use the synchronous client rather than the asynchronous client.

> **TIP** *Rust is still an immature language that is regularly evolving. Because of that, it's probably helpful to keep the Rust installation up to date. This came up during the course of writing this chapter. Building this program generated errors in the underlying* `mongodb` *crate. Updating the Rust installation ended up resolving the problem, even though it had been updated a couple of months before. To keep your Rust installation up to date, just as a reminder, you can use the following command:*
>
> ```
> rustup update
> ```
>
> *This will pull all of the latest versions of the software and install them. It's a simple process and shouldn't be very time-consuming. In lieu of regularly checking the Rust website to determine whether there is a new version, you can periodically check using this command.*

Because we are going to be using what is effectively a data structure, we need to declare a data structure. This locks us into a schema rather than allowing a freeform JSON object. Because we are going to work with files and also create binary versions of JSON, we need to have traits that will do the serialization and deserialization of these data structures. We are going to allow the Rust compiler to create these traits for us, as shown in the following code, since we can ask by adding an attribute. You may recall that `#[derive]` is a directive indicating what the compiler should just take care of for us, so we don't have to:

```
#[derive(Serialize, Deserialize)]
struct Person {
    name: String,
    age: i32,
    occupation: String,
    location: String,
    phone: String
}
```

We will be reading in a file, so we need both the `file` crate from the standard libraries as well as `BufReader` to take care of reading in from the file in a controlled way. The primary reason for using `BufReader` is because it's used to take care of pulling the JSON in. We also are serializing and deserializing data, meaning we will be taking a data structure and storing that data as well as retrieving it. *Serializing* is taking a complex data structure and writing it to a storage or communications medium in a way it can be read by another process. This reading in process is called *deserialization*, meaning the data that was serialized is having that process reversed, so all the individual data components are placed into the memory allocated for the information.

Reading in Data from a File

We are going to start with a data file stored as JSON objects. These are in plaintext, meaning they are easy to read and parse. We are not going to be using a catalog, meaning a collection of JSON objects that are put together in a meaningful way (i.e. the data objects are all related in a way that makes sense to an application reading the JSON). Rather than a catalog, we will be working with all of the JSON objects on individual lines. Doing it this way makes it slightly harder to read visually, but the program we are writing can only handle it if the object is on an individual line. As it turns out, we don't really need to read the file ourselves since the program is going to take care of that for us. However, the JSON objects we will be working with follow:

```
{ "name": "Steve Hogarth", "age": 61, "occupation": "Musician", "location": "UK",
"phone": "0114455891" }
{ "name": "Steven Wilson",  "age": 53, "occupation": "Producer/Musician",
"location": "UK", "phone": "01188937300" }
{ "name": "Emma Stone", "age": 32, "occupation": "Actor", "location": "USA",
"phone": "8189900234" }
{ "name": "Joe Schmo", "age": 58, "occupation": "Plumber", "location": "USA",
"phone": "7158892340" }
```

The function that is going to take care of reading in this file follows here. This function takes in a single parameter providing the filename. We've worked on reading in from files before, so the first two lines in this function won't be anything new. Since this is where we are going to be deserializing data from what's in a file, in JSON format, into a data structure, which we looked at earlier, we need to use `serde_json::Deserializer`. One way to make use of this is to pass in the `BufReader` struct. What we end up with is all of our JSON objects in a collection. We need to get to each individual record.

```
fn read_records(filename: &str)  {

    let file = File::open(filename).unwrap();
    let buf_reader = BufReader::new(file);

    let deserializer = serde_json::Deserializer::from_reader(buf_reader);
    let iterator = deserializer.into_iter::<serde_json::Value>();
    for item in iterator {
        let p: Person = serde_json::from_str(&item.unwrap().to_string()).unwrap();
        match db_populate(p) {
            Ok(_o) => (),
            Err(e) => println!("Unable to insert data because of {}", e)
        };
    }
}
```

To get to the individual records from the file, we need an iterator. Each line is going to have the type `serde_json::Value`. This is indicated because it's the type between the `<>` in the call to the trait `into_iter()`. Now we have an iterator over a collection of JSON objects. Getting to each one of these, so we can do something with them, we're going to use a `for` loop. We will get an identifier called item, which has a data type of serde_json::Value. To convert from that data type into the data structure Person, we need to use the following line:

```
let p: Person = serde_json::from_str(&item.unwrap().to_string()).unwrap();
```

There is a lot to pull apart here. You could do this in multiple lines to make it easier to see what is happening, but we can take this in pieces to make it easier to understand. First, we have an identifier p, which has the type Person. We are going to use the function serde_jason::from_str() to perform the conversion from Value to Person. We need to take the item, which is a Result containing a Value, and unwrap it to get the Value out. We need this value to be a String because we are using the from_str() function. To get a String, we call the to_string() trait on the Value structure. The to_string() trait, though, doesn't actually return a String, so we have to unwrap it from the Result that does come back.

Putting all of that into plain English, we take the individual line from our collection of lines, convert it to a string, and then allow the deserializer to convert the string into the data structure. This means the deserializer understands JSON and can convert what it finds in each line of our file into the Person data structure, returning an instance of that data structure.

This takes us to the function call inside of the for loop. This is the next function we are going to take a look at, but it returns values we need to deal with. Most importantly, it returns errors. This is why we are going to perform a match on the return value from the function call. If we get an Ok() back from the function, we don't need to do anything. All the work is done in the function, so there is nothing to return in a success. In the case of an error, we just print the error and a note indicating we couldn't go any further. We don't want to call panic!() in this case, because it could have been a case of one object failing. We don't know anything beyond that, so no need to let the program fail.

Populating the Database

The function being called is the one we are going to take a look at here. The entire function follows. The signature is straightforward. We need to pass in the data structure we created in the previous function. This function we're going to look at is meant to be called for each record rather than creating a complete document that contains all of the records in order to store them all at once. We'll get to how to do that from the perspective of interacting with the database shortly. The other part of the signature, though, is the return. This is all about the error, as noted before, which is an error from the MongoDB driver:

```
fn db_populate(record: Person) -> mongodb::error::Result<()> {
    let client = Client::with_uri_str("mongodb://localhost:27017")?;
    let collection = client.database("customer_info").collection("people");

    let data = bson::to_bson(&record).unwrap();
    let document = data.as_document().unwrap();
    let insert_result = collection.insert_one(document.to_owned(), None)?;

    let data_insert_id = insert_result
        .inserted_id
        .as_object_id()
        .expect("Retrieved _id should have been of type ObjectId");
    println!("Inserted ID is {}", data_insert_id);

    Ok(())
}
```

The first couple of lines are all about creating the connection to the database. Keep in mind, we are using the synchronous driver rather than the asynchronous driver. If we were going to use the asynchronous connection, we would connect in a different way and also have to make adjustments to the function because it would have to be flagged as an asynchronous function. We are going to create a client from a universal resource identifier (URI) string. The URI string, in this case, indicates the protocol or type of connection (mongodb). We also need to provide the hostname or IP address we are going to connect to. In this case, the MongoDB server is in a Docker container on the same system where the application is running, although the localhost hostname can be adjusted as needed. Finally, we need to provide the port number. Port 27017 is the default port used by MongoDB, so there is nothing special here.

What we really need, though, is a collection to work with. Remember, we need a database and a collection. This is similar to a database and a table in a relational database. This takes care of getting to the collection in a single line, although we could easily have done this one line in multiple lines to make it clearer. Following is another way to get to the same result:

```
let client = Client::with_uri_str("mongodb://localhost:27017")?;
let db = client.database("customer_info");
let collection = client.collection("people");
```

This does the same thing but uses another line and another identifier to get a database struct. Using multiple lines for the collection definition is a way that is readable to those who may not be able to understand what they are looking at. You may notice that none of these functions return a `Result`, so there is no need to unwrap anything. We get the struct we need without having to add any unwraps in the middle. Once we have the collection, we can move on with adding data. Following are the two lines used to convert the data structure into a format expected by the MongoDB driver:

```
let data = bson::to_bson(&record).unwrap();
let document = data.as_document().unwrap();
```

First, MongoDB uses binary JSON. This is why we need to use the `bson` crate. We are going to call the function `to_bson()` out of that function, passing in a reference to the data structure. This function returns a `Result` that needs to be unwrapped, but the `bson` struct is stored in the identifier `data`. Converting to the binary JSON format is not everything, though. We need to create a BSON document in order to store it into MongoDB using this driver. This formats the raw BSON into a document that can be provided to the database. Once we have the BSON document, we can move onto storing it in the database. The two lines needed to store our document follow:

```
let insert_result = collection.insert_one(document.to_owned(), None)?;

let data_insert_id = insert_result
    .inserted_id
    .as_object_id()
    .expect("Retrieved _id should have been of type ObjectId");
println!("Inserted ID is {}", data_insert_id);
```

You'll see we are going to call the `insert_one()` trait on the `collection` struct. If we had more than one document to insert, we could call `insert_many()`, instead. While it's possible to do that, it was easier to demonstrate inserting data into the database a single document at a time, although you might argue that bouncing back and forth between getting an individual record and writing it out is inefficient. The one tricky part of the first line, where we insert the document, is the `to_owned()`

piece. Remember that every piece of memory is owned by one single entity. We need to convert the `document` identifier to one that is owned. If you leave that call out, you will get an error about trying to make use of a reference.

The second parameter in this call is the write concern. This is a way of letting the MongoDB server know that you need some special acknowledgment from the server on the write operation. We aren't looking for anything special here, so we are going to pass in `None`, indicating we don't need any additional write acknowledgment. You might use this value if you were working with a clustered server to make sure you knew the write operation had succeeded across all of the shards in the cluster.

While we have created a BSON document from a data structure, you can also create the document using a macro. Following is the code to create a BSON document using that macro. This takes the JSON structure we've been using and converts it into the binary JSON needed to put into MongoDB. We can take the `doc` identifier here and provide that to the `insert_one()` function:

```
let doc = doc! { "name": "Anna Kendrick", "age": "35", "occupation":
"singer/actor",
"location": "USA", "phone": "8768890011" };
```

Once the record is inserted, it's assigned an object identifier. We can retrieve the object identifier using `insert_result`. We want the `inserted_id` back from the result, and that identifier should be returned as an object identifier, so we call `as_object_id()`. Finally, you will see `.expect()` on the end. What this says is, if there is an error, print the message provided as a parameter. Once we have the object identifier back, we print it out. This demonstrates that the insertion was successful. It also provides the one piece of information in the record that wasn't provided from the file. Figure 9.4 shows the result of populating the collection with all of the data from the file of JSON records.

As the function is providing a `Result` and we've gotten to the end of the function without any errors, we need to provide an `Ok()` to indicate the success of the function. We aren't providing any value back to the calling function, so we send back an empty set, meaning there is no value—just the `Result` with nothing in it.

Finally, from the perspective of this program, there is the `main` function, which follows here. It's a simple function, with a constant value providing the filename that contains the JSON values. We also call the function that reads the records from that filename. This does all the work of the program, including, as we've seen, calling the function that inserts the data into the database:

```
fn main() {

    const FILENAME: &str = "people.json";

    read_records(FILENAME);

}
```

Retrieving Values

Once we have a populated collection in the database, we need a way to get it back out. We can reuse some of the same code as in the last program we looked at. We still need to connect to the database. We still need to work with a collection because that's where the data is stored. The process of retrieving information from the collection, though, is to create a BSON document that contains a parameter

```
    _id: ObjectId("5f5835bb00372ab20093ea82")
    name: "Steven Wilson"
    age: 53
    occupation: "Producer/Musician"
    location: "UK"
    phone: "01188937300"


    _id: ObjectId("5f5835bb009a8cd90093ea83")
    name: "Emma Stone"
    age: 32
    occupation: "Actor"
    location: "USA"
    phone: "8189900234"


    _id: ObjectId("5f5835bb00cff2de0093ea84")
    name: "Joe Schmo"
    age: 58
    occupation: "Plumber"
    location: "USA"
    phone: "7158892340"


    _id: ObjectId("5f5835bb00d798080093ea81")
    name: "Steve Hogarth"
    age: 61
    occupation: "Musician"
    location: "UK"
    phone: "0114455891"
```

FIGURE 9.4: Records in MongoDB

that we are looking for. Basically, we create a partial JSON record and send it to the database in order to get any record that matches back out. Following is the entire program. It starts with a slightly different way to indicate the crates we are going to make use of. This is a nested approach to the crates. Both bson and sync are components of the mongodb crate, so we can indicate all of them together rather than having to do them individually on separate lines. Without this approach, you would use something like use mongodb::bson::doc, for instance:

```
use mongodb::{
    bson::{doc, Bson},
    sync::Client,
};
use std::io;


fn main() -> mongodb::error::Result<()> {
    let client = Client::with_uri_str("mongodb://localhost:27017")?;
    let collection = client.database("customer_info").collection("people");
```

```
        println!("What person would you like to look up? ");
        let mut input = String::new();
        match io::stdin().read_line(&mut input) {
            Ok(_n) => {
                input = input.trim().to_string();
            },
            Err(error) => println!("error: {}", error)
        }

        let results = collection.find(doc! { "name": input }, None)?;
        for result in results {
            match result {
                Ok(document) => {
                    if let Some(location) = document.get("location").and_
then(Bson::as_str) {
                        println!("location: {}", location);
                    } else {
                        println!("no location listed");
                    }
                }
                Err(e) => return Err(e.into()),
                }
            }

        Ok(())
}
```

The first part of the `main()` function should look familiar and straightforward. It is the way we connected to the database and collection in the previous program. There is no particular reason for creating the connection to the database before we have anything to look up, other than if we can't get a connection to the database, there is no reason to ask the user for any information they may want to look up. It would be frustrating from a user experience perspective to be asked a question, provide an answer, and then be told, "Sorry, the database is unavailable, so we can't fulfill your request." Sometimes you need to think about what the user experience is going to be as you are developing your programs. As before, we have set up the `main()` function to be able to return errors, which means we can use the `?` notation at the end of function calls that provide a `Result`.

The next block of code is also similar to something we have seen in a previous chapter. We are going to provide a prompt to the user to let them know what we are looking for and then accept input. Since we are getting a `Result` back, we need to make sure we don't get an error, so this time we're going to use a `match` statement to look for the `Ok()` and the `Err()`. There is no value that comes back inside the `Ok()`, though. This is because we sent a `String` identifier into the `read_line()` trait and sent it in as mutable so it could be changed. Rather than returning the `String` value inside the `Ok()`, this particular trait just changes the `String` that gets passed into the trait. However, if we do get an `Ok()`, the function was successful, and there would be a changed value in the identifier. The problem we have, though, is there is going to be a newline character at the end of the line that is read in. We need to remove that; so if we get an `Ok()`, we call `trim()` on the `String` value to remove that newline.

Once we have the value from the user in a clean state, we can move on to construct the BSON document. We are going to do that using the `doc!()` macro, as discussed previously. What we looked at before was constructing a document from plaintext values known at the time the program was written. This time around, we are going to construct a BSON document from programmatic content, meaning we are going to construct the BSON document using a value that was not known when the program was written. The following line is how we create the document that has to be passed into the database as well as how we pass that document into the database:

```
let results = collection.find(doc! { "name": input }, None)?;
```

As usual, you can break this into multiple lines. You can use the `doc!()` macro on one line and create an identifier to store the BSON document. There's no particular reason to write another line of code since we aren't going to do anything with the identifier other than pass it into the `collection` `.find()` trait. May as well just skip the middleman and pass the document directly into the `find()` trait. When we create the document, you will see that we use a string value, `"name"`, to indicate the property we are looking for. The value that is associated with that property is contained in the `input` identifier. What we will end up with is a BSON document that contains JSON that looks like this:

```
"name" : "input_value" }
```

In place of `input_value` will be the value provided by the user. When we perform the `find` operation, we get a set of results. Depending on what we are looking for, there could be many records that come back from this query. Essentially, we could have a vector of records, which means we need an iterator to run through them along with a `for` loop to get each individual record out. What we get back from the `find()` trait is a data structure called a `Cursor`. The cursor is a common database concept. It's a pointer to the current location in the database. You move the cursor around the database, and you move to different records. In this case, what we have is a pointer to a vector of records. It's the same thing as an iterator because we can use the cursor value to move from one record to the next in the set of values we retrieved from the database.

When we get a result, it's actually a `Result`, which means we need to make sure we got a value back, stored inside the `Ok()` enumeration. Assuming we didn't get an error and we have a value, we can take a look at the document that came back. We sent a document into the database with a partial set of data. The database will have sent back any records that match that partial set of data. Keep in mind, we have a document that is JSON-based. This means we have property/value combinations. We can query that document to get the values associated with different properties. This is the line where we do that query:

```
if let Some(location) = document.get("location").and_then(Bson::as_str)
```

Performing a `document.get()` returns an `Option` enumeration. We get either `Some` or `None`. If there is no value associated with the property being requested, we will get a `None` back. If there is a value, we will get `Some`, and the value will be kept inside the enumeration. Working on that line from left to right, we want to create an identifier called `location`, so we use the `let` keyword. However, we only have a value if what comes back is `Some`, so we need to indicate that. `Some(location)` indicates that there is a `Some`, and `location` is the identifier the value will be kept in if we did get a `Some` back.

Once we have the location value back, we need to take it out of the binary JSON format. We do this with `and_then`, which is a combinator. This is used to protect against chainable values where you might end up with `Option<Option<value>>`, for instance. Using `and_then` allows us to perform a trait chain and get a single value back rather than nested enumerations, which would require some unraveling. This unraveling can end up in long lines of unwraps, which can be confusing to figure out. Instead of that, we call `and_then` with the wrapped type and get an `Option` back. Essentially, this is a way of easily getting the value we want back through all of the wrapping in enumerations.

One last line we need to get through, and then we can call it quits on this short program. Error handling can be complicated. This is especially true when you get into specific error implementations. In other words, once you start creating data types that are errors specific to a crate or handling a data type, you need to be able to convert between them. Remember, Rust is not object-oriented. Object-oriented languages typically implement inheritance, which means you can take a class and make changes to it, creating a whole new class that implements some features of the original class but adds some additional features. With inheritance, you get parent and child classes. When you create a child class, you can still take on the traits or features of the parent class and move between one and the other.

Since we don't have inheritance the same way in Rust, we need to be able to move between one type and another type. When it comes to errors, all we need to do is use the trait into(). This takes one type of error and makes sure it is converted to another error type. Following is the way we return an error in the correct error type expected to be returned by the function. We call into() on the identifier e, which contains the error that may have resulted from checking the result from the list of results from the database:

```
Err(e) => return Err(e.into())
```

With that, we are at the bottom of the function, where we return an Ok(()). This just returns a success value back to the operating system, which called the program.

SUMMARY

Writing programs is a complex endeavor, and learning to write programs in any given language is not necessarily as straightforward as learning the syntax and going on your merry way. Each language has a different way of interacting with the world around it. Some impose a way of viewing data and any actions that interact with that data, like object-oriented languages. Some are just very straightforward and take a procedural approach to the world around them. We provide a set of instructions, and those instructions get followed one step at a time. There are a number of languages that fall into this category, like C, Pascal, FORTRAN, and others.

Some languages enable the ability to ensure that data falls within specific bounds. This keeps programs in a correct state. Not all languages offer that functionality. Rust provides it in the way of assertions, which is how some other languages provide the same functionality. This is not to say that assertions, in the form of the assert() function, are necessarily easy to follow clearly. You can get the behavior you want, but programming isn't entirely about getting the behavior you want. It's almost as much about readability and maintainability. You can make use of the contracts crate to implement design by contract. This may be more readable and straightforward to read and maintain than just plain assertions. It also makes it clear what is a pre-condition and what is a post-condition, which can be valuable.

Database programming is an essential task today because so many types of programs use one sort of database backend or another. Not everything today is a relational database. There are other kinds of data storage, commonly grouped together in a classification called NoSQL. These databases may include document-store databases like MongoDB. MongoDB uses binary-formatted JSON documents. Rather than databases, tables, columns, and rows, MongoDB takes documents, which may be collections of JSON objects. JSON is a good data format because it is self-describing. This means each value in a JSON document also has an attribute name to go with the value. You don't have to use a rigid data schema with JSON documents because there are no columns you have to adhere to, as would be the case in a relational database.

Storing data in MongoDB requires a database and then a collection in that database. Each collection is a collection of JSON documents. Storing data in a MongoDB collection means creating a binary JSON document (BSON) and inserting that into the database. You can also insert multiple documents at the same time if you want to do insertions in bulk.

When it comes to retrieving documents from the database, you create a new document with partial data filled in. You have a property/value in a JSON document where you indicate which property you are searching for and the value in that property. You pass that document into the database, indicating that the document should be used so the database could find the data requested. The database server then replies if it's able to find anything, with a collection of results. You will need to get an iterator through the results. When you are working with databases, these iterators are called cursors.

You don't have to put a lot of effort into getting yourself a database server. This means you don't have to get a whole new server or virtual machine. You can do application virtualization with containers. To develop the programs for this chapter, I installed an instance of a MongoDB server in a Docker container. I didn't have to go through a lot of effort in installing the server on my desktop. I installed Docker and then pulled the image down and ran it. No configuration was necessary to get it up and running. To work with the database, you can also grab a copy of MongoDB Compass, which is free from the MongoDB website.

EXERCISES

1. Modify the existing data storage program to accept input from the user for new records rather than reading data in from a file.

2. Modify the data retrieval program to print the entire record rather than simply a single value.

3. Modify the existing data storage program to take complete JSON-formatted input from the user to store a variable-length document rather than one bound by the data structure presented.

4. Modify the existing data storage program to add more attributes to the data structure, and then modify the data file to support the additional attributes.

ADDITIONAL RESOURCES

Design by Contract Introduction - `www.eiffel.com/values/design-by-contract/introduction/`

Design by Contract Part 1 - `www.leadingagile.com/2018/05/design-by-contract-part-one/`

What is a Document Database? - `www.mongodb.com/document-databases`

Fundamentals of Document Databases - `www.dataversity.net/fundamentals-of-document-databases/`

MongoDB Tutorial - `www.tutorialspoint.com/mongodb/index.htm`

10

Web Communications

IN THIS CHAPTER, YOU WILL LEARN THE FOLLOWING:

➤ How to use style guides to make code consistent

➤ How to communicate with web servers using client functions

➤ Extracting data from a web page

➤ Synchronous communication

To paraphrase Irwin M. Fletcher as Gordon Liddy, it's all web communications. While it seems like the web is shiny and new because it keeps evolving in what it is being used for, it's actually about three decades old now. To be clear, the web is an overlay on the Internet, which is more than fifty years old. When we say *web*, we mean the broad collection of servers that use Hypertext Transfer Protocol (HTTP) to communicate between server and client. Even HTTP is now becoming a foundation for another overlay of servers that provide more complex services than where web services started—primarily simple, static pages that mostly were a way to share research and documentation between scientists.

Today's web servers not only provide static content but also can be the foundation for mobile applications to communicate with, offering a richer set of features to users without over-consuming limited-capability devices. Additionally, web servers can be used as a way of offering programmatic functionality that anyone can make use of in the way that makes the most sense to them through exposing application programming interfaces (APIs) to both web pages as well as any other application that wants to consume the API.

All of this is to say that learning how to communicate with web servers is essential. Even if you are working primarily with developing native applications, meaning applications that run directly on a system using its processor, you may still want to communicate with a web server at some point. This may simply be a way of providing help services to a user. Many applications have moved from offering help files for documentation on the local system to just pulling documentation from a web server and displaying a web page within the application.

One reason for using Rust as a programming language is because of its safety, meaning it may be less prone to common vulnerabilities that lead to exploitation. This is not to say that there is no way for exploits to happen in Rust programs. Even in cases where vulnerabilities don't happen in Rust programs, there may be ways for a Rust program to pass a problem through to another system. There are ways to address this along with getting more readable programs. One way is to introduce the use of style guides, which can provide guidance around consistency in programming as well as a unified way to solve common problems that may be security-related.

In this chapter, we are going to develop a client program that can communicate with a web server, sending requests, getting responses, and parsing them. We will also take a look at the potential use of style guides to improve overall consistency in your programming efforts. This may be useful even if you are a solo programmer since you can adopt an existing style guide and make sure you are always adhering to that style guide so your programs are consistent, making them easier to follow even for you.

STYLE GUIDES

One problem with writing programs is walking away from a program for a period of time and then coming back to it later and trying to figure out what you were thinking when you wrote it. Yes, you can follow the code, but maybe it's not clear why you made the stylistic decisions that you made. There has long been a minor debate about whether the correct term is *computer science* when there is so much art to writing programs. In other words, since there isn't just one way to solve any particular problem (write a program that solves a problem), it's more of an art than a science.

As soon as you can start being expressive when you write programs, you potentially run into issues of understanding what a program is doing. This may be truer of languages other than Rust, but even with Rust, you need to be concerned with readability so programs can be maintained and bugs fixed after the initial write. One way of addressing this is to make use of something called a *style guide*. Some people will tell you that style guides are all about simple things like defining a preferred approach to writing. For instance, the following two fragments are identical in terms of getting the code compiled, but there may be a preference from a style perspective for one over the other:

```
fn func1() {
println!("This is a function!");
}
fn func1()
{
println!("This is a function!");
}
```

The difference is where the curly brace goes—at the end of the function definition line or on the next line all by itself. You may think this is inconsequential, but in reality, style guides are far more than stylistic differences like where you place your curly braces. There are a lot of reasons to use style guides. Here's an example, which helps make your program more understandable. You may have noticed through the course of the book that there is very little consistency to the naming of identifiers. As long as they have a name that is understandable, that is sufficient from my perspective. However, there are a lot of other ways to think about how you may name your identifiers.

First, think about the types of identifiers there are. You have local identifiers, meaning identifiers that belong to a function. Second, you have identifiers that belong to a data structure. Even there, you may have two types of identifiers: an identifier that is only ever accessed or manipulated through a trait, meaning it is never used directly by any function, and also an identifier that is used directly and may not have any trait used to access or manipulate it. You may want to create different naming conventions for those two types of identifiers that belong to structs. As you can see, there may be a lot of different ways of thinking about identifier names, and following a consistent format for that will help in clearly calling out the type of identifier being used.

Speaking of types of identifiers, Microsoft used to follow a specific way of naming variables in its code. This was before style guides as they are today became popular. The naming style was called *Hungarian notation*, so-called because the creator was Charles Simonyi, who had Hungarian heritage. A classic feature of Hungarian notation was that the data type is the first part of the variable name or, when we are talking about Rust, the identifier name. As an example, if we had a string that contained a name, the variable name would be `strName`. If you had a Boolean value indicating that something had been chosen, you might use the variable name `bChosen`.

> **NOTE** Unlike in most other European countries, Hungarian names are "reversed" in the sense that the surname or family name comes first and the given name or first name comes second. Charles Simonyi in Hungarian would have been Simonyi Károly. Similarly, in Hungarian notation, the given name comes second while the family name or data type is first.

You can see how this may make code easier to understand, because you don't have to go back to figure out what type a variable is in order to understand the context for how it's used. This, again, seems like more of how something looks than how it works, even if there is a lot of value in controlling how something looks. Style guides can also be used to declare choices in programming behaviors. A good repository for style guides in a number of programming languages comes from Google. This is not to say Google the search engine, but instead, Google the company (even if the company makes the search engine). The style guides are stored in GitHub, but Google maintains style guides for a number of languages it commonly uses, including C++, C#, Swift, Java, Python, JavaScript, and Common Lisp, among others. Taking a look at these different style guides, you can see some of the breadth of how you can use a style guide.

In the C++ style guide, Google says to only use inline functions in cases where the function is short—10 lines or less. This is a programming behavior rather than strictly how something looks on the page. Another example of something from the C++ style guide Google maintains for its programmers is avoiding virtual method calls in constructors. You can also define ways to handle functionality that may impact either security or user interaction. The C++ style guide specifically states that C++ exceptions will not be used. Figure 10.1 shows more details about this style guide rule.

∞**Exceptions**

We do not use C++ exceptions.

Pros:

- Exceptions allow higher levels of an application to decide how to handle "can't happen" failures in deeply nested functions, without the obscuring and error-prone bookkeeping of error codes.
- Exceptions are used by most other modern languages. Using them in C++ would make it more consistent with Python, Java, and the C++ that others are familiar with.
- Some third-party C++ libraries use exceptions, and turning them off internally makes it harder to integrate with those libraries.
- Exceptions are the only way for a constructor to fail. We can simulate this with a factory function or an `Init()` method, but these require heap allocation or a new "invalid" state, respectively.
- Exceptions are really handy in testing frameworks.

FIGURE 10.1: C++ exception style rule

This can be a way to protect the program from abuse. Exceptions can be a way for an attacker to find details about the program and how that program might be used. Details can leak out from an exception that can provide insight into how to break the program in such a way that the attacker can control the flow of the program. Beyond just the use of exceptions, which can be employed to gather information, is the use of structured exception handling, which allows a program to call a function as part of processing an exception. This feature can be misused easily, allowing the attacker to redirect the function that gets called when an exception happens.

Style guides can be used to not only define behavior but also to compare a program's implementation against. Once you have defined how programs should be written, you can compare that definition against how a program is actually written. You can think of it as auditing code against a standard. There are a number of tools that can be used to perform this comparison. Often, static code analysis tools will perform this comparison, although many of them perform the comparison against their own defined style guides. Think of the style guide as a set of coding rules. Once we have the rules, we can check for compliance with those rules. Using a style guide, you can almost automate some of the writing of your code. Some editors allow for snippets, which means you can have shortcuts for blocks of statements that you commonly use. If you know that a section of code has to look a certain way, you may be able to get your preferred editor to help with that. Both Visual Studio Code and Atom have snippets capabilities, and if you prefer other editors, those editors may support similar functionality. Anything that can make your life writing software easier and more consistent is a good thing.

We can certainly use style guides with Rust. In fact, there is a style guide already available for Rust, although it's not one of the Google style guides since Google apparently doesn't use Rust as one of its development languages. This may not be especially surprising, considering Google has a language that was developed by scientists at the company, including Ken Thompson, one of the people responsible for Unix and the C programming language (since he created the precursor language, B). Some of

If a block has an attribute, it should be on its own line:

```
fn block_as_stmt() {
    #[an_attribute]
    {
        #![an_inner_attribute]

        // a comment in a block
        the_value
    }
}
```

FIGURE 10.2: Rust style guide

the Rust development team have created a style guide, stored on GitHub, defining how to write Rust programs. In some cases, they are simple visual style considerations like the number of blank lines in between statements (zero or one). Other cases, as shown in Figure 10.2, suggest that any attributes belonging to a block of code should be on a line by themselves.

Much of the Rust style guide is about creating consistency in formatting the language. As mentioned before, this makes it easier to read and understand. It's been stated several times, but it's hard to overstate the value of writing readable and understandable code.

HYPERTEXT TRANSFER PROTOCOL

The Hypertext Transfer Protocol (HTTP) was developed as a way to communicate hypertext documents. Hypertext itself is a concept that goes back to the 1960s, taking the idea of *hyper* from the Greek for "over" or "above." Think about the idea of hyperspace or hypercubes, which aren't larger versions of space or cubes but, instead, space or cubes with more dimensions. The same is true of *hypertext*, which is a word coined by Ted Nelson in 1965. Take a text document and add some additional dimensions to it, and you have hypertext. Today, we are very used to hypertext documents, but in the 1960s, it was a revolutionary idea; and if you think about someone conceiving of a way to take a static document and be able to hop up and out of that document, it was an astounding way to look at the world.

In the late 1980s, the Internet was just taking its form out of a collection of semi-interconnected research and academic networks. This was in part because of the National Science Foundation (NSF), which created a high-speed network called the NSFNET based on 1.5 Mb per second data connections. This was significantly faster than the previous connection speeds, which may have been 56 Kb per second or even slower.

> **NOTE** This seems like a reasonable place to clear up a misconception. In 2000, Al Gore was running for president, and said he took the initiative in creating the Internet. This was misconstrued to suggesting Gore claimed to have invented the Internet, which was not the case. The reality was that Gore was a leading advocate and sponsor for legislation while he was in the US Senate that created the NSFNET, which became the initial backbone of what is today the Internet. It's unfortunate that someone who had such a strong voice in leading the charge to create these connections we rely on today has been turned into a punchline because of a deliberate misquote of his comments. Political allegiances aside, Gore had a major role in a lot of information technology initiatives in the US Senate in the 1980s and beyond.

Up to that point, these wide area networks were used for research purposes so researchers could collaborate and share information. All of this is to say that there was a need for more efficient ways of sharing information. In the late 1980s, a team at the European Organization for Nuclear Research (CERN, after the French) started the WorldWideWeb project, which resulted in the creation of the Hypertext Markup Language (HTML) as a way to create text-based pages that included links to other documents. This page-formatting language offered a way for documents to be viewed easily before doing something with them. This was unlike the File Transfer Protocol (FTP), which allowed for moving files around but required the transfer to happen before opening the file in a local application. HTML allowed for the possibility of it happening all at once in a single application.

When the researchers at CERN created the markup language, they also needed a server application to serve up these pages, as well as the application that would talk to the server. This resulted in the creation of HTTP so the client application could send requests to the server and get documents returned from the server. The early version of HTTP only allowed for a single request type, GET. Only later versions began adding in other request types.

Like any other protocol, there is a grammar that has to be followed because the server expects requests to be well-formatted in order to understand the requests and fulfill them unambiguously. There are different versions of HTTP at this point, and each of them has different requirements when it comes to requests. We're going to skip the early versions of HTTP and start with HTTP version 1.0. A simple request in that version of HTTP looks like this:

```
GET /page.html HTTP/1.0
```

This request is composed of three elements. The first element is the verb. This is the request type being made. We are making a GET request, which means we are requesting a document for retrieval. The second part of the request is the resource. In this context, the resource commonly refers to a page, which may include a relative path, meaning it's the path starting at the top of the directory tree the web server knows about. Finally, the last part of the request is the version of HTTP the request will be using. Different versions have different requirements. The reason for using version 1.0 is it's the simplest version to use when interacting with the server. The only elements of a request that are necessary are the ones indicated here. If you want to bump up to version 1.1, which is the version that was most widely used since the late 1990s, you need to add another line. Following is a request using version HTTP 1.1:

```
GET /page.html HTTP/1.1
Host: www.server.com
```

This doesn't change the request line, aside from the version number, but it does add an additional line. The reason is that in version 1.0, you could only serve up content for a single host on a single system. This is very inefficient, all things considered. I have a second domain or hostname I want to serve up content on, and I need a whole new server, which required a whole new piece of hardware in the 1990s because virtualization, especially application virtualization, wasn't anywhere near the thing it is today. It was possible to have multiple services serving up on separate IP addresses, but it was harder to do.

With HTTP 1.1, virtual servers became possible. All you needed to do was have multiple fully qualified domain names (FQDNs) point to one IP address and configure the web server to be able to point requests to a hostname at a directory where the content for that server was. Figure 10.3 shows what that might look like. Out in front is the web server. If a request comes into www.wubble.com, the web server knows where in the filesystem the content for that server is located. The web server will then find the right file on disk and send it back to the client, based on what resource was requested.

GET is not the only request you can perform now that we have moved on from version 1.0. The following table includes the verbs that are commonly used in HTTP, as well as what they are used for:

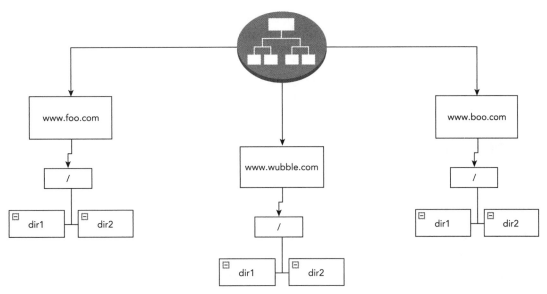

FIGURE 10.3: Web server directory tree

HTTP Verbs

VERB	FUNCTION
GET	Retrieve a file from the server.
POST	Send data from the client to the server.
HEAD	Retrieve data without getting the data, only the headers.
OPTIONS	Retrieve the options available on the remote server.
TRACE	Follow the path within the server when parameters are sent.

There are other methods or verbs that can be used, some of which require extensions to be enabled on the remote server. These are the ones that are most commonly used. GET and POST are the most common, and HEAD is good for testing to see if the resource being requested exists. If you use HEAD, you are only going to get a set of headers back. Servers respond to requests with information about the server and the data. Following are the headers that come back from the server at www.google.com when you request the main page at that server. This brings up a note about resource requests. You are always requesting a page. If you ask for a directory, as in the request for the top directory /, you are really requesting whatever is defined as the index page for that server. In many cases, that would be something like index.html. The request that generated this response was GET / HTTP/1.1:

```
HTTP/1.1 200 OK
Date: Sat, 19 Sep 2020 19:44:39 GMT
```

continues

(continued)

```
Expires: -1
Cache-Control: private, max-age=0
Content-Type: text/html; charset=ISO-8859-1
P3P: CP="This is not a P3P policy! See g.co/p3phelp for more info."
Server: gws
X-XSS-Protection: 0
X-Frame-Options: SAMEORIGIN
Set-Cookie: 1P_JAR=2020-09-19-19; expires=Mon, 19-Oct-2020 19:44:39 GMT; path=/;
domain=.google.com; Secure
Set-Cookie: NID=204=kPsqLWWAoe7Zz_aA6bYwU_K3RkzvgIelXf1qorRZQu8P7srC8RkdVoup8hUsbXT
ZZcF1DSq9yNLK19tkSHGJaIplVT-efnZlAXULHcJaA5t9y_EtCpukEEHckorybYimUo6f_
Ahcl229jDN17Cr0LNddGMN6cmi9OXmnNbXe2Hg; expires=Sun, 21-Mar-2021 19:44:39 GMT;
path=/; domain=.google.com; HttpOnly
Accept-Ranges: none
Vary: Accept-Encoding
Transfer-Encoding: chunked
```

HTTP servers respond with numeric status codes, much like FTP servers do. A common response would be 200, which means OK, indicating it was a successful request, and the server can respond with what was asked for. HTTP uses a series of numeric values, meaning values between defined ranges mean similar things. Anything between 100 and 199, for instance, is an informational response. Anything in the 200s would be a success. A 300 series response would indicate multiple choices. This might be a response indicating the requested resource has moved, for instance, whether temporarily or permanently. Along with the status code in the response shown previously, you can see the version of HTTP the server is responding with. The 400 and 500 series are error codes, and you may see these while testing. A 400-level error typically indicates some problem with the application, meaning in the code that is written by the application developer. A 500-level error is generally something to do with the server itself, which does not mean you can't get a 500 error from an application problem.

There are a lot of other headers in this response indicating how the client should handle the data coming back, including how the data has been encoded. The server also indicates whether data can be cached on the client or not. This is useful for keeping track of static versus dynamic content. If content is dynamic, that means it is potentially changing a lot, and there is no value in caching it locally because any cached data would be outdated if it were used. Caching helps with the speed of page rendering on the client side. One other piece of data that is useful in the headers is the server. This indicates the application that you are communicating with. This happens to be the Google web server (gws). Finally, the server provides the content type so the client knows how to render the content that is being returned. This is expressed as a Multipart Internet Mail Extension (MIME) type.

Programmatic Communication

The headers returned by the server shown previously were retrieved using a manual exchange with the server. This means I connected to the server using a piece of software called netcat and typed the request in by hand, which resulted in the set of headers from the server. There are other ways of doing this, of course. If you want the content, you can use a tool like wget or curl to retrieve just the content. Sometimes you want to get both, especially if you are doing this programmatically. Python is a scripting language that makes it easy to do things quickly, so we can take a look at how to issue a web request using Python. Following is a very simple script to make a request to `www.google.com` asking for the top index page. If the request results in a success code, 200, the script will print the headers:

```
#!/usr/bin/python3

import requests

r = requests.get("http://www.google.com/")
if r.status_code == 200:
    print(r.headers)
    print(r.text)
else:
    print("Unable to find the requested document")
    print(r.headers)
```

This does require the installation of the `requests` module. The program pip is the easiest way to install the package so Python knows where it is and can make use of it when requested. This is the package that will do all of the work for us. After importing requests, we create a variable that is going to carry the response from the GET request. To create the GET request, all we need to do is call the `get()` function from the `requests` library. We will have to provide the universal resource locator (URL), which consists of the protocol (`http`) followed by a delimiter (`://`), then the fully qualified domain name (FQDN), and the resource being requested. The universal resource identifier (URI), by the way, is the `protocol://` portion of the URL. In the case of this request, it would be `http://`.

Once we have the response, which is broken out into elements that can be addressed or requested, we can start doing something with it. First, we want to know whether the status code is a 200, meaning it was a successful request, so there will be a response. If that's the case, we will print out the headers we get back from the servers, followed by the text of the response, which may otherwise be referred to as the *body*. The headers here will be printed in JavaScript Object Notation (JSON) format. Since the headers are in JSON, we can retrieve elements of the headers individually. For example, if we wanted to know the MIME type of the document returned, we could use `print (r.headers['content-type'])` to get the program to print out the MIME type so we can see and maybe even retrieve the MIME type in order to do something about it. Different content types may require different handlers, for instance.

Another scripting language that can do the same thing in a similar way is Go, the programming language, sometimes called Golang, presumably to differentiate it from the game or another use of the word *Go*. Using Go, we can perform the same task in about the same number of lines of code. The following Go code will do essentially the same thing we did with the Python script earlier. Go is a little different, even though both Python and Go take some of their language design cues from the C programming language. Go is more of a direct descendant than Python is:

```
package main

import (
        "fmt"
        "io/ioutil"
        "net/http"
)

func main() {
        resp, err := http.Get("http://www.google.com/")
        if err == nil {
            body, err := ioutil.ReadAll(resp.Body)
```

continues

(continued)

```
                    if err == nil {
                        fmt.Printf("%s\n", body)
                    }
            }
    }
```

First, because it's a Go program, we need to define a package to include everything in. This is a standalone script, so we're going to say this is a package named `main`. Once we have created the package, we can import all the external libraries we need. First, we need `fmt` because we are going to print some of our content to the console, and that function is in this library. Second, we need `ioutil` to be able to extract the content from a response. Finally, the package that takes care of issuing the request and then managing the response is in `net/http`. Unlike in Python, we need to define a `main` function. Once there, we can get a pair of results from the call to `http.Get()`. The first return value is the response, including the headers and body, if there is one. The second is an error, in case the function call resulted in an error. You may notice we use `:=` to perform an assignment of value from the right-side value to the left-side value. This is a shorthand notation. Normally, we would indicate that we are declaring variables using the `var` keyword. Using `:=`, we can do the declaration and assignment in the same line without using the `var` keyword to indicate that we are declaring a variable.

Similar to the Python script, we use the `Get()` method from the `http` library. Just as with Python, we send in the URL we want to retrieve content from. Before we do anything, we need to check to see if we got an error. The line `if err == nil` is how we check to see if there was no error. If there was an error, the variable `err` would not be nil, meaning there is no value in the variable. Before we can print the body, we need to extract it from the data structure `resp`. We do this using `ioutil.ReadAll()`. Once we have the full text of the response body, we can use `fmt.Printf()` to print the value. This is similar to the approach to printing that the C language uses, meaning we use a `print` statement that includes a format string. We are printing a string value followed by a newline character. Once the format string has been provided, we can just send in the variable `body` that has the text contents of the page.

Now that we've seen Python and Go, we can take a look at Rust by comparison. The following code is how we could issue a request to a web server using Rust. In fairness, this is a more manual approach, and later on we will look at how to use crates to take care of much of the protocol and decipher work in Rust. However, unlike in Go, there is no built-in means to handle HTTP communication in Rust. We need to resort to pulling in external crates to handle the lower-level communications. Following is the code that will perform the request to the web server and print the results:

```rust
use std::io::prelude::*;
use std::net::TcpStream;
use std::str;


fn main() -> std::io::Result<()> {
    let mut stream = TcpStream::connect("www.google.com:80")
                        .expect("Unable to connect to the server");

    let request = String::from("GET / HTTP/1.1\r\nHost: www.google.com\r\n\r\n");

    let mut response: [u8; 4096] = [0; 4096];
```

```
        stream.write(request.as_bytes())?;
        stream.read(&mut response)?;

        println!("{}", str::from_utf8(&response).unwrap());

        Ok(())
    }
```

As we did before in a previous chapter when we were writing Transmission Control Protocol (TCP) client communications, we need to bring in some additional crates. The first is the `io::prelude` contents. This brings in a number of traits that are used across other traits, so we need to use this crate to have the definitions ahead of the implementations in other crates. Next, we need to bring in `TcpStream` from `std::net` to get the functionality to handle the network communication easily. Finally, we need to do some conversions of data types, so we need `std::str`.

The first thing we are going to do is to create a socket connection with a stream capability, meaning buffered input/output, wrapped around it. At the very bottom is a socket connection, but there are also some input/output capabilities that we need, or at least that will make life easier than doing raw sends and receives. This is a call we could use a `?` on to handle the error or unwrap the stream structure to pass back to the identifier named `stream`. This needs to be mutable since it is going to be changed as we interact with it. Instead of using `?` as the shorthand for automatically taking care of errors and unwraps, we are going to use the `expect()` trait, instead. This is going to handle the error condition if it happens.

We have a stream, so we need to create a communication. We are going to create a `String`, as you can see in the following line. This is going to create the complete request, so we don't have to send lines one at a time. It looks ugly, but we're going to take a look at what it really looks like in a moment. All the parts that may not be particularly clear are the control characters necessary to send a carriage return and line feed combinations or newline characters:

```
let request = String::from("GET / HTTP/1.1\r\nHost: www.google.com\r\n\r\n");
```

It may be easier to break this out into what it would look like to the server. The following block is what it would look like if you were to write it out without the special characters, having converted them to what they really are:

```
GET / HTTP/1.1
Host: www.google.com
```

There is a blank line in that block that is not a mistake. It is there deliberately to indicate that we are sending a blank line to the server to indicate that the request is complete and the server can respond. Once we have a request to send, we need to create a space to hold the response. We are going to have to convert the `String` we have into bytes because we can't send complex data structures. We have to break them down into bytes because, ultimately, what we need to send is a set of characters as single bytes with a numeric value that represents the ASCII (American Standard Code for Information Interchange) value of the printable character we want the other side to receive. Because we send bytes, it shouldn't be unexpected to recognize that we also receive bytes. Because of that, we need a buffer to store those bytes in. The following line creates that buffer. This is a buffer that is 4096 bytes long, so we are going to hope the response, including headers and body, isn't longer than 4 KB. If it is longer, whatever is left over will simply get lost because it hasn't been put into the buffer we have created to hold it:

```
let mut response: [u8; 4096] = [0; 4096];
```

The following two lines do the sending and receiving. You will notice here that we are handling the potential error conditions using the `?` shorthand. On the first line, we have to convert the `String` to a stream or array of bytes. This pulls the characters out of the complex structure that is a `String` and just sends the individual ASCII values in their numeric byte state. The second line reads whatever response comes back from the server and puts it into the byte array we created. As we are writing into it, we need to specify that the value is mutable. This is a case where the identifier or memory location being passed into the trait is going to take the resulting value rather than returning the resulting value out of the trait:

```
stream.write(request.as_bytes())?;
stream.read(&mut response)?;
```

Finally, we can print the value we have. This requires some conversion because we simply have a byte array with no indication that it is anything other than an array of numeric values where each numeric value happens to fit into 8 bits. Each value or location in the area is discrete and separate from every other location. We need to convert that to a string. This is separate from a `String`, which is a Rust data type that has attributes and traits. Instead, we are going to convert to something more like a character array—basically telling the `print()` statement that each byte value is actually a UTF-8 character. UTF is the Unicode Transformation Format, and a UTF-8 character indicates that we have a Unicode character that is only 8 bits wide. The Latin alphabet is one character set that fits into that 8 bits, which is what we are using. Following is the line that does the conversion and prints the result out in printable characters that we can understand:

```
println!("{}", str::from_utf8(&response).unwrap());
```

Finally, we need to return an `Ok(())` from the function because we have indicated that we are going to return a `Result()`. Running this program returns a result, as you can see in the following. This is only a portion of the response, since there is so much more to the complete HTML that was returned from the server. Even if it's only 4 KB, that's a lot of data. It would be roughly an entire page, and you'll get the gist of what the result looks like from the sample. This includes the complete set of headers as well as some of the HTML:

```
PS C:\Users\kilro\Documents> .\webreq.exe
HTTP/1.1 200 OK
Date: Sun, 20 Sep 2020 00:06:12 GMT
Expires: -1
Cache-Control: private, max-age=0
Content-Type: text/html; charset=ISO-8859-1
P3P: CP="This is not a P3P policy! See g.co/p3phelp for more info."
Server: gws
X-XSS-Protection: 0
X-Frame-Options: SAMEORIGIN
Set-Cookie: 1P_JAR=2020-09-20-00; expires=Tue, 20-Oct-2020 00:06:12 GMT; path=/;
domain=.google.com; Secure
Set-Cookie: NID=204=iB_7uGx1wJm7L4QfwYO71j-FrV9Sj2QLn3LAanT2wXRNnE32XhiVdCCOmatkVJ_
8I8F9QTswkye-nloLr69xNOh3mjqv6DXXERLtUdx_9dwQQ1BohzsLWlISIe9xhxaQf7nejWM9KpjENRwaaz
wA0nvFmqO5vy-zI81InJSUITg; expires=Mon, 22-Mar-2021 00:06:12 GMT; path=/; domain=.
google.com; HttpOnly
```

```
Accept-Ranges: none
Vary: Accept-Encoding
Transfer-Encoding: chunked

4b57
<!doctype html><html itemscope="" itemtype="http://schema.org/WebPage"
lang="en"><head><meta content="Search the world's information, including webpages,
images, videos and more. Google has many special features to help you find exactly
what you're looking for." name="description"><meta content="noodp"
name="robots"><meta content="text/html; charset=UTF-8" http-equiv="Content-
Type"><meta content="/images/branding/googleg/1x/googleg_standard_color_128dp.png"
itemprop="image">
```

What you may have noticed is that we are using unencrypted communication to the web server so far. This isn't terribly realistic. Web servers today generally prefer to communicate using Transport Layer Security (TLS). It's actually surprising that the Google server didn't do a redirect to an encrypted port and away from the cleartext communication stream. To be realistic, we need to do our communication over a TLS encrypted communication channel.

Web Communication Over TLS

We have the foundations of our programs at this point. It's not hard to make changes to the programs we have. Actually, some programs are even easier than you might think. Following is the Python program altered to use TLS instead of plaintext HTTP. You can flip back and forth to do the stare and compare if you like, but I can tell you there is only a one-letter difference between what we looked at before and what you are looking at here. The only difference is in the URL string. Instead of http:// for the URI, we change to https://, and that tells the underlying library to not only use TLS but also communicate over port 443 instead of port 80, since that's the default TLS port for HTTP communications:

```
#!/usr/bin/python3

import requests

r = requests.get("https://www.google.com/foo")
if r.status_code == 200:
    print(r.headers)
    print(r.text)
else:
    print("Unable to find the requested document")
    print(r.headers)
```

Now, let's take a look at the Go program, adjusted for TLS. Following is the corrected program. Again, the only change is a switch from http:// to https://. The underlying library takes care of the rest by setting up the TLS channel when it needs to and using the correct port by default since we didn't make any changes to the port. As a note, if you needed to change the port, you would do it in the URL string. You could move from port 443 using HTTPS to port 4433 by using the URL string www.google.com:4433/:

```
package main

import (
        "fmt"
```

continues

(continued)

```
            "io/ioutil"
            "net/http"
    )

    func main() {
            resp, err := http.Get("https://www.google.com/")
            if err == nil {
                    body, err := ioutil.ReadAll(resp.Body)
                    if err == nil {
                            fmt.Printf("%s\n", body)
                    }
            }
    }
```

We can now move on to the Rust implementation. Following is the rewritten implementation for Rust. You'll see differences in this implementation on top of just using a TLS library instead of the TcpStream crate by itself. Again, you can flip back to look at the earlier implementation, but I can save you a little bit of hassle. This is considerably different just to get the TLS management built into it. It starts with the statements at the top importing the necessary crates. First, we need the TlsConnector from native-tls (seen as native_tls here but native-tls in Cargo.toml). Then, we need to bring in Read and Write from the std::io crate because it has the definitions for those traits, which are needed to take care of the implementation in the TLS crate. Finally, we are going to still need TcpStream from std::net:

```
    use native_tls::TlsConnector;
    use std::io::{Read, Write};
    use std::net::TcpStream;

    fn main() -> std::io::Result<()> {
        let tlsconn = TlsConnector::new().unwrap();

        let stream = TcpStream::connect("www.google.com:443")
                            .expect("Unable to connect to the server");
        let mut tlsstream = tlsconn.connect("google.com", stream)
                            .expect("Can't create TLS connection");

        let request = String::from("GET / HTTP/1.1\r\nHost: www.google.com\r\n\r\n");

        let mut response = vec![];

        tlsstream.write_all(request.as_bytes())?;

        tlsstream.read_to_end(&mut response).unwrap();

        println!("{}", String::from_utf8_lossy(&response));

        Ok(())
    }
```

First, we need to create an identifier for the TLS connection. To do that, we need to call the new() trait on the TlsConnector structure. This gives us an instance of the TlsConnector structure stored in the identifier named tlsconn. Once we have that, we are going to create the TcpStream as we did earlier. This is going to be fed into the connect() trait of our TlsConnector struct instance. We need to call `connect()`, passing in the domain name of the request as well as the `TcpStream` instance. This then gives us a `TlsStream` instance. This is what we are going to be using to read and write with. Just as we did with the `TcpStream`, we are going to use the `expect()` trait to handle any potential error condition that may arise.

Using the `TlsStream` instance, `tlsstream`, we are calling the trait `write_all()` and passing the `String` in byte form using the `as_bytes()` trait. We then need to call `read_to_end()` on the `tlsstream` identifier. The function will read all the bytes until the stream comes to an end. This returns a value into an empty vector that got skipped over in the rush to start writing to our exciting TLS connection. A vector is different from an empty byte array, but it's what the `read_to_end()` trait takes as a parameter. The parameter is expected to be a vector of unsigned 8-bit integers. If you think about it, an unsigned 8-bit integer is just a byte. So, we have a vector of bytes that we are passing as a mutable value to our read function. The read returns the response from the server into that identifier.

Because we have a vector of unsigned 8-bit values, we will call a different converter function than we did previously. The `String` crate includes a trait called `from_utf8_lossy()`. This is what we need to use to convert the byte vector to a `String`. The `String` can then be printed because there is a default formatter for a `String` data type with the `print!()` macro.

The problem we have with this implementation—well, one of the problems—is that `read_to_end()` keeps reading until the input channel indicates there is an end. This is simple when it comes to reading a file, because there is an end-of-file indicator somewhere when the end of the file is reached. When it comes to reading to the end of a communication channel over the network, the only way we know there is an end is when the channel closes. HTTP connections may be left open, though, meaning the TCP socket is kept open rather than closing it, because the expectation is that the client will have other requests to make or maybe there is data to be sent from the server to the client. Rather than having to spend time reopening the connection, just leave it open. In the case of a server that has an application that is constantly sending updates to the client, the server can't open a connection to the client, so the only way the data can be sent is to keep that communication channel open so anything that has to go from server to client or vice versa can just go over the existing connection. This means it takes a long time to get to the end. If we use `read_to_end()`, it may take a long time before we ever get the end of the communication, closing the read.

Using `read()` on the `TlsStream` doesn't work either, because it's just going to check to see if there is any data in the stream, and if there isn't, the read isn't going to return any data. We have to use `read_to_end()` to get everything, but we have timing issues. This is why it's better to use an HTTP-specific library rather than trying to handle HTTP communications using lower-level TCP connection mechanisms.

CLIENT COMMUNICATION

We're going to take a look at how to use HTTP libraries to handle that communication. More specifically, we need to be able to use TLS-enabled HTTP libraries, because if we want to communicate with web servers today, we need to support encryption to that web server. This is fairly simplistic, though, so we want to be able to support additional functions. As mentioned earlier, there are a couple of utility programs that can be used to interact with web servers on the command line. This is useful if you want to be able to download files from a web server and store those files on disk. If it's an HTML file, you may not care so much about storing the file; but if it's something like a PDF or some sort of compressed file, you may want to store it without having to use a browser and go through the save to file process. We may also want just the text of a web page without all of the HTML tags in the file.

We are going to write a program that uses an HTTP crate to manage the request and the response without needing to do any of the TCP socket or even TLS work. We will also add the capability to write the remote file to a local file. Additionally, we need to add the capability to print the contents of the remote file out to the screen without the HTML tags, and we will do a little string replacing to try to clean up the output after removing the HTML tags. Once you've removed HTML tags, you may end up with a lot of blank lines. Following is the complete program. As always, we will break it down a little at a time:

```
use hyper::{Client, body::HttpBody as _};
use hyper_tls::HttpsConnector;
use tokio::io::{AsyncWriteExt as _};
use tokio::fs::File;
use std::env;
use voca_rs::*;

async fn write_to_file(data: &String) -> Result<(), Box<dyn std::error::Error>> {
    let mut output_file = File::create("resp-output.txt").await?;
    output_file.write_all(data.as_bytes()).await?;

    Ok(())
}

fn print_to_screen(data: &String) {
    let stripped = strip::strip_tags(data);
    let clean = stripped.replace("\n\n", "");
    println!("{}", clean);
}

#[tokio::main]
async fn main() -> Result<(), Box<dyn std::error::Error>> {
    let https = HttpsConnector::new();
    let client = Client::builder().build::<_, hyper::Body>(https);
    let mut hostname = String::new();
    let mut write_file = false;
    let mut print_file = false;
    let mut body = String::new();

    let args: Vec<String> = env::args().collect();
    for position in 1..(args.len()) {
        if position == args.len()-1 {
            hostname = String::from(&args[position]);
        }
        match args[position].as_str() {
            "-w" => write_file = true,
            "-p" => print_file = true,
            _ => ()
        }
    }
```

```
    let mut res = client.get(hostname.parse()?).await?;
    println!("Headers:\n{:#?}", res.headers());

    while let Some(chunk) = res.body_mut().data().await {
        let chunk = chunk?;
        body.push_str(&(String::from_utf8_lossy(&chunk)));
    }

    if write_file {
        write_to_file(&body).await?;
    }
    if print_file {
        print_to_screen(&body);
    }

    Ok(())
}
```

Before we get into breaking down the import statements, we need to include the following in the Cargo.toml file. Because tokio is a collection of different crates, we need to specify which elements of that broader package we want to include. We do this by using the features parameter, indicating which crates within the tokio project we want to use. If you don't indicate specifically what you want to include, you can bring in the broader namespace, but you will have to refer to the individual elements specifically. As an example, previously you saw File::create() being referred to. This is clarifying which namespace to pull create() from. You'd have to do the same thing if you didn't pull in specific namespaces out of tokio:

```
[dependencies]
"hyper" = "*"
tokio = { version = "*", features = ["macros", "tcp", "fs"] }
"hyper-tls" = "*"
"voca_rs" = "*"
```

This brings us to the block at the top of the source code, where we bring in additional functionality. This has been discussed in previous chapters, of course, but there is a new wrinkle here that highlights a little how this works. You may remember that when you are writing a C program, there is a directive telling the preprocessor to include another file. This brings in the contents of that file, so all the appropriate declarations are in a place where they are needed. In Rust, use is a little different because it's not just about bringing in a bunch of declarations so they are known when the source code you have written comes to them. There are namespaces that get brought in unless you make it clear you don't care about the namespace.

A namespace is a way of referring to an entity in a way that includes the container the entity resides in. Each crate you use external to your program has a namespace of the crate. All of the structures, traits, and functions that exist within that crate are members of the namespace the crate defines. We have seen this in many places over the course of several chapters. As an example, previously we used String::from_utf8_lossy(), which is a trait within the String namespace, and the namespace is clearly identified. We didn't just call from_utf8_lossy(); we included the namespace the trait belongs to.

In some cases, you may have a set of traits that belong to a specific namespace, but because of the way the namespace and crate were created, they may overlap with other traits or structures. This may be true in the case of I/O-based functionality, because there are crates and namespaces that are defined in an abstract way in a crate whose whole reason for existing is just to create the definitions. All of the implementations are left for other developers. You can think of this as defining the interface to a set of functions, and any developer who wants to use the same set of functions has to use the same interface, or else it's confusing to programmers trying to use good external functionality without having to re-create it themselves.

Now, hopefully, we've set the stage for a conversation about conflicts. If you are bringing in a lot of external functionality, at some point you may run into conflicts with symbols, meaning the way something is named. This was true in the course of writing the program we are discussing here. We'll get into where this happened later on, but there was a point where there was a name conflict between two crates being used in the program. This resulted in simply finding another way to do it rather than correcting the namespaces. One way to fix the problem of namespace overlap is to import the traits without importing the namespace symbol, meaning you aren't bringing in the name of the bucket the trait sits in; you are just bringing in the trait. You do that using the technique seen in the first line of the source code:

```
use hyper::{Client, body::HttpBody as _};
```

When we write `as _`, what we are saying is the same thing we have said in the past when using the underscore, although it may not have always been clear. The underscore says this doesn't matter. When you compile a Rust program where you store a value in an identifier but then don't use the identifier, the compiler says to start the identifier with `_` to indicate that this doesn't really matter, although that's not specifically what the compiler says. There are a lot of places when we are writing programs that we do things simply because we have to but not because we care about the result, meaning we are looking for the side effect, and the result may be irrelevant. When we import functionality saying `as _`, it means the symbol or namespace name doesn't matter here. Just bring in the traits so they can be used, because we may have a conflict with symbol names.

As far as the other crates being used, most of them are related to functionality necessary to be able to handle HTTP requests without having to create that functionality ourselves, since HTTP is not a simple protocol from an implementation standpoint. It would be a lot of work, and since someone else has done it and that implementation has been tested and used by a lot of other people, it's likely more reliable and certainly more battle-tested than anything we could do. What you will see later on is that the functionality we have brought in introduces asynchronous communication. This is why we had to use `tokio`'s file capabilities—because once you start down the asynchronous communication path, everything has to be asynchronous to make sure you get safety in process execution.

Jumping Ahead

We're going to skip ahead in the program and move to the `main` function, because it will help make the two smaller functions more understandable. Compared to other `main` functions we have written in the past, this one is long, but in some ways, it was easier to keep all of this functionality together and only call out to other functions when we wanted to do something with the data we were gathering. What you will see is that a good chunk of this `main` function is defining identifiers that need to be used to help with the execution flow of the program. Following is the `main` function in its entirety so you don't have to go back to refer to it:

```rust
#[tokio::main]
async fn main() -> Result<(), Box<dyn std::error::Error>> {
    let https = HttpsConnector::new();
    let client = Client::builder().build::<_, hyper::Body>(https);
    let mut desturl = String::new();
    let mut write_file = false;
    let mut print_file = false;
    let mut body = String::new();

    let args: Vec<String> = env::args().collect();
    for position in 1..(args.len()) {
        if position == args.len()-1 {
            desturl = String::from(&args[position]);
        }
        match args[position].as_str() {
            "-w" => write_file = true,
            "-p" => print_file = true,
            _ => ()
        }
    }

    let mut res = client.get(desturl.parse()?).await?;
    println!("Headers:\n{:#?}", res.headers());

    while let Some(chunk) = res.body_mut().data().await {
        let chunk = chunk?;
        body.push_str(&(String::from_utf8_lossy(&chunk)));
    }

    if write_file {
        write_to_file(&body).await?;
    }
    if print_file {
        print_to_screen(&body);
    }

    Ok(())
}
```

The first thing you will see is an attribute, `#[tokio::main]`. This is from the `tokio` crate, and it tells the compiler that the `main` function needs to be fixed. We are going to go write the `main` function the way we would normally run the `main` function. When the compiler runs, though, `tokio` is going to replace what we have written, or rather it's going to put what we have written into another function and put in its own `main` function that creates a multithreaded approach, starting up the different threads that are necessary to maintain the asynchronous nature of the communications that are happening. Each time a trait gets called that could be asynchronous, it needs to be in a separate thread, and `tokio` manages all of that for us.

The main function is also going to return some values. As usual, we need to mostly be concerned with the errors that are going to be returned from some of the functions we will be using. The only result we will be returning that isn't an error is an empty Ok() indicating that the program completed successfully. Because we are going to be returning several potential errors of different types, we need to return a generic error. We do this by creating a box around the error and returning an error::Error rather than the specific errors that might have resulted from the individual traits that are used in this function. You will also note the main function has an extra notation indicating that it's asynchronous. This goes back to what tokio is doing for us. We will be engaged in an asynchronous way with a remote server, so the main function needs to know that it can't just exit until all the threads are complete.

To start, we need to create an HttpsConnector. We have assigned the identifier https to the instance of the HttpsConnector structure. Next, we are going to create an instance of a Client module. We will do this using a Builder struct from the Client module to get the Client instance. The specific trait we will use from the Builder struct is build(). We need to provide some additional details in order to get the correct Client back. We need to indicate a connector, which we don't care about because the connector indicates the destination. Because the destination will be taken care of later, we provide a _ as a way of providing a value that is irrelevant or not necessary. We also need to indicate the payload.

To make sure we get the right client, we are going to specify the instance of the Client by specifying the types we are using so we get the right instance back. As mentioned, the first type doesn't matter. The second type is going to be hyper::Body. Finally, in the builder, we need to pass the HttpsConnector instance, https, that was created in the previous line. With all of that, we have created an instance of Client in the identifier client.

The next lines create identifiers we will need. These have to be initialized ahead of putting anything we care about into them. Basically, we need to allocate space to store data. We do this in the case of String by using the new() trait. This allocates some space for a String without putting anything into that space yet. We are doing this twice—once for the hostname that we will get from the command line, and the second time for the body of the response. The other set of identifiers we need are Boolean values that will be set based on command-line switches that will get passed into the program. These will get initialized with a false value initially because we aren't going to assume the function the user wants to execute. A command-line switch passed to the program will change that value once we know what has been requested.

To determine what the user wants to do, as well as identify the URL being requested, we need to collect the command-line parameters from the environment that are passed into the program. We do this using the line that follows. This collection of parameters is going to be put into a vector of String values:

```
let args: Vec<String> = env::args().collect();
```

We now have a vector that we need to iterate through. One problem with the vector we get of the command-line parameters is that the very first parameter is the program that is being run. The other problem is that the vector is indexed starting at 0. We could use an iterator to select each argument, one at a time. However, at some point, we need to know the index in the vector because the last parameter is going to be the URL we expect to go to. This means we need to know when we have hit that parameter. We can use a `for` loop with a range of values where we start at 1, because we are skipping the name of the program. The last of the range is the length of the vector:

```
for position in 1..(args.len()) {
    if position == args.len()-1 {
        desturl = String::from(&args[position]);
    }
    match args[position].as_str() {
        "-w" => write_file = true,
        "-p" => print_file = true,
        _ => ()
    }
}
```

Inside the loop, we check to see whether the position is the last position in the vector. Since we start at 0, the last position is going to be one less than the length of the vector. If we have five parameters, for instance, the last parameter would be position 4 because 0 is the first, 1 is the second, and so forth. We take the `String` at that position and place it into the identifier `desturl`. If we aren't at the last position, we need to see what we have for switches. We can do this using a `match` statement. We do have to do a conversion first, though. Each argument is going to be a `String`, but the `match` statement expects a `str`, instead. We use the `as_str()` trait to get a `str` back. If we get a `-w`, we set the identifier `write_file` to true. If we get a `-p`, we set the identifier `print_file` to true. If we get anything else, including the destination URL, which is the last parameter, we do nothing in the `match` statement.

Now we have set the destination URL and also set Boolean values to indicate what has been requested from the user. We can move on to issuing the request. We have the `client` identifier, which is an instance of `Client`. We are going to issue a GET request using the `get()` trait. We need to pass in a value of `Http::Uri`, but we have a string. We can use the `parse()` trait in the `String` struct to get the correct data type back. Since the `parse()` trait returns a `Result`, we need to unwrap or handle the error. Since we don't particularly care about errors in the sense of the type of the error, we can just use the `?` to automatically handle errors and unwrap the value from the `Result`. This is an asynchronous request; we are using `await` to indicate that we will wait for the result, rather than needing to provide a callback to another function to take care of the return from this call. Again, we have the case where we may need to handle an error or unwrap a value, so we are using the `?` to take care of both of those possibilities. Once we get the result back, we print out the headers just to see what the result was before doing anything else:

```
let mut res = client.get(desturl.parse()?).await?;
println!("Headers:\n{:#?}", res.headers());
```

At this point, we have issued the request and received the response. We need to do something with the response other than print out the headers. Ultimately, we need the body of the response. HTTP messages are, or at least can be, communicated in chunks. The reason for this is because TCP messages have a maximum size, and the HTTP response may be larger than that maximum size. The operating system can only aggregate a single message before passing it up to the application. If there are multiple messages, meaning TCP segments, that constitute the complete HTTP body, it's up to the application to take care of putting them all back together. We are going to need to read through all of the chunks that came back in the HTTP response. Following is the code that does that:

```
while let Some(chunk) = res.body_mut().data().await {
    let chunk = chunk?;
    body.push_str(&(String::from_utf8_lossy(&chunk)));
}
```

Again, we are dealing with an asynchronous message, in part because of what was mentioned earlier—each chunk of the body may come in at a different time. We have to handle them as they arrive. Again, we are going to await the result. We may get data back, or we may not get data back. This means an `Option`, so if there is data, it will be encapsulated in `Some()`. If there isn't, it will be in `None()`. To get the data, we call `body_mut()` to get a mutable reference to the body; and on that, we call `data()` to get the data out of the body. If there is data, we check to make sure we get a `Some()` back and then place the data into the identifier `chunk`. We still need to pull the value out of the `Some()` enumerator, so we have to either unwrap it or handle any potential error; we use `?` and place the result back into the identifier `chunk`.

We may have multiple chunks, but we want a single `String` value that we can do something with, depending on what the user has requested. This means we need to take the `str` we got in `chunk` and push it onto the empty string we initialized at the beginning of the program. There are two ways to do this. The first is to use `from_utf8()` from `String`. The problem with this, as discovered in writing the program, is that you'll get a UTF-8 error in the last chunk having to do with the size of the chunk. The way to fix that is to use `String::from_utf8_lossy()` instead. This takes a UTF-8 value, meaning a collection of bytes, and returns a `String` that can be pushed onto the `String` value. What we end up with after we have pushed on all the individual chunks is a single `String` value.

The last two clauses in this function are where we check to see what the user wanted to do. Following are the last two clauses so we can take a closer look at them. The first of these clauses is where we check to see whether we are going to write the chunks out to a file. This is another case where we are doing an asynchronous action, so we need to treat it that way. We are going to `await` a response. We'll get into what that means a little more when we look at the function itself:

```
if write_file {
    write_to_file(&body).await?;
}
if print_file {
    print_to_screen(&body);
}
```

You may notice that we are passing in a reference to `body`. The reason for doing this is that there is nothing to prevent us from both writing the contents out to a file as well as printing the contents to the screen or console. We can't reuse the `body` identifier if we don't pass it into `write_file()` as a reference. Without passing it as a reference, it will become owned by that function. As soon as the function returns, the identifier will be lost. Remember the idea of ownership and how all of those rules work. Once we pass an identifier into a function, the called function owns the memory the identifier points to. The way around that is to pass the identifier as a reference, meaning we are passing the value rather than the address of the memory location.

The last clause in this function is another `if` statement. In this case, we are just going to do a `print` statement, so there is nothing asynchronous about that. We don't need to use the `await` trait or call the function in any particular way. We can just perform a straight call on the function.

Jumping Back

We can jump back to the two functions we just got set up to call. These are reasonably easy to talk about since there isn't much going on in them. One of the considerations is that the `tokio` crate takes over I/O functions for the program. This means everything we are doing from an I/O perspective, like reading and writing to files or network communication streams, gets managed by `tokio`. File access is now a `tokio` thing and not just a plain old file write as we've done in the past. Before we go too much further, the last two functions follow so you can see them without having to bounce back to find the full program:

```
async fn write_to_file(data: &String) -> Result<(), Box<dyn std::error::Error>> {
    let mut output_file = File::create("resp-output.txt").await?;
    output_file.write_all(data.as_bytes()).await?;

    Ok(())
}

fn print_to_screen(data: &String) {
    let stripped = strip::strip_tags(data);
    let clean = stripped.replace("\n\n", "");
    println!("{}", clean);
}
```

Again, as we did with the `main` function, we have marked the `write_to_file()` function as `async`. What this means is, not only is it asynchronous, which is easy enough to determine on its face, but in order to be asynchronous, it has to implement some traits that are based on an abstract crate that is part of Rust called `Futures`. `Futures` are basically definitions that have to be implemented for any crate that wants to do asynchronous programming. Of course, `tokio` is one of those crates. One problem with asynchronous programming is that you need to be able to continue processing as best you can while some other process is outperforming some computation or task.

When it comes to `Futures`, you have what are essentially placeholders. When we perform a task, that task may go off and do some work, but we still need to have a way to go forward, because we are asynchronous. In asynchronous programming, you might do something called *polling*. This means we keep going back and checking on the process that got sent off to do some work. Once it's complete, we get whatever the result of the task was. In the meantime, we need a placeholder until we get the final result. This is what `Futures` are about. They're a way to start up a task while still having a way to move forward with tasks that need to happen that may not rely on that result.

Speaking of results, we are doing I/O, which often has the potential to generate errors. This may be especially true with I/O with files or communication streams. Once we've left the context of our process space and start trying to interact with the world at large, or at least the world inside of our computer in, say, the disk, we have the chance for bad things to happen. All of this is to say we might generate an error. While we could say we are going to return a file-based error, we're just going to use Box to wrap up a generic error and return that error. Because we are potentially returning an error, we need to also be able to return an Ok() for a successful result. The return from this function will look exactly like the return from the main function.

The first thing we need to do is create a file. We are going to assume a file doesn't exist, so we will use File::create(). This trait opens the file in write-only mode. If the file doesn't exist, create() will create it. If the file does exist, create() will essentially create it anyway. It would be the same result if we deleted the existing file and then created a new file. Anything in the existing file will no longer exist once we're done. One thing you could do if you wanted to add to an existing file would be to use OpenOptions. This would look like the following line of code:

```
let mut file = OpenOptions::new().append(true).open("resp-output.txt").await?;
```

The problem with this approach is it won't create a file that doesn't exist. If the file doesn't exist, you need to use create(). Other options in OpenOptions are read() and write(). If you need to do something like append to a file, you need to use OpenOptions. The append() trait opens the file in write mode since you can't append if you can't write.

Once we have the file open, we can write to it. In this case, we are going to use write_all() to write the entire string out to the file. Again, this is an I/O function, and tokio is taking care of all I/O for us, so we are performing an asynchronous action. This is why, again, you will see await? on the end of each of the file-based calls in this function. Files have to be written as bytes because we are storing the characters from the string and not the entire String structure, which wouldn't make a lot of sense in a text file. The complete structure is really only meaningful for a Rust program. To write the bytes from the String out, we have to use the as_bytes() trait.

The final function is very straightforward. It's really just a println!() call, passing the String that contains all of the chunks we read from the remote server. There is nothing else that needs to happen in this function. We could have done this in the if statement from the main function, but this gives us the flexibility to perform other tasks as needed. It never hurts to create a function for a task since the compiler will optimize back and not do a pair of jumps or calls just because we happened to write it that way in the higher-level source code.

You now have a program that will send requests to a remote server and take the response back, printing it out to the console or writing it out to a file.

SUMMARY

Web servers are how a lot of business happens today. Even if you have a mobile application, it may be communicating with a web server to perform tasks like authentication or maybe data storage. This makes the ability to communicate with a web server an important arrow to have in your quiver. To communicate with web servers, we use the Hypertext Transfer Protocol (HTTP). This is a text-based protocol that uses a verb resource version grammar to issue requests. You tell the server what you want to do (GET, POST, etc.) then the resource you want to interact with (/, /wubble.html, etc.). Finally, you tell the server the version of HTTP you are using, since the version will indicate what else you need to supply.

HTTP is how we interact with the server to issue requests and get responses. The responses will be a combination of a numeric status code indicating how the server feels about the request and a short text message providing more details about the status code. There is a lot of other information that the server will send back in response to the request. This information comes in the form of headers, and the headers will give some additional context to the response, including how it may be encoded as well as the server application that was used to respond.

HTTP is also how data is transmitted. The headers provide status information and other details the client may use to interpret the response. The body is the data the client should be using. This might be an HTML file that would need to be rendered, typically, by the client. The client would commonly be a web browser, but not always. In our case, we wrote an application that interacted with the server, sending HTTP requests and receiving responses. We did this using HTTP over TLS, which is HTTPS, or HTTP Secure.

Rust has a number of crates that will handle HTTP requests and responses for you. In our case, we used `tokio`, which is really a framework for communication that takes care of a lot of different I/O aspects. Mostly, it handles communications in an asynchronous way, meaning we issue communication messages without necessarily expecting it's going to be a "you talk, I talk, you talk, I talk" conversation. With asynchronous communications, you never know when the response may come back, which means you really need to have a separate process to take care of handling the response as compared with sending the request. Fortunately, `tokio` handles all of the scaffolding needed to set up that asynchronous work.

Finally, style guides are good programming practices, especially if you are working in a team. Consistency is important when it comes to quality code. Consistency also helps with readability and maintainability, and these are both important features of software development. Getting used to working with style guides can help you be more useful as a programmer on a software development project. Style guides are not exclusively about how to format your source code. There can be guidance about important decisions in programming, including how to handle identifiers and how to handle errors as well as returning values from functions. No matter how you are choosing to provide guidance to the software team, a style guide can be a good decision.

EXERCISES

1. Add a check to see whether neither of the command-line parameters for functions has been submitted. If neither is submitted, provide a message to the user indicating the options they have.

2. Add a check to see if the file exists. If the file exists, open it in append mode. If it doesn't exist, create it.

3. Allow the user to provide a filename as an additional parameter. You can assume the parameter immediately following the `-w` is going to be the name of the file.

ADDITIONAL RESOURCES

Hypertext Transfer Protocol - `developer.mozilla.org/en-US/docs/Web/HTTP`

What is HTTP? - `whatis.techtarget.com/definition/HTTP-Hypertext-Transfer-Protocol`

Web Client Programming - `www.alan-g.me.uk/tutor/tutwebc.htm`

Client-Side vs Server-Side Programming Languages - `www.c-sharpcorner.com/UploadFile/2072a9/client-side-vs-server-side-programming-languages/`

11

Web Server

IN THIS CHAPTER, YOU WILL LEARN THE FOLLOWING:

- ➤ Differences between offensive versus defensive programming
- ➤ Implementing application programming interfaces (APIs)
- ➤ How to use Representational State Transfer (REST) programming
- ➤ How to build a web server

Writing web application clients is a good skill to have, although in fairness, you may be less likely to be writing those clients unless you are developing a mobile application. The other side of the client, of course, is the server. You don't need to use a traditional web server like Apache or Microsoft's Internet Information Server (IIS) or Nginx to develop web applications on the server side. In fact, it may actually be better to develop the application using a language like Rust in order to protect the server and all of its data. Fortunately, there are ways to write these types of servers using Rust. In this chapter, we will take a look at writing a web application server using Rust.

This brings up the issue of writing applications in general, whether they are web or otherwise. To write any application, you are probably going to use an application programming interface (API). Anytime you are talking to the operating system, you are working through an API. This includes doing any input/output operations. There are a lot of other APIs you are probably familiar with. In fact, when we write the web application server, we are laying the foundation of an API ourselves, since we could be developing something a client could interface with to perform a task. Before getting too far down that road, though, we will talk about exactly what an API is a little later on. This will include the concept of writing Representational State Transfer (REST) applications, as they are a common way of writing web applications today.

As with other chapters, we will also talk about some programming strategies beyond just the syntax of the Rust programming language. Rust, as you will have seen mentioned once or twice in these very pages, is all about safe programming. This not only includes language features—both syntactically as well as in the implementation—but also should include good programming practices. We've been talking about a lot of them, but perhaps it's helpful to look at two ways to think about developing good programs that are resistant to both crashing and also attack in case they do happen to crash. You can and should be thinking about both offensive and defensive methods when you are writing programs, whether they are written in Rust or any other language.

OFFENSIVE VS. DEFENSIVE PROGRAMMING

We've actually been talking about these concepts throughout the course of the book, but it's probably time to put names to the techniques we've been using. Both offensive and defensive techniques are helpful, and in fact, offensive programming is an aspect of defensive programming. It's best to factor in both types of programming rather than only considering defensive programming or offensive programming in isolation. Together, you can think about how you can improve the overall quality of your code and protect the application as well as the underlying operating system and any data that may be available, either stored on disk or in memory.

The goal of defensive programming is improving the quality of code in a program. Programs that have been written using these strategies are, ideally, more readable. Or another way to think about it is, programs that are more readable are in a better place for getting through code audits easily. A good strategy for programming in general is to make the program predictable. This means no unexpected side effects resulting from any code that is executed.

This is challenging because user behavior is unpredictable. If we can't guarantee data will look a particular way, meaning it will fall into acceptable bounds and always look the way we expect it will look, we can't always predict the way a program will behave. This is why defensive programming is important. Programmers can follow some practices to ensure that programs don't fail in unsafe ways, even in the face of unexpected or unpredictable input.

There are some fundamental ideas behind defensive programming, although they may be hard for some to consider or accept. The first is that programmers are fallible. Yes, this includes you. And me. And anyone else who writes code at any level. We all make mistakes. We can't always see the implications of actions we take, certainly within a program we are writing. Any program or module or library contains mistakes of one sort or another. Sometimes these are minor mistakes where no harm results, simply because the program is too small or maybe the mistake is too minor. Sometimes they are much greater and may be mistakes that are only understood much later on because of the magnification of the mistake through other functions that may get called over the course of running the program.

Another fact of life that is fundamental to defensive programming is software is flawed. In fact, more complex software will have more bugs. Frederick Brooks, the author of *The Mythical Man-Month*, made several observations about issues with large, complex systems. He based these observations on his time as part of the development team of the OS/360 at IBM. This was an operating system for a new mainframe design at IBM in the 1960s. He made a couple of related observations about software defects. The first is that in sufficiently complex systems, there comes a point where some bugs simply can't be fixed. Brooks refers to this as the tendency toward an irreducible number of errors. He says that in fixing observable errors, additional errors are introduced. Other people have taken this idea of an irreducible number of errors to suggest that for every bug fix, two new bugs will be introduced. This may not be correct, but it highlights the difficulty of fixing problems in complex systems.

This is not to say that all software is plagued by unfixable errors, but once you learn a language, you are unlikely to stick with small, simple programs like the ones we have been working on. You will want to take some of these building-block ideas and build something that is more useful and, by extension, more complex. Working on following some of the practices of defensive programming will help make your software more reliable. At a minimum, crashes shouldn't be able to be manipulated so an attacker can gain remote access to the software and the system the software is running on.

Defensive programming starts in the design phase. You design programs to be safe; programs don't just magically become safe after the fact. This means thinking not only about how you are going to structure the program (data and functions) but also about how you are going to implement additional functionality. This means making intelligent decisions about code you are going to reuse. Libraries (crates, in our case) are ways you can introduce functionality easily without having to work really hard on developing the functionality yourself. However, code reuse itself isn't the best answer. Just because you find a crate doesn't mean that crate isn't loaded with bugs. Good design means making intelligent, informed decisions, which includes doing some investigation about the external components you are using. In some cases, you may not have much choice if there is only one crate available for the one piece of functionality you need. It's still your responsibility to assess all external code you introduce.

Proactive design and programming is important. This includes some basic beliefs. The first is that all data is invalid until proven otherwise. Once you assume data is invalid, you have to check the data before you do anything with it. Along the same lines, you should assume all code is untrustworthy until proven otherwise. If you assume code is untrustworthy, you don't just blindly accept output from a function that is called. You would need to validate the output, demonstrating that it's outside the bounds that should be expected based on the input provided.

How do we do this? We go back to the idea of design by contract. Design by contract uses pre-conditions, post-conditions, and invariants to expect data passed to or returned from a function falls within acceptable boundaries. This helps to ensure programs are predictable or provable—demonstrating correctness. A way to implement design by contract in Rust or other languages is through the use of assertions. Assertions are generally a good practice because when an assertion fails, the program fails. This aligns with an idea called fail fast. It's generally considered a good idea to fail as quickly as possible when it looks like something is going awry. The reason for this is you can end up causing additional problems if you think you'll be able to recover. The following is an example of an assertion in Rust:

```
fn main() {
    let x: i32 = 95;

    assert!(x < 30, "x is not less than 30 as expected, instead it is {}", x);

}
```

> **NOTE** *Invariants in programming are a way to ensure a condition is true during the period of code execution. This is not something you can define in the sense of declaring an invariant. Instead, it's a way for a program to behave, much like pre-conditions and post-conditions in functions. If you expect a condition to be true, such as a variable having a particular value throughout the execution of a block of code, you need to implement checks to make sure that it is true.*

Both assertions and design by contract are good practices to get into wherever you can, and both are considered implementations of defensive programming. While assertions are good to ensure that you are getting good data into your functions, you should also consider proving code correctness. This also goes back to design and the importance of designing software, meaning writing requirements and specifications up front rather than writing the code as you go. When you have a specification, meaning a set of requirements you are writing to, you can check the requirements against the code you are writing; or even better, someone else can check the requirements against the code you are writing. First, you may have a bias for your own code and may read the requirements the same way both times. Someone else may have a different take on the requirements and so can provide insight that can improve the overall code quality. Second, you need to prove correctness, not incorrectness. That's a whole other task.

We should also use exceptions rather than return codes. Returning a value from a function is easy to do, demonstrating success or not success. However, returning a value from a function means you have to correct any problems that may exist. Exceptions, though, can be used to cause a program failure with a cause. As mentioned before, trying to limp along with an error condition or guess the right path forward is probably not a good idea. You can't guess what a user intended to do with incorrect data. It's better to fail on the data and maybe indicate why you are failing so the user can try again with correct data and you don't leave your program in a broken state.

This brings up another way of thinking about defensive programming, even though it's called offensive programming. Offensive programming is a philosophy around error handling. While it sounds like it's in opposition to defensive programming because *offense* tends to be the opposite of *defense*, offensive programming is just another way of protecting your application. Offensive security is focused on application failure.

An interesting idea from offensive security is to keep applications simple in the sense of not performing a lot of checks that might generate errors. Some errors are going to cause the program to fail (crash) anyway. Checks that are going to find these failures and cause them anyway add complexity (more code) to programs. An offensive programming strategy may be to simply let a program fail from an error condition. The priority in offensive programming is to not allow errors in wrong places. These can be prevented at times by getting rid of additional code that handles fallback conditions, which may include setting default values to prevent the program from failing. In fact, program failure may be desirable if it can fail in safe or clean ways.

Where offensive programming and defensive programming strategies agree is in the use of assertions. One reason assertions are considered preferable in offensive programming is that they can be disabled. As an example, following is a debug assertion, which shows a way to validate a program during testing. While testing a program, you can cause errors through these assertions, which may cause errors further down the execution path in normal operation. This can allow you to address the failure in the design of the program. Offensive programming also prefers design by contract to handle checks and cause failure. Remember that assertions are fundamental to design by contract in Rust, so making use of assertions consistently is a good programming practice.

WEB APPLICATION COMMUNICATIONS

In the last chapter, we did some very basic communication with a web server. This is important, but it was based on static content, which isn't as useful in today's world. Today, when we interact with web servers, we are doing it in a programmatic way, meaning functions are being called on the web server, and data is being passed back and forth between the server and the client. As a result, we should be adding to what we learned about simple client communication and talk about how to interact with a web server in a more modern way.

First, we need to talk about how to pass data in very simple ways to a web server. That means using parameters and sending those into a web application. On top of straightforward parameters, there are other ways of getting data to servers and back. One is the use of semi-structured data and being able to get that data back and forth from the client to the server. Finally, we have Representational State Transfer (REST), which is a common way of handling communication between a client and server when we want to get functionality that is similar to that we would get from a native application where everything is stored in a single package on the local system.

Web Application Parameters

Before we talk about web applications, we need to talk about passing parameters. Web applications are built around forms. A web form is a collection of input fields where a user provides data to be sent to the web server. You are familiar with these fields, of course. All you need to do is visit a web search page, and you will see an edit box where you can provide data to pass to the server. Let's take a look at a simple web form, though. Figure 11.1 shows a simple web application with two fields and a submit button. Not very fancy, but more than sufficient for our purposes.

Keep in mind that there are different types of requests you make to a web server, meaning you would use a different verb depending on what you wanted the server to do for you. A common request handled by your browser is a GET request, meaning you are telling the server you want to get some information from it. This is not as straightforward as it may seem, though. In fact, in addition to asking for information with a GET request, you also send data into the server. You do this by passing parameters via the uniform resource locator (URL). Following is a URL that passes parameters into the page seen in Figure 11.1:

```
http://192.168.4.15/welcome_get.php?name=Ric&email=foo%40foo.com
```

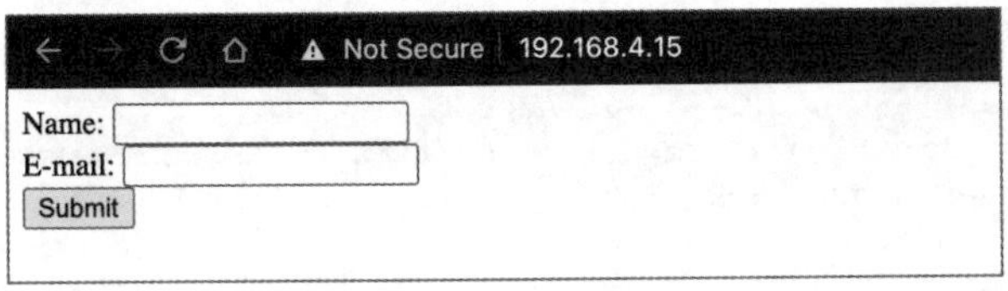

FIGURE 11.1: Simple web form

The server is located at 192.168.4.15, and the page being requested is `welcome_get.php`. PHP is Hypertext Preprocessor, which is a simple language meant to be used for interacting with web clients like browsers in cases where there needs to be something programmatic that happens, including extracting parameters from a web request. Following is the PHP that is used to extract the parameters from the request. The rest of the URL includes the parameters that get passed into the `.php` file. The `?` is the delimiter indicating that the name of the file is done and parameters are to follow. Each parameter is named with the value following the equal sign. When there are multiple parameters, you separate the parameters with a `&`:

```
<html>
<body>

Welcome <?php echo $_GET["name"]; ?><br>
Your email address is: <?php echo $_GET["email"]; ?>

</body>
</html>
```

> **NOTE** Because of the use of characters like `?` and `&` by the script, and other meanings for other characters, we have to do something for these special characters, which is why you can see `%40` in the parameters. This is called URL encoding. You preface a URL-encoded character with a `%` and then provide the hexadecimal value for the ASCII character.

You can see in the PHP source that we are pulling field names out of the GET request. `_GET` is an array or vector of key/value pairs. You retrieve the value by referring to the name provided in the HTML for the edit box. Of course, GET is not the only type of request you can provide. We can change the request to a POST rather than a GET. This changes two things. First, it changes the request type, which also changes the way parameters are passed. Second, it requires us to get data out of the `_POST` variable rather than `_GET`, although the process is still the same. Instead of passing parameters in the URL, as we saw earlier, we pass them as though they were part of the set of headers. Following are the headers for the request when we do a POST instead of a GET:

```
POST /welcome_post.php
HTTP/1.1
Host: 192.168.4.15
Connection: keep-alive
Content-Length: 37
Cache-Control: max-age=0
Upgrade-Insecure-Requests: 1
Origin: http://192.168.4.15
Content-Type: application/x-www-form-urlencoded
User-Agent: Mozilla/5.0 (Macintosh; Intel Mac OS X 10_15_7) AppleWebKit/537.36
(KHTML, like Gecko) Chrome/86.0.4240.68 Safari/537.36 Accept:
text/html,application/xhtml+xml,application/xml;q=0.9,image/avif,image/webp,image/
apng,*/*;q=0.8,application/signed-exchange;v=b3;q=0.9
Referer: http://192.168.4.15/index.html
Accept-Encoding: gzip, deflate Accept-Language: en-US,en;q=0.9

name=Wubble&email=wubble%40wubble.com
```

With the script in place, we can now write some simple programs that can interact with the script on that server. First, let's take a look at Python, simply because it's a common language to write such things in today. Following is the Python script that will make a POST request to the server. We provide the URL being interacted with, welcome_post.php. We then create a hash or dictionary of the parameters. In Python, this hash is the collection of key/value pairs. We're using a module called requests. Using that module, you call the posts function from the requests module, passing the URL as well as the hash of the parameters. The return from that call is the response from the server, without the headers. In our case, it's just simple HTML that comes back:

```python
import requests

url = 'http://192.168.4.15/welcome_post.php'
parms = {'name': 'Ric', "email": "wubble@wubble.com"}

x = requests.post(url, data = parms)

print(x.text)
```

Moving on, we can take a look at how to do the same thing in Rust. Following is a Rust program to interact with the page we have been using so far. We are going to use the reqwest crate for this, although we still need tokio to handle all the asynchronous management for us, as we did in the last chapter. The reqwest crate provides all the functions we need to implement an HTTP client. The assumption in Rust, using the crates we have used so far, is that we should send a request out and go about our merry way doing other things since Rust is built around the idea that we should be able to perform multiple tasks at the same time (more or less) using multitasking.

```rust
use reqwest;

#[tokio::main]
async fn main() -> Result<(), reqwest::Error>   {
    let req = reqwest::Client::new();
    let response = req.get("http://192.168.4.15/welcome_get.php")
        .query(&[("name", "Ric"), ("email", "ric@wubble.com")])
        .send()
        .await?;

    let body = response.text().await?;
    println!("{}", body);

    Ok(())
}
```

As before, we need the tokio crate and its functions to set up the actual main function for us that will handle the asynchronous communications. The wrapper that gets built by the tokio attribute is going to create functions that will spawn additional threads as needed. We need to be able to support error responses from the main function since we are doing everything in that function. The reqwest crate has its own error, which is what we will be returning from the program in case something bad happens.

We are creating a new reqwest::Client that will handle issuing the request to the server. Once we have the Client struct created, we can issue the request to the server. We're going to issue a GET request here. We need to provide the URL to the get() trait. On top of just saying we are going to send a GET request, we need to provide the query parameters. This is done by creating a sequence.

The sequence in our case is a serialized hash collection. We are providing each parameter being passed as a key/value pair. The key/value pair will be sent in a GET request using URL encoding. Following is the response we get from the server using the earlier program:

```
kilroy@milobloom $ target/debug/httpreq
<html>
<body>

Welcome Ric<br>
Your email address is: ric@wubble.com
</body>
</html>
```

Because we are using asynchronous communications, we don't necessarily get the response right away. That means we need to use await when trying to call text() to get the response body. As we have the potential for an error, we need to make sure we are extracting the String from the Result, which is why we use ? at the end of the statement. Finally, we can print the HTML that we have received from the server.

These are simple parameters and how you'd handle them. Web applications have become complex over the years since HTTP and HTML were first introduced. To support robust and rich application experiences using web architectures, we need to be able to support better ways of passing data back and forth between the server and the client.

Asynchronous JavaScript and XML

One of the long-standing problems with the Hypertext Transfer Protocol (HTTP) is that it is stateful. This means the client sends a request to the server, and the server fulfills the request. That is the entire extent of the transaction. The server doesn't naturally maintain any awareness of the client. What if you want truly dynamic content, meaning the contents of pages will be updated without any request from the client? You have problems because HTTP doesn't support any means for the server to send back data to the client without the client initiating a request. To better understand how all of this works, we should take a look at what a common web architecture looks like. Figure 11.2 shows a simple web architecture.

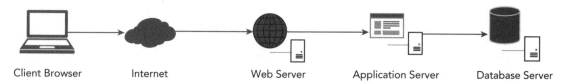

| Client Browser | Internet | Web Server | Application Server | Database Server |

FIGURE 11.2: Web application architecture

While the different elements are represented as systems, you should think of them more as services since they may not be implemented as individual systems. They may be implemented as services that all reside on a single system. They may also be implemented as containers without servers. Ultimately, what you will commonly get when you are engaging with a web application is a web server that takes the request from the client and maybe handles all static content. Behind the web server is an application server that takes care of all programmatic content. Finally, you have a database that stores a lot of information that supports the application. Even though the database may store some information related to the client, there is nothing in HTTP that allows the server to create information that can be stored in the database.

This is where we have to start getting creative in terms of extending what we can do with just HTTP and HTML. We start adding some scripting (meaning small programmatic functions) in, and we may be able to keep connections open. This requires a way to directly interact with the page that is being displayed; this requires the document object model (DOM). The DOM provides a way to directly get to the elements on a page. You don't need to know where in the text something is from the standpoint of offset from the top of the page. Instead, all you need to know is the type of element you are looking for or, even better, the name of the element, and you can interact with that element directly. This may include replacing the text with something more up to date.

One way to make all of this happen is by using Asynchronous JavaScript and XML (AJAX). Using AJAX, the server can bundle up data using the self-documenting format XML and send it off to the client. This doesn't require the client (meaning the user) to initiate a request (meaning visit a URL directly by entering it in or by clicking on a link on another page). Instead, you use JavaScript to keep up communication with the server, checking periodically for updated data to display on the page. The XML provides all the hints as to what each piece of the data is. If you have a section of a page where you have some element that has a name, you may have the same name in the XML, and the contents of that element could be replaced by the value of the element in the XML.

Again, AJAX is one way of making sure that you can maintain dynamic interaction between the server and the client. When it comes to using AJAX, it relies on the server to manage the overall interaction with the server. This is not the only approach to handling a web application.

Representational State Transfer

You will often hear how web applications are RESTful, which means they have a number of properties that are characteristic of the Representational State Transfer (REST) model. This is a way of developing web applications that was developed in the late 1990s alongside the development of HTTP 1.1. There are some constraints that define a RESTful architecture, and they are constraints forced by the use of HTTP and a traditional web architecture.

The following are the six constraints that drive the use of REST when it comes to implementing a web application:

➤ **Client-server architecture:** As shown in Figure 11.2, web applications use a client-server architecture. The client is the web browser, while the server is either a web server or an application server; but no matter what server is on the other end, it's the place where content and most functionality are stored.

➤ **Statelessness:** HTTP has no native ability to store state, which means every request to the server is effectively a standalone request. While this has some advantages, especially when it comes to highly available implementations—since state doesn't have to be shared across instances of servers to support the client connecting to any of those servers—it makes maintaining a useful application difficult.

➤ **Cacheability:** To make application performance faster, clients can store web pages. This may result in data that is outdated being presented to the client through the browser. While speed is improved, it can cause confusion on the part of the user if the browser pulls from cache.

➤ **Layered design:** As seen before, there are multiple layers or tiers to a web application design. Beyond the functional layers, there may also be additional layers like load balancers or even reverse proxies that may handle requests from the client before handing those requests over to the web server or application server to handle. This means the client never has any idea what layer of the application design it is communicating with.

➤ **Uniform interface:** No matter what the application is or what its needs are, the interface to the user is always going to be the browser. Developers will be constrained by whatever they can do in HTML and any other dynamic content they can use, depending on what a user may have installed on their system.

➤ **Code on demand:** One way to get around the uniform interface is for the server to send additional functionality to the browser that can be run inside the context of the browser. This may be something like a Java applet, for instance, that needs to be sent to the client to run there.

These constraints can end up forcing more functionality to the client, including keeping track of the state and not worrying about whether the server can keep track of that information. One way of allowing this to happen, while also enabling mobile clients to consume functionality on a web server, is to implement an API through the web server. You can implement a RESTful API by implementing endpoints through an address that can be contacted (e.g. `www.server.com/endpoint/`), using standard HTTP methods (e.g. `GET`, `POST`, `PUT`, `DELETE`), and using media that can send data containing state information from the server to the client or vice versa. In the case of implementing an API, you may use a network design more like what you see in Figure 11.3.

Client Browser   Internet   Application Server   Database Server

FIGURE 11.3: API architecture

APIs in Node.js and Python

These APIs can be easily implemented using multiple languages and don't even need a traditional web server (i.e. Microsoft's Internet Information Server or the Apache web server). You can implement these API servers entirely in code. One really simple way to do this is to use a language called Node.js, which is based on JavaScript, allowing web servers to be created simply and easily. A very simple REST API follows, written in Node.js, using the Express web server module. JavaScript, especially in Node.js, can be difficult to understand because it is focused on responding to actions rather than being more procedural:

```
var express = require('express');
var app = express();
var fs = require("fs");

app.get('/bacon', function (req, res) {
    fs.readFile( __dirname + "/" + "bacon.txt", 'utf8', function (err, data) {
        console.log( data );
```

```
            res.end( data );
        });
    })

    var server = app.listen(8080, function () {
        var host = server.address().address
        var port = server.address().port
        console.log("Bacon app listening at http://%s:%s", host, port)
    })
```

First, we create what appear to be identifiers or variables that are based on importing modules. This syntax effectively places the entire namespace of the module into a variable so it can be called from that variable. The variable express takes in the contents of the module express. When we need a specific instance of express, we can call express(), which would be like instantiating a new struct or object in Rust or C++. Once we have the instance of express named app, we write a response to a GET request. We do this by creating a function that responds to the message app.get. The endpoint is /bacon, and we define an inline function that has the parameters req and res passed into it. This is the complete request as well as the response that needs to be populated.

For our response, we are going to read in a file and just send that back. As part of reading in the file, we call another inline function with the results from reading in the file. This logs the data read from the file to the console as well as sends the data back in the response using the function res.end(), indicating that the response is complete and can be sent back to the requesting user.

Finally, we create the instance of the server that is going to listen for incoming connections. This is done by creating a variable named server that will be the result of the call to app.listen(). This function is told to listen on port 8080 and then sets the variables host and port to the address and port of the listening server. This information is logged to the console. The app.listen() function handles the loop of listening and then dispatching messages as requests come in.

We can also very simply write a program in Python that will do the same thing. With Python, we're going to use Flask to take care of handling the requests, similar to using Express with Node.js. Following is the Python script that listens for requests and provides a response if the endpoint requested is /bacon. We are responding with the same information (a Bacon Ipsum document) as we did with the previous Node.js program:

```python
import flask

app = flask.Flask(__name__)

@app.route('/bacon', methods=['GET'])
def bacon():
    f = open('bacon.txt', 'r')
    return f.read()
```

To get started, we import the flask module and then create an instance of it, using the name of the script as the value that initiates the instance. The variable __name__ in Python is the name of the running script. With Python, we can use decorators as syntactic sugar to make readability a little easier. The @app.route('/bacon', methods=['GET']) line indicates that when a GET request arrives at the server for the endpoint /bacon, the application should take care of that by using the function bacon(). This may not be immediately obvious because there is no parameter for the app.route()

function. That's what the @ line is for. It indicates that the handler for the GET request for the /bacon endpoint should be the function that follows.

> **NOTE** *Running the Flask server with the script provided requires you to set the* FLASK_APP *environmental variable to the name of the script. In my case, I used* export FLASK_APP=myapi.py. *Once you set the* FLASK_APP *variable, you can use* flask run *to start the flask server.*

Once the function is called to respond to the request, the program will read in the file bacon.txt. The contents of that file will be returned to the user. By default, the Flask server in this script will run on port 5000, meaning you need to connect to http://127.0.0.1:5000/bacon to get the response.

API Server in Rust

We can do the same thing in Rust. In fact, there are a number of crates that will handle REST APIs in Rust. We'll take a deeper look at another one later on, but for now, we're going to take a look at the warp crate. The following is a simple server that will take a request to the endpoint /bacon and handle it using warp as the framework for managing the connection to the client as well as mapping the request to the endpoint and the code that handles that endpoint:

```
use warp::Filter;
use std::fs;

#[tokio::main]
async fn main() {

let bacon_contents = fs::read_to_string("bacon.txt")
    .expect("Unable to open bacon.txt file");

let bacon = warp::path("bacon").map(move || format!("{}", &bacon_contents));

warp::serve(bacon)
    .run(([127, 0, 0, 1], 8080))
    .await;

}
```

First, we need to use warp::Filter, since that's the crate that carries the functionality needed to handle the server and add a path, which we will get into in a moment. As warp is built on top of hyper, which we used in the last chapter, we will be making use of tokio again, because hyper uses tokio. Again, any web-based communication is going to use an asynchronous model, regardless of how we choose to handle it in our code. We can write a completely synchronous program where we always wait for the responses to come back, but the underlying crates are going to be asynchronous simply because web-based communication can leave gaps that could easily be filled with other tasks in more complicated programs. Our sole purpose is to receive requests and respond to them. There is nothing more complicated going on. We still need to adjust to writing code that is asynchronous.

As usual, we use an attribute to have `tokio` create its version of a `main` function for us while we also indicate that the `main` function we are writing is flagged as `async`. As it turns out, `warp` doesn't generate errors in the functions we are using, so we don't need to return anything from the `main` function. The first thing we do in the `main` function is to read in the contents of the `bacon.txt` file we are going to be sending back to the client. This will be stored in a `String` value that we'll use later.

The important part is the line that follows here. We need to create a mapping between the endpoint, meaning the part of the URL after the hostname and the function that the endpoint refers to. The trait `warp::path()` is a filter that returns an iterator. Any request that comes in matching the filter specified will be added to the collection of structs the iterator points to. Effectively, you get a `for` loop working through all the elements in the collection. In normal use, you would use syntax like `.map(|x| wubble(x))` to indicate that each element would be put into the identifier named `x` and passed into the function named `wubble()`:

```
let bacon = warp::path("/bacon").map(move || format!("{}", &bacon_contents));
```

In our case, we don't have any identifier we are going to do anything with. Instead, we just need to hand back something that will be returned to the filter so it can be handed back to the requesting client. There are some nuances here that are worth talking through. First, remember that we are sending data back through the network. This means we can't just return a `String` value. It needs to be converted to something that can be consumed by the function sending the data. We have a problem, though. First, we have the usual considerations around ownership. Second, we have an issue around scoping because we are using asynchronous functions.

The way to address these issues is to do something other than just passing a `String` back or even converting that `String` to bytes and sending the bytes back. Instead, we are going to use the `format!()` macro to take the `String` value and create output from it that will be sent back to the client. By using `format!()`, we fix the scope issues. We aren't passing an identifier or even a reference to an identifier back to the handler. We are allowing the macro to create what is essentially an anonymous value that can be safely sent back to the responder.

> **NOTE** When we use asynchronous functions, we have two functions existing simultaneously. When we call an asynchronous function, as we are effectively doing with the `path()` trait, we have a case where the called function may exist longer than the calling function. If the identifier is defined in the calling function, there is the possibility of that identifier going out of scope when the calling function ends, but the called function, still existing. While this isn't possible in the case of the calling function being the `main` function (when it ends, the entire program should come to an end), the Rust compiler will still flag passing identifiers into asynchronous functions because of the possibility of the calling function ending, meaning all connected memory being destroyed.

Once we create the path mapping, meaning the name of the endpoint for the filter to look for as well as the response that will be sent back to the client, we can start the server. This is done using the following lines. We need to call `warp::serve()`, passing in the identifier that holds the path. We need to run the server, so we call the `run()` trait, passing in a `SocketAddr`. We don't need to create an identifier to hold the address. Instead, we can pass in the four octets that create an `Ipv4Addr` value. The `Ipv4Addr` that results from `[127, 0, 0, 1]` along with a numeric value for the port value ends up creating an instance of a `SocketAddr`. This creates the address the server will listen on. Keep in mind that you can listen on any port, but if you listen on any port number below 1024, you will need to run the program with administrative privileges because those port numbers are privileged ports. We are going to await the server, meaning we are going to just sit and hold until the server ends (or, in this case, is killed by the user):

```
warp::serve(bacon)
    .run(([127, 0, 0, 1], 8080))
    .await;
```

A single endpoint does not an API make, however. The way we called `serve()` only allows for a single endpoint. We need to create a collection of filters that we can then pass to `serve()`. The following revised program allows for multiple endpoints that are passed into the `serve()` trait. We've also added some different ways to create filters to this program, so you have some options. This includes taking parameters as well as nested endpoints, meaning it's not just /bacon; it could be /wubble/foo, for instance. This allows you to be more expressive in your endpoints to make it clear what you are performing. It also allows you to group endpoints in a way that makes it look like several of them are collected under what would normally be a directory listing:

```
use warp::Filter;
use std::fs;

#[tokio::main]
async fn main() {

let bacon_contents = fs::read_to_string("bacon.txt")
    .expect("Unable to open bacon.txt file");

let bacon = warp::path("bacon").map(move || format!("{}", &bacon_contents));
let hello = warp::path!("hello" / "you").map(|| "Hello, you\n");

let bye = warp::path("bye")
        .and(warp::path::param())
        .map(|name: String| format!("Goodbye, {}!\n", name));

let routes = warp::get().and(bacon.or(hello).or(bye));

warp::serve(routes)
    .run(([127, 0, 0, 1], 8080))
    .await;

}
```

The first new filter is put into an identifier called `hello`. This appears like a nested path, meaning you would issue a `GET` /hello/you request to the server to call this endpoint. Note that in order to accept the multiple parameters to the filter, we need to call the macro version of `path()`, which has the form `path!()` just like other macros we've used have had. The last endpoint we are creating takes a parameter. The following is the code that will create the filter for the endpoint and then accept the parameter. Remember that map takes an iterator, and normally you would have an identifier in between the ||, which we didn't do before because there was no value that needed to be passed to the closure. In this case, we do need to pass a value in. We are going to call the identifier name and declare it as a String. The closure (the anonymous function that is the second part of the map() parameter) is the same as we have used before, meaning it's the format!() macro:

```
let bye = warp::path("bye")
        .and(warp::path::param())
        .map(|name: String| format!("Goodbye, {}!\n", name));
```

Finally, to create the collection of endpoints, we have to use the warp::get() function. The syntax of this to get the right chaining may seem odd, but this is how it works: you call warp::get() and add the and() trait. This, though, is where it gets weird. The first endpoint we are passing to and() is bacon. This is the identifier created for the filter. This is a struct, so we can call a trait on it. We are going to call the or() trait on the bacon struct. We need to pass a value into this trait, so we are going to pass the identifier hello. We have one more endpoint to add, so we call or() on the result from the previous or() trait. What looks odd is the inconsistency of bacon.or() followed by or(hello).or(). You call a trait on the filter without it being a parameter and use the other filters as parameters. This makes more sense when you think that all of it is a parameter to the and() trait. This is the way, though, that warp expects to get a collection of filters together:

```
let routes = warp::get().and(bacon.or(hello).or(bye));
```

Once we have the collection of filters together, we can call serve(), passing in the identifier for that collection of filters we just created. Same as before, we will call run() on the result from the serve() trait. Just as before, we need to specify the IP address and port number we want the server to listen on. Perhaps it goes without saying, but you need to make sure the IP address you specify belongs to the system where you are running the server. In this case, the 127.0.0.1 address will always belong to whatever system you are running the server on. Every networked device has a loopback interface, which would commonly carry the 127.0.0.1 address.

RUST ROCKET

As noted earlier, there are a lot of different ways to support writing a web server in Rust. This includes multiple frameworks that will take care of routing, meaning you can indicate the name of an endpoint and specify how that endpoint should be handled. We're going to makes use of a framework called Rocket that should make the process of building a complete web server that has routing as well as static file capabilities a lot easier than what we were looking at. This is not to say that warp is at all a bad framework for creating these web servers. The advantage of Rocket is that it is more readable once you get into the routing because of how it handles defining routes. Following is the complete source code for the program:

```
#![feature(proc_macro_hygiene, decl_macro)]

#[macro_use] extern crate rocket;
```

continues

(continued)

```rust
use rocket::Data;
use std::fs;

#[get("/")]
fn index() -> &'static str {
    "Welcome to your very own server, but there is nothing at the main branch\n"
}

#[get("/bacon")]
fn bacon() -> String {
    let bacon_contents = fs::read_to_string("bacon.txt")
        .expect("Unable to open file");

    format!("{}\n", bacon_contents)
}

#[post("/upload", format = "plain", data = "<data>")]
fn upload(data: Data) -> Result<String, std::io::Error> {
    data.stream_to_file("/tmp/data.txt").map(|num_bytes| format!("Wrote {} bytes
out to file", num_bytes))
}

#[get("/greetz/<name>/<age>")]
fn greetz(name: String, age: u8) -> String {
    format!("Greetz, {} year old named {}!", age, name)
}

#[get("/ofage/<name>/<age>")]
fn ofage(name: String, age: u8) -> String {
    if age > 18 {
        format!("Welcome, {}, your age {} means you can view this content!", name, age)
    }
    else {
        format!("Sorry, {}, you are not the right age, since you are only {} years
old", name, age)
    }
}

fn main() {
    rocket::ignite().mount("/", routes![index,greetz,upload,bacon,ofage])
    .launch();
}
```

NOTE *Before you get started, it's important to know that Rocket requires some additional work with your Rust installation. Rocket requires some features that may not be in the stable build. The Rocket developers are using the most cutting-edge versions of the Rust tools, which means in order to use Rocket, you need to be doing the same thing to ensure that*

Rocket programs install. You will need to run the following command, which will switch you from using stable builds of the tools to using nightly builds, which may not be stable and may cause breakage:

```
rustup default nightly
```

If you end up having issues or simply want to switch back once you are done working with Rocket, you can run the following command to move back to stable builds. You could also move to something in the middle, which would be beta, if that's your preference over the long term. Rocket requires the nightly build setting, though:

```
rustup default stable
```

Starting at the top, we should talk about the attributes that start off the program. The first, the feature attribute, is used to enable experimental features. Rocket is using some features that are not in the stable versions of Rust, so the compiler needs to be told that these features have to be enabled and allowed. The first of these is proc_macro_hygiene, and the other is decl_macro. Both of these features have to do with the use of macros and how they are declared and used. Over time, the use of macros in Rust has evolved and continues to evolve. The decl_macros feature was created to enable and standardize a declarative macro system, including how these macros are named. Basically, the feature is needed if the modules being used are going to declare macros, so the compiler knows how to handle the macro definition. The first feature listed is actually a collection of other issues, mostly having to do with providing some additional structure around the creation of macros. The short answer to the inclusion of these features at the top of this source code is that Rocket is going to use macros, and the compiler needs to know that.

Similarly, in the next line, we are using the crate rocket, but we need to provide some additional context for the use of that crate. What we set up in the previous line was the runway for the compiler to be able to handle macros correctly. In this line, we are providing an attribute saying not only that we are using an external crate but that the crate is going to be declaring and using some macros. In general, as of Rust 2018, there is no reason to use the syntax extern crate unless you are needing to set specific parameters, as we are doing here. The right way to tell the compiler you are using external functionality that is in a crate is to set the requirements in the Cargo.toml file and then just use the crate. The compiler pulls in the external functionality from the Cargo.toml file. The keyword use is only for pulling in the namespace from the library, so you don't have to use the :: to specify which namespace you are referring to when using something out of that external library.

Speaking of use, we are only using two external libraries for this program. The first is the specific Data library from the Rocket framework. Again, we aren't saying we are using those features from the Rocket library but not other ones. We specify rocket::Data as a convenience so we don't later have to use Data::Data when we make use of the Data struct. You can think of it as a convenience as much as anything else, although there is something that also makes it more readable if you aren't cluttering the program with a lot of references to external namespaces. This may be a matter of preference, though, since you could also argue that Data::Data provides more specificity and clarity than just Data.

We can get into the different routes we are going to be using at this point. You may recall from `warp` previously that we had to create filters that `warp` would use to send requests to the right place. We also had to use what were effectively closures, meaning anonymous functions, that were called from the `map()` trait on an iterator that was created from the `warp` filter. Rocket does something different from how `warp` handles things. Following, you can see how Rocket handles setting up routes to endpoints. First, we are using an attribute, which is similar in some ways to the decorators from Python. This allows Rocket to know a couple of things very easily. It makes for an uncomplicated way of setting up the path to a request coming into the server. First, we indicate the request type. In this route, we are expecting a `GET` request. We also need to know what the resource being requested is. For this route, we are using the / resource, meaning we are expecting the index for the top level of our web server. Since this isn't a traditional web server, which would just be reading files from disk and serving them up, we need to provide some content to return to the client. You can see the return type from the function is a `static str`, meaning it's a string literal:

```
#[get("/")]
fn index() -> &'static str {
    "Welcome to your very own server, but there is nothing at the main branch\n"
}
```

You will also notice here that we are not using an anonymous function. The attribute provided at the top of this function, which is an outer attribute because it is declared outside of the function, indicates the function that follows is what should be called if that request (`GET /`) is the one that arrives at the server. This makes developing content quite a bit easier, perhaps, than what we were doing before. I have a complete function to work with, which may be easier to implement or understand. All you need to do is make sure you are passing a return value that Rocket can handle to provide the response to the client. You can name this function anything you like because you are going to tell Rocket later what routes to set up, but it may be helpful to name it something that makes sense. In this case, the client is requesting the primary index page. Therefore, naming it `index` makes some sense.

Each of the endpoints we are looking at in this program offers slightly different functionality, so we can see some of the capabilities of using Rocket. The endpoint that follows is the same one we have been using in other examples—if someone requests /bacon using a `GET` request, we are going to return the contents of `bacon.txt`, just as we have before. Remember that the contents of `bacon.txt` are a number of paragraphs of Bacon Ipsum, just because it's funny. As we've done before, we are going to read the contents of that file into a `String` value. Because the `Responder` trait from Rocket has been implemented for `String`, we can just pass a `String` value back, and Rocket will provide the `String` to the client. As before, so we don't run into any ownership issues, we are going to use the `format!()` macro to create a brand-new string. Since we're already using `format!()`, we can take advantage of that call to also send a newline character at the end, just in case, so we aren't leaving a line hanging:

```
#[get("/bacon")]
fn bacon() -> String {
    let bacon_contents = fs::read_to_string("bacon.txt")
        .expect("Unable to open file");

    format!("{}\n", bacon_contents)
}
```

We are not limited to just GET requests, of course. We can use other methods specified by the HTTP protocol. In the function that follows, we are going to accept a POST request. Remember that a POST request generally means you are sending data from the client to the server. The attribute for this has gotten more complex than the ones we have seen so far. Because we expect to be getting data back from the server, that means we need to be able to accept that data. First, we need to specify the format the data is coming back in. We are accepting a plaintext value, but we could specify any content type, which mostly means you indicate the Multipart Internet Mail Extension (MIME) type of the content you expect back, and that's the format that will be accepted. As an example, we could specify application/json, and that would indicate we were going to get a JSON document back from the client:

```
#[post("/upload", format = "plain", data = "<data>")]
fn upload(data: Data) -> Result<String, std::io::Error> {
    data.stream_to_file("/tmp/data.txt").map(|num_bytes| format!("Wrote {} bytes
out to file", num_bytes))
}
```

Since we are going to get data back from the client, we probably want to do something about it. That means we are going to be passing a parameter into the function so the function can do something with the data. In the attribute, we need to indicate the name of the parameter so the server knows what parameter to put the data into. You may have multiple parameters, after all, which means you need to give names to the parameters so the right data goes to the right place.

We are going to take the data, which is plaintext, and write it out to a file. Because this is an input/output operation, we have a chance of running into an error. After all, the program the user is running may not have permissions to write to that file after all, as one example of an error that may occur. The trait stream_to_file() is going to return the number of bytes that were written. We are going to take that value and just send it back to the client. Well, we're going to provide a little more context than just the numeric value of the number of bytes. We're going to tell the client the number of bytes that were written out to a file. This user on the client can then check the number of bytes written with the number of bytes sent if they choose to do that. At least with a little context, they aren't just getting a number without knowing what it means or what to do about it.

Our next endpoint is going to accept parameters from the client. As before, we are going to specify the attribute indicating the request type as well as the resource that is being requested. In this case, though, we are going to take some parameters that will look like they are part of the path for the resource. Following is what the declaration of the function and the endpoint definition looks like. Again, because we are going to be taking multiple parameters, we need to give them names. We specify the name by bracketing it in the attribute. As an example, we are going to take a name from the user, and the parameter will be called name, so it looks like <name> in the attribute. This doesn't mean we expect the parameter from the user to be placed inside the angle brackets. Instead, the brackets just indicate that inside is the name of the parameter to look for in the function definition. We are also going to take an age, which means we are looking for a numeric value. That is reflected in the parameter to the function declaration. Age shouldn't be that big, so we can allocate 8 bits to it and be fine:

```
#[get("/greetz/<name>/<age>")]
fn greetz(name: String, age: u8) -> String {
    format!("Greetz, {} year old named {}!", age, name)
}
```

This function is very simple. Again, we are going to use the `format!()` macro to generate a string to return to the client. We are going to use the name and age provided to send a greeting back to the client. This isn't hugely interesting, but we can take that idea and make it a little more interesting by doing something with the age. After all, there is nothing about these functions that says we can't perform some computations or comparisons. Following is the next endpoint we are going to take a look at. It's only slightly more complicated than the one before, but it raises at least one issue for us:

```
#[get("/ofage/<name>/<age>")]
fn ofage(name: String, age: u8) -> String {
    if age > 18 {
        format!("Welcome, {}, your age {} means you can view this content!",
name, age)
    }
    else {
        format!("Sorry, {}, you are not the right age, since you are only {} years
old", name, age)
    }
}
```

As before, we are accepting a GET request, and we are going to take some parameters. These are the same parameters we accepted in the `greetz` endpoint. Inside the function body, though, we are going to see if the age is greater than 18, meaning the person issuing the request is technically an adult for some purposes. If the person is older than 18, we send one response, but if they are less than 18, we send back a different response. This brings up an important point. Remember, with function returns in Rust, we are using an expression. Typically, this expression would go on the last line of the function. In this case, the expression is on what would be the last line of code in the function executed rather than the actual last line of code in the function. Inside the conditional statement, we create an expression, effectively, by not including a statement terminator (the `;`). This tells the compiler that this is the value to be returned from the function. Since we are using a conditional, we have two potential expressions that could be called. There is no way to get to both of these expressions in the same call of the function, so there is no conflict that could come from trying to return multiple times. Every call of the function is only going to result in a single expression, meaning a single return value.

To call this endpoint, we just provide the parameters as though they were parts of a directory path. Following is what that would look like using a manual interaction with the server. This makes it clear what the request would look like between the client and the server. The program being used is `netcat`, which allows a direct connection to the port specified: in this case, port 8000. Because the second parameter is 23, the person provided here is an adult and can view whatever content is behind this endpoint:

```
kilroy@milobloom $ nc localhost 8000
GET /ofage/kilroy/23 HTTP/1.1
Host: localhost

HTTP/1.1 200 OK
Content-Type: text/plain; charset=utf-8
Server: Rocket
Content-Length: 61
Date: Thu, 08 Oct 2020 00:31:52 GMT

Welcome, kilroy, your age 23 means you can view this content!
```

We are now down to the last piece of the program, which is the following `main` function that launches the Rocket server. We are going to use `rocket::ignite()` to get Rocket started up. We need to provide some endpoints to the server, though. We do that using the `mount()` trait. We could call `mount()` multiple times in a chained fashion if we had different types of servers we needed to create. This could include creating the ability to serve up files directly from the filesystem. In this case, though, we are just specifying routes to endpoints. To do that, we pass in the names of the functions to the `routes!()` macro:

```
fn main() {
    rocket::ignite().mount("/", routes![index,greetz,upload,bacon,ofage])
    .launch();
}
```

Now we have a program that can run and serve up content for us. One nice thing about Rocket is that you get content back from running the program, meaning it provides you with status. This includes details about the manner in which it is starting, like the address and port, as well as details about requests that come into the server and have been handled. Following is an example of starting this server and serving up content. You will also get any error messages if, for example, in testing, you happen to leave off one of the parameters to a request so it doesn't match what was specified in the endpoint definition. This highlights the specificity of the request, though. If you don't exactly match how it was defined in your program, the request will simply fail:

```
kilroy@milobloom $ target/debug/ch11_rocketsrv
🔧 Configured for development.
    => address: localhost
    => port: 8000
    => log: normal
    => workers: 32
    => secret key: generated
    => limits: forms = 32KiB
    => keep-alive: 5s
    => tls: disabled
🛰  Mounting /:
    => GET / (index)
    => GET /greetz/<name>/<age> (greetz)
    => POST /upload text/plain; charset=utf-8 (upload)
    => GET /bacon (bacon)
    => GET /ofage/<name>/<age> (ofage)
🚀 Rocket has launched from http://localhost:8000
GET /ofage/kilroy/23:
    => Matched: GET /ofage/<name>/<age> (ofage)
    => Outcome: Success
    => Response succeeded.
```

What you can see in this output is all of the endpoints that have been configured in the server, so you can easily tell if you have mistakenly left one of your definitions out, in case you didn't notice it in the code. You will get all of the endpoints, their definitions, and the name of the function that will be called when the endpoint is matched by a request.

SUMMARY

One of the great things about the modern programming landscape is that we are no longer bound to traditional web servers or even application servers to create programmatic content that can be consumed by different types of clients. You are also no longer bound by the traditional client endpoint, which is the web browser. Today, you can create mobile applications that can consume content from a server without the content necessarily being HTML. Instead, you can ship data back and forth between the client and the server in the background without the user even being aware of the brains on the back end of the application, residing on a server on the Internet somewhere.

Rust has a lot of options in this regard. While we looked at two here, Rocket and warp, there are many others. Each is going to be a little different in terms of how you write code that uses the functionality. You can see that just by looking at the differences between the two programs we saw in this chapter. Your programming tastes will vary from those of other programmers. You may prefer one way of interacting with the server over the other. If you don't like either of the two on offer here, there are other crates you can take a look at.

No matter what crate you choose to develop your server in, you know that you can build out very useful server functionality using Rust. You don't have to use PHP or C# or Java, and you also don't have to install any other application as you would to serve up Java, for instance. With C#, you'd be bound to use Microsoft's Internet Information Server and make sure you had the functionality to serve up .NET-based applications enabled, and everything would happen inside the web server itself. In our case, we can just write our very own application server and do everything in one place.

Any programming you do is going to cause you to make decisions when you are designing it. Ideally, you aren't writing on the fly and thinking that's a good way to create well-constructed applications that are going to be as free of bugs as possible. Getting in the habit of making decisions that will reduce the number of bugs and increase the reliability of your programs will be important. You can do this by factoring into your design concepts from defensive programming or offensive programming. Either path will require you to make decisions during the design phase that will increase overall readability and, along with it, reliability of the design.

If you take nothing else away from the discussion of defensive and offensive programming, think about the problems associated with trying to hobble along with bad data or data you think may be bad. It will always be better to just error on the data when you have determined it's bad. If you suspect it may be bad, check that it conforms to the parameters you have specified, and error if it doesn't meet those parameters. One way to do that is to use design by contract, which means you can create conditions before entering a function or after exiting the function. Either way, you have guaranteed as best as possible that the data you are working with will be clean and won't cause unexpected side effects later on when you try to work with it.

EXERCISES

1. Change the `greetz` endpoint from the Rocket program to check for a specific name and send a special greeting to that person.

2. Add another endpoint to the Rocket server that takes multiple parameters and does something based on those parameters.

3. Add a line to the `upload` endpoint in the Rocket server so the data is written out to the screen as well as being written out to a file.

4. Add an endpoint to the `warp` server that provides static content back to the client.

ADDITIONAL RESOURCES

Here are some useful resources to learn more about the topics in this chapter:

"AJAX Introduction" - `www.w3schools.com/xml/ajax_intro.asp`

"Introduction to AJAX for Java for Web Applications" - `netbeans.apache.org/kb/docs/web/ajax-quickstart.html`

"What Is REST" - `restfulapi.net/`

"What Is REST?" - `www.codecademy.com/articles/what-is-rest`

"Offensive Programming" - `wiki.c2.com/?OffensiveProgramming`

"Offensive Programming" - `johannesbrodwall.com/2013/09/25/offensive-programming`

"Is 'Defensive Programming' Actually Healthy?" - `dev.to/cubiclebuddha/is-defensive-programming-actually-healthy-5flj`

"Defensive Programming: the Good, the Bad, and the Ugly" - `enterprisecraftsmanship.com/posts/defensive-programming`

12

Getting to the System

IN THIS CHAPTER, YOU WILL LEARN THE FOLLOWING:

- ➤ How to read and write from the Windows Registry
- ➤ How to get information about system components
- ➤ How to get process listings
- ➤ How to add traits to existing structs

There are some people who consider Rust a systems programming language. Systems programming differs from application programming in that application programming is focused on providing some useful functionality to an end user. Systems programming is more behind the scenes. You may be developing a service that other applications may be consuming. You could also be performing lower-level tasks that interact directly with lower-level operating system components or elements. Some may think that systems programming requires using a very low-level language, along the lines of assembly where you are writing directly in the language the processor understands without having to go through a compiler to get from the language you are using to the one the processor understands.

The reason for using assembly language is that it's thought to be faster, because the compiler may introduce inefficiencies into the resulting program. Some may use a language like C to be able to be more expressive in their program but still get some of the perceived power that comes with assembly. C is thought to be between assembly and a higher-level language like FORTRAN (which was a dominant language when C was developed). The problem with this belief is that it assumes the programmer writing in either assembly language or C is highly skilled. Writing highly optimized code in assembly language takes years of practice—and directed practice, at that, meaning constantly evaluating the programs you are writing to find better ways of doing it.

C programmers are no better off. It's easy to write really bad C programs, and even the best-optimizing compiler can't always fix problems with bad C code. The same is true for other languages as well. Well-written programs in a well-designed language can be just as efficient as badly written programs in lower-level languages. Perceived power is not everything there is.

We can just as easily write systems programs—where speed is considered to be of the essence—in Rust and get all the benefits Rust provides. Again, C does no one any favors with all the so-called power it offers because very few programmers know how to write in C so as to avoid vulnerabilities in the code, especially in more complex programs. Better to have a safe program that conceivably runs a little slower than one that is loaded with vulnerabilities because of the weaknesses in the C language.

Of course, in reality, modern processors are so fast that better-constructed, safer languages like Rust don't introduce nearly enough lag that any user would notice the difference. The performance problems are far more likely to be a result of input/output or graphics with a user interface than they are with anything the program may be doing to hold up the proceedings.

So, we are going to use Rust to do some lower-level work. We're going to take a look at interacting with various system components like gathering information about disks attached to a system. We are also going to spend a little time working with the Windows Registry, since it's such an important part of interacting with a Windows system. A lot of information is stored in the Windows Registry, not only strictly related to Windows itself but also to just about every application that is installed.

Finally, we're going to take a look at some other features of Rust that can help you be a little more expressive when you are writing programs. One thing you may have been struggling with throughout the course of the book—especially if you come from an object-oriented background—is, why isn't Rust object-oriented? Or is it really object-oriented? That probably depends on how you define *object-oriented languages*. There are certainly elements of Rust that are like object-oriented languages, but there are also pieces of object-oriented languages that either aren't present or aren't fully present in Rust. We're going to take a look at something Rust supports that is similar to but not quite the same as object-oriented languages.

EXTENDING FUNCTIONALITY

Why bother banging on about object-oriented languages in the context of Rust? It's easier to understand one thing if you can compare or liken it to something else that is understood. Object-oriented languages have been around for decades now, and a lot of programming today happens in these languages, including Java and C++ as well as others that have object-oriented capabilities but may not be inherently object-oriented in nature, like Python or even PowerShell. These two scripting languages can be used in a procedural manner while also having the capability of having objects written and consumed within any script. They are comfortable going in either direction.

Object-oriented (OO for short) languages come from a desire to separate data from code in a way. Rather than having any code in a program be able to act directly on a piece of data, there is an idea of *encapsulation*, meaning you create a bubble around the data so anything outside the bubble can't get to it directly. Instead, you have a semipermeable membrane using functions (sometimes called methods). To get at the data inside the bubble, you interact with a function that has direct access to the data inside the bubble. You can see a visual representation of this in Figure 12.1. The functions sit on the edge of the bubble, catching requests and then acting directly on the data

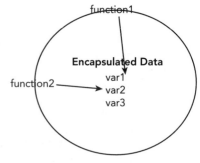

FIGURE 12.1: Encapsulated data

inside the bubble. This way, the data stays protected because no one can perform any action on the data anytime they want. The functions created on the edge of the bubble present the actions that are allowed to be taken.

When you perform this encapsulation of data, you are binding code with the data that the code acts on. You create data that may be represented in any way that makes sense within the bubble, and then you define methods that can be used to interact with the data. The bubble can be made as opaque or transparent as you would like. You may want a complete black box, for instance, where anyone using the data simply has no idea what the data is or how it is represented. They just know what actions they want to perform. This aggregation of data and associated methods is considered an object.

FIGURE 12.2: Magic card box

We can look at a specific example. Let's say we have a box of playing cards, as shown in Figure 12.2. Consider this box our object. We don't know exactly what is inside. We know that if we want a card, we ask the box for a playing card, and it provides one. If we want to reorder the cards, we ask the box to shuffle, and whatever is inside the box is reordered in some new way. You can't see inside the box. The box does all the work for you. Of course, you could open the box (which may mean doing some debugging, for instance, in order to see the internal representation of the cards), but it makes working with the box harder and slows down the process. You can think of an object as a magic box: you ask the box to perform some predefined capability, and the box takes care of it for you without having to trouble you with what is inside the box.

Encapsulation is an important aspect of OO programming and is really a foundational element. However, there are other aspects of what are commonly considered object-oriented languages that are worth talking about here, just so we can toss Rust up against them in order to understand Rust a little better. The first is the implementation of objects. An object, remember, is a definition of data and the functions that can act on that data. Objects are typically implemented in classes. You create a class, define the data that is at the core of that class, and then define the methods that anyone outside the class can use. You may also define methods that are solely for the use of other methods inside the class. When you want to define a new set of data within the parameters of that defined by the class, you will create a new instance of that class. You can have multiple instances of a class in any given program.

From the Rust perspective, we define associated data in *structs*. These are data structures defined by the programmer where all of the identifiers in the struct are related to one another. Rather than methods, as might be common in OO languages, Rust uses *traits*. Okay, so both are essentially functions. In Rust, you can create as many instances of a struct as you like. Any trait that has been defined for the struct can be accessed through the instance of the struct. The way Rust works is a little inside-out compared to OO. With OO languages, you have an object that probably has some data at its core, and then you interact with the data using methods. In Rust, you have a data structure. It's very clear that what you are working with is a representation of data. You can perform actions on that data through the use of traits, but you are always referring to the data representation, even if it's a specific instance of that representation.

> **NOTE** *OO languages may differentiate between data that belongs to the class, meaning data that is identical across all instances of the class, and data that belongs only to the instance of the class. A class variable is a value that belongs to all instances of the class. No matter how many instances of the class there are, the value in that variable will be identical. In an instance variable, the value is exclusive to the instance of the class and can't be seen by any other instance of the class.*

OO programming languages typically include some capability for inheritance. That means you can define a class in an OO language and then declare a subsequent class that uses all the same characteristics of the original class. It inherits them but then adds characteristics like additional data or methods that can be called. To help make this clear, we can take a look at the following example, written in C#. What is declared here is a class called `Person`. It has two properties: a string value that holds the person's name and an integer that holds the person's age. We don't want anyone outside of this class to muck around with the variables declared in the class, so we write *accessor methods*. These are ways to get to the data stored in the class without touching the variable directly.

```
public class Person {
    string name;
    int age;

    public string Name() {
        return name;
    }

    public int Age() {
        return age;
    }
}
```

We now have a base class, which we can inherit from. Following is another class that inherits from the Person class. It is an Employee. This class inherits all of the properties and methods of the Person class, so we can still get the name and age of the Employee, just as we can with a Person. In addition, an employee earns a wage, so we can keep track of that. It's not especially helpful to store a value you do nothing with, so we may as well include an accessor method that returns the value of the salary property. Some OO languages will also implement something called *polymorphism*, although we aren't going to spend many words talking about it. Effectively, you can take an Employee instance and cast it to a variable declared as a Person. You can still retain access to everything that a Person class knows about, but you can no longer get access to the Employee methods from the Person instance. It can be a little confusing, so we aren't going to spend any additional time on it.

```
public class Employee: Person {
    int salary;

    public int Salary() {
        return salary;
    }
}
```

The reason for bringing up any of this is to simply say that Rust doesn't have inheritance in the sense that you can declare a whole new type that takes on all the characteristics of the original type so you can extend it with some additional properties and methods. Because Rust doesn't have inheritance, there is also no polymorphism. And perhaps that's just as well, because it can be confusing trying to keep track of which instance type you are referring to an object from so you know what data you can get access to. No one needs that level of confusion and problem-inflicting behavior in their programs.

Instead, Rust does something different, which is why Rust isn't really an OO language. A lack of inheritance effectively kicks Rust out of the club, although that's not such a bad thing. Instead of using inheritance, you can tack functionality onto a data structure. You can't add additional properties to the struct, which you could do with proper inheritance, but you can add additional methods that act exclusively on that data structure. In fact, you can extend the capabilities of built-in functions. Following is a small program that takes a `String` struct and adds some additional traits to it, extending the capabilities of the `String`:

```
trait ReverseIt {
    fn reverseit(&self) -> String;
}

trait Half {
    fn half(&self) -> String;
    fn half(&self) -> u16;
}

impl ReverseIt for String {
    fn reverseit(&self) -> String {
        let mut rev_str = String::new();
        for c in self.chars().rev() {
            rev_str.push(c);
        }
        rev_str
    }
}

impl Half for String {
    fn half(&self) -> String {
        let mut half_str = String::new();
        let mut half: bool = true;
        for c in self.chars() {
            if half {
                half_str.push(c);
            }
            half = !half;
        }
        half_str
    }
}

/*
impl Half for u16 {
    fn half(&self) -> u16 {
        (self / 2) as u16
    }
}
*/

fn main() {

    let first_str = String::from("This is a string");
    let full: u16 = 250;
    println!("{}\n", first_str.reverseit());
    println!("{}\n", first_str.half());

}
```

First, we declare that we are creating a new trait. Remember that a trait is effectively a method in OO parlance that acts on the data within the `struct` it has been implemented for. We're going to declare two traits here. The first is going to take any existing `String` and reverse all the characters. The second trait, showing the power of traits, is going to provide half a value back. The power comes from being able to identify a trait, meaning we declare an interface and then provide specific implementations across multiple data structures. You can see that in the code that follows. We are implementing the `ReverseIt` trait for a `String` struct:

```
impl ReverseIt for String {
    fn reverseit(&self) -> String {
        let mut rev_str = String::new();
        for c in self.chars().rev() {
            rev_str.push(c);
        }
        rev_str
    }
}
```

The code here takes the existing `String` and gets an iterator to all of the characters but in reverse order, meaning starting from the end of the `String`. Now that we are working through the characters from back to front, we can take each character and push it into a new `String` value. This, once we are done with it, becomes the value we return from the function.

The second trait we are going to look at shows the value of the Rust way of doing things but also highlights how Rust isn't object-oriented. You can see there is a trait defined called `Half`. There are two functions defined in `Half`, both named `half`. Some languages will look at the complete signature of a function before determining if there is a name clash. This means the compiler will look at the name of the function, the parameters provided, and the return type before determining if a function has been re-declared. This is called *overloading*. It means you are taking a name and giving it multiple potential definitions. The compiler has to correctly identify the correct definition and function call based on how the function has been called. Rust only looks at the name. There is no way to overload function names in Rust, at least if you are trying to do it in the same namespace. If you were to uncomment the lines (remove the `//` or the `/* */` pieces from the source code shown previously), you would get compiler errors about redefining functions.

That doesn't mean you can't have multiple definitions. You can take the trait definition and the implementation in `u16` and move them to a completely different program or provide them with a different namespace. It's not overloading in the same way other languages do it, but you can take these interfaces and apply them to other data structures using the same interface and providing essentially the same functionality. Calling a trait applies to the specific data structure the trait is being applied to so you can have the same trait name that has implementations for multiple data structures.

The trait system in Rust isn't at all the same thing as objects and object-oriented practices, but you get a lot of capability to extend the functionality of the data types in question. We have two interesting capabilities that we can call against an instance of a `String`. Following, you can see the output from the program shown previously, with the `u16` implementations commented out. The first line of output shows the original string value "This is a string" in reverse. The second line of output shows what happens when you only take alternate letters from a string and put them into a new value:

```
PS C:\Users\kilroy\Documents> .\reversestr.exe
gnirts a si sihT

Ti sasrn
```

WINDOWS REGISTRY

The Windows Registry is an important feature of the Windows operating system. It is a repository of configuration information for the system. Rather than having a lot of individual configuration files in different file formats, as would be the case on a Unix-like operating system, Windows puts all of the configuration data in a single place and makes accessing that information completely uniform. The Registry is also interesting in that it can be stored on disk, but much of the data in the Registry exists only in memory at the time the operating system is running. You may consider it similar to the pseudo filesystems of Unix-like systems, where there is a collection of files that only ever exist in memory, although they appear to be files on disk just like any other file on the disk. If you were to shut down the system and look at everything on the physical disk, you wouldn't find any of those files you saw when the system was running. The same is true of the Windows Registry. There is simply some data that is only in place when the system is running.

Prior to the Registry, Windows had a large number of `.INI` files, which were used to initialize programs and system components with default configuration parameters. Microsoft decided to standardize on the Registry for configuration information around Windows 95. The Registry is organized in a hierarchical manner, much like a filesystem is traditionally represented. You have folders at the top level with folders underneath them and data (or files) potentially in each of the levels of folders. You can see how the Registry is represented in the Registry Editor in Figure 12.3. One thing about the Registry, unlike the filesystem, is that there are multiple top-level items.

From the perspective of the Registry Editor, there are five top-level items in the Registry. The Registry is composed of keys and values. When you look at the editor and the hierarchy, what you are looking at are the keys, which are represented as folders. These keys can contain multiple additional keys or even values. Each value has a name and the contents of the value, which are structured into data types, which we'll get to in a moment. For now, let's take a look at the top-level or root keys within the Registry. There are others, but since these are the ones the Registry Editor presents, they are the ones we are going to look at, especially since these are the ones you are most likely to interact with in a programmatic fashion:

➤ `HKEY_LOCAL_MACHINE` (**HKLM**): A collection of keys and values that contain settings that belong to the machine as a whole. These may be considered operating system settings primarily, although you will also find configuration settings related to system services. Inside HKLM are additional important keys. One of them is SAM, which is the Security Accounts Manager, and this key includes information about users and accounts in addition to other information. The `SECURITY` key includes information about the security policy settings on the system, such as audit policy settings and other user account controls that are configured above or outside of the individual users. The `SYSTEM` key contains information about hardware or other devices. The `Software` key includes information related to software that has been installed on the system, but the configuration is across the system as a whole rather than settings specific to an individual user since there are settings that are user-specific in software. All of those are in a different root key.

➤ `HKEY_CURRENT_CONFIG` (**HCC**): A root key that is not stored on disk at all. It only exists at runtime and contains information about the hardware configuration of the system as it is currently running.

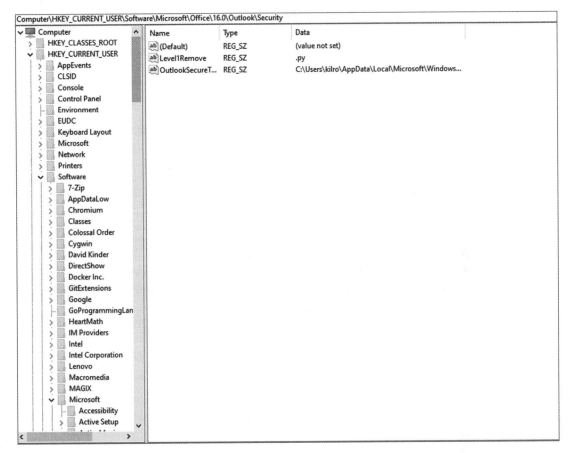

FIGURE 12.3: Registry editor

➤ `HKEY_CLASSES_ROOT` (**HKCR**): When applications are installed, they may register with the system, which means they may have some system-level configuration details that need to be stored. These are outside of the application-specific configuration itself but are details that the system as a whole needs to know about. One example of this would be registering handlers for file extensions. All of the handlers for different file extensions are registered in this key. One fun fact about this key is that the `.exe` file extension, which executable files have, is registered here. The handler for it is a universally unique identifier (UUID), which points to the application or system component that is going to handle that file type. Malicious software may be able to hijack that handler to sit in between the actual executable and the operating system so the malicious software always runs ahead of the program the user intends to run.

➤ `HKEY_USERS` (**HKU**): Your system may have multiple users configured on it, which may include your user account, a local administrator account, and a guest account. In an enterprise environment, there may be many other accounts that your system knows about. All of these accounts are stored here.

➤ `HKEY_CURRENT_USER` (**HKCU**): Stores information about the user who is currently logged in or at least the user who is interacting with the Registry. You would never get to another user's settings by using the HKCU root key. Any user-specific application settings go under this root key as well as any other system settings specific to the user, including things like the desktop background, screen saver, and any other user interface settings the user has configured.

Most of these root keys exist in some manner on disk. They are stored in files called *hives*. These hives do not correspond to the top-level keys. Instead, they are stored in a different way. All of the hives under HKLM are typically stored in `C:\Windows\system32\config`. If your Windows installation is in a different directory, it would be located there, which is why it's usually represented as `%SystemRoot%\system32\config`. The `%SystemRoot%` part is a variable that just says wherever the Windows installation is actually stored, no matter what directory that happens to be. Figure 12.4 shows a list of the files in that directory on a Windows 10 system. These are binary files, so you would not interact with them directly; nor would you be able to, because the system would protect itself from that level of contamination. The `.log` files are there because they store transactional information related to changes to the Registry. This is because these files are databases, so transactions are logged in case of a failure. The changes can be rolled back into the Registry if needed to recover from the failure.

SAM	10/7/2020 8:22 PM	File	128 KB
SAM.LOG1	10/3/2020 2:55 AM	LOG1 File	78 KB
SAM.LOG2	10/3/2020 2:55 AM	LOG2 File	64 KB
SAM{899818f5-0551-11eb-a810-000d3...	10/3/2020 4:48 AM	BLF File	64 KB
SAM{899818f5-0551-11eb-a810-000d3...	10/3/2020 4:48 AM	REGTRANS-MS File	512 KB
SAM{899818f5-0551-11eb-a810-000d3...	10/3/2020 4:48 AM	REGTRANS-MS File	512 KB
SECURITY	10/7/2020 8:22 PM	File	32 KB
SECURITY.LOG1	10/3/2020 2:55 AM	LOG1 File	88 KB
SECURITY.LOG2	10/3/2020 2:55 AM	LOG2 File	8 KB
SECURITY{899818e8-0551-11eb-a810-0...	10/3/2020 4:48 AM	BLF File	64 KB
SECURITY{899818e8-0551-11eb-a810-0...	10/3/2020 4:48 AM	REGTRANS-MS File	512 KB
SECURITY{899818e8-0551-11eb-a810-0...	10/3/2020 4:48 AM	REGTRANS-MS File	512 KB
SOFTWARE	10/7/2020 8:22 PM	File	120,064 KB
SOFTWARE.LOG1	10/3/2020 2:55 AM	LOG1 File	25,392 KB
SOFTWARE.LOG2	10/3/2020 2:55 AM	LOG2 File	26,016 KB
SOFTWARE{899818d0-0551-11eb-a810...	10/3/2020 4:48 AM	BLF File	64 KB
SOFTWARE{899818d0-0551-11eb-a810...	10/3/2020 4:48 AM	REGTRANS-MS File	512 KB
SOFTWARE{899818d0-0551-11eb-a810...	10/3/2020 4:48 AM	REGTRANS-MS File	512 KB
SYSTEM	10/7/2020 8:22 PM	File	27,648 KB

FIGURE 12.4: Registry hive files

There are also files related to the individual user. The entries that belong in HKCU are found in a file called `ntuser.dat` in the user's home directory. This file exists even if the user isn't logged into the system. The only way to see the entries under HKCU is to log in and look at that Registry key. Otherwise, it's an inert file on the disk that can be pulled off and parsed in an offline fashion as needed.

Programmatic Access to the Registry

Because Windows is such a dominant operating system around the world and the Registry is such a critical component of its successful operation, it's probably not surprising that there are many ways of interacting with the Windows Registry. We're going to start by taking a look at a native way to programmatically access the Windows Registry, just by way of comparison so you can see similarities and differences. PowerShell is a language that was developed by Microsoft as a way for system administrators to perform essential administrative functions in a programmatic way on Windows systems. Other systems had languages like the Bourne (and later, the Bourne Again) Shell on Unix-like systems, which is a scripting language for doing repetitive tasks that may be especially related to system administration. Microsoft wanted to offer the same thing for Windows administrators so they could write powerful scripts without having to get another language system on board.

Today, PowerShell is a cross-platform language that runs on Windows as well as macOS and Linux. It has become much more powerful than it used to be, to the point that it has become the language of choice for attackers who want to use programs to perform functions on compromised systems like downloading files or performing reconnaissance on other systems on the network. Why bother getting another language that requires installing additional software when there is already a powerful language built into the operating system? We can use this language ourselves to write some quick scripts to interact with the Windows Registry.

The nice thing about PowerShell is that it is similar to shell languages on Unix-like operating systems. There are some constructs that come from programming languages, but there are also built-in commands that can be called. In the case of PowerShell, these are called *cmdlets*, and they expose functionality to the user that makes querying the system or even making changes to the system very easy. We don't even necessarily need to write a program to get information. As an example, to print out the keys and values within a key in the Registry, all we need to do is use the Get-ChildItem cmdlet. Following is the output of this cmdlet on the HKCU key:

```
PS C:\Users\kilro> Get-ChildItem -Path Registry::HKEY_CURRENT_USER


    Hive: HKEY_CURRENT_USER

Name                           Property
----                           --------
AppEvents
CLSID
Console                        ColorTable00    : 789516
                               ColorTable01    : 14300928
                               ColorTable02    : 958739
                               ColorTable03    : 14521914
                               ColorTable04    : 2035653
                               ColorTable05    : 9967496
                               ColorTable06    : 40129
                               ColorTable07    : 13421772
                               ColorTable08    : 7763574
                               ColorTable09    : 16742459
                               ColorTable10    : 837142
                               ColorTable11    : 14079585
                               ColorTable12    : 5654759
```

continues

(continued)

```
                               ColorTable13              : 10354868
                               ColorTable14              : 10875385
                               ColorTable15              : 15921906
                               CtrlKeyShortcutsDisabled  : 0
                               CursorColor               : 4294967295
                               CursorSize                : 25
                               DefaultBackground         : 4294967295
                               DefaultForeground         : 4294967295
                               EnableColorSelection      : 0
```

This is not a recursive function, meaning we are only going to get keys and values that are directly in the HKCU key. This doesn't reach into additional keys and provide information from inside them. However, it's easy enough to just add on another key we want to look at more closely. Following is the output from looking into the EventLabels key underneath HKCU:

```
PS C:\Users\kilro> Get-ChildItem -Path Registry::HKEY_CURRENT_USER\AppEvents\
EventLabels


        Hive: HKEY_CURRENT_USER\AppEvents\EventLabels

Name                          Property
----                          --------
.Default                      (default)     : Default Beep
                              DispFileName  : @mmres.dll,-5824
ActivatingDocument            (default)     : Complete Navigation
                              DispFileName  : @ieframe.dll,-10321
AppGPFault                    (default)     : Program Error
                              DispFileName  : @mmres.dll,-5825
BlockedPopup                  (default)     : Blocked Pop-up Window
                              DispFileName  : @ieframe.dll,-10325
CCSelect                      (default)     : Select
                              DispFileName  : @ieframe.dll,-10323
ChangeTheme                   (default)     : Change Theme
                              DispFileName  : @mmres.dll,-5860
Close                         (default)     : Close Program
                              DispFileName  : @mmres.dll,-5826
CriticalBatteryAlarm          (default)     : Critical Battery Alarm
                              DispFileName  : @mmres.dll,-5827
DeviceConnect                 (default)     : Device Connect
                              DispFileName  : @mmres.dll,-5828
DeviceDisconnect              (default)     : Device Disconnect
                              DispFileName  : @mmres.dll,-5829
```

We could write a PowerShell program to enumerate through all the keys in the Registry underneath any given key, but that would be a lot of information that would be difficult to read through, so there isn't a lot of value to doing so. Just knowing you can easily use a single cmdlet to get a lot of detail from inside the Registry is nice. One thing we didn't talk about before, though we hinted at it, is that the Registry uses data types. The following are some of the data types you will see used in the Windows Registry:

➤ REG_SZ: A string value that is zero or null-terminated, meaning the last character in the string has the ASCII value of 0.

➤ REG_BINARY: Any arbitrary binary data of any length.

➤ REG_DWORD: A binary value that is 32 bits in length. This is an unsigned integer, meaning it can have the values of 0 and 4,294,967,295.

➤ REG_MULTI_SZ: A collection of strings, which means you would have a list of zero-terminated strings. If you were to display them, each would typically be on a line by itself.

➤ REG_QWORD: A binary value that is 64 bits long. This is an integer, just like the DWORD value, which means it's a whole number and doesn't include a decimal value.

Using Rust to Access the Registry

Now that you know what the Registry is all about and how it is constructed, we can take a look at how to get access to keys and values using Rust. We're going to take a look at a simple program written in Rust that performs some basic functions in the Registry. Following is the complete program that demonstrates the use of the winreg crate, which we will break down a little at a time. The winreg crate has the code that interfaces with the Windows API functions that give us access to the Registry:

```
use std::io;
use std::path::Path;
use std::env;
use winreg::enums::*;
use winreg::RegKey;

fn enumerate_run() -> io::Result<()> {
    let hklm = RegKey::predef(HKEY_LOCAL_MACHINE);
    let runkey = hklm.open_subkey("Software\\Microsoft\\Windows\\CurrentVersion\\Run")?;

    for (name, value) in runkey.enum_values().map(|entry| entry.unwrap()) {
        println!("{} = {:?}", name, value);
    }

    Ok(())
}

fn write_value() -> io::Result<()> {

    let hkcu = RegKey::predef(HKEY_CURRENT_USER);
    let path = Path::new("Software").join("KilroySoft");
    let (key, reg_resp) = hkcu.create_subkey(&path)?;

    match reg_resp {
        REG_CREATED_NEW_KEY => println!("A new key has been created"),
        REG_OPENED_EXISTING_KEY => println!("An existing key has been opened"),
    }

    let working_dir = env::current_dir()?;
    let display_dir = working_dir.to_str().unwrap();

    key.set_value("location", &display_dir)?;

    Ok(())
}
```

continues

(continued)

```
fn read_value() -> io::Result<()> {
    let hkcu = RegKey::predef(HKEY_CURRENT_USER);
    let read_key = hkcu.open_subkey("Software\\kilroySoft")?;

    let location: String = read_key.get_value("location")?;
    println!("Location: {}", location);

    Ok(())

}

fn main() -> io::Result<()> {

    enumerate_run()?;
    write_value()?;
    read_value()?;

    Ok(())
}
```

First, the use statements. We'll be using three out of the std crate. We could just provide the statement use std::* and pull in everything we need, but some of the modules we're going to be using are nested in the crate; so, again, we have a namespace issue. To use any of the input/output functionality, we'd have to preface it with io:: if we just pulled in everything. The same would be true with any of the path features. We'd have to use path:: rather than just referring to them as though they were a part of the program proper. While it seems more specific, which leads to an easier understanding of the purpose of the program, it's probably a little more readable to not have to parse the path through the crate and modules for specific structs and traits. That's why we get to specific modules in the crate.

The next module we pull in, std::path, is a way to work with different paths in an abstract way. Anything that is stored or referred to in a hierarchical fashion will have a path, meaning you need to start at a top-level item and work through successively lower items until you get to the item you want. Anything in a filesystem will have a path associated with it. The same thing is true with the Registry because it is organized in a hierarchical fashion. Since we are going to need to get to items in the Registry, we need to pull in the std::path module for the functions that let us use path references.

The other modules we are using will be pulled in with specific functionality rather than as the high-level crate because, again, it may aid readability to not have to parse through the path in a module to get to a struct or a trait. These are all from the winreg crate, which is not a standard crate, so a line needs to be added in Cargo.toml to be sure cargo builds that crate when you perform a build.

One important key in the Windows Registry tells the operating system a list of programs that should run when the system boots up. This is stored in HKEY_LOCAL_MACHINE in the Software hive. The Software hive is organized by vendor, so all of the Windows configuration settings fall under the Microsoft key. We are looking for the key HKLM\Software\Microsoft\Windows\CurrentVersion\Run.

This will have potentially many values stored under it, one for each program that is configured to run. Following is the function that is going to enumerate all the values in that key:

```rust
fn enumerate_run() -> io::Result<()> {
    let hklm = RegKey::predef(HKEY_LOCAL_MACHINE);
    let runkey = hklm.open_subkey("Software\\Microsoft\\Windows\\CurrentVersion\\Run")?;

    for (name, value) in runkey.enum_values().map(|entry| entry.unwrap()) {
        println!("{} = {:?}", name, value);
    }

    Ok(())
}
```

Since we are using input/output functions, we need to be able to return IO errors. So the return is going to be `io::Result<()>`, which allows the function to terminate if any IO errors happen, returning the error. In `winreg`, there are some predefined keys. This allows us a starting point in the Registry. We are going to start by creating an identifier that stores what is effectively a pointer to the `HKEY_LOCAL_MACHINE` key. Once we have that in place, we can use the `open_subkey()` trait to open keys that are under the top-level key. It may be helpful to think of this as opening a file. The line including `hklm.open_subkey()` is similar to opening a file. We need to have a handle on the key so we can read from it.

Since there are multiple potential values inside that key, we need to enumerate through those values, which means we need an iterator. If `runkey` is our handle to the key, we can call the `enum_values()` trait on that handle in order to get values back. First, we need the name of the value, and then we need the contents of that named value. This means we will get a tuple, which is stored in `(name, value)`. Our iterator is going to return a `Result` for each entry in the key, and that `Result` needs to be unwrapped, so we are going to use `map()` on the results from the iterator to get the value we need. Once we have the contents of each value, we can just print them out. Each line of output here will be the name of a program and then the path to that program.

Writing values to the Registry is slightly more cumbersome but not onerous. Following is the function where we write a value into the Registry. As before, we are performing IO functions, so there is a chance of generating an error, which means we need to be able to handle those errors. As before, we are starting with a handle to a predefined key. We are going to tack onto that top-level key—in this case, `HKEY_CURRENT_USER`—a path to a new key. We are going to create a key, or perhaps just open the key if it already exists, named `KilroySoft` underneath the `Software` key. This will give us a full path of `HKEY_CURRENT_USER\Software\KilroySoft`. That's just the key. We still need a value.

```rust
fn write_value() -> io::Result<()> {

    let hkcu = RegKey::predef(HKEY_CURRENT_USER);
    let path = Path::new("Software").join("KilroySoft");
    let (key, reg_resp) = hkcu.create_subkey(&path)?;

    match reg_resp {
        REG_CREATED_NEW_KEY => println!("A new key has been created"),
        REG_OPENED_EXISTING_KEY => println!("An existing key has been opened"),
    }
```

continues

(continued)

```
        let working_dir = env::current_dir()?;
        let display_dir = working_dir.to_str().unwrap();

        key.set_value("location", &display_dir)?;

        Ok(())
    }
```

Before we get to the value, we are going to create the subkey based on the `Path` that we created. `create_subkey()` requires an `OsStr` value, which is the result of calling `Path::new()`. The trait `create_subkey()` also returns a pair of responses. First is the handle to the key we are going to use when we write the value out to the Registry. The second is a response value indicating whether the key already existed or not. If the key already existed, `create_subkey()` will resort to simply opening the existing key rather than trying to create the key again, which could end up overwriting some data. We can use a `match()` statement to determine whether we created the key or just opened it.

The only reason for checking with the `match()` statement is to let us know whether the key existed or not. From the perspective of wanting to write out a value, it doesn't matter if the key the value is in needed to be created or if it already existed. All we need to know is that we have the key and we have a handle to it, so we can write a value into it. This is a case, as was also true with other trait calls in this function, where we are going to just drop out of the function if we run into a problem. As we've seen before, the `?` at the end of the statement indicates that the `Result` should be unwrapped if that's what comes back; otherwise the function should simply fail, with an error being returned. You may note that this is an example of offensive programming. If there is a hint of a problem, we're simply going to fail and not try to make do with what we have. We aren't going to spend a lot of time trying to determine whether everything looks exactly right. We try out what we are trying to accomplish, and if it doesn't work, we just fail and let the user figure it out.

We have a handle to a key where we want to write a value. We need a value to write. Rather than making up a string to write out, let's do something interesting and get the current working directory. This is an environment variable, meaning it is information that came from what was in place in the environment when the program ran. We are going to use the `env` module to get that information. This raises an interesting point about the `use` keyword and how it works with namespaces. You will have noticed that we have indicated we are going to use `std::env`. Surely that should mean we wouldn't need to refer to anything in `env` by clarifying. In fact, if you wanted to refer to `current_dir()` without prefixing it with the module it came out of, you would need to write `use std::env::*` instead of `use std::env`. The way we have written it now, all we've done is bring in the `env` namespace. We still need to prefix anything out of that module with `env::` to make it clear what module any trait used comes from.

Of course, just getting the current working directory is not sufficient, because what we have for a data type from that call is a `PathBuf`. You may recall from earlier that `PathBuf` is not one of the data types the Registry understands, so we need to convert the `PathBuf` to something we can make use of. We will use the `to_str()` trait to get a string value (note the lowercase string rather than the uppercase `String`, meaning it's just an array of characters rather than a Rust struct). This is something we can pass into the `set_value()` trait called on the `key` handle we had previously created. We are passing a reference to the string rather than passing the actual string (meaning the memory location of the data) into the trait.

Finally, we have another function to look at, which is going to pull the value that we just created out of the Registry to demonstrate it was written in to begin with. Following is the function that will read a value out of the Registry:

```
fn read_value() -> io::Result<()> {
    let hkcu = RegKey::predef(HKEY_CURRENT_USER);
    let read_key = hkcu.open_subkey("Software\\kilroySoft")?;

    let location: String = read_key.get_value("location")?;
    println!("Location: {}", location);

    Ok(())

}
```

As before, this is going to return `io::Result<()>` because we are interacting with the Registry and performing input/output functions. First, we start with getting a handle to the top-level key `HKEY_CURRENT_USER`, meaning we are looking at settings specific to the user who is currently logged in or, more specifically, executing the program. Once we have the handle, we can call the `open_subkey()` trait on it to select a key that is underneath the top-level key. We are going to be using the `Software` key, because we are writing software, and a key underneath that named `kilroySoft`. This call gives us a second handle to the specific key we want to read from.

The next line is the important one. We create a new identifier and declare it as a `String`, placing the result of `get_value()` into it. We need to specify the value we are trying to read. That's passed in as a string literal. We called the value `"location"` before, so of course that's what we are going to use here.

One thing you may have noticed throughout this program is that we specified the path in the Registry using \\ instead of \. That's because Windows uses the backslash (\) as a delimiter between levels in any hierarchy, whether it's in the filesystem or in the Registry. The problem with that is, in the rest of the computing world, the backslash is used as an escape character. That means in cases where a character means something specific, but we want to use it literally, we need to *escape* it, telling whatever is interpreting the value that we mean it as the character rather than whatever function or purpose the character has that's different from the literal purpose of the character. In this case, because the backslash character is an escape character, we need to escape it, which results in using \\ rather than the \ that is really what is meant.

We can take a quick look at the `main` function so as not to completely ignore it, although it's really just a driver, meaning its sole purpose is to drive (or call) the other functions where we were demonstrating capabilities. Following is the `main` function:

```
fn main() -> io::Result<()> {

    enumerate_run()?;
    write_value()?;
    read_value()?;

    Ok(())
}
```

Again, we are calling functions that can return errors, so we need to be able to handle errors in the main function as well. We are going to do the same return from this function as we have with the others just because that's the error the other functions will return, so we need to match it. There are three statements of substance, which are just calls to the three functions that we looked at earlier. Each of them is terminated by a ? because each of those functions will return a Result, whether it's an error or just an empty Ok(). Speaking of empty Ok(), the last line in this program is the expression Ok(), indicating a successful run through the function, which is also a successful run through the program.

SYSTEM INFORMATION WITH RUST

We're working on doing system programming, so we will need to take a look at getting information about the system. Modern operating systems are very complex things. The operating system, meaning the kernel, has to keep track of a lot of information, so there are a lot of data structures in memory to maintain all of that information so it's available. Of course, not all of the details about the operating system are stored in memory. Some of them are stored in configuration databases, such as the Security Accounts Manager (SAM) in the Windows Registry in the case of user account information. There is a crate available to us, called sysinfo, which can be used to extract a lot of information about the operating system. While these details may well be stored in the operating system portion of memory—which is a special piece of memory, since it's the first memory available to the system when it boots, before the entire amount of memory becomes addressable—the traits and data structures referred to in the sysinfo crate are going to be pulled using application programming interface (API) calls to the operating system. This is another example of data encapsulation, but this isn't only about protecting the data from being misused or tampered with. Because the memory is owned by the operating system, it requires the highest level of permissions to get access to it. However, the operating system will happily provide details for the information we are requesting. All we need to do is ask it in the right way, meaning we use the provided API calls to get the data rather than trying to reach out for it directly:

```rust
use sysinfo::{ProcessExt, SystemExt, UserExt};
use std::env;

fn display_memory() {
    let mut system = sysinfo::System::new_all();
    system.refresh_memory();

    println!("System memory:\t {} KB", system.get_total_memory());
    println!("Used memory:\t {} KB", system.get_used_memory());
    println!("Total swap:\t {} KB", system.get_total_swap());
    println!("Used swap:\t {} KB", system.get_used_swap());
}

fn display_disks() {
    let mut system = sysinfo::System::new_all();
    system.refresh_disks_list();

    for disk in system.get_disks() {
        println!("{:?}", disk);
    }
}
```

```
fn list_processes() {
    let mut system = sysinfo::System::new_all();
    system.refresh_all();

    for (pid, proc_entry) in system.get_processes() {
        println!("{}:{}, status: {:?}", pid, proc_entry.name(), proc_entry.status());
    }
}

fn display_users() {
    let mut system = sysinfo::System::new_all();
    system.refresh_all();

    for user in system.get_users() {
        println!("{} is in {} groups", user.get_name(), user.get_groups().len());
    }
}

fn main() {

    let s = sysinfo::System::new();
    println!("This system has been up {} seconds", s.get_boot_time());
    println!("The current process id is {}", sysinfo::get_current_pid().unwrap());

    let args: Vec<String> = env::args().collect();

    match args[1].as_str() {
        "disks" => display_disks(),
        "memory" => display_memory(),
        "process" => list_processes(),
        "users" => display_users(),
        _ => println!("You haven't provided an acceptable parameter")
    }

}
```

As usual, we have use statements at the top of the file. We are going to be using command-line arguments, so we need to make sure to pull that functionality into the program. We are also going to be using a number of modules from the sysinfo crate, so we will pull those in specifically so all of the data structures and traits will work when we call them. We'll be using ProcessExt, SystemExt, and UserExt for this program. There are others, including NetworkExt, for getting network information from the system.

We can start with the main function for this one because it will introduce us to the use of the sysinfo crate, as well as refresh our memories on the use of command-line parameters. The first thing we are going to do is to pull some system information. We need to create a new instance of a struct that is going to hold all of the current system information for us. To get that struct instance, we are going to call the sysinfo::System::new() trait, which is going to populate that new instance for us. A couple of pieces of information that are just general purpose are how long the system has been up as well as the process identification number for the process currently executing (the running instance of this program).

Printing this information is done with a couple of println!() statements, calling two traits. The first is the System struct instance we have, called s. This is the amount of time the system has been up, meaning the number of seconds since the system booted up. The second piece of information is in the `sysinfo` module itself, so we need to call `get_process_id()` out of the module directly. You may wonder why we aren't pulling this out of the instance of the `System` struct we have. The process ID for the current process has to be extracted from the system, but it isn't a collection of information belonging to the system overall. Instead, it's a system-provided piece of information that belongs to the process we are running.

We are going to pull in the command-line parameters now using the `env::args()` trait. Since we want all of the arguments together in a `Vector`, we are going to use the `collect()` trait. That's going to take each individual argument and push it onto the `Vector` so it can be referred to either directly or through an iterator later on. When writing text-based programs like this, you are often going to need to pull command-line parameters to direct the way the program runs. This little chunk of code we're using here in the `main` function is helpful to pull and reuse as you need it. This is similar to a chunk of code we have used in other programs written in this book.

Once we have the collection, we could iterate through all the provided command-line parameters, but in this case, the design decision is to just accept a single parameter. This means for each run of the program, we are only going to call a single function, at most. If one of the allowed parameters isn't provided, we're going to tell the user they haven't specified an allowed function. This means all we need to do is check the second parameter in our vector. The first parameter, you may recall, is always the name of the called program. Also, the vector of parameters is 0-based, which means the first position in the vector is 0. Every position is will be offset backward by 1. We start at 0, so the second parameter is going to be 1. This means we can pull the only parameter we care about using `args[1]`, which should be the function the user wants to run.

We are comparing the provided function name to a string literal, which is different from the Rust `String` data structure. Because we have what is essentially an ordered collection of characters, or a character string, we need to convert the command-line parameter to a `str` data type rather than the `String` it currently is. We do this by calling the `as_str()` trait on the parameter we have extracted from the vector. We can then use `match()` to perform the comparison and call the correct function based on the parameter provided by the user. You may notice we are expecting the case to be exact. Any difference in case, such as providing `Disks`, for instance, isn't going to match. This is something that could be corrected easily, but rather than compensating for something strange the user may be doing, we can draw a hard line and say, "Do it my way, or the program is just going to fail." Remember, it's not always a virtue to compensate for unexpected output.

We can move on to looking at the first function that's going to provide us with system information. We'll jump back up to the top of the file to look at the function that will provide us memory information. Following is the function we'll be looking at:

```
fn display_memory() {
    let mut system = sysinfo::System::new_all();
    system.refresh_memory();

    println!("System memory:\t {} KB", system.get_total_memory());
    println!("Used memory:\t {} KB", system.get_used_memory());
    println!("Total swap:\t {} KB", system.get_total_swap());
    println!("Used swap:\t {} KB", system.get_used_swap());
}
```

As we did before, we are going to create an instance of the `System` struct. To make sure we have the latest information, we are going to call `refresh_memory()` to be sure we've populated the right places in the struct. Once we have called that, we can just run through and print out the memory information. These calls are very simple and straightforward because there is no collection of information associated with any of the information, unlike what we will see later on. First, we want to print the total amount of memory in the system, which is expressed in kilobytes. Second, we are going to get the amount of used memory, meaning the amount of memory that is being consumed by all the applications that are running on the system. To determine the amount of free memory, you could easily subtract the used memory from the total.

Swap space is the amount of space that has been allocated on disk to temporarily store data or programs that need to be pulled out of main memory to make room for other data or programs. Today, most systems have adequate memory installed so that they don't need swap space; but if you have a system without a lot of memory installed in it, say 4 GB or less, your operating system may need to keep shuffling programs in and out of memory. Programs that haven't made use of the processor, meaning they aren't actively running, may be swapped out to disk. The last two calls in this function will give us the total amount of swap space configured as well as the amount of swap space currently being used.

Following is the function for getting disk information. Since systems may have multiple disks installed, we will have a collection that comes back when we call `get_disks()` on the instance of `System` that we have again created (don't worry, we aren't really creating that many instances of this data structure because we are only calling a single function, and the data structure is destroyed when the function ends anyway). Because we have a collection, we need an iterator to run through them all. We will use a `for ... in` loop to work through all the results in the collection of disks. The `:?` in the format statement inside the `println!()` call means there is a collection of information and to print all of it. This saves us from needing to put multiple `{}` sections into the `println!()` statement, trying to format it ourselves. Rust will take care of correctly formatting the complete collection of information, which is effectively a tuple with multiple values in it:

```
fn display_disks() {
    let mut system = sysinfo::System::new_all();
    system.refresh_disks_list();

    for disk in system.get_disks() {
        println!("{:?}", disk);
    }
}
```

We're going to get another collection of information in this next function. The operating system maintains a process table, which contains information about all of the processes that are currently known by the operating system, meaning they are in some running state. This means they have been executed, although perhaps they are sitting waiting for something, which means they are idle. *Running* in this context doesn't necessarily mean they are actively in the processor with operation codes executing merrily along. Following is the function to list information out of the process table:

```
fn list_processes() {
    let mut system = sysinfo::System::new_all();
    system.refresh_all();
```

continues

(continued)
```
        for (pid, proc_entry) in system.get_processes() {
            println!("{}:{}, status: {:?}", pid, proc_entry.name(), proc_entry.
    status());
        }
    }
```

As before, we get an instance of the System structure. We call the get_processes() trait on that structure to get the complete list of the processes on the system. This returns a collection of information to the function. Again, we will use a for .. in loop to look at each entry. Each process entry is going to have a process identifier, often shortened to pid. There will also be a data structure that contains a lot of information about the process. We are going to pull both of those out of the process table we get back. First, we refer to pid as the process ID. We will also create an identifier named proc_entry for the individual entry out of the process table. As noted, proc_entry is going to be a struct itself, so we need to get individual pieces of information from it directly. While there are a lot of ways to look at a process, we will be checking the name of the process. The name of the process is going to be the name of the file that was executed to create the running process as well as getting a status on that process. In most cases, the status will be that the process is running, although sometimes you will get other statuses. This may also be dependent on the operating system you are executing this program on.

The final function to look at is the list of users configured on the system. This may not be an interesting list in most cases, because today, most systems are effectively single-user, even though the operating system can support multiple users being configured to use the system. In some cases, multiple users can be using the system at the same time. In fact, this is actually true if you consider that every system service has to run as a user, and it's unlikely the system service is going to be running as your user. Even if you aren't aware, there are probably at least three users configured on your Windows system and quite a few more than that if you are using a Unix-like operating system like Linux.

The function, as all the others have, gets a System instance, and we refresh the data to make sure all the latest information has been populated into the struct. Following is the code for this function. As we've done in other functions, we are going to get a collection of information back when we call get_users(). We will handle this the same way as we have by using the iterator built into the results from get_users() to get each entry in the results. For each pass through the for loop, we are going to call get_name() to get the name of the user—just the username, not the real name. We will also call get_groups(), which is going to provide us another collection because it's a list of groups rather than a single group. We're only going to get the total number of groups a user has been configured with here rather than printing out all the groups:

```
    fn display_users() {
        let mut system = sysinfo::System::new_all();
        system.refresh_all();

        for user in system.get_users() {
            println!("{} is in {} groups", user.get_name(), user.get_groups().len());
        }
    }
```

We can now see what it looks like to run the program. This run is going to be on a Windows system. The output may look different on another operating system. Following is a portion of the output from the call to look at the processes:

```
PS C:\Users\kilro\Documents\rust\ch12_systemdetails>
.\target\debug\ch12_systemdetails.exe process
This system has been up 1602356061 seconds
The current process id is 14824
1372:msedge.exe => status: Run
4468:Lenovo.Modern.ImController.exe => status: Run
2884:svchost.exe => status: Run
9472:GoogleCrashHandler64.exe => status: Run
13644:Lenovo.Modern.ImController.PluginHost.Device.exe => status: Run
5940:svchost.exe => status: Run
1956:WinStore.App.exe => status: Run
4824:LockApp.exe => status: Run
104:Secure System => status: Run
4296:svchost.exe => status: Run
1040:svchost.exe => status: Run
11288:svchost.exe => status: Run
```

This program could easily be extended to provide additional system information, and you could have yourself a nice utility to provide you with a lot of useful details about any system you ran it on.

PERSISTENCE (FOR FUN)

One other thing you can do using the Windows Registry is to ensure programs keep running from one boot of a system to another. This is a very common technique that malware uses. We can add functionality to any program we write that will ensure the program continues to run every time the system is booted or rebooted. The following is the code that makes that possible. It contains a function that makes sure the correct Registry key is in place as well as a main function that calls that function. We're going to reuse some of the techniques we've looked at earlier in this chapter. We're going to use the functions from the winreg crate. We also need to be able to get the current executable, so we are going to use some features out of the std crate that let us get the path to the program that is running:

```
use winreg::enums::*;
use winreg::RegKey;
use std::path;
use std::io;

fn persist() -> io::Result<()> {
    let hkcu = RegKey::predef(HKEY_CURRENT_USER);
    let cur_ver = hkcu.open_subkey_with_flags("Software\\Microsoft\\Windows\\
CurrentVersion\\Run", KEY_WRITE)?;

    let mut exe_string = String::new();

    match std::env::current_exe() {
        Ok(this_exe) => exe_string = format!("{}", this_exe.display()),
        Err(e) => println!("failed to get current exe {}", e)
    };

    match cur_ver.set_value("MyProcess", &exe_string) {
```

continues

(continued)

```
            Ok(_) => println!("Successfully added value"),
            Err(e) => println!("There was an error {}", e)
        };

        Ok(())
    }


    fn main() {

        match persist() {
            Ok(o) => o,
            Err(e) => panic!("Error! {}", e)
        };


    }
```

There are a few Registry keys that will allow you to make sure a program runs when the system starts. The first key is `HKEY_LOCAL_MACHINE\Software\Microsoft\Windows\CurrentVersion\Run`. This ensures that the program starts at boot time. Another—the one we will be using—is `HKEY_CURRENT_USER\Software\Microsoft\Windows\CurrentVersion\Run`. There are two differences between this and the first one. First, this one doesn't require administrator privileges to add to the Registry since each user will have access to the Registry keys for their own configuration settings. Second, any program loaded into the `Run` key for the user will require the user to log in before it starts. The system can't know the current user until a user logs in, after all.

The function that sets the persistence follows here. Just as before, we need to open a key. This is going to be the `Run` key for the user that runs the program. Once we have an identifier for the `Run` key, we can get the current process. This requires calling `std::env::current_exe()`. This function returns a complete path to the executable, which is what we need since we can't run the program without the full path. Once we have the current path, we can set a value in the `Run` key. It doesn't matter what we name the value, as long as the contents of the value are the path to the executable. This requires converting the `PathBuf` struct that is returned from the `current_exe()` call to a `String`, which is needed to write to the Registry.

Accessing the Registry can generate errors. This may be especially true if you don't have permissions to the keys you want to write to. We need to handle the errors in the `persist()` function, which means we need to accept the same errors in the `main` function. All we need to do is create a `match()` to handle the `Result` that comes back from the `persist()` function, and we're okay. Of course, the only thing this does is make sure the program (this one) starts up when the user logs in. We'd probably want the actual program to do more than just this, since a program that just executes and makes sure it is going to execute each time the user logs in isn't especially useful. Figure 12.5 shows the value that has been added to the Registry.

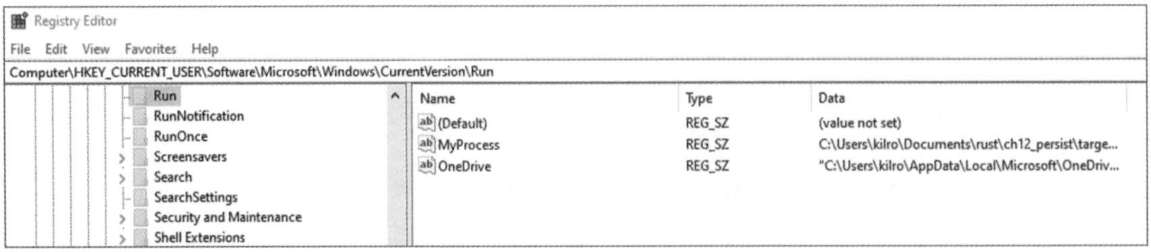

FIGURE 12.5: Value added to the Registry

SUMMARY

While there may not be a lot of value in either the debate or even knowing the answer, there is sometimes a debate about whether Rust is object-oriented or not. The only reason to have this discussion at all, it seems, is to make it easier to understand Rust by trying to fit it into some preconceived ideas about what an object-oriented language is and how it works. There are a lot of features in object-oriented languages, but one feature that is commonly believed to be important is inheritance. This allows you to create a class that has some properties and methods (data and functionality). You can then extend that class by creating a child class that inherits all the characteristics of the parent (the class you originally created). This may allow you to get more specific in terms of functionality offered by the class. You can also get into polymorphism once you start down the inheritance road, meaning you can refer to the parent class and get one set of information or functionality for the child class. This can get complicated.

Fortunately, Rust doesn't do inheritance, which means we don't need to deal with polymorphism in that sense. Instead, Rust offers a different way to extend functionality. Rust uses the struct as a foundational way to collect data. Data often doesn't exist by itself, meaning you don't often have single, unconnected variables in complex software. Instead, data is often related, so it makes sense to create complex data structures that put together all the related data. To allow something like data encapsulation, where data is stored together with functions that act on that data, Rust uses traits. These are abstract definitions of functionality that then need to be implemented for specific data types. Using these traits, you can extend functionality for any given data structure by providing a function that will act on the data structure. This is not the same as using classes and methods, but it can perform a similar function, and the use of traits offers some flexibility that the class model of object-oriented languages doesn't offer.

Rust is sometimes referred to as a systems programming language. This may mean several different things, so we aren't going to spend a lot of time on trying to debate the semantics of what it means. For our purposes, it means we have the ability to interact directly with the operating system to create interesting and useful programs that can help us out. On a Windows system, the Windows Registry is a critical collection of configuration information. Fortunately, as with many other interesting or important functions, there is a crate for that. The `winreg` crate offers us the ability to interrogate the Registry for information. Because the Registry is organized as a hierarchical database of sorts, we need to be able to handle using paths and navigating through the tree of data that the Registry is.

Using `winreg`, we can not only pull data out of the Registry but also create keys and values—the essential ways data is stored in the Registry, which you may think of as folders and files. There is a lot more in `winreg` that we didn't touch, but if you are going to do programming on a Windows system and feel you want to store and retrieve configuration settings, this is going to be an invaluable crate for you to get familiar with.

Similarly, if you want to interrogate the operating system itself to get details about what is going on with the running system, you will want to get familiar with the `sysinfo` crate. We looked at processes, users, disks, and memory, as well as some other pieces of information. We only scratched the surface of what you can pull out of the operating system. Fortunately, operating systems expose application programming interfaces to request this information, which means we aren't having to nose around in operating system memory space to get any of the information back.

1. Add some other pieces of information to store in the Registry using other data types supported by Windows.

2. Look up the documentation for the `sysinfo` crate and add another function to print out some additional information about your system.

3. Add a function to provide help to the user if they specify help on the command line for the system information program.

4. Fix the match in the `main` function of the system information program so it doesn't matter what case is provided by the user. You should consider converting the provided input to one case or the other (upper or lower) and then comparing it to what you expect.

5. Add the process path to the `list_processes()` output in the system information program. You can get this with the `exe()` trait.

6. Modify the `display_users()` function to list all the groups rather than just the number of groups that have been configured for the user.

ADDITIONAL RESOURCES

Here are some additional resources to learn more about the topics in this chapter:

About the Windows Registry - `docs.microsoft.com/en-us/windows/win32/sysinfo/registry`

winreg crate - `crates.io/crates/winreg`

sysinfo crate - `crates.io/crates/sysinfo`

"Windows Registry Information for Advanced Users" - `support.microsoft.com/en-us/help/256986/windows-registry-information-for-advanced-users`

"Windows Registry Demystified" - `www.howtogeek.com/370022/windows-registry-demystified-what-you-can-do-with-it`

13

Device Programming

IN THIS CHAPTER, YOU WILL LEARN THE FOLLOWING:

➤   How to interact with hardware devices like the Raspberry Pi

➤   How to use syslog on Unix-like systems to log from the application

➤   How to log to the Windows Event subsystem

A word you hear a lot today is *maker*, especially if you are listening in the right places. Technology has opened a lot of doors for a lot of people to go make things—all manner of things. The price of 3-D printers has dropped significantly since they were introduced many years ago. That has allowed people to make physical structures that are limited only by the size of the printer and the capabilities of the person designing the 3-D model that will be printed. You don't even have to do any design yourself if you don't want to or aren't capable. You can use someone else's design since there are so many places to download these files.

People with 3-D printers aren't the only ones who are experiencing a richness of opportunities. First, there are a number of communities to provide support, designs, and inspiration. If what you really want to do is mechanical automation, there are now low-cost computing platforms and ways to create electronic devices that can be programmed using different programming languages. While Python is a common language that is used in these situations, Rust has capabilities here as well.

One of the electronic devices that can be used to build mechanical creations is the Raspberry Pi, although it is not at all the only one. The Pi is what is called a *single-board computer*, meaning that on a single, small board that may be able to fit into the palm of your hand (it fits in mine, certainly), you have memory, processor, video, network, and a slot to insert a small memory card that serves as storage. Effectively, we use a microSD card as the hard drive in the system. It may not be as fast or capable as desktop systems, but one thing the Pi does is expose a hardware interface that allows us to plug in additional components, including low-level electronic components like LED lights and resistors, to build a variety of different things.

In this chapter, we are going to look at the hardware interface the Raspberry Pi has and, more importantly for our purposes, the library available for Rust to communicate with that hardware interface to interact with a number of different components.

One thing we haven't talked about so far is the importance of logging. Logging is an essential part of any application development. There are a couple of reasons to consider this. The first is that applications can run into issues. An application that doesn't log is going to be a lot harder to troubleshoot. Logging, when done well, provides essential information for when anyone running the application or managing the system needs to figure out why the application is misbehaving. Second, logging is essential when it comes to security. If an application happens to be compromised, logging can help us understand when the compromise happened. There are many other security considerations when it comes to logging, including authenticating users as well as providing access to resources. All of this is to say that logging is important, so we're going to take a look at how to generate logs for both Windows and Unix-like systems.

LOGGING

When you are developing a program, you need to be concerned with a number of different things. One of those things is input/output (I/O). You may think of I/O as only something you do with a user, meaning you are taking input from a user or displaying something for the user's consumption. Application programs may be highly concerned with that sort of I/O. As discussed in the last chapter, though, Rust can be used as a systems programming language, which means it may be used for services or other system-level components. In that case, there isn't really a user to be concerned about interacting with. You may be interacting silently with other devices for I/O, including the disk to write out or read files.

Even in cases where you are writing application programs and interacting with the user, you should still consider leaving a trail of activity in a log somewhere. In the case of system services, it's definitely true that you should be logging activities. In the case of system services, as noted earlier, you may not have a console to write out to for any visibility, so the only place you may have available to you for any sort of output may be a log. While you can certainly write out your own logs, typically to a file on disk, there are also system-provided logging facilities available. In the case of Windows, the Windows Event Log is where you would send log information. In the case of Unix-like operating systems, you would use syslog, which is a decades-old service that provides a lot of capabilities that applications can use, whether they are user-focused or system services.

Using syslog

In the 1980s, a lot of network protocols were still in development—or even if protocols had been mostly settled on, there weren't standard implementations of them, meaning there weren't applications that were dominant providers of those protocols. An early—and later, dominant—implementation of the Simple Mail Transfer Protocol (SMTP) was Sendmail. This was a program written by Eric Allman that became the de facto implementation for SMTP servers for many years. Also keep in mind that when Sendmail was written, there was no such thing as a Windows server, so Microsoft hadn't created its own SMTP implementation. That would come years and years later. One element of that Sendmail project was a way for Sendmail to log messages. This service was called *syslog*.

Syslog was originally an application that eventually became a logging protocol and then, over time, a logging standard. Today, if you are working on a Unix-like operating system, including Linux and macOS, you have syslog running, taking care of log messages for you. There are now many different implementations of syslog available, and even other products have implemented syslog capabilities. These include security information and event management (SIEM) systems, which may provide the capability to set up a syslog listener for systems to send log messages to.

Syslog has two vectors that can be used to define any given message. The first is the facility, meaning the type of message that is coming in. This commonly defines the type of program that is generating the message. Syslog not only defines 16 facilities but also allows an additional 8 user-defined facilities for messages that may not fall into the 16 predefined facilities. Table 13.1 shows all of the facilities defined by syslog.

TABLE 13.1: Syslog facilities

CODE	FACILITY	DESCRIPTION
0	kern	Messages from the kernel
1	user	Messages from the user level
2	mail	Mail system messages
3	daemon	Any system daemon messages
4	auth	Authentication or security messages
5	syslog	Messages from syslog itself
6	lpr	Messages from the line printer subsystem
7	news	Network news subsystem messages
8	uucp	Messages from Unix-to-Unix copy
9	cron	Scheduling (cron) system messages
10	authpriv	Security or authentication messages
11	ftp	Messages from the File Transfer Protocol server
12	ntp	Messages from the Network Time Protocol server
13	security	Log audit messages
14	console	Log alert messages
15	solaris-cron	Scheduling system from Solaris
16–23	local0–local7	User-defined messages

Many of these are simply archaic, highlighting the age of the syslog protocol. It's unlikely you will see any Unix-to-Unix copy (UUCP) messages these days. The same is true of the network news systems since network news hasn't been much of a thing in a long time. However, these are the facilities we have to work with. We don't only have to work with the facility, however. We can also set a priority, meaning we can specify how severe we believe a message is. More specifically, we would indicate how serious an issue that led to the log message would be. Table 13.2 shows the different severities defined by syslog.

TABLE 13.2: Severity table

VALUE	SEVERITY	KEYWORD	DESCRIPTION
0	Emergency	emerg	System unusable.
1	Alert	alert	Action has to be taken immediately.
2	Critical	crit	Critical situation.
3	Error	err	An error has occurred, not critical.
4	Warning	warning	An event that isn't an error.
5	Notice	notice	Normal condition that should be seen.
6	Informational	info	Informational message.
7	Debug	debug	When debug logging has been enabled.

All of this is relevant because anytime you generate a log message using syslog, you need to specify the facility as well as the severity. Both of these pieces of information also allow a syslog server to determine what happens to the log messages when they arrive at the server. Not everything is handled the same, after all. If you were to write everything that arrived at a syslog server out to disk, you might get far too many messages to be able to process, depending on the scale of the implementation. The following configuration of the syslog server on an Ubuntu Linux installation shows us how we can indicate what happens to messages that come in:

```
auth,authpriv.*.          /var/log/auth.log
*.*;auth,authpriv.none     -/var/log/syslog
#cron.*                    /var/log/cron.log
#daemon.*                  -/var/log/daemon.log
kern.*                     -/var/log/kern.log
#lpr.*                     -/var/log/lpr.log
mail.*                     -/var/log/mail.log
#user.*                    -/var/log/user.log
```

This shows filters by facility. The severity is not taken into consideration because the * indicates the severity doesn't matter; everything is logged. All `authpriv` messages are written out to the `/var/log/auth.log` file. Other facilities are commented out with the # character, meaning nothing happens with messages using those facilities. If you wanted to, for example, send critical messages from the kernel to a different file, you would use the line that follows:

```
kern.crit        -/var/log/kern.crit.log
```

This would direct critical kernel messages to the file `kern.crit.log`, while—assuming the other line was still in place—everything else would be sent to the file `kern.log`. Using these two vectors, you have a lot of control over where messages show up using syslog. However, we aren't here to talk about configuring a syslog server. We are here to talk about writing out messages using a syslog server. Before we get into writing a Rust program to write to syslog, let's take a quick look at the way some other languages do it. First, we can start with Python. There is a module called syslog that we need to import to get the syslog functions. Following is a program that shows some different ways we can write to syslog using a Python script:

```
#!/usr/bin/python3

import syslog

syslog.syslog("Logging some syslog messages")

syslog.syslog(syslog.LOG_ERR, "OMG!! An error occurred")

syslog.syslog(syslog.LOG_CRIT, "OMG!! A critical error has occurred")

syslog.openlog(logoption=syslog.LOG_PID, facility=syslog.LOG_DAEMON)
syslog.syslog(syslog.LOG_CRIT, "One of the cross beams has gone out of skew")
```

First, we can just write out a syslog message. This is going to write to a local syslog server. Remember that syslog uses facility and severity to determine how messages are written. In the first line, you see where we write out a message, syslog.syslog("Logging some syslog messages"). No facility or severity is specified, so it defaults to the User facility with severity of Info. We don't have to rely on the defaults, however. We can indicate a different severity, as you can see on the two subsequent lines. First we will use a defined value, syslog.LOG_ERR, to indicate an error and then syslog.LOG_CRIT to send an error message followed by a critical message.

That still doesn't address the case where we want to use a different facility. In that case, we need to use syslog.openlog() to specify the facility. We can also provide the process ID that will be included in the log message. Once we have a handle to syslog open with the correct facility, we use the same function as we had previously to write out a log message with the severity we would like to use. Following is what the execution of this program looks like in the log file:

```
Oct 19 01:59:39 hodgepodge /sysl.py: Logging some syslog messages
Oct 19 01:59:39 hodgepodge /sysl.py: OMG!! An error occurred
Oct 19 01:59:39 hodgepodge /sysl.py: OMG!! A critical has occurred
Oct 19 01:59:39 hodgepodge /sysl.py[14038]: One of the cross beams has gone
out of skew
```

We can also take a look at writing a Go program. Go is not a scripting language. Instead, it's a compiled program, just as Rust is. Following is the program that demonstrates how you would write a syslog message in Go. Go uses packages to define namespaces, so we are going to create a namespace called main to put into it the one function that defines the program. We will need to import the log and log/syslog packages for the additional functionality we need to write to a syslog server. Again, just as we did with the Python program, this is writing to a local syslog server rather than using a network connection:

```
package main

import (
    "log"
```

continues

(continued)

```
        "log/syslog"
    )

func main() {
    syslogger, err := syslog.New(syslog.LOG_ERR, "sysl")
    if err != nil {
        log.Fatalln(err)
    }

    log.SetOutput(syslogger)
    log.Println("Out of skew error, treadle failure")
}
```

Go is a little closer to an object-oriented programming language than Rust is, although it's still not completely an object-oriented language. We need to create an instance of—basically meaning a handle to—a syslog object, which knows how to communicate with the local syslog instance. In this case, we are going to create an error message using the defined LOG_ERR value. We also need to provide the name that will be attached to the log message. This is the process name. Like other modern languages, Go will allow multiple return values. We will get our instance to a syslog connection along with an error. This is similar to the way Rust handles return values. A function can return a value or an error. We should check to see if there is an error stored in the err variable. If there is no error, the err variable will not exist, meaning it will have a nil value. This is like pointer-based languages. If there is no memory address assigned to a variable, it has a null or nil value. The variable contains the address of the memory where the value is stored.

Once we are sure there is no error, we need to tell the log module the handle of the object that is going to handle the actual logging for us. In this case, it's the syslogger variable, which contains the syslog instance handle. This allows us to move on to writing out the log message. We're going to use the log module interface to do that for us. We can just use the log.Println() function to write out the log message.

Now that you've seen how syslog works in other languages, including a language you may already know something about, we can move on to writing the same functionality in Rust. We're going to go in a little more depth with Rust, in part because the module we'll use requires us to but also because we're going to look at setting up a little program that we can use over and over if we want to. Following is a simple program that will send a message out to our local syslog server instance. The program uses a small driver function that has a meaningless string that gets written out. You can, of course, adjust the logging function to support different types of severities or even facilities:

```
use syslog::{Facility, Formatter3164};
use sysinfo::get_current_pid;

fn get_process_name() -> String {
    let this_process = std::env::current_exe().unwrap();
    let this_file = this_process.file_name().unwrap();

    String::from(this_file.to_str().unwrap())
}

fn logger(message: &str) {
    let this_pid = get_current_pid().unwrap();
    let formatter = Formatter3164 {
```

```
            facility: Facility::LOG_USER,
            hostname: None,
            process: get_process_name(),
            pid: this_pid,
        };
    match syslog::unix(formatter) {
        Err(e) => println!("Unable to connect to syslog: {:?}", e),
        Ok(mut writer) => {
            writer.err(message).expect("could not write error message");
        }
    }
}

fn main() {

    logger("This is a log message");

}
```

One thing we haven't done yet is to look at a syslog message, although we will shortly. The reason for mentioning it is, you can see at the top of the file that, in addition to the modules from the syslog crate, we are going to go back a chapter and look at some information from the sysinfo crate. In addition to just the log message, we will need to feed some additional information to the call to log a message. This includes some information about the process that is going to be sending the log. You'll see why, if you don't already know, when we look at the result of logging the message.

To get the name of the process so we can feed that into our logging function, we need to pull it from the environment variable. The problem with what we get back from our environment variable for the name of the process is that we get the entire path to the executable rather than just the executable itself. The call to get the process name gets us a Result, which needs to be unwrapped to get the value out. Inside the Result is a PathBuf. To get the filename out of the full path, we are going to call the trait file_name() on the PathBuf identifier. This will result in an Option that contains the struct OsStr. We can safely assume that we are going to get a valid result back, meaning a Some() and not a None(), since there has to be a filename in the name of the executable. This is why we aren't going to check the Option to see which it was. We know what we are getting back, so we can just assume the response and move on without cluttering up code with match() statements to be sure.

The OsStr struct has to be converted to a character string, which is done using the to_str() trait. However, later we will need a Rust String, which is the full struct that contains the character array rather than just the character array itself. Once we get the str value back from to_str(), we can feed it into the constructor String::from() to get a String value. This is what gets returned from the function get_process_name().

Now that we have some of the information we need to create a syslog message, we can move to the function that generates that log message. This is the sort of function you could dump into any of your programs and use if you were working on a Unix-like system. Following is the function where we write the message. It takes a single parameter—the string that contains the message. Everything else is in the body of the function, although you may want to alter it:

```
fn logger(message: &str) {
    let this_pid = get_current_pid().unwrap();
```

continues

(continued)

```
        let formatter = Formatter3164 {
            facility: Facility::LOG_USER,
            hostname: None,
            process: get_process_name(),
            pid: this_pid,
        };
        match syslog::unix(formatter) {
            Err(e) => println!("Unable to connect to syslog: {:?}", e),
            Ok(mut writer) => {
                writer.err(message).expect("could not write error message");
            }
        }
    }
```

We start by getting the process identifier (pid) from the `sysinfo` crate. We will use this inside the data structure we are creating starting on the next line. The `syslog` crate offers two ways to format a syslog message. This is based on the version of the syslog protocol you are using. There is one that is defined by Request for Comments (RFC) document number 3164. The other one is based on RFC 5424. The more recent RFC has superseded the older one, but for our purposes, either should be fine; so we are going to stick with the format specified by RFC 3164. If you want to change it, you are going to use the struct named `Formatter5424` instead.

The struct we are creating stores pieces of information that are essential for a syslog message. The first is the facility. Facilities are defined in the `syslog` crate from the `Facility` module. Since we are a user-based application, we are going to use the `LOG_USER` facility. We also need to provide a hostname. This is used in case you are logging into a remote system rather than a local system. If you were to log into a remote system, you might want that remote system to have a reference to the system the log message was sourced from. When we provide a value for this identifier, that value will show up in the log message. For the purposes of this data structure, this is an `Option`, which means we need to provide a `Some()` or a `None`. If we want to provide a value in the `hostname` field, we would have to supply it with something like `Some(String::from("stevedallas"))`. This assigns an `Option` along with the associated value, which has to be a `String`, to the identifier.

The last two pieces of information are ones we have collected about the process. The first is the process name, shorn of its full path, leaving just the name of the executable. The second is the process ID, or pid. Once we have the struct in place with all the information needed, we can create the struct we will use to write out the value. This is done using `syslog::unix(formatter)`, which will return a `Logger` that will give us the ability to write out the message. The call to the `unix()` trait indicates we are going to connect to syslog using Unix sockets, meaning our program will try to connect to `/dev/syslog` or `/var/run/syslog`; both of these are file representations of the socket to communicate with. This does not mean we are limited to doing this.

In theory, you could replace the call to `unix()` with a call to `tcp()` or `udp()`. This is not a particularly straightforward process, however, since you are relying on networking functionality. At a minimum, you would need to do the following:

```
use std::net::{ToSocketAddrs, SocketAddr};

let addr = SocketAddr::from(([192, 168, 4, 10], 601));
let mut remote_addr = addr.to_socket_addrs().unwrap();
match syslog::tcp(remote_addr, remote_addr)
```

The first line would be used to make sure you had the socket address functionality in place, since you would need to create addresses. The fourth line is to replace the `unix()` call with one to `tcp()`. The `tcp()` trait requires not only the formatter but also the address you want to connect to, which is a `ToSocketAddr`. This is what is created in the second and third lines. We create a `SocketAddr` and then convert it to a `ToSocketAddr`. Using this code, though (which consists of fragments that would need to be put in the correct places in the existing source), generates errors about unsatisfied trait bounds.

What you can do is to just write out to your local syslog server on a Unix-like operating system and let the server take care of forwarding. That would be where it would typically happen anyway, rather than a developer deciding to push messages out to a remote server without passing through the local one. So, we can skip back to our `logger()` function. Once we have a handle back to a `Logger`, we can use that to write out the message we have. First, we need to catch an error. If there is no syslog server running or there is no Unix socket available to connect to, meaning the existing server is only listening on the network and not over a local socket, we need to be able to error on that condition. We aren't going to throw an error ourselves. Instead, we'll just print out that we couldn't connect to the syslog server and be done with the function.

What you will notice in the call is that the severity has been defined by the trait called on the `Logger` struct we have. The `Logger` implementation in the `syslog` trait defines calls for each of the different severities, based on the keywords in Table 13.2. So, we have `emerg()`, `alert()`, `crit()`, `err()`, `warning()`, `notice()`, `info()`, and `debug()` traits that can be called, depending on the severity you want to communicate.

Following are the messages as they show up in log files. The first is the message written without a hostname provided. The second is an error message with the hostname provided, and the third is a warning that also has the hostname provided. You will notice that there is no difference between the second and third messages. The severity is available only if you happen to separate your log files based on severity. Similarly, the facility is only known based on the log file you are looking at and knowing what facilities go to what log files. This log file catches a lot of different facilities, so the facility is ultimately lost:

```
Oct 12 16:04:14 hodgepodge ch12_syslog[27316]: This is a log message
Oct 12 16:48:39 hodgepodge stevedallas ch12_syslog[27732]: This is a log message
Oct 12 18:59:21 hodgepodge stevedallas ch12_syslog[29046]: This is a log message
```

What you get in these entries is the timestamp when the log entry was written. Next is the name of the hostname the syslog server is running on. The third value is the hostname that seems to have sent the message. Remember that we talked about changing `None` to `Some()` and providing a value. The last log entries here were generated with that `Some()` field in place. The next field is the name of the program that generated the log message. In brackets after the process name is the process ID. Following that is the log message itself.

Using Windows Event Logs

The syslog service typically runs on Unix-like operating systems, including Linux and macOS. You can get a syslog service for a Windows system, but Windows already comes with extensive functionality for logging. The Windows Event Log, typically accessed using the Windows Event Viewer application, is the service or subsystem provided by Windows for logging messages. Figure 13.1 shows what the Windows Event Viewer looks like. This is different from the text-based logs we've been looking at with syslog. With syslog, there really is no need to develop a special viewer application to look at the logs because they are all text-based and generally readable. There aren't a lot of fields, and what fields there are can be distinguished easily enough. Every log message is going to look the same as the others. While this is also true of the Windows Event Log, in the sense that there is a clearly defined set of information provided with each entry in the Windows Event Log, it's true that there is simply a lot more detail conveyed with each entry on Windows systems.

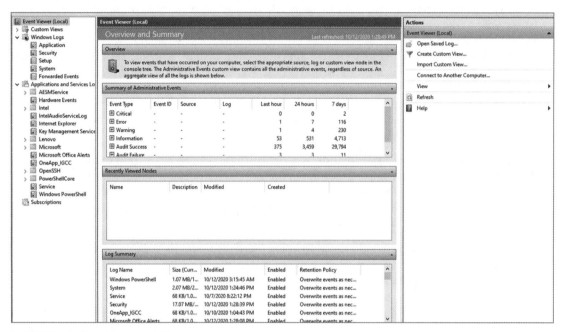

FIGURE 13.1: Windows Event Viewer

Windows breaks out the logs into both Windows logs as well as application logs. This wasn't always the case, but with more recent versions of Windows, it is. The historic Windows logs are Application, Security, System, and Setup. You'll also see a Forwarded Events log if you look closely at Figure 13.1. On top of the Windows logs, there are application and service logs. This is where you can find vendor-specific logs. Each vendor that generates its own logs using the Windows Event Log subsystem, meaning it uses the Windows application programming interface (API) to create a log entry, will get an entry here once it has registered its log.

Each log entry is going to contain the same sorts of information that you'll get with syslog, including the message and the severity—but with Windows, we get much more. This includes the source, which is the service or process that has generated the message. Figure 13.2 shows an example of a single log message that has been opened up from the list of all of the log messages. One thing you will see is the name of the log. This would be one of the logs mentioned earlier. You will also see the name of the user the process is running as. As with syslog, it's possible to get messages from other systems, so the name of the computer that generated the log is available.

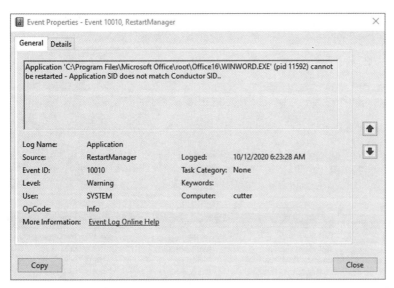

FIGURE 13.2: Windows Event Log entry

Another piece of data you can see with each entry is the event ID. This is a number that uniquely identifies a particular event, rather than an instance of an event. Let's say, for instance, that a service is being restarted. Every time that service is restarted, the event ID for the log entry will be the same. This is actually convenient. Whereas with syslog, we can use text-searching tools like grep to get all of the entries from a log file, it's not a perfect solution, because if we happened to have an event ID in syslog, that event ID would be a number, and that number could be found in other places in the log. With Windows, we have a tabular view with a column for each piece of information. This includes the event ID; so if we wanted to look for all instances of one event ID, we could sort on the column header and get something like what you can see in Figure 13.3. This retains all of the same information we have had. It's just a convenient way of reordering the log entries we have.

Since we are storing a lot more information with a Windows Event Log entry, it stands to reason we have to collect a lot more of that information to write out an entry. As before, we'll take a quick look at writing out an entry using Python first. Following is a simple program that writes an entry to the Windows Event Log. This could be restructured to be a function to take a parameter that is expected to be written out. It demonstrates, though, the amount of information required to create an event entry:

```
import win32api
import win32con
import win32security
import win32evtlogutil
import win32evtlog

proc_handle = win32api.GetCurrentProcess()
token_handle = win32security.OpenProcessToken(proc_handle, win32con.TOKEN_READ)
curr_sid = win32security.GetTokenInformation(token_handle, win32security.
TokenUser)[0]
```

continues

(continued)

```
win32evtlog.RegisterEventSource("localhost", "WasHere Source")

appname = "Test Application"
event_id = 9100
event_category = 19
description = ["This is the first line of a description", "But something bad
happened"]
event_data = b"This is a data"

win32evtlogutil.ReportEvent(appname, event_id, eventCategory=event_category,
eventType=win32evtlog.EVENTLOG_WARNING_TYPE, strings=description, data=event_data,
sid=curr_sid)
```

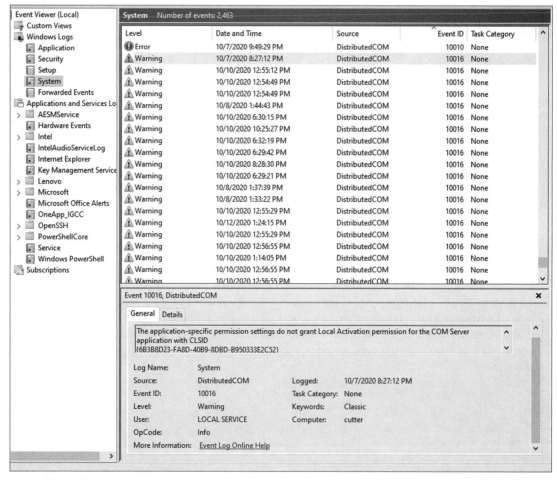

FIGURE 13.3: Reordered log entries

The package Pywin32 is necessary to generate event log messages on Windows. You can install it using the pip utility. That package will provide all of the necessary imports for this script. Some of these are needed for writing the log entry itself, while others are needed to acquire the information that will be put into the log entry. The first thing we do is to get a handle to the current process. This is necessary because we are going to get the user who owns the process so the username can be used in the log message being created. Once we have the process handle, we can get a token from the process. This will allow us to pull security information about the process. It will take three steps—getting a handle to the current process, getting a token for the process, and then getting the security identifier from the token—but in the end, we will get the security identifier for the current user.

When it comes to working with a Windows Event Log, you can register an event source. A common way of doing this is to store the event source in the Windows Registry. What you see in this script just registers the source for the duration of the script's run. Another way to approach this is to use the `AddSourcetoRegistry()` function, which not only registers the source but also stores the source in the registry for future use. Remember that the source in a Windows event entry is going to be the application or service that is generating the event.

As mentioned several times, we are going to need a lot of information when we create an event log entry. First, we are going to create a variable containing the name of the application. We also need an event identifier value. This should uniquely identify the type of error, meaning we have run across an error condition and, as many times as we get instances of that error, we are going to be using the same identifier. This is going to be a numeric value. Similarly, when you are writing an application, you should clearly define the errors you are going to be generating, so you should know all the errors and also the different categories those errors may fall into. We set a category the event will fall into in a variable named `event_category`. Both the category and identifier are numeric values that are controlled by the application developer.

Last, we add a description as well as some data. You don't have to have the data added, but you can, so it's shown here. Once all the variables have been populated with the information we are going to put into the event log, we can call `win32evtlogutil.ReportEvent()`. Python allows for the use of named parameters, rather than parameters being in specific positions in the function call. Once we have called the function with all of the data we have passed into it, we will end up with an event log entry that looks like what's shown in Figure 13.4.

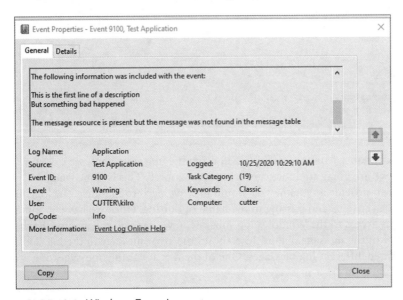

FIGURE 13.4: Windows Event Log entry

Rust also has a crate that allows us to write entries into the Windows Event Log. The crate winlog provides functionality to register an event source as well as to write event entries out to the event log. According to the documentation, it makes use of macros to determine the log level based on the macro that is called. To write a program using winlog, you need to add it to the Cargo.toml file just as we have with other crates.

> **NOTE** When using community-provided libraries, you can run into issues. Unfortunately, what happens a lot is that the documentation is poor because the developer is focused on making the library, module, or program work. An advantage of using community-provided libraries, though, is that you can often get in touch with the developer to ask questions if you get stuck because the documentation is incomplete or maybe incorrect, which happens sometimes. With Rust crates that have been supplied by developers around the world, you should be able to get contact information for the crate's developer if you look at the information page on crates.io for the crate you are trying to work with.

We can write a simple function that handles logging to the Windows Event Log. Following is a very simple program that demonstrates that logging. The first thing to note is that in addition to the winlog crate needing to be referenced in Cargo.toml, we also need to add the log crate. The log crate is a standard crate that provides the infrastructure (meaning functions and macros) that enables a generic logging platform. The winlog crate becomes a provider for the log crate by offering the calls to the logging platform that have been specified by the program. We still need the log crate, though, because we are going to use the standard macros from that crate to issue our log requests. In turn, those macros will call the winlog functions to write out the logs:

```
use log::{info, error, warn};
use winlog;

fn main() {

    winlog::register("WasHere Log");
    winlog::init("WasHere Log").unwrap();
    warn!("This is a log message");
    error!("This is a serious error message");
    info!("Just some information");

}
```

Once we have added the functionality from log and winlog using the use statement, we can start our program. The first thing we are going to do is register an event source. This is done using winlog::register(). You can provide any name you would like. We need to initialize our logging system, though, using winlog::init() and passing in the name of our log. Once we have an initialized identifier that provides us access to the Windows log subsystem, we can call the macros. Each macro is based on the severity of the message. Figure 13.5 shows the error message in the log. This program actually generates three different log messages. One of them is a warning message, one is an informational message, and one is an error message.

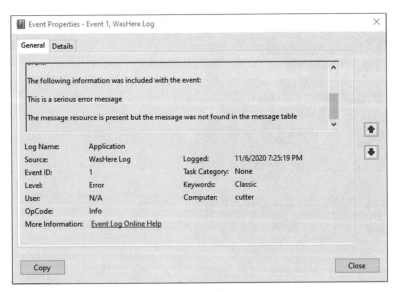

FIGURE 13.5: Error message in Windows Event Log

You can see the Event ID is 1. The `winlog` crate is fairly limited, in part because it relies on the providers from the `log` crate. The Windows API call, as seen earlier, expects a lot of data. The `winlog` crate offers no access to the different information that can be provided to the Windows Event Log. Instead, it assumes some defaults, which result in messages in the log that aren't as expressive as they could be. However, you do get the message that you decide to write, and the message is going to the logging subsystem, so there is still a lot of value in doing this.

WORKING WITH RASPBERRY PI

The Raspberry Pi is a low-cost, single-board computer, which means you have a computer that contains a processor, memory, input/output (in the form of USB ports), storage (in the form of a microSD card slot), a network, video, and audio all on a single board. While you can find computers today that have nearly all of those components on a single board, typically memory requires a different set of cards that slot into the motherboard. More than that, though, is the size of the Raspberry Pi. It is a single-board computer that fits into a space the size of a playing card, as you can see in Figure 13.6. The photo shows a Raspberry Pi Model 4 lying next to a standard-sized deck of playing cards.

There are a few reasons the Raspberry Pi can be as small as it is. One is that it doesn't support additional boards to provide more functionality, as a more traditional computer does. This means there doesn't have to be space on the board for slots for those other boards to fit into. Additionally, there are no connectors for multiple storage devices. This simplifies the input/output requirements. There is no need to have all the wiring and ports required to support multiple Serial AT Attachment (SATA) drives. The Raspberry Pi has video built in, in the form of a mini HDMI port. It's a simple computing device, so it doesn't need to be large.

FIGURE 13.6: Raspberry Pi

If you were to look at a modern motherboard, what you might see is a large processor. In fact, the processor is not large. However, modern processors generate a lot of heat; the bulk of the space taken up by a processor today is for heat dissipation. It used to be that processors could get away with using a heat sink to disperse the heat generated by the processor. Today, not only are heat sinks necessary, but fans are also needed to actively draw the heat away from the processor to keep it from effectively melting. The Raspberry Pi gets away without the need for a heat sink by using a different kind of processor than the ones seen in desktops or even laptops today. Figure 13.7 shows you how large the fan is over the AMD Ryzen processor, which takes up only a portion of the area consumed by the fan on the top.

FIGURE 13.7: AMD processor with a fan

An Intel-based processor, including the compatible AMD processors, uses a complex instruction set, meaning there are a large number of instructions supported by the processor. Every processor family has a defined set of instructions, known to the processor as *operation codes* (opcodes). Each instruction in a complex instruction set computing (CISC) device may perform several tasks, which may consume multiple clock cycles to complete. This makes each instruction powerful but also makes it harder to determine the number of instructions per second that can be handled by a processor, because each instruction will take a variable number of clock cycles (the change in voltage that indicates when tasks should be performed is a clock cycle).

The Raspberry Pi uses a technology called *reduced instruction set computing* (RISC). This is defined by the philosophy that each instruction should perform a simple, clearly defined task. The Raspberry Pi uses a processor developed by the company ARM, which develops these RISC-based processors. You will also see ARM processors in mobile devices. One advantage of these processors over the more complex Intel-derived ones is that they consume less power. Since they consume less power, they generate less heat and don't need the power-dissipation capabilities of the larger systems. All of this is to say that there simply isn't the need for the Raspberry Pi to be very large to get a powerful computer system that fits into a small space. Just to highlight this, you can see a Raspberry Pi in its case, without the top cover just to show what it is, sitting on top of the fan inside a traditional computer in Figure 13.8. The Raspberry Pi fits into less space than just the space needed for the processor in a traditional desktop.

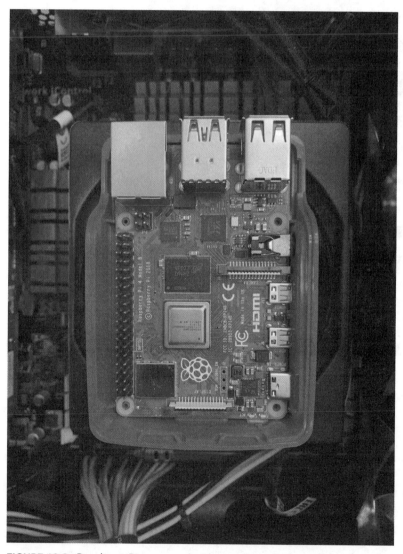

FIGURE 13.8: Raspberry Pi compared with a traditional processor

The Raspberry Pi also offers something else that is unique in modern computing devices. If you look back at Figure 13.6, you will see a set of pins that look like they are ready to take a connector. This is a general-purpose input/output (GPIO) header that is ready to take either a number of individual connectors to the pins in the header or a connector on the end of a ribbon cable. This ribbon cable may lead to a breadboard, which allows for wiring circuits in a more comfortable space rather than trying to wire the circuit with a number of small jumper cables directly to the GPIO header. You can see an example of a breadboard in Figure 13.9. This shows the connector the ribbon cable would plug into, as well as some components that would be wired into the breadboard to make a circuit that provided specific functionality.

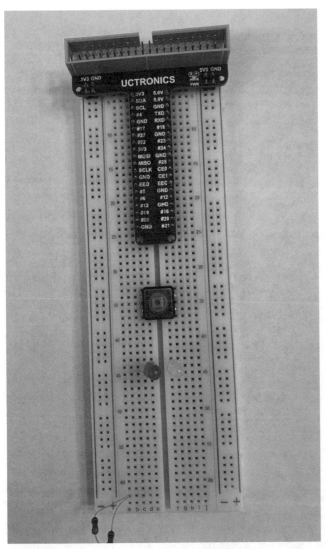

FIGURE 13.9: Breadboard for a Raspberry Pi

Using the breadboard, we can put in some electronic components and interact with them using a programming language. The Raspberry Pi can run a number of different operating systems. First, there are a handful of Linux-based distributions. This includes Raspbian, a Debian-based distribution specifically for the Raspberry Pi. You can also use a copy of Kali Linux, which is a security-oriented distribution. There are other versions of Linux that have Raspberry Pi implementations (remember that the Raspberry Pi doesn't use an Intel-based processor, so all of the software has to be recompiled for the ARM-based processor). You can also get an embedded version of Windows for the Raspberry Pi. The easiest one to use for the purpose of this exercise is Raspbian, because it has the needed packages to support the GPIO interface. The package `wiringpi` has the libraries necessary to interface with the GPIO header, although you may need to use a different version of the package than the one provided in the standard repository if you are using a newer version of the Raspberry Pi.

Lighting Lights

Once you have the `wiringpi` package installed, you will get the libraries needed to interface with the GPIO header, as noted already. You will also get a utility called `gpio` that will allow you to interact with the GPIO header on the command line. As an example, reading the state of all the pins in the GPIO header uses the `gpio readall` command. You can see the output from this command here:

```
quiche ~ » gpio readall
 +-----+-----+---------+------+---+---Pi 4B--+---+------+---------+-----+-----+
 | BCM | wPi |   Name  | Mode | V | Physical | V | Mode |  Name   | wPi | BCM |
 +-----+-----+---------+------+---+----++----+---+------+---------+-----+-----+
 |     |     |    3.3v |      |   |  1 || 2  |   |      | 5v      |     |     |
 |   2 |   8 |   SDA.1 |   IN | 1 |  3 || 4  |   |      | 5v      |     |     |
 |   3 |   9 |   SCL.1 |   IN | 1 |  5 || 6  |   |      | 0v      |     |     |
 |   4 |   7 | GPIO. 7 |   IN | 1 |  7 || 8  | 1 |   IN | TxD     | 15  | 14  |
 |     |     |      0v |      |   |  9 || 10 | 1 |   IN | RxD     | 16  | 15  |
 |  17 |   0 | GPIO. 0 |  OUT | 0 | 11 || 12 | 0 |   IN | GPIO. 1 | 1   | 18  |
 |  27 |   2 | GPIO. 2 |   IN | 0 | 13 || 14 |   |      | 0v      |     |     |
 |  22 |   3 | GPIO. 3 |   IN | 0 | 15 || 16 | 0 |   IN | GPIO. 4 | 4   | 23  |
 |     |     |    3.3v |      |   | 17 || 18 | 0 |   IN | GPIO. 5 | 5   | 24  |
 |  10 |  12 |    MOSI |   IN | 0 | 19 || 20 |   |      | 0v      |     |     |
 |   9 |  13 |    MISO |   IN | 0 | 21 || 22 | 0 |   IN | GPIO. 6 | 6   | 25  |
 |  11 |  14 |    SCLK |  OUT | 0 | 23 || 24 | 1 |   IN | CE0     | 10  | 8   |
 |     |     |      0v |      |   | 25 || 26 | 1 |   IN | CE1     | 11  | 7   |
 |   0 |  30 |   SDA.0 |   IN | 1 | 27 || 28 | 1 |   IN | SCL.0   | 31  | 1   |
 |   5 |  21 | GPIO.21 |   IN | 1 | 29 || 30 |   |      | 0v      |     |     |
 |   6 |  22 | GPIO.22 |   IN | 1 | 31 || 32 | 0 |   IN | GPIO.26 | 26  | 12  |
 |  13 |  23 | GPIO.23 |   IN | 0 | 33 || 34 |   |      | 0v      |     |     |
 |  19 |  24 | GPIO.24 |   IN | 0 | 35 || 36 | 0 |   IN | GPIO.27 | 27  | 16  |
 |  26 |  25 | GPIO.25 |   IN | 0 | 37 || 38 | 0 |   IN | GPIO.28 | 28  | 20  |
 |     |     |      0v |      |   | 39 || 40 | 0 |   IN | GPIO.29 | 29  | 21  |
 +-----+-----+---------+------+---+----++----+---+------+---------+-----+-----+
 | BCM | wPi |   Name  | Mode | V | Physical | V | Mode |  Name   | wPi | BCM |
 +-----+-----+---------+------+---+---Pi 4B--+---+------+---------+-----+-----+
```

At this point, we have all the foundations in place so we can work on wiring up a little circuit to do something simple, just to demonstrate how to interact with the GPIO header. One thing you may note in the previous output is that some of the headers indicate voltage (e.g. 3.3 v). This means power is carried to that pin. If we are going to do something with electronics, we need power. Using a kit with different electronic components (available from Amazon as well as other locations), we're going to wire up a circuit that will allow us to turn on a light-emitting diode (LED). This is going to require an LED as well as a resistor and jumper wires. Figure 13.10 shows how it's wired.

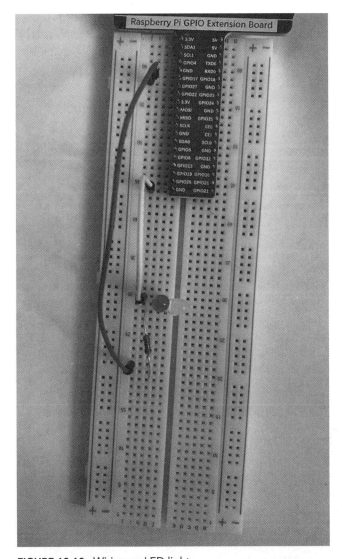

FIGURE 13.10: Wiring an LED light

NOTE *If you look closely, you may see there are two LEDs wired up here. As long as you have enough pins and wire them all the same, you can turn on multiple LEDs at the same time. In this case, I have a yellow LED and a red LED wired up in parallel, so both will turn on and off as the voltage is turned on and off.*

We're going to use a jumper wire to connect one of the holes alongside pin #11, which is GPIO #17, to one end of a 220 ohm resistor. The other end of the resistor requires a jumper wire to connect to one leg of the LED. The long end of the LED (one of the two legs of the LED should be longer than the other) should go into a hole on the same line as the resistor. The other leg of the LED should go into a hole on the same line as a jumper wire that then runs to a GND (ground) pin, indicated on the small board that connects to the breadboard. We now have a power side, which we will control programmatically by sending a signal to the 11th pin, and we have a ground side for the power to return to. Let's move on to the program. The following is a simple Python script that turns the light on and off:

```python
#!/usr/bin/env python3

import RPi.GPIO as GPIO
import time

def restoreclean():
    GPIO.cleanup()

if __name__ == '__main__':
    GPIO.setmode(GPIO.BOARD)
    GPIO.setup(11, GPIO.OUT)
    GPIO.output(11, GPIO.LOW)

    try:
        while True:
            GPIO.output(11, GPIO.HIGH)
            time.sleep(5)
            GPIO.output(11, GPIO.LOW)
            time.sleep(5)
    except KeyboardInterrupt:
        restoreclean()
```

First, we are going to be using Python 3 rather than Python 2 for this, although in practice, there isn't much difference for our purposes. We are going to import the RPi.GPIO package using the name GPIO to refer to it later on. We are also going to import the time package. This will let us set a timer so we can turn the light on and off in a loop.

We're going to create a function that will clean up after the program has been killed. This will reset everything in the GPIO header so the LED isn't left on. We're going to set up a signal handler in the main part of the program that will call this function when Ctrl-C is pressed on the keyboard. The GPIO package includes a function that will handle resetting everything for us.

> **NOTE** This is a limitation of the Rust programming language, although Rust isn't alone in this regard. Rust does not have the ability to handle signals, so we can't create a function that will perform program cleanup in case an interrupt signal is sent. When you see the Rust program later on, you will notice it doesn't have this function. This can leave the GPIO in an odd state, thinking it's under the control of a program that is no longer running, as well as leaving an LED lit.

If the call is for the function named __main__, we are going to run the main function. Python does not allow for the clean definition of a main function, so to distinguish the main function, we have to check what the interpreter is calling. The first thing we do once we enter the main function is to configure the GPIO package. We are going to indicate that the addressing we will be using will be physical addressing, which means we will use physical pin numbers rather than a GPIO number, which may be assigned to a different physical pin. Then we indicate that we want to communicate with pin 11, which will be the sixth pin down on the left-hand side. We want to make sure the power is off to that pin, so we set the output to GPIO.LOW, which means no power is being sent to that pin.

Since we are going to catch a signal from outside the program, we need to use a try/except block. The code inside the try portion will continue executing until there is an exception. The exception we're looking for in this case is a KeyboardException, meaning (more than likely) Ctrl-C was pressed on the keyboard, sending an interrupt signal to the process. Inside the try block, we're going to run an infinite loop, meaning the code will continue to execute forever because there is no condition within the loop to break out. Breaking out will require sending the interrupt signal (pressing Ctrl-C) as previously indicated. Inside the loop, we set the pin output to high voltage, which will turn on the light, and then sleep for 5 seconds before turning the light off.

We can do the same thing using Rust, of course. At least, we can write a program that turns the light on and off. We'll take it a little further than we did in Python, though. Before we get there, we need to add some dependencies in the Cargo.toml file. Some of what you see here is related to the fact that we're not going to be writing to the console as the program runs. Instead, because we are running this on a Linux system, we can use our syslog logger from earlier in the chapter:

```
[dependencies]
"sysfs_gpio" = "0.5"
"rand" = "*"
"syslog" = "*"
"sysinfo" = "*"
```

The first line is the crate needed to communicate with the GPIO header on the Raspberry Pi. The second line is needed because we are going to randomly set a delay on turning the LED on and off. Finally, because we are going to be writing out to syslog the same way we did earlier in the chapter, we need the last two crates in the Cargo.toml file shown earlier. Following, now that we have the dependencies set, is the program we're going to be working with:

```
use sysfs_gpio::{Direction, Pin};
use std::thread::sleep;
use std::time::Duration;
use rand::Rng;
use syslog::{Formatter3164, Facility};
use sysinfo::get_current_pid;

fn get_process_name() -> String {
    let this_process = std::env::current_exe().unwrap();
    let this_file = this_process.file_name().unwrap();

    String::from(this_file.to_str().unwrap())
}
```

continues

(continued)

```
    fn logger(message: &str) {
        let this_pid = get_current_pid().unwrap();
        let formatter = Formatter3164 {
            facility: Facility::LOG_USER,
            hostname: None,
            process: get_process_name(),
            pid: this_pid,
        };
        match syslog::unix(formatter) {
            Err(e) => println!("Unable to connect to syslog: {:?}", e),
            Ok(mut writer) => {
                writer.err(message).expect("could not write error message");
            }
        }
    }


    fn main() {
        let mut rand_instance = rand::thread_rng();

        let my_led = Pin::new(17);
        my_led.with_exported(|| {
            my_led.set_direction(Direction::Out).unwrap();
            loop {
                my_led.set_value(0).unwrap();
                let length: u64 = rand_instance.gen_range(150,500);
                logger(format!("Waiting {} milliseconds before resetting the light",
length).as_str());
                sleep(Duration::from_millis(length));
                my_led.set_value(1).unwrap();
                sleep(Duration::from_millis(length));
            }
        }).unwrap();
    }
```

The first line of the program is going to bring in `Direction` and `Pin` from the `sysfs_gpio` crate. This will let us determine whether we are setting output values as well as sending the output value to a specific pin. We're also going to use `sleep()` from the `std::thread` crate because we will need to pause between turning the LED on and turning it off. The other imports at the top of the program are going to be used to send our output to syslog rather than to the window we are running the program in.

Because we looked at them closely earlier in the chapter, we are going to skip over the first two functions. Instead, we'll just jump straight to the `main` function. We need to create an instance of a random number generator, which is what we do in the first line of the function, storing the instance in the `rand_instance` identifier. Once we have that, we are going to create an instance of a `Pin`, which is a struct defined as part of the `sysfs_gpio` crate.

With the `Pin` instance in place, we want to do something with it. We're going to use the `with_exported()` trait on the `Pin` instance to execute a closure using that instance. This means we are going to take the pin in the GPIO header and create a logical representation of it in our program and then create an anonymous function to use that logical pin. Once we have the `Pin` instance, we need to indicate whether we are reading from the `Pin` or writing to it. We indicate that with the following line, which uses the `Direction::Out` value to let our logical pin know to expect output from our program being sent to the pin:

```
my_led.set_direction(Direction::Out).unwrap();
```

Following the direction setting, we enter our loop. This is also an infinite loop, although you could easily set a loop that executed some predefined number of times. The first thing we are going to do is shut off the LED. We do this by sending a 0 to the pin. This sets the voltage to low, turning off the pin. This is done using the following line. We get a `Result` from this call, so we need to unwrap the `Result`:

```
my_led.set_value(0).unwrap();
```

The following lines create a new random value between 150 and 500, which will be the number of milliseconds we go to sleep. In the middle of this, we are going to log the amount of time we are waiting before we turn on the light. Finally, we need to wait that amount of time. We do this using the `sleep()` function. This function requires a `Duration` struct to function correctly. We take our value—which we assume is in milliseconds—and return a `Duration` instance using the trait `from_millis()`, passing in the numeric value generated by our random number generator. The program will wait the specified number of milliseconds before moving on:

```
let length: u64 = rand_instance.gen_range(150,500);
logger(format!("Waiting {} milliseconds before resetting the light",
length).as_str());
sleep(Duration::from_millis(length));
```

Once it moves on, we are going to turn on the power. This is done using the same `set_value()` trait used earlier. Instead of the 0 passed in before, we are going to pass in a 1 to turn on the power. This loop will continue until we kill the program in some way, which may include pressing Ctrl-C on the keyboard. Since this is Linux, there are other ways to have the same effect, including using the `kill` command with the process identifier for the program. Usually, Ctrl-C is easier, and there is nothing that would prevent it from working with this program.

Reading GPIO

Turning on LEDs is interesting, but it's far from the only thing we can do with GPIO. We can also read values from the GPIO. We can take a look at how to wire up the breadboard to read a value from a switch. This is a pushbutton device that will change the value when the right pin has its value read. First, we need to wire everything up correctly. There are a number of ways to do this. If you search the web for using a push-button with the GPIO on a Raspberry Pi, you will find a lot of different wiring diagrams. For our purposes, we're going to do this simply. One end of the button device is going to be wired to GPIO #23. The other end is going to be wired to ground. You can see the breadboard in Figure 13.11 with the button wired. You'll also see LEDs wired up since you could use the wiring to have the button turn the LED on and turn off. We won't be using the entire wiring setup here since we're just going to look at reading from one of the GPIO pins.

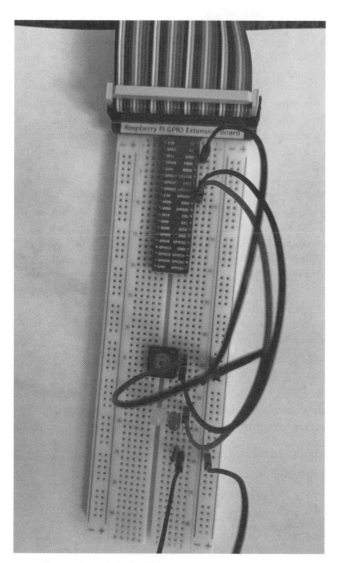

FIGURE 13.11: Push-button wiring

Now that we have the wiring in place, we can look at the program, which follows. As before, we need to make sure we have sysfs_gpio as a dependency in the Cargo.toml file. We are also going to be doing a time-based loop, so we need the same time dependencies as before. The reason for this is because the check for the GPIO device is non-blocking since there will always be a value to read. We are looking for a state change, which we are going to have to determine ourselves:

```
use sysfs_gpio::{Direction, Pin};
use std::thread::sleep;
use std::time::Duration;

fn main()  -> sysfs_gpio::Result<()> {
```

```
        let inpin = Pin::new(23);

        inpin.with_exported(|| {
            inpin.set_direction(Direction::In)?;
            let mut prev_val: u8 = 255;
            loop {
                let val = inpin.get_value()?;
                if val != prev_val {
                    println!("Button has been pushed with a value of {}", val);
                    prev_val = val;
                }
                sleep(Duration::from_millis(10));
            }
        })
    }
```

The program is going to look a lot like the one we saw before because we are using the same structs and traits. The big difference is that we are going to be changing the direction we set on the `Pin` struct. Let's not get too far ahead of ourselves, though. First, we are going to set the `use` lines for the crates and components of those crates necessary for the program to work. The first difference is that we are going to allow the program to handle errors that may result from reading the value in GPIO. There may be a number of reasons we could get errors. Of course, even if you don't have anything wired up to the pin, you will still get a value, but there could be other reasons you might get errors. Either way, it's a good idea to handle errors, especially when you are dealing with hardware.

As before, we create a new `Pin` struct, using the value 23. This refers to the GPIO value and not the pin number in the header. This can get confusing, so it's important to know which you are referring to when you are passing these values in. When we looked at the Python script previously, we set the numbers to be the ones on the board, meaning the numeric value of the pin if you were to number from top to bottom, left to right. In the case of the Rust crate, we are using the GPIO number. If you look at a diagram of the GPIO header, you will see that there are several GPIO pins that have names like GPIO #11. These are the only pins we can communicate with programmatically. Other pins, like the ones labeled GND, are used for things like carrying current back to ground or other electrical functions.

We need to create a closure using the `with_exported()` trait on the `Pin` struct. Once we have the closure created, we can set the direction on the `Pin`. We are reading from the pin, so we need to use `Direction::In` where before we used `Direction::Out` because we were sending values.

We are looking for a change in value on the device, so we need to have something to compare to the first time we run through the comparison. You will see when you run the program that the two values you get are 0 and 1. We are going to use a value that isn't one of the possible values so we are guaranteed to pass the comparison when we look for a value change. As a result, we set the value to the maximum possible on a `u8`, which will hold all the potential values that come back from a read on a GPIO pin. This is 255.

We need to set up a loop because we are going to keep checking the value on that pin. The first thing we do is to read the value, which is done using the trait shown here:

```
        let val = inpin.get_value()?;
```

This is a place where we might get an error. Because we have already set up the function to support an error return, we are going to call the trait with a ? appended to allow Rust to either unwrap the Result or handle the error by just terminating the function we are in. Once we have the current value on the pin, we can compare it against the previous value, as seen in the short block of code the follows. In this case, we're just going to print out a statement that the value has changed and display the current value so you can see that it has changed. Once we have displayed the current value, we are going to set the current value to the prev_val identifier. This is because the next time through the loop, our current value will be the previous value, and there will be a different current value:

```
if val != prev_val {
    println!("Button has been pushed with a value of {}", val);
    prev_val = val;
}
```

As we did with the program used to blink the LEDs, we are going to sleep just to pause for a brief period. In this case, we are going to pause for 10 ms. You could change this if you preferred, but 10 ms seems like a reasonable value. If you were to bump up to 100 ms, you might miss a state change just because pressing is a state change, and releasing is another state change. If you miss that press, which can be really fast, you won't know that it happened. Anything shorter, like 1 ms, seems like overkill. Of course, you could write it so there isn't any sleep, and you are constantly polling the GPIO pin for a value.

Because we need to provide a Result from the function, the closure is left as an expression. This means we aren't unwrapping the Result. We are returning it as it is from the function. There's no reason at this point to try to retrieve the Result and do something with it.

One last note here: as Rust has no ability to handle signals, the way to break this program is to use Ctrl-C as we did before. This means the GPIO device is going to be left in an unclean state. The next time you run through a program, it's possible to get an error about the state the GPIO device is in. This shouldn't cause any issues with running, but you may receive a notification depending on the language you are using and the way you are handling any error conditions.

SUMMARY

Logging is an important factor in writing programs. While you could write your own log files, this isn't necessary or advisable since there are ways to log that are already standardized. The first is syslog on Unix-like operating systems. Even if you are running on a Windows system, you can still write to a syslog server over the network. This requires the remote server to be listening for the connection, although syslog supports both TCP and UDP for network protocols, so setting up a network server isn't that problematic. One of the problems with syslog, though, is that the only way you know the severity of a syslog message by looking at log files is if you are filtering into different log files based on severity. This makes it harder to differentiate between informational messages and critical errors.

Windows has its own logging subsystem. You write out to the Windows Event Log using a Windows API call to interface with that subsystem. The Windows Event Log has been around for decades, although not as long as syslog has. While the underlying format used to store the messages on disk may have changed, and there may be more log buckets to write to, the Windows Event Log format hasn't changed all that much in that time. There are a lot of details stored with each event. These include the severity of the message, the user, the system, and the time, as well as an identifier that will allow you to collect all instances of the same error. You can also categorize your errors by defining a category that may let you collect multiple event identifiers to give you a better understanding of what is happening in the application.

The Raspberry Pi is an interesting computing device. This is a low cost, single-board computer. By paying usually less than $50, you can get a powerful computing device. You need a microSD card, keyboard, monitor, and mouse, just as you would with a desktop system, but the computer itself is inexpensive.

The nice thing about the Raspberry Pi, in addition to its low cost and small size, is that we get a set of headers we can programmatically interact with. If you get a breadboard, you can build electronic circuits that have a collection of output devices, like the LED lights we interacted with, as well as a number of sensors. We looked at interacting with a push button, but there are countless sensors available for these low-cost, single-board computers. You just need some jumper wires and wiring diagrams, and you can create your own electronic projects that you can programmatically interact with.

Perhaps the easiest thing to do is to use the Raspbian operating system, making sure you have the latest `wiringpi` package. Once you have your operating system and interface library in place, you can start writing programs to send signals to the GPIO headers or read values from those headers. As each of these is general-purpose, indicated by the name, you can read or write using any of the pins. You are not bound by using only a single set of pins for output or input.

There is also an active community around the Raspberry Pi. With a little bit of looking, you can probably find wiring diagrams for a lot of different projects. There are usually Python scripts written around these projects, but you should be able to convert the Python to Rust and build your program using a fast, safe, compiled language.

EXERCISES

1. Alter the `logger()` function for syslog so you can pass in the facility rather than having it hard-coded.

2. Alter the `logger()` function for syslog so you can pass in the severity in addition to the facility.

3. Alter the program that blinks the LED to take a parameter on the command line for the number of times to blink the LED, and then change the loop to run only that number of times.

4. Reverse the order in which the light turns on and off to see if it makes a difference in how the LED operates.

ADDITIONAL RESOURCES

Syslog Protocol - `tools.ietf.org/html/rfc5424`

"What Is Syslog? Syslog Server vs. Event Log Explained + Recommended Syslog Management Tool" - `www.dnsstuff.com/what-is-syslog`

"Windows Logging Basics" - `www.loggly.com/ultimate-guide/windows-logging-basics`

Windows Event Log API - `docs.microsoft.com/en-us/windows/win32/wes/windows-event-log`

`Winlog` crate - `crates.io/crates/winlog`

Raspberry Pi - `www.raspberrypi.org`

GPIO documentation - `www.raspberrypi.org/documentation/usage/gpio`

Breadboard tutorial - `magpi.raspberrypi.org/articles/breadboard-tutorial`

14

Collecting Stuff

IN THIS CHAPTER, YOU WILL LEARN THE FOLLOWING:

➤   How to use collections in Rust

➤   How to use traditional data structures like linked lists

➤   How to implement a binary search tree

The thing about data is that it wants to be together with other data. You have some information you want to store, and it's almost never just one thing. For instance, this chapter is being written in Microsoft Word, which is a program that isn't storing just a single letter or word. In fact, it's not just storing thousands of words. There is a lot of other data that is stored with every Word document, including metadata like the name of the person who has registered the copy of the application and, thus, is probably the person who wrote the document. All of this is to say that having data types is great, and being able to instantiate those data types into identifiers that can be manipulated in a program is great. Additionally, the fact that Rust lets us collect disparate pieces of information that are related somehow into a complex data type called a *struct*, defined by the programmer, makes life significantly easier for us.

The problem is that, as already stated, data just seems to want to collect and be together with other data. Even if you have a struct in Rust, the chances are that you won't have a single instance of that struct. If you did, you probably wouldn't need a struct. You'd just have individual identifiers. This means we need something above individual data types—we need *collections*. A collection is not only a data type in and of itself. It also provides methods to manipulate the collection in different ways, including inserting information into the collection.

We've already spent some time talking about collections, because we've been using them. However, there are some classic collections, meaning some collection types that have been implemented in multiple languages because they are foundational to the way problems are commonly solved. In some cases, the language itself implements these features as core parts of the language. In other cases, you make use of libraries or modules that implement these collections. This is, perhaps, because the language itself doesn't have some elements to facilitate these collection types.

When it comes to programming languages, there are a number of common collection types. There are some linear types, including stacks, queues, and lists. You may also find variations on these linear collections. There are also sets or associative arrays, which are associative collections. This means you associate one piece of data with another piece of data and collect all of those associations. Finally, we have graphs, which include trees. Trees are ways of collecting data in a semi-organized manner that can be used to help find data quickly.

We're going to take a pass through some of the collection types we've already seen in other chapters, but looking at them again helps to set the stage for collections we haven't looked at, including a binary search tree. Using a binary search tree can help us take some of what we've done in previous chapters and make it more efficient.

ARRAYS AND VECTORS

An array is perhaps the simplest of data collections in programming. Using an array, we take a single data type and create a single identifier that collects together a number of instances of that data type. You may, for instance, need to collect 30 days' worth of temperature readings so you can do something with them later, like generating statistics, including average, high, low, and median. Before we get into looking at it in Rust, we will take a look at it in C and then Python. The C code follows here. This creates an array with a size of 30 that will store integer values. The first line in the main() function defines the array. The next line assigns a value to the first entry in the array:

```
#include <stdio.h>

int main(int argc, char **argv) {
    int daily_temps[30];

    daily_temps[0] = 72;

    printf("Today's temp: %d", daily_temps[0]);

}
```

There are two problems with this code that require a programmer to be on her or his toes. First, the array is entirely uninitialized, although a portion of memory has been assigned to the array. If we had reversed the order of the assignment and the printf() statement, you'd get an undefined value, meaning there is no way of knowing at compile time or even runtime what that value would be. Every pass through a program would get a completely different value because it would be whatever happened to be in that memory location before the program ran.

The second problem we have with this program is that it's possible to access a part of memory that was not allocated to the array. There is nothing in C that would prevent the following code from compiling, for instance. We create but don't initialize an array, which means all the elements in the array will have values that can't be predicted, meaning they may make no sense at all for the use of the program. We then access a portion of memory that does not belong to the array. In this instance, nothing bad happens because it's a very small program. One thing to keep in mind, though, is that the data that belongs to this function will be placed on the stack in line with other data, which would include the return pointer if it had been a function that had been called, creating another frame on the stack. If we happened to overwrite the return address from the function, the program would attempt to jump to a memory location that might not belong to the program. This would cause the program to crash. It's also possible that making this assignment here would just overwrite another memory location that belonged to another variable. When this variable was accessed later, it would have an unexpected value. This could cause the program to crash or at least cause the program to behave in an unexpected way with an unexpected value.

```c
#include <stdio.h>

int main(int argc, char **argv) {
    int daily_temps[30];

    printf("Today's temp: %d", daily_temps[0]);

    daily_temps[0] = 72;

    daily_temps[40] = 55;

}
```

Let's take a look at another programming language doing the same thing. This language doesn't require quite so much care and feeding. Following is a very short Python script. In it, we declare an array of indeterminate size. Python protects us, though, by requiring data to be placed into the location before it can be accessed. In short, Python takes care of memory management. This is why we call append() on the array to add a value to it. We can't just access the first location as we did in C using temps[0] = 42. As far as Python is concerned, there is no memory associated with temps[0], so it would be entirely inappropriate to access it:

```python
temps = []
temps.append(42)
print(temps[0])
```

Now we can move on to Rust, and we will see how Rust protects us from the sins of C and the potential it has to cause program crashes from even simple programs if the programmer isn't very careful and neglects to do bounds-checking. We are going to create a collection of floating-point values, and the collection is going to be able to store 30 values. The reason for the fixed point is because you may have an accurate thermometer, such as the one shown in Figure 14.1, that can register temperature in tenths. If you didn't have such a thermometer, you could adjust the data type to be i8 instead of f32. You shouldn't use an unsigned data type like u8 or u16. Remember that unsigned values won't accept negative numbers, and if you live in part of the world where it gets cold, you'll need to store negative numbers:

```rust
let daily_temps: [f32; 30];
```

> **NOTE** *You could use any size numeric data type you want. As we are storing temperature values, it's unlikely they would get into the 200s, much less higher, so 8 bits should be more than adequate to accept the range of values. Memory being so cheap, though, there is no harm at all in using a larger data type. You should consider the traits and functions you would like to use on the data since some of these functions, such as those that may be in crates you might need, may not implement traits and functions for all widths of numeric values. Using floating-point values, though, requires that you use at least 32 bits because that's the smallest floating-point value available.*

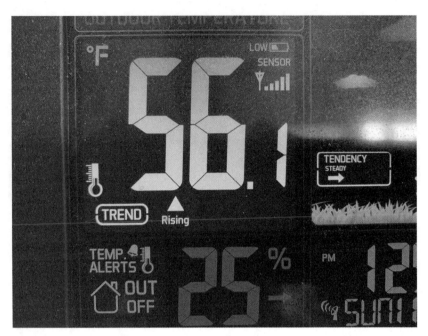

FIGURE 14.1: Daily temperature including tenths.

There is a problem with this definition, although it works well enough on its own. Rust doesn't allow you to make use of any value that hasn't been initialized. Even though we've defined the array and indicated the size, Rust requires that there be values in all of the places before it will create the instance of the array. Following is how you might fix that problem. You define the identifier that gives you access to the array, followed by an initializer that puts a default value into all of the elements in the array. Accessing an element in the array would look something like the second line in the code that follows:

```
let mut daily_temps: [f32; 30] = [0.0; 30];
daily_temps[0] = 59.8;
```

Even getting to an array we can use doesn't help us a lot, though. It's ambiguous, for a start. What is a daily temperature? Is it the high? The low? Is it just the temperature taken at a particular point in the day, regardless of maximum or minimum? Perhaps a better approach here would be to create an array of structs where the struct defines the minimum and the maximum each day. Then we could have a collection of highs and lows for each day of the month. Following is the definition of the structure for this approach, as well as the definition of an array of the struct:

```
struct DailyTemperature {
    minimum: f32,
    maximum: f32
}

let mut daily_temps: [DailyTemperature; 30];
```

There is a problem with this code, though. While you have created an array of the DailyTemperature struct, the array is again uninitialized. This means you can't try to access anything in the array. We can fix this, though. The following lines take care of defining the array of structs while at the same time initializing each element in the array with a pair of values. This is a little cumbersome, however. This may not be the most readable code in the world. Additionally, it requires a redefinition of the `Daily-Temperature` struct, which you can see here as well. Because of Rust's memory rules, we can't just create an instance of `DailyTemperature` and assign it to an element in the array we are creating. We need the ability to copy the value rather than just trying to make an assignment. This requires implementing a `Copy` trait on the struct we have created. Fortunately, Rust will take care of this for us if we add `#[derive(Copy)]` before the struct. This code also adds the `Clone` trait, although it's not strictly necessary for this assignment:

```
#[derive(Copy,Clone)]
struct DailyTemperature {
    minimum: f32,
    maximum: f32
}

let mut daily_temps_array: [DailyTemperature; 30] = [DailyTemperature{ minimum: 0.0,
        maximum: 0.0 }; 30];
```

Given how much work you have to put in to get an array of structs working, when it comes to creating a collection of data—especially data you don't have a way of initializing right away—it may be better to use a `Vector`. The `Vector` takes care of all memory management and initialization. In that sense, it's much like the Python array. Let's take a look at how we would implement a `Vector` for the same task we have been working on accomplishing:

```
struct DailyTemperature {
    minimum: f32,
    maximum: f32
}

    let mut daily_temps: Vec<DailyTemperature> = Vec::new();

    let today = DailyTemperature { minimum: 45.3, maximum: 82.1 };
    daily_temps.push(today);
```

Now that we have a `Vector` of temperature values, we can do something with it. Since we've started down the path of storing temperatures, we can read values in from a file, store them in the `Vector`, and then do something with that `Vector` of values. Following is the complete program that does all of that. Most of the work is done in the `main()` function here, but we can pass the `Vector` around to perform calculations. We can also pass the `Vector` to a function if we want to display all the values in the `Vector`. For what we are trying to accomplish, there is a single function implemented that will calculate the average from all the values. There will be something new in this program that we haven't done before that is something like a collection, although it's a much smaller scale than things like arrays and vectors, so hang on for that:

```
use std::fs::File;
use std::io::{self, BufRead};

#[derive(Copy,Clone)]
struct Temperature {
    minimum: f32,
    maximum: f32
}
```

continues

(continued)

```
    fn get_average(temps: Vec<Temperature>) -> (f32, f32) {

        let mut min_total: f32 = 0.0;
        let mut max_total: f32 = 0.0;
        let mut count = 0;
        for t in temps {
            min_total = min_total + t.minimum;
            max_total = max_total + t.maximum;
            count = count + 1;
        }

        (min_total / count as f32, max_total / count as f32)
    }

    fn main() {

        let file = match File::open("temperatures.txt") {
            Err(e) => panic!("Unable to open file: {}", e),
            Ok(file) => file
        };

        let mut daily_temps: Vec<Temperature> = Vec::new();

        let lines = io::BufReader::new(file).lines();

        for line in lines {
            let line = line.unwrap();
            let mut split_line = line.as_str().split(',');
            let left = split_line.next().unwrap();
            let right = split_line.next().unwrap();
            let today = Temperature { minimum: left.parse::<f32>().unwrap(),
                maximum: right.parse::<f32>().unwrap()
            };
            daily_temps.push(today);
        }

        let avgs = get_average(daily_temps);
        println!("Average daily low: {}, average daily high: {}", avgs.0, avgs.1);

    }
```

We're going to be using a file to read in all of our values, which means we need features from the fs and io crates. You can see those in the use statements at the top of the file. From there, we're going to jump down to the main() function and look at reading the temperature values from the file. The first thing we need to do is open the file. The handful of lines that will open the file follow. Since we're going to be working with a file, there are a number of error conditions that could take place. Rather than just letting the compiler take care of it for us, we're going to handle the error possibility using a match statement. If there is no error, the match statement will return the identifier named file with a handle to the file that has been opened. If there is an error, there's no point in continuing, so we're going to just cause the program to fail by using a panic!() with an indication of what the error was. If we print out the error condition, it provides some details for the user without having to run through a lot of effort trying to figure out programmatically exactly what the error was. Capturing the error and printing it as part of the `panic!()` statement should give all the details needed:

```
let file = match File::open("temperatures.txt") {
    Err(e) => panic!("Unable to open file: {}", e),
    Ok(file) => file
};
```

Once the file is open, we can create the `Vector` of our `Temperature` struct. We'll make use of that in a bit. We also need to read the contents of the file. This is done using the `lines()` trait on the `File` struct. This provides us with a collection of all the lines as individual strings. We're going to need to iterate through all of those strings. You can see the `for` loop that takes care of all of that in the following. The `lines` identifier provides us with an iterator that will drive the `for` loop, giving us a single `String`. The problem with the `String` is, it's a pair of values that have been separated by a comma. You could put the two values on separate lines, but that might get confusing in the file since there is no way to clearly identify the values we're looking at. It's easy to lose track of what line represents which value. It's easier to put the two values on a single line:

```
for line in lines {
    let line = line.unwrap();
    let mut split_line = line.as_str().split(',');
    let left = split_line.next().unwrap();
    let right = split_line.next().unwrap();
    let today = Temperature { minimum: left.parse::<f32>().unwrap(),
        maximum: right.parse::<f32>().unwrap()
    };
    daily_temps.push(today);
}
```

The first thing we need to do in the `for` loop is to extract the `String` from the enumeration it's stored in. This is done, as always, with an `unwrap()`. Once we have the `String` value out, we need to split it in two. This is done by converting the `String` to an `str` value and then calling the `split()` trait on that, passing in the delimiter, which is a comma here. We get a collection back from the call to the trait, so we need to extract the individual values. That's done using `next()`, which is effectively an iterator that returns the value in the next position in the collection. This comes back as a `Result` enumeration value, so we need to extract the value using `unwrap()`. Once we get those two values out, we have a new problem. We have a pair of `String` values, but we need floating-point values instead. The following line will perform that conversion for us:

```
let today = Temperature { minimum: left.parse::<f32>().unwrap(),
    maximum: right.parse::<f32>().unwrap()
```

The `String` struct comes with a `parse()` trait, letting us perform a conversion from `String` to another type. We will need to indicate the type being parsed out of the `String`, so the correct trait implementation gets called. The trait is specified in between the angle brackets, also known as the *less than* and *greater than* symbols. We are using floating-point values for our temperatures since we are going to assume we have a thermometer that will give us those more detailed temperatures. The data type for the floating point is `f32`. The call to the `parse()` trait gives us a `Result`, so that needs to be extracted using `unwrap()`. The two floating-point values are stored in the `Temperature` struct and assigned to an instance of that struct named `today`. The next line in the code pushes that instance onto the `Vector`.

Once we have the `Vector` full of the contents of the file, we can do something with all of the values. We're going to call the `get_average()` function to get the two averages. The code for this function follows, and you can see in this code that we are passing in the `Vector` of `Temperature`. This function takes over the `Vector` from the calling function since we aren't indicating that we only want a reference to it and not the `Vector` itself. What you will see is that the function returns a tuple. We'll skip back to the `main` function in a bit and look at how to handle that:

```
fn get_average(temps: Vec<Temperature>) -> (f32, f32) {

    let mut min_total: f32 = 0.0;
    let mut max_total: f32 = 0.0;
    let mut count = 0;
    for t in temps {
        min_total = min_total + t.minimum;
        max_total = max_total + t.maximum;
        count = count + 1;
    }

    (min_total / count as f32, max_total / count as f32)
}
```

This is a reasonably straightforward function. We need some identifiers to keep track of incrementing values, so we need to define and initialize those. The identifiers `min_total`, `max_total`, and `count` are all mutable because each of them is going to increase with every temperature we need to add to the collection. You may notice that we're going to keep track of the count of temperature pairs. In theory, we could pull the length of the vector and get back the number of entries. The problem there is that we need to do something with the resulting length because we need to convert it to a floating point since it comes back from `len()` as a `usize`. Calling `len()` and trying to convert it generated errors related to borrowing. For clarity of code, it was easier to just keep track of the number of temperature pairs rather than trying to dereference a reference that would have been required to get back the length.

Each pass through the `Vector` using a built-in iterator gives us a single instance of a `Temperature` struct. We increment the `min_total` identifier by the `minimum` value in that struct instance. The same thing happens with `max_total` and `maximum`. Once we have calculated the totals of each temperature and the total number of pairs, we can return the average. This is done by converting the integer value that is the `count` identifier to a floating-point value. We use the clause `count as f32` to get a floating-point value out of the integer. This is necessary because you have to perform arithmetic on the same data types. You can't mix floating points and integers when you are doing math. Since we are working with temperatures that are floating-point values and expect to get floating points for averages, it only makes sense to convert the `count` to floating point to make it all match.

You'll see that the return is a tuple, indicated by providing the two values inside `()`. This creates a single value out of multiple values. In a way, this is a small collection, which means we need to get the individual values out of that collection. Following is the code from the `main()` function that retrieves the tuple value and then extracts each part of the tuple:

```
let avgs = get_average(daily_temps);
println!("Average daily low: {}, average daily high: {}", avgs.0, avgs.1);
```

You might expect that, as it's a collection, you would retrieve the individual values just as you would with other collections, including arrays and vectors. That would look like avgs[0] and avgs[1]. This doesn't work with a tuple. Instead, you refer to them by numeric values dotted against the tuple identifier. Rather than avgs[0], you get the first value out of the tuple using avgs.1. You then use avgs.2 to get the second value from the tuple. While this may seem inconsistent from a language perspective, it perhaps highlights that Rust considers tuples to be different from other collections it handles. In reality, a collection is usually consistent with data types, meaning all the entries in a collection are the same data type. The problem with a tuple is that you can have different data types all being part of the tuple. That means we need to get the different elements out of the tuple differently than we do with traditional collections.

LINKED LISTS

We didn't spend a lot of time on arrays, in part because they are more limited than the Vector collection in Rust. When you define an array, as discussed earlier, you have to know how big the array is and then initialize it. This makes it a fixed thing. It is located in one place in memory and is of a known size. If you want to grow the array, you need to create a new array and move or copy values out of the existing array into it. This is a pain. It's much easier to do things dynamically, especially when you may have no idea at all how many values you are going to be storing at compile time. If you don't know at compile time how big your array is going to be, you end up with memory problems. You'll need to be able to allocate on the fly. This typically requires the programmer to have more control over memory allocation and deallocation than Rust allows. In the end, this is a good thing, because most programmers do a very bad job of managing memory. It's much easier to let the language take care of that management.

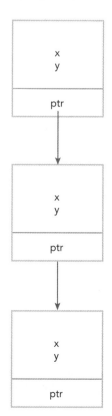

A *linked list* is a collection that typically puts control over the collection of data in the hands of the programmer. The one thing you have control over as a programmer is the individual instances of data. A linked list is where you take individual instances of data and connect them to one another. This typically requires that you have access to the memory location of each instance. This is normally through a data type called a *pointer*. A pointer is simply a memory address. The pointer tells you where the data you are looking for is located, but you then have to dereference the data in that memory location. To create a linked list, you need to have a data structure, because you need to keep track of the next entry in your list by storing the address of that next entry somewhere.

Because we now have a pointer value to store in addition to whatever else we want to store, we need a struct. Even if you only had a single value you wanted to keep a dynamic list for, you would need a struct because you would immediately have at least two values—the first value you wanted to store as well as the pointer to the next value. You may have a pair of pointers, but we'll get to that in a bit. Let's first take an example of a data structure that has two integer values named x and y as well as the pointer to the next entry in the list. Figure 14.2 shows a linked list of three entries of that structure.

FIGURE 14.2: Linked list.

An advantage of using this approach is that you can control the order of all the entries, which you can't easily do with an array. As you are creating entries in your list, you can insert a new entry into the existing list by just reassigning the pointer to the next entry. You can see an example of that in Figure 14.3. We take the existing list and insert a third value between the first and second by just reassigning the pointers. We take the next pointer from the second entry, named B, and point it at the fourth entry, named D, and then point the next value for D to C, which is the previous third entry. The order of the entries will then be A, B, D, C. If you wanted an ordered list of entries, a linked list would be a good way to keep everything in the right order. You just run through the list until you find the place you need to insert the value and then change the pointers.

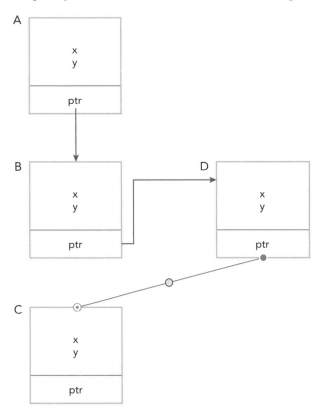

FIGURE 14.3: Reordered linked list.

Let's take a look at some code that will create a linked list and then insert a new value into the list. This code is written in C since it's one language that gives you control over the memory addresses, which is necessary to get pointer values for linked lists. The first thing we do after we have included functionality from the C libraries we need is to define our structure. This is going to contain our two integer variables named x and y as well as the pointer to the next entry in the list. This variable is named next. As mentioned earlier, C doesn't do or require any initialization. When we define a pointer value, we can just define it, and we'll be pointing at some random value that may point to something completely outside of the program we are writing. A better approach is to assign the value NULL to any pointer before it's been properly initialized. This means it doesn't go anywhere. Trying to dereference a NULL value will generate a program crash.

```
#include <stdio.h>
#include <stdlib.h>

struct Entry {
    int x;
    int y;
    struct Entry *next;
};

int main(int argc, char **argv) {
    struct Entry* first = NULL;
    struct Entry* second = NULL;
    struct Entry* third = NULL;
    struct Entry* current = NULL;

    first = (struct Entry*)malloc(sizeof(struct Entry));
    first->x = 5;
    first->y = 10;

    second = (struct Entry*)malloc(sizeof(struct Entry));
    second->x = 92;
    second->y = 45;
    first->next = second;
    second->next = NULL;

    third = (struct Entry*)malloc(sizeof(struct Entry));
    third->x = 42;
    third->y = 19;
    third->next = second;

    first->next = third;
    second->next = NULL;

    current = first;
    printf("Value: %d\n", current->x);
    current = first->next;
    printf("Value: %d\n", current->x);

}
```

With C, you need to allocate any dynamic memory. We do that using the malloc() function. This requires a single parameter, which is the size of the memory we want to be allocated. The sizeof() function will provide the size of the Entry data structure, and that amount of memory, in bytes, will be allocated on the heap. The malloc() function not only allocates memory that can be used later to assign values into but also provides the address to that memory location. The variable gets assigned the address, and getting access to any data eventually stored there has to be done by dereferencing the memory address. You can see an example of this with the line first->x = 5;, for instance. The variable first contains the memory address of the entire structure. To get to the address where the x element is stored, we need to call first->x. Then we can assign a value into that memory location.

Much of the rest of this program is the same. Create a new instance of the structure multiple times. Keep in mind this is a linked list, though. The idea is to connect together each instance of the structure. The address of the second instance, for example, gets assigned to the next field of the instance named first. As shown earlier, we can easily reorder the list by assigning new addresses to the next field. You can see this in the following lines:

```
third->next = second;

first->next = third;
```

Where we started with a linked list that had first connected to second, we end up with first connected to third and third connected to second. The list looks like first->third->second once we are all done reassigning the different next fields.

To work our way through the list, we can assign a new variable with the address of the first instance. This gives us a variable we can keep changing addresses in without losing track of the address of the first instance. If the address of the first instance got lost, the entire list could be lost, leaving a lot of memory orphaned in the program with no way to get back to it for access, much less to release it. We can keep changing the value of current to continue moving through the list. This is a version of an iterator that we've been using in Rust. Rather than the data structure taking care of it, though, we have to move through the list manually. First, we assign the address of first to the variable current. To get to the next entry in the list, we assign the address stored in current->next to current. This effectively places the address of second into the variable current. The way we know we are at the end of the list is if the next value is equal to NULL. This does require a lot of discipline on the part of the programmer to ensure that the last item in the list always has the next variable set to NULL; otherwise, trying to iterate through the list will result in attempts to access memory that has no values and may not even belong to the program.

We can do the same thing in Rust as we did in C. The reason for showing C first is to show all the things that Rust takes care of for us. Following is a short section of code that implements a linked list in Rust, adds some entries, and then extracts the entries. Everything comes out of the crate std::collections::LinkedList, so that's all we need to import into the program. If we create a mutable instance of a LinkedList using the new() trait, we can immediately start using it. You should note that we are creating a LinkedList with no data type associated with it. A linked list is a collection of the same data type. We can't just assign any value we want. In this case, since we didn't specify, Rust imputes the data type by the first data that is assigned to the list:

```rust
use std::collections::LinkedList;

fn main() {

    let mut list_collection = LinkedList::new();
    list_collection.push_back("Our first entry");
    list_collection.push_back("Our second entry");
    list_collection.push_back("Our third entry");

    for entry in list_collection {
        println!("{}", entry);
    }
}
```

If you were to try to do something like `list_collection.push_back(42)` in the middle of all of those string values, the compiler would complain and fail to complete the compilation. Rust assigns the data type automatically and keeps track of whether or not the data being added to the list is the same type. If you wanted to, though, you could assign a data type to be safe and also explicit. Following is a slightly rewritten version of the program that explicitly assigns a data type to the linked list. One reason to be explicit is that there is a little ambiguity in the earlier program. If you weren't paying close enough attention, you might not recognize that the data type in this linked list is `str` and not `String`. The bare character string presented is not a `String` struct but instead a more traditional character string. The following program rectifies that by not only being explicit about the data type but also creating actual `String` values and adding them to the list:

```
use std::collections::LinkedList;

fn main() {

    let mut list_collection = LinkedList::new();
    list_collection.push_back("Our first entry");
    list_collection.push_back("Our second entry");
    list_collection.push_back("Our third entry");

    for entry in list_collection {
        println!("{}", entry);
    }
}
```

What we've been talking about so far has been a single linked list. This means we can only move in one direction through the list. Languages that require you, the programmer, to manage all the memory yourself might also necessitate the implementation of a doubly linked list. This means that each entry in the list has a link to the entry before and after it. Following is a redefinition of the C structure that was defined earlier. This adds a new variable in the structure that provides a way to get to the last entry as well as the next entry. This keeps us from having to start back at the beginning again, which can be painful in really long lists. Keep in mind that working your way through a list is a serial process. You don't jump straight to an entry as we can with an array or a `Vector` in Rust:

```
struct Entry {
    struct Entry *previous;
    int x;
    int y;
    struct Entry *next;
};
```

Stacks

Another common collection type is a stack. We've been talking about stacks for a while when we've been discussing memory management. Remember each time a function gets called, a new frame is pushed onto the stack. Working with the stack involves using a pair of functions. Adding entries onto the stack requires a *push*. Removing the value from the stack is a *pop*. This means you are adding values to and removing values from your collection rather than just letting them always sit in memory,

moving your way through the entries. You can see an
example of using a stack in Figure 14.4. The left side
shows four entries that have been pushed onto the stack.
When we pop a value off the stack in order to get access
to it, the entry is removed altogether, so it's no longer
available in the collection. However, removing one entry
does give us access to the next value down.

The concept of a stack and how it operates is often
explained by comparison to trays in a cafeteria. This
is probably in part because, in a cafeteria, the trays are
often stored in a mechanism that is spring-loaded. This
makes the idea of *push* and *pop* easier to observe. You
push a tray onto the stack of trays, and the stack goes
down. You take a tray off, and the stack rebounds to
a slightly higher level without the weight of the tray

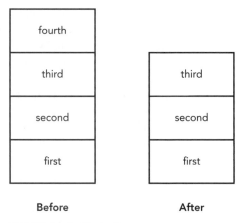

Before   **After**

FIGURE 14.4: Stack diagram

that was taken off. However, it's just as easy to see the stack by looking at the plates in Figure 14.5.
This is also a stack and represents how a stack in computing works just as well. You take your clean
plates out of the dishwasher and add them to the pile—you are pushing plates onto the stack. This
increases the size of the stack until it's time to eat, at which point you take a plate or several plates
off the stack. Figure 14.5 shows two white plates, followed by three red plates, followed by a white
plate. When you are removing from the stack, you take the top plate off, reducing the size of the
stack by one. We do the same thing with data. We push an entry, or plate, onto the stack, making
the size of the stack larger. When we want to retrieve an entry, we pop it off, reducing the size of the
stack by one.

FIGURE 14.5: Real-life stack

> **NOTE** One implementation of a stack can be found in some calculators that use something called reverse Polish notation (RPN). This is sometimes called postfix notation. With postfix notation, you push values onto the stack such as operands. When an operator is called, the number of operands needed to use the operator is popped off. As an example, if we saw 2 2 +, that would translate to 2 + 2. The result would then get pushed onto the stack again. Something more complex would be 8 2 2 + –. When the calculator that uses postfix notation sees the +, it pops off the 2 and the 2, resulting in 4, which is pushed back onto the stack. Then the calculator sees, so it calculates 8 – 4. The result of 8 2 2 + – should be 4.

We can, unsurprisingly, implement a stack in Rust. In fact, we've used the collection that implements a stack several times in previous chapters. Rust provides the same dynamic collection capabilities of a stack in the `Vector` that we've used before. When you add data to the `Vector`, you push it on. You can also pop the data off and remove it. The following program demonstrates the implementation of a stack using the `Vector` data collection type we've been using in previous chapters:

```
use std::vec::Vec;

fn main() {

    let mut vec_stack = Vec::new();
    vec_stack.push("First entry on");
    vec_stack.push("Second entry on");
    vec_stack.push("Third entry on");
    vec_stack.push("Fourth entry on");

    while let Some(top_entry) = vec_stack.pop() {
        println!("{}", top_entry);
    }

    if let Some(another_entry) = vec_stack.pop() {
        println!("Final entry: {}", another_entry);
    }
    else {
        println!("No entries left");
    }
}
```

You can see that we push the `string` values on in numeric order: First, Second, Third, and then Fourth. Following is the output from running the program. You can see that when we pop off the values, they come out in reverse order from the way they were pushed on. This is the same as plates that are taken out of the dishwasher. The last plate put on the stack is the first one that will be taken off when you go to set the table. What you will also see in the output is the demonstration that once we have popped all the values off the stack, the stack is truly empty. There are no values left to remove. Unless we save them in some way, once they are popped off the stack, they are gone:

```
Fourth entry on
Third entry on
Second entry on
First entry on
No entries left
```

Jumping back up to the code, you can see the creation of the Vector, followed by pushing four character strings onto the Vector that was created with the identifier vec_stack. When we take the values off the stack again, we check to see whether we are done by checking the Option that is returned from the pop() trait. If there is a value to be returned from the stack, pop() returns a Some enumeration, with the value contained. If not, there will be a None returned. This will cause the loop to fail. Just to demonstrate that the stack is empty, there is a check for another value. Since there is no other value on the stack, we get the response, "No entries left."

While Rust does have something called *smart pointers*, they are generally not used because it's safer to let Rust take care of memory management; we can get an effect similar to pointers using the Option enumeration data type. You can determine that you are at the end of a list in a traditional language like C by seeing if your pointer value is NULL, meaning there is no memory location being pointed to. In Rust, you create a list by wrapping a value inside a Some enumeration. If there is no value, you get a None, which is similar in concept to NULL, meaning there is nothing there.

Queues

If you look at it from the perspective of the data, a stack is last in, first out (LIFO). The last value placed on the stack is the first value that is removed. This isn't always what you want, though. Sometimes you want a first-come, first-served model, called first in, first out (FIFO). This type of data collection is called a *queue* because it acts the same way as a line (or queue) at a grocery store or bank. The first person in line is the first person to the checkout or teller. The same is true with the queue data structure. It is similar to the stack in the sense that it is a collection of data that is removed from the collection one element at a time. The difference is the order in which the data goes into the collection compared with the way it comes out. We add data onto a queue, and the first elements added are the first that are removed. In Rust, the queue is implemented in the VecDeque crate. We can take a look at how we'd implement a queue in the following code:

```
use std::collections::VecDeque;

let mut queue:VecDeque<String> = VecDeque::new();
queue.push_back(String::from("first"));
queue.push_back(String::from("second"));
queue.push_back(String::from("third"));
queue.push_back(String::from("fourth"));
queue.push_front(String::from("zeroth"));

while let Some(q_entry) = queue.pop_front() {
    println!("{}", q_entry);
}
```

This implementation of a Vector gives us more control over where we add data into the collection. You will notice that there are traits to add both to the front of the collection and to the back. This gives us a way to cheat and allow line hopping in our queue. A strict queue would only push onto the back of the queue, leaving those who were already in line exactly where they are. However, we may discover that an element has come along that belongs at the front of the line. Looking at the code, you can see everything gets pushed to the back once the queue identifier has been created as an instance of VecDeque. Just to show that we can also add to the other end as well, there is a push_front() example at the end. As before, iterating through the Vector will generate a Some enumeration response when there are values to remove and a None when everything is gone. Following is the output from this little program segment, and you can see that the word "zeroth" shows up at the front of the list of values, just as you'd expect when you push it onto the front of the queue:

```
zeroth
first
second
third
fourth
```

Having a collection data structure that can act as both queue and stack, depending on the traits that you call, gives you a lot of flexibility. If you like, you can use the same data structure regardless of whether you need a stack or a queue.

Sorting

One problem with using these types of collections is that very often, they have values entirely out of order. Being able to sort the collection is often helpful. If we jump back to the C program, we can see a very simple way to perform a sort. This is called an *insertion sort*, and it reorders the list as entries are added to it. Following is a section of the code where we perform a comparison between the existing head of the list and the new entry. If the new entry is smaller than the existing entry, the existing entry becomes the new head of the list. This requires, as you can see, that all the moving around is done manually by adjusting the head of the list and the next pointers in each entry to make sure that the list is structured correctly:

```c
first = (struct Entry*)malloc(sizeof(struct Entry));
    head = first;
    first->x = 500;
    first->y = 10;
    first->next = NULL;

    second = (struct Entry*)malloc(sizeof(struct Entry));
    second->x = 92;
    second->y = 45;
    if (head->x > second->x) {
        second->next = first;
        head = second;
        first->next = NULL;
    }
    else {
        first->next = second;
        second->next = NULL;
    }

    third = (struct Entry*)malloc(sizeof(struct Entry));
    third->x = 42;
    third->y = 19;

    if (head->x > third->x) {
        third->next = head;
        head = third;
    }
    else {
        second->next = third;
        third->next = NULL;
    }
```

There are some problems with this, of course. First, it's a very simple example. You wouldn't normally do it in this brute-force sort of way. You'd get an entry at a time rather than putting all of your entries into your code at once. It would be more dynamic than what we are doing here, meaning you might get the values from user input or from a file. You wouldn't get your entries directly from the source code. More importantly, though, this doesn't leave the entire list sorted. It just makes sure the first entry is the smallest out of all the entries that are being added to the list. You'd want something more generic to search the list until you found the right location, and then you'd insert the entry between two existing entries, assuming it didn't belong at the head of the list.

Fortunately, we have easier ways to take care of the out-of-order problem. Let's say we have a stack implemented with a `Vector` in Rust. It contains a list of animals, but the list is out of order. We can use a built-in trait, `sort()`, to handle sorting them into alphabetical order. Once it's done, we can pop all the values off the stack and print them out. Following is the code that creates an instance of a `Vector` and then populates it with animal species before sorting it and then popping all the values off the stack:

```
let mut sort_stack = Vec::new();
sort_stack.push("anteater");
sort_stack.push("zebra");
sort_stack.push("tapir");
sort_stack.push("elephant");
sort_stack.push("coati");
sort_stack.push("leopard");
sort_stack.sort();

while let Some(animal) = sort_stack.pop() {
    println!("{}", animal);
}
```

The interesting thing about this code is what happens when you print out the values. Following is the output from the code fragment you just looked at. Based on an initial inspection, this may look wrong. It looks backward, right? You need to keep in mind the collection type we are using. This is a stack. When you sort, it sorts from the perspective of the bottom of the stack, meaning the first entry. However, we are printing the stack from the top, meaning the last entry. The printing process goes from the top of the stack to the bottom, so it's going from the last entry:

```
zebra
tapir
leopard
elephant
coati
anteater
```

We can control the way things are sorted if we like, though. Let's say we had a data structure that we wanted to add to a `Vector` we were treating like a stack. First, we would need to define the data structure, but, more importantly, we would need to define how it was going to be sorted. After all, with a struct, we have more than one value we would need to be concerned with. Which value do you want to sort by? You need a way to compare one struct against another. This requires implementing some traits that will handle the comparisons. Fortunately, Rust can derive its own implementations of common traits, including those used to compare one struct instance against another. Following is the code that demonstrates a simple data structure where Rust will derive some traits for us:

```
use std::vec::Vec;

#[derive(Debug, Eq, Ord, PartialEq, PartialOrd)]
struct DVD {
    title: String,
    year: u32
}

impl DVD {
    pub fn new(title: String, year: u32) -> Self {
        DVD {
            title,
            year
        }
    }
}

fn main() {
    let mut movies = vec![
        DVD::new("Buckaroo Banzai Across the 8th Dimension".to_string(), 1984),
        DVD::new("Captain America".to_string(), 2011),
        DVD::new("Stargate".to_string(), 1994),
        DVD::new("When Harry Met Sally".to_string(), 1989),
        DVD::new("Kiss Kiss Bang Bang".to_string(), 2005),
        DVD::new("The Dark Knight".to_string(), 2008),
        DVD::new("Boys Night Out".to_string(), 1962),
        DVD::new("The Glass Bottom Boat".to_string(), 1966)
    ];

    movies.sort_by(|a,b| b.year.cmp(&a.year));

    while let Some(movie) = movies.pop() {
        println!("{:?}", movie);
    }

}
```

At the top of the source code, we define a simple data structure for a DVD, although you could just as easily call it a Movie since it amounts to the same thing. The struct contains a title and a year. In addition to the traits that Rust will take care of for us, there is a trait for new() that is implemented. This trait takes two parameters for the two values in the struct and creates a new instance of DVD, returning that instance back from the trait call. This makes it easier to create a new instance of our struct, although we certainly could also create an instance by hand by using the lines of code inside that trait each time we wanted to create an instance. In our case, it's not very onerous to do that, but if you had a large struct, it would just be easier to use the new() trait. Additionally, it makes the code in your program easier to read, which is always preferable.

In the main() function, we create a Vector using the vec!() macro and passing it a collection of instances of the DVD struct. Once we have the Vector created, we can sort it on our terms. This is easy enough to do using the `sort_by()` trait. This trait hands in a pair of parameters that consist of a pair of entries that need to be compared to determine their correct order. We don't get any control over the sorting algorithm being used. However, we do have control over what field we are going to sort by. In our case, we are choosing to use the `cmp()` trait that was created for us, comparing the years of the two struct instances. If you wanted to compare in a different way, you could implement your own trait for `cmp()`. This would allow you to go in a different order than the order provided by the standard Rust implementation. The results of this program are shown in the following:

```
DVD { title: "Boys Night Out", year: 1962 }
DVD { title: "The Glass Bottom Boat", year: 1966 }
DVD { title: "Buckaroo Banzai Across the 8th Dimension", year: 1984 }
DVD { title: "When Harry Met Sally", year: 1989 }
DVD { title: "Stargate", year: 1994 }
DVD { title: "Kiss Kiss Bang Bang", year: 2005 }
DVD { title: "The Dark Knight", year: 2008 }
DVD { title: "Captain America", year: 2011 }
```

You can see it is in numeric order from earlier year to later year. Keep in mind, again, that this is a stack, so the order is going to be reversed. Knowing that, the program specifically compares b with a rather than a with b. The order matters because of the way the comparison works. Since the stack was going to be in reverse order based on the way the values were going to be popped off, it was important to compare the second value with the first rather than the first with the second. If you reverse the comparison line so it reads `movies.sort_by(|a,b| a.cmp(&b.year))`, you will get output that looks like what follows. Normally, you would compare a with b, meaning you would call the `cmp()` trait on a, passing in the value of `b.year`. That, though, assumes you have a queue rather than a stack, meaning the top of the list is the first value rather than the last value.

SEARCH TREES

There are other ways of sorting through the use of data collections that may be better-suited to the task. A common data collection type in computer science is the *binary tree*. Rather than a list of values, as would be the case with a linked list, queue, or stack, we have something that looks like what its name implies—a tree. At least, it looks like the roots of a tree. When computer scientists refer to a tree, they usually refer to a structure that looks like roots emanating from a single node at the top. In the case of a binary tree, each node has a pair of nodes coming off of it, as you can see in Figure 14.6. Typically, the tree would be sorted as it was being constructed. The parent node would stay the same, but the subsequent nodes would be placed based on their values relative to the parent. Usually, any value that was less than the parent node would move to the left. It would then be compared to the next node down, moving left for a lesser value and right for a greater value.

If you look at the top of the tree in Figure 14.6, just off to the side, there is a new entry. This one hasn't been placed yet. The value 8 is larger than 5, so it moves to the right side of the tree. The next node we encounter is 12. We know 8 is less than 12, so we're going to move to the left branch. There is no node there, so we can place 8 there. You can see the result of this operation in Figure 14.7.

We can see what a data structure that implements a binary tree looks like, based on the tree we have seen previously—a single integer value as the contents. Since Rust is going to take care of all of this for us when we get to writing the Rust program, it's easier to see it in C. The format of the definition is similar enough to Rust that even if you aren't familiar with C, you can see what is going on. First, we create a data structure, the definition of which follows. Inside the data structure is a single integer, which is called x for simplicity. There are two other values stored in the structure. First is a pointer called left, which holds the address of the node to the left of this one as we follow down the tree. The other value, unsurprisingly, is called right and holds the address of the node that is to the right at the next layer of the tree:

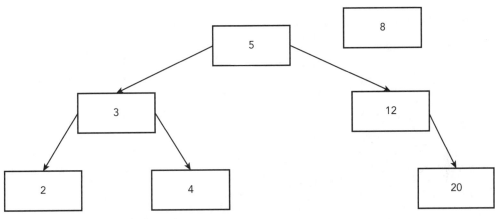

FIGURE 14.6: Binary tree before placement

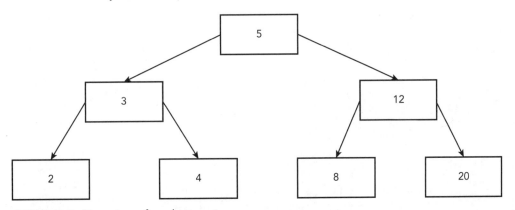

FIGURE 14.7: Binary tree after placement

```
struct Node {
    int x;
    struct Node *left;
    struct Node *right;
};
```

As usual with C, you as the programmer would need to maintain the addresses and also ensure that the pointers were set to NULL at the bottom of the tree so your functions that were trying to traverse the tree would know when to stop. Rust makes life easier for us because we don't have to take care of all the memory address management to make sure we aren't referring to an address in memory that doesn't exist. Following is a program that implements a binary tree. This is going to be a variation on the DVD program that was in Chapter 3, "Building a Library." Rather than just storing information about the movies in a list, we can store them in a binary tree, which makes it quicker to find entries:

```rust
use std::collections::BTreeMap;
use std::fs::File;
use std::io::{self, BufRead};
use std::iter::FromIterator;


fn fill_tree() -> BTreeMap<String, i32> {

    let file = match File::open("values.txt") {
        Err(e) => panic!("Unable to open file: {}", e),
        Ok(file) => file
    };

    let mut movie_entries: BTreeMap<String, i32> = BTreeMap::new();

    let lines = io::BufReader::new(file).lines();

    for line in lines {
        let line = line.unwrap();
        let mut split_line = line.as_str().split('\t');
        let left = split_line.next().unwrap();
        let right = split_line.next().unwrap();
        let year = right.parse::<i32>().unwrap();
        movie_entries.insert(String::from(left), year);
    }

    movie_entries
}

fn main() {
    let movies: BTreeMap<String, i32> = fill_tree();

    println!("We have {} movies", movies.len());

    match movies.get("Captain America") {
        Some(year) => println!("{}", year),
        None => println!("Unable to find that movie")
    }

    for (movie, year) in &movies {
        println!("{}: {}", movie, year);
    }

    let mut movie_vec = Vec::from_iter(movies);
    movie_vec.sort_by(|&(_, a), &(_, b)| a.cmp(&b));
    println!("{:?}", movie_vec);
}
```

You may recognize pieces of this program, since the file-reading part is taken from other programs you've seen, including the program demonstrating the use of the Vector earlier in this chapter. Code reuse makes life a lot easier and speeds the time of completion. Because we've seen that part before, we can skip over the bulk of the function that creates the BTreeMap, except for a couple of notes. First, the function returns a BTreeMap that contains a string and an integer. One note about the data types used: wherever possible, use managed data types. While it's possible to use an str value, you will find it a lot harder to move around from function to function because of the ownership rules. An str created in a function will continue to live in that function, no matter how much manipulation you do to it and how you try to assign the results to new identifiers. The base value is an unowned data type and doesn't contain traits that allow you to easily copy it and move it around. Second, once we have our two values—the name of the movie and the year of its release—we use the insert() trait to add it to our tree.

The BTreeMap is a map, meaning it expects two values where one is mapped to the other in some way. Think of it as a hash or a dictionary—to find one piece of information, you need to search based on another piece of information. What we are creating here is a way to look up the year of a movie based on its name. Just to highlight that, we can look at the code fragment that follows. We will be searching for a movie based on the title, and this requires an exact match:

```
match movies.get("Captain America") {
    Some(year) => println!("{}", year),
    None => println!("Unable to find that movie")
}
```

Remember, this is a map or a dictionary. The results from the get() trait only show you the data associated with the key that was provided. To get back both values, you need to use a different trait. If we were to use get_key_value() instead of get(), we'd get a tuple with both values. Following is the same block of code that gets back both of the values in a tuple and then prints out the two values rather than just the year. This uses the same Some, None approach as the other collections we have looked at to know when we are done with the tree. To get the value out of the Option, we use a match clause. The contents of the Option will be placed in the identifier named in parentheses with Some(). For the code fragment seen here, we use two identifiers because we are getting back a tuple. Those identifiers are named name and year. If we didn't have names for them, we wouldn't be able to print the contents of the identifier:

```
match movies.get_key_value("Boys Night Out") {
    Some((name, year)) => println!("{} : {}", name, year),
    None => println!("Unable to find that movie")
}
```

Just as we have done with other collections, we can print the entire collection. The BTreeMap struct includes an iterator, so we can run through the entire tree, printing out the key and value as we go. The following code uses the iterator and prints the values. As before, since we are getting a pair of values, they come back in a tuple, requiring the two identifiers to be placed inside () to indicate that they are two parts of a whole. Trying to use the two identifiers without the parentheses to indicate that they are a tuple will result in a compiler error:

```
for (movie, year) in &movies {
    println!("{}: {}", movie, year);
}
```

You can see a little of the structure of the tree in the output from the program. The output isn't really sorted, although it's not in the order from the file that was used to create the tree. Following are the two sets of output so you can compare them. The first output is from the program where we ran through the tree using the iterator and printed out all the values. The second set of output is the order the values were in on disk in the file that was read to create the tree:

```
Program output:
Boys Night Out: 1962
Buckaroo Banzai Across the 8th Dimension: 1984
Captain America: 2011
Kiss Kiss Bang Bang: 2005
La La Land: 2016
Stargate: 1994
The Dark Knight: 2008
The Glass Bottom Boat: 1966
When Harry Met Sally: 1989

Contents of values.txt:
Buckaroo Banzai Across the 8th Dimension        1984
Captain America 2011
La La Land      2016
Stargate        1994
When Harry Met Sally    1989
Kiss Kiss Bang Bang     2005
The Dark Knight 2008
Boys Night Out  1962
The Glass Bottom Boat   1966
```

This may not be what you want. You may want to be able to print the output where it's sorted. Sorting a BTreeMap isn't nearly as straightforward as sorting a Vector, so it is easier to just dump the contents of the tree into a Vector and then sort that. Because the BTreeMap is a collection and has an iterator, we can use that iterator to collect the contents of the map and put them into the Vector. This is done using the from_iter() trait from the Vector struct. Following are the two lines used to map the tree into a Vector:

```
let mut movie_vec = Vec::from_iter(movies);
movie_vec.sort_by(|&(_, a), &(_, b)| a.cmp(&b));
```

Remember that when we did the sort before, we had a struct that had been created and needed to be able to compare one against the other. This was done by comparing an element of the struct against another element of the struct. In this case, we don't have a struct; we have a tuple, because the BTreeMap is a connection or mapping from one element to another element that are stored together. When we call sort_by() on the Vector, we need to be able to provide a closure that the trait can use to determine the ordering of values. We define the values we are comparing by providing identifier names that we can call the cmp() trait on.

This is one of those places where it can be hard to follow what's going on, so hang on as we go through it step by step. When the sort_by() trait is called, it has to have a pair of values that need to be compared. In the closure definition (remember that a closure is an anonymous function), the first part, in between the || symbols, is the mapping to the two values that will be passed to the anonymous function. Each value in the vector is a tuple, so we'll have a pair of tuples that are being mapped. We only care about one half of each of the tuples. Additionally, we are going to borrow the value rather than take ownership of it. Because we don't care about one half of the tuple, we provide the name of each identifier that will be used by discarding one of the two values in the tuple by naming it with a _. That's why you see &(_,a) for the first part of the map and &(_,b) for the second part. What that says is that we're borrowing the tuple (the & part), discarding the name (the _ part), and naming the year so we can perform the comparison.

Once we have our two identifiers, we can perform the comparison. As before, we need to know which order we want the values to come out in, so it matters which value the `cmp()` trait is called on. Also as before, we are borrowing the value to pass into the trait, so we need to prepend the ampersand when we provide the parameter.

Now that we have the `Vector` sorted, we can display the collection. Rather than working through the collection using the iterator, we're going to let `println!()` take care of it for us. When we provide the formatter with `{:?}`, it tells the `println!()` macro to pull apart the tuple and present the contents pre-formatted without any additional work on our part. The output is presented as a collection, as you can see from the output that follows. If you want something that looks better than what you see, you can rewrite the output portion so it has the look that you prefer. It does not, after all, look very appealing as it is here:

```
[("Boys Night Out", 1962), ("The Glass Bottom Boat", 1966), ("Buckaroo Banzai
Across the 8th Dimension", 1984), ("When Harry Met Sally", 1989), ("Stargate",
1994), ("Kiss Kiss Bang Bang", 2005), ("The Dark Knight", 2008), ("Captain
America", 2011), ("La La Land", 2016)]
```

SUMMARY

Collections are important concepts in programming. When you have a programming language like Rust, there are a lot of collections that are either built in or provided in a standard library. Rust provides a number of collections in the standard library. They include sequences, maps, and sets. The sequences that Rust defines are the same as lists in other languages. These include linked lists, queues, and stacks. One of the maps provided by Rust is a binary tree map, which uses a standard binary tree to allow you to implement an efficient dictionary or hash. This means when you provide the key, you will get the value that is associated with the key. The hash just happens to be stored as a binary tree to make searching more efficient.

Linked lists are commonly implemented in languages that support them with pointers. This typically requires the programmer to manage the memory. The linked list is a collection of values where each entry in the list is created dynamically and connected together by keeping track of where all the entries are located in memory. Rust does support linked lists using the `LinkedList` crate from the standard library. A linked list can allow you to insert values into the list since it's dynamic, and the list is entirely controlled by connecting one entry to another with memory addresses. If you want to insert a new value into the list at a location, you change the next pointer of the new entry to the location of entry B while you change the next pointer of location A to the new entry. This inserts the new entry in between entries A and B.

Other types of lists or sequences are queues and stacks. These are often represented or thought of as linear collections. A queue is first in, first out, while a stack is last in, first out. The stack is implemented in Rust with a `Vector`, while a queue is implemented as a `VecDeque`. With a stack, you push values onto the stack and then pop them off. Both the push and pop happen from the top of the stack. With a queue, usually you push onto the queue at the back of the queue while removing values from the front of the queue. With the `VecDeque` collection, though, you can push or pop from either the front or the back, which makes it a versatile collection, capable of acting as either a stack or a queue. It just requires that you know how you are using it, so you know where the values you want to use are.

Collecting data is nice, but at some point, you probably want it in some order. There are a lot of ways to sort data. The `Vector` collection type in Rust includes two functions that will perform sorts.

The first is a trait named sort(). This assumes an ordering based on the data type being stored in the Vector. If you want to sort in your own direction, or if you are trying to sort a struct you have created yourself, you will want to use sort_by(). This trait uses a map to assign values that are then passed into a closure or anonymous function. The closure defines how the comparison is done, which should provide the correct order as specified by you based on the data in the struct.

EXERCISES

1. Add a function to the temperature vector program that calculates and displays the total temperature values.

2. Add a function to the temperature vector program that displays all the values from the file.

3. Add a check in the temperature vector program to ensure that the maximum is higher than the minimum. If it's not, you should swap the values, although you could also decide to discard them.

4. Write a program that takes numeric input from the user or from a file, puts the data into a Vector or VecDeque, and then presents a sorted list to the user followed by the average, obtained by popping the values off the collection.

5. Add an additional field to the DVD data structure in the sort program for a length in minutes. Make sure to populate that field, and then change the sort _ by() parameter to sort on the year.

6. Add the ability for the user to insert more values into the BTreeMap by taking input, creating a new entry, and then inserting it.

7. Add the ability for the user to ask for the year based on a movie name provided.

ADDITIONAL RESOURCES

Queue Definition - computersciencewiki.org/index.php/Queue

Queue Data Structure - www.geeksforgeeks.org/queue-data-structure

Stacks and Queues - everythingcomputerscience.com/discrete_mathematics/Stacks_and_Queues.html

Stack Definition - computersciencewiki.org/index.php/Stack

Stack Data Structure - www.geeksforgeeks.org/stack-data-structure

Binary Tree Data Structure - www.geeksforgeeks.org/binary-tree-data-structure

"Introduction to the Binary Tree Data Structure" - www.baeldung.com/cs/binary-tree-intro

Linked List Data Structure - www.geeksforgeeks.org/data-structures/linked-list

Linked List Definition - computersciencewiki.org/index.php/Linked_list

15

Odds and Sods

➤ Introducing unit testing to your code

➤ Solving problems with recursion

➤ Using machine learning

There are a handful of utterly unrelated topics to discuss in this chapter. One is essential. The second is not essential, but it's a useful concept that is often used in challenging problems. Finally, we take a look at one other area of solving problems with programs just for fun. The first topic is unit testing, which is an essential technique used in software development. Recursion is a classic computer science technique; Rust does not support all versions of it directly, but we can still solve problems in Rust through the use of a crate that allows us to do recursive-like things. There are also some types of recursion that are directly supported in Rust. Finally, you'll likely have heard about machine learning, as it's all the rage in the more fashionable and even not so fashionable areas of information technology and development.

There are a lot of problems in math and, by extension, computer science that make use of *recursion*, which is the process of repeatedly calling the same function over and over from inside the function itself. We'll take a look at different types of recursion as well as ways we can use recursion in Rust, regardless of the type of recursion.

Machine learning is a bit of a loaded term today. It's very popular in data science because of the promise machine learning has to let programs learn from large data sets in ways that we may not be able to teach directly. This is a topic that takes entire books to cover completely, but we can certainly take a pass at using some machine learning modules and techniques inside Rust.

Testing hasn't been left until last because it's less important but mostly because all the essential syntax and techniques in Rust can be implemented without doing testing other than standard debugging—trying to remove compiler errors in the process of writing code and getting it working. Now that we've covered syntax and usage in Rust as well as a number of useful crates, we can talk about how to go about testing the software you are writing. You don't have to wait until you are writing very big programs to jump into unit testing. Some languages require additional add-on libraries to take care of unit testing for you. Rust has the capability built into it. Hooray for us! We can create unit tests right in our code without adding any additional crates to support them.

UNIT TESTING

Testing is a big topic. It's not left until last lightly. It's essential when it comes to software development. You may think that testing is the province of quality assurance engineers, meaning you write the code, get it compiling, and then toss it over the fence to the testing team to deal with. The testing team then has to run the software through its paces to make sure it does everything it's supposed to do as well as not do things it's not supposed to do. While we are going to be focusing on unit testing, there are other types of testing to think about as well.

Before we get too far ahead of ourselves, we should take a look at a software development lifecycle. Figure 15.1 shows a simplified lifecycle that has the essential elements of most lifecycles you will run across. No matter which development methodology you are going to be using, you will need to perform some version of these steps in order to get your software from ideation to functional and in production. Skipping any of these steps introduces the possibility of bad software or a lot of bugs that will later need to be sorted out. It's a well-worn saw that the earlier in the development process bugs are identified, the less expensive they are to fix.

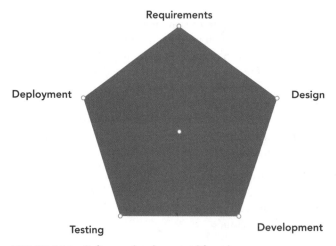

FIGURE 15.1: Software development lifecycle

Speaking of cost, it's worth driving this point home. According to the National Institute of Science and Technology (NIST), Figure 15.2 shows the dramatic increases in the cost of fixing software/ system defects as you progress through the different stages. NIST was tracking the phases a little differently than the ones shown in Figure 15.2, but they are easy enough to map. Requirements are still requirements. According to NIST, requirements and architecture go together, but requirements should drive the architecture, which is why design (this may be thought of as architecture) is decoupled from requirements in the model shown earlier. From a cost perspective, though, it is going to be roughly equivalent to fix a defect in either stage that early in the process.

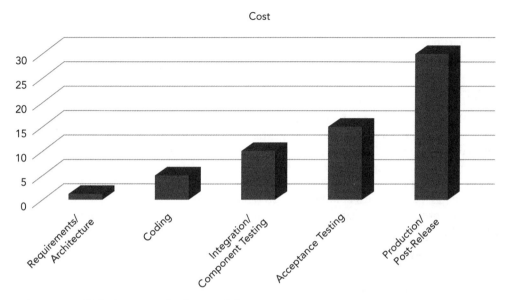

FIGURE 15.2: Relative cost of software defects

Once you hit the development (or coding) stage, fixing a defect that might have been caught earlier or at least might have been introduced earlier by a bad requirement costs five times as much as it would have had it been caught and resolved earlier. By the time you get to an integration or component testing phase, where different elements of the overall project are being tested with each other, the multiple rises to 10. This means something that might have cost $100, as a very inexpensive example, suddenly costs $1000. If the defect isn't caught until the entire system is being tested and the project is getting a go/no-go decision, that $100 is now $1500. This, of course, is inexpensive compared to the $3000 it would cost once the product is in the hands of end users.

Now, take that $100 and make it something more realistic, given the cost of software development. You're talking at least tens of thousands if not many millions of dollars. While NIST says 30 times, IBM—an expert on large-scale software development if ever there was one, considering the legendary OS/360 project from the 1960s, which introduced a lot of learning around software development—says a defect post-deployment could cost 100 times what it would cost if that same defect had been caught in requirements or design. This highlights the importance of planning and really thinking about your software before you start writing it.

There has long been a push to move security to the left in the software development process. To understand what that means, you'd need to unbend the pentagon from Figure 15.1 to get a straight line. Then start on the left end of the line and write out the different phases, as you would with any process you wanted to read in order. English is a language that is read from left to right, after all. So, if you think about the process starting at the left side of the line moving to the right over time, moving to the left means starting earlier in the process. When it comes to security, we can start at the requirements phase.

The same holds true when it comes to testing. We don't have to limit ourselves to testing in the phases in our lifecycle that are named *testing*. It's less likely to be testing in the requirements phase, but we can certainly start pushing testing into the development phase. However, before we start getting into testing in the development stage, we should back up again.

Testing Types

There are several ways of thinking about testing. Let's look at some of the types of testing that we have already talked about. First—and you may get dizzy thinking about the different buckets we can talk about to put different testing types into—we should talk about the differences between functional and non-functional testing. *Functional* testing means you define a set of functions that a piece of software is intended to perform. Functional testing verifies that the software actually achieves that set of functionalities. However, it's not always as straightforward as "Here is what the software does; go make sure the software does what we say it's going to do." Let's take a look at some other ways of thinking about functional testing:

➤ **Component testing:** Software is composed of multiple components. These may be libraries or modules or even different services, depending on how the software is constructed. Component testing takes each of the individual libraries, modules, or other components and tests it as it stands. This testing is done without any regard for any other component that may be included in the software. It is all done standalone.

➤ **Integration testing:** At some point, all the components need to be put together and tested as a coherent whole. The focus of integration testing is making sure all the different components talk to one another. Anywhere there is an intersection point of sets of components, the communication between those components needs to be tested to ensure that there are no unexpected failures.

➤ **Performance testing:** Software is expected to perform in a reasonable way, meaning users want responses to requests in a timely fashion. Performance testing does a lot of timing to make sure the software is going to be responsive to the user and they won't have to wait for responses for undue amounts of time in normal operating conditions.

➤ **Stress testing:** Similar to performance testing, the idea of stress testing is to push the software to its limits to see how it performs. In the case of a network service, for example, you might send as many requests as possible to the network service in as short a period of time.

➤ **Anomaly testing:** You may think of this as *fuzz testing* since that's what it is often called. This is a type of security testing since the idea is to send a bad request to an application—it could be an actual request, as in the case of a network service, or it could just be bad data, as in the case of an application that reads and parses the contents of a file. Poorly written or unforgiving software may crash when it shouldn't be based on this bad data.

➤ **Smoke testing:** This is typically a surface level of testing that validates a critical set of functionality to ensure that functionality is functional. This requires prioritization of what the software is meant to do.

➤ **Regression testing:** This is a much deeper level of testing. In some cases, testing focuses on new functionality to be sure that new functionality works as expected. Regression testing goes back over all the older components and functions. This can be time-consuming, but it is also essential to ensure that nothing was broken with the new development. As with many types of testing, this may be automated.

➤ **Usability testing:** This type of testing is commonly focused on the user interface, such as it may be. The idea of usability testing is to make sure users will find the user interface usable.

➤ **Acceptance testing:** At some point, the software has to be ready for production, meaning it needs to be in a state that can be put in front of users. This means there is some bar that has been set—here are the things the software absolutely has to do before it's ready for production. This may not be testing in the traditional set of testing. It can be someone sitting in front of the software to make sure it behaves as it is expected to before it can be moved to released or production status.

When it comes to software testing, and perhaps especially security testing, we can also think about the level of detail the testers may have. Not all testing is done with a complete understanding of the software right down to the source code. As a result, we often talk about black, white, and gray box testing:

➤ **Black box:** The testers have no idea what the software looks like or how it's expected to behave at a low level. They may get no access to documentation and may only have a top-level idea of what the software is expected to do. Testers are expected to not only determine what the software can do but also attempt to find bugs or break the software.

➤ **White box:** White box testers are in full collaboration with the software developers. These testers will probably have complete access to the source code to be able to follow testing pathways through the software. At a minimum, white box testers may have access to the documentation that may describe in detail what the software will do.

➤ **Gray box:** As you might expect, gray box testing is testing with a variable level of knowledge of the software on the part of the testers. This is fairly common, especially when it comes to security testing of software.

Test Plans

All testing, ideally, is done from plans. You'll find that the best results in most things come from plans. Well, at least when it comes to software development. In real life, spontaneity and making decisions on nothing but a whim can be fun. In the software development world, it means something is going to get missed. A common way to measure the effectiveness of software testing is something called *code coverage*. This means the percentage of lines of code that have been tested in some way, whether it's component testing, regression testing, or some other type of testing. The more code coverage you get, the better you can feel about the number of bugs that may remain in the software after testing. Lower code coverage numbers probably mean more bugs in the code that has been released to the outside world.

So, the way we address this is by developing test plans. Based on the number of different types of software testing, you might expect that you could find a lot of different ways to develop test plans. There, again, are probably multiple ways of thinking about test plans. One way is to think about use cases. This means you think about something you expect the software to do, so you develop a plan to test whether the software does that thing or not. One way of looking at this is very often neglected, and that is to develop misuse cases. This is a type of negative testing, whereby you are trying to find breakages in the software by doing things the software wasn't necessarily designed to do but that a user might do. *Positive testing* is where you say the software is expected to take numeric input and generate a sum based on the input provided, and then you validate that the sum provided by the software is correct based on the input. *Negative testing* is where you say, "I'm going to send a letter into the program when I know it is expecting a number, just to see how it handles it."

Once we have created a number of use cases—and many of these can be developed based on simple things like requirements—we need to develop the plans. In fact, the very first place you should start with your testing is by developing use cases around all the requirements. If the software is supposed to do X, Y, and Z, then your three use cases are validating that it does in fact do X, Y, and Z, not foo, wubble, and bar instead.

Documentation is helpful when it comes to test cases. It helps you to keep track of what you have done. In larger software projects, you are going to be running your tests a lot, most likely, and you should have the test results from previous runs so you can compare one set of results against another set of results to make sure nothing has changed unexpectedly. When you are creating test plans, you should consider the following data points to be in your documentation:

- ➤ **Title:** This is a short version or description of the test to uniquely distinguish it and make sure it can be found.

- ➤ **Description:** This is a more detailed description of the test, which may provide specifics about the components being tested or the requirements the test is based on.

- ➤ **Procedure:** This should be the steps taken to perform the test. This allows anyone to pick up a test plan and run through it from top to bottom.

- ➤ **Assumptions:** This is a document of everything that needs to be in place before the test can be successfully completed. There may be other software that has to be in place, or there may be services running on other systems that are needed. You may also have assumptions about versions or other software that needs to be in place or users that need to be created. Anything that needs to be in place that you are assuming will be there.

- ➤ **Expected outcome:** This provides an exact description of what the test should result in. As a tester, you should always know what the outcome of the test should be.

- ➤ **Actual outcome:** When you run the test, you should document what the actual outcome of the test is to compare it against the expected outcome. From this, you can also indicate whether the test was a success or a failure. This could be a separate line item if you like.

- ➤ **Details:** You should provide as many details about the test as possible. This should include all output from the run of the test. As always, the more documentation you can create, the better position you will be in when you need to remember how a test went.

One way to do this is to create a table with all of the details. Once you have a table in place, you can copy and paste it over and over, filling in the sections you need to for each test. Table 15.1 shows an example of what that might look like.

TABLE 15.1: Rust test plan

UNIT TEST 001	
TITLE	**VALIDATING AREA FUNCTION**
Description	The struct `Room` has a trait to calculate the area based on the stored length and width. This test validates that it works as expected.
Procedure	Run `cargo test test_area`.
Assumptions	Ensure that `cargo build` has been executed to get the current source code built into an executable with the test code in it.
Expected outcomes	The run of the test should result in `test result: ok`. A failure will result in an error.
Actual outcome	`test result: ok. 1 passed;`
Details	The test was executed without issue and resulted in a pass. The test was executed against software build 20201031.005.

You can see in the details that the software version was included. This helps you track what you were actually testing against. If you want, you can break it out into a separate line item in the table. As always, you can add or change what you keep track of to suit your needs. This is just one example of some essential data points to keep track of. The most important elements here are procedure and expected outcomes. You need to know how to run the tests. You should also always know what you expect to happen when you run the tests. You need to know the expected outcome so you can compare it against the actual outcome. Not all tests will give you an easy way to determine success like the one provided in the example here.

Unit Tests

A short admission here: there was an omission earlier when talking about different types of testing. The reason is this very section. Since it was going to get a complete section to talk about testing, it seemed reasonable to give it a miss earlier. No point in spoiling the surprise after all. Unit testing is a type of functional testing. Typically, you would create unit tests either alongside the functions you are creating or, better, you would create the tests before you've written the function you will be testing. The reason for this is if you write the test first, you know what the expected outcome of the test will be.

Think here about the design-by-contract idea. When you write the function, you should know what the pre-condition is, meaning you need to know what needs to be in place before the function should run, as well as the post-condition, meaning the expected outcome from the function or trait. The same is true when it comes to unit testing. In fact, a unit test is just a way of validating that the function does what it says it does without generating a panic or error condition when the function runs. Writing the unit test allows you to validate the correct behavior of the function ahead of the release of the software rather than just expecting the contract conditions, if you are using them, to make sure the functions behave as they should.

Every function should have a unit test to go along with it. Actually, each function should probably have multiple unit tests. If all you are doing is verifying that the function takes expected and good input and generates expected output, you can get away with a single unit test. Functions aren't always that simple, though. There are probably multiple paths through a function, and you'd need to at least run a unit test multiple times with varied input in order to trigger the different paths through the function. This requires that the person writing the unit test fully understands the function. This is one reason it's a good idea for the software developer to be the one who writes the unit test. They know the code they are writing the best and should be best able to write tests. Another reason why the developer should be writing the unit test is because if you are thinking about how you are going to be testing the function, you may also be thinking about how to defend against software failure.

This brings up a common approach to developing test cases. You start with something called a *use case*. You think about how the software or the function is going to be used. You should think about all of the different ways it could be used or, in the case of a function, it could be called. Each of those use cases should be a test. What is often overlooked, though, is *misuse cases*. Software is misused a lot. This doesn't have to be malicious misuse. It could just be a user who thinks about the software differently than the developers did. They are trying to use something in a way it wasn't necessarily meant to be used. Developers should be encouraged to think about misuse cases when they are developing unit tests rather than just validating that what they did worked the way they said it would work.

Let's take a look at how we can write unit tests. We're going to start with Python again just to have a point of comparison when we look at the way Rust does unit tests. The short script that follows here is a very simple function as well as the code needed to be able to test that function. To perform the test, we need to import the `unittest` package. This package is going to provide the means to drive the tests that we write. For this example, there is just one function, and it's really simple, so we only have a single test case that we're going to be running:

```python
#!/usr/bin/env python3

import unittest

def area(x, y):
    return x * y

class AreaTest(unittest.TestCase):
    def test(self):
        self.assertEqual(area(4,5), 10)

if __name__ == '__main__':
    unittest.main()
```

First, we define a function. This is a simple function that takes two integers, ideally, and returns an area calculation where the two integers are multiplied together. Because Python is an untyped language, we have no way to indicate that we expect integers here. Theoretically, you could pass in a character value and get something other than an area, simply because of the way Python understands characters and multiplication. We'll take a look at that in a little more detail shortly. Before we go further, we need to talk about how we are going to write the unit test.

To create a unit test using the `unittest` package, we need to create a class. Python is not necessarily an object-oriented language by its nature, but it does support objects, and you can create classes, which is a common way of defining objects. One reason for using a class to define a unit test is because it allows us to define the class as a child of `unittest.TestCase`. With any child class, it inherits all the properties and methods of the parent. This ensures that the class we create has all the wrapper bits needed to be able to run the test cases. Effectively, we have a test harness we are going to be sticking tests into, and the harness will take care of knowing what tests to run and then running them.

Inside the class definition, we create functions that define the unit test. Our one unit test is going to call our `area()` function. We're going to use an assertion to determine whether the result from the function call is what we expect it to be. What you will see in the previous code is an invalid assertion, just to demonstrate what it looks like when you get an error. Following is the result of running the test as it is written in the listing you've seen:

```
kilroy@hodgepodge $ python3 pytest.py
F
======================================================================
FAIL: test (__main__.AreaTest)
----------------------------------------------------------------------
Traceback (most recent call last):
  File "pytest.py", line 10, in test
    self.assertEqual(area(4,5), 10)
AssertionError: 20 != 10


----------------------------------------------------------------------
Ran 1 test in 0.000s

FAILED (failures=1)
```

You can see that the unit test fails. You can also see why it fails, if you look through the output. At the end of the traceback, you can see why this failure occurred. It says `AssertionError: 20 != 10`. The unit test says the value from the call to the function should be 10. In fact, 4 times 5 is 20. The test says 10 is not equal to 20, and since we said we were expecting to get 10, the assertion fails. We only had a single test that was run, so we have just the one failure. You will get a readout of the number of successful tests as well as the number of failed tests.

The fact that Python supports the ability to multiply a character by a number may mean you need to consider that fact as you are writing software. A function called `area` probably should only accept valid integer values. However, let's say you wanted to test whether you were able to send in a character. The following line will actually succeed. If it shouldn't be based on requirements to the software, you may get a success from the test, but you should flag it as a failure:

```
self.assertEqual(area(4,5), 10)
```

Before moving on to look at how we would do the same thing in Rust, it's worth noting how you run the unit tests using the framework in Python. You'll see at the bottom of the script that we call `unittest.main()`. This is potentially confusing on first read, and it certainly isn't transparent from a coding perspective. Nowhere in the code you see is there a `unittest.main()` function. The reason for this is because it's in the `unittest.TestCase` parent class. Effectively, we call the function out of the parent class to trigger the test harness.

Let's take a look now at how to write the same test in Rust. Following is a small program that takes advantage of the way Rust is constructed. This means rather than just writing a function, we've got a struct that defines a room. While there may be other pieces of data you could assign to a room, we're only going to be keeping the width and length. Once we have a struct, we have the ability to add a trait to that struct. This lets you create an instance of the Room and then have that instance calculate the area of the room for you:

```rust
struct Room {
    width: u16,
    length: u16
}

pub trait Area {
    fn area(&self) -> u16;
}

impl Area for Room {
    fn area(&self) -> u16 {
        self.width * self.length
    }
}

#[cfg(test)]
mod tests {
    use super::*;

    #[test]
    fn test_area() {
        let a = Room {
            width: 5,
            length: 5
        };
        assert_eq!(a.area(), 25)
    }
}

fn main() {

}
```

Unlike Python, where we had to use a package, we aren't having to import any outside functionality when we write unit tests in Rust. To define tests in Rust, we use attributes. These attributes will then be read by cargo to know what test to use. To separate the unit tests from the rest of the code, we create a module using the mod keyword. The module we are creating is called tests, and it's where all the testing functions will be. The attribute used on the module is #[cfg[test]], which tells cargo that the module contains testing functions. You will see the line use super::* at the top of the module definition. This is a namespace issue. Remember that you are creating a module, which is separate from the rest of the code in the program when you are thinking about a namespace. To refer to anything in the code outside of the module, you need to refer to it specifically to be clear what you are calling. When we use super::*, it says to import everything outside of the module as a local namespace.

Once we have imported all the outside functions and data, we can start writing unit tests. Again, we have a single data structure and a single trait on that data structure, so we are only going to write a single test. The test, isolated from the rest of the program, follows. We are going to use an attribute to identify that the function following is a test, so when you use cargo to run tests, cargo knows what functions to call. The attribute you need to use to identify the function as a unit test is #[test]:

```
#[test]
fn test_area() {
    let a = Room {
        width: 5,
        length: 5
    };
    assert_eq!(a.area(), 25)
}
```

Just as we did with the Python unit test and as we've done in programs in the past, we are going to use assertions. We could use the assert!() macro and include the comparison in the macro, but we're going to use assert_eq!() instead. This may be a matter of preference since there probably isn't anything that is clearer about using assert_eq!(a.area(), 25) as compared with assert!(a.area() == 25). What you are saying is, if the two values—the return from the function and the supplied value—match, the assertion succeeds, which means the unit test succeeds. Whichever approach makes the most sense to you when you are writing, from the perspective of reading it and understanding what it is saying, is the approach you should use.

The negative approach may be less obvious in some cases because you are saying, effectively, "This is not true"; but you can definitely use that if it makes the most sense. In some cases, it's just easier to use a not equal rather than trying to write a comparison based on whether values are equal. From a testing perspective, it may be clearer to say that you expect these two values to not be equal based on the test case you are working on. If you need to write a not-equal test case, you can use the assert_ne!() macro or just use the assert!() macro and use the != comparison inside the assertion.

When you run the tests, you are going to use the cargo program and just pass the parameter test to call all the tests that have been defined in the program. Following is the output from a run of the test in the program we've been looking at:

```
PS C:\Users\kilro\Documents\unittest> cargo test
    Finished test [unoptimized + debuginfo] target(s) in 0.08s
     Running target\debug\deps\unittest-d9db9632b0c76f8a.exe

running 1 test
test tests::test_area ... ok

test result: ok. 1 passed; 0 failed; 0 ignored; 0 measured; 0 filtered out
```

This assumes you want to run all tests that have been defined. You can also run individual tests using cargo. Following is a call to the specific unit test. The program has been altered so the assertion fails so that you can see what a failure looks like. You can see, without looking at the code, what change was made. The output indicates that the right side of the comparison is 20. Previously it was 25, which is the correct value for multiplying 5 by 5:

```
PS C:\Users\kilro\Documents\unittest> cargo test test_area
    Compiling unittest v0.1.0 (C:\Users\kilro\Documents\unittest)
     Finished test [unoptimized + debuginfo] target(s) in 0.28s
      Running target\debug\deps\unittest-d9db9632b0c76f8a.exe

running 1 test
test tests::test_area ... FAILED

failures:

---- tests::test_area stdout ----
thread 'tests::test_area' panicked at 'assertion failed: `(left == right)`
  left: `25`,
 right: `20`', src\main.rs:27:9
note: run with `RUST_BACKTRACE=1` environment variable to display a backtrace


failures:
    tests::test_area

test result: FAILED. 0 passed; 1 failed; 0 ignored; 0 measured; 0 filtered out

error: test failed, to rerun pass '--bin unittest'
```

At the very bottom of the output, you will see the statistics. There isn't much to look at here because we only have one test that is being run. You can see the one failed test listed. Nothing has been ignored or filtered out. This way of testing just checks the output from a function, though. In some cases, you don't really want to check the output. You want to make sure a function panics in the right place. Remember that sometimes, perhaps often, you want to die cleanly rather than try to limp through making guesses about correct behavior. This means when you are checking for correct values and issuing a panic if you don't get what you expect to see. Let's rewrite this program slightly to add in some contracts and then check to make sure the panic happens as expected. Following is the rewritten program:

```
use contracts::*;

struct Room {
    width: i16,
    length: i16
}

pub trait Area {
    fn area(&self) -> i16;
}

impl Area for Room {
    #[requires(self.width > 0, "value must be a valid measurement")]
    #[requires(self.length > 0, "value must be a valid measurement")]
    fn area(&self) -> i16 {
```

```
            self.width * self.length
        }
    }

    #[cfg(test)]
    mod tests {
        use super::*;

        #[test]
        #[should_panic(expected = "value must be a valid measurement")]
        fn test_area() {
            let a = Room {
                width: -1,
                length: 5
            };
            assert_eq!(a.area(), 20)
        }
    }

    fn main() {
        let a = Room {
            width: -1,
            length: 5
        };
        let _x = a.area();

    }
```

We are going to use the `contracts` crate to provide us with the attributes needed to check for the right conditions being in place to enter functions. We're going to use these conditions alongside our unit tests to make sure the contracts are working correctly. The differences start by introducing the possibility to have negative numbers. Previously, we were using unsigned integers, which means there is no possibility of using negative numbers. If there is no sign value allowed, everything is a positive number. As a result, all `u16` definitions have been changed to `i16` instead. This is a 16-bit integer rather than a 16-bit unsigned integer. Without this change, we wouldn't be able to assign a –1 to either the `length` or `width` identifier in our struct.

There are two new conditions in place ahead of the `area()` trait implementation. The attributes tell us to create a contract requiring both the `width` and `length` properties in the struct to be greater than 0. After all, if you are talking about a room, you can't have either the width or the length be zero or a negative number. That doesn't make sense. You might argue that if we are talking about a room, it probably doesn't make a lot of sense for the value to be 1 or maybe 2. If you wanted, you could rewrite the contract if you have a definition for a room with one of the properties being at least, say, 6, for example. These conditions are going to result in a panic being generated if we get zero or negative values for either property.

Since we have a place where we can generate a panic, we can test to make sure that panic is actually generated. We can write a unit test that verifies the panic. All we need to do is add an attribute ahead of the function that has our test. The following line is that attribute, which says the function should generate a panic. Not only that, it indicates what the text of the panic should be. This may be important if you have the possibility of multiple panics being generated. In our case, we have created the text of the panic as part of the condition in the contract for the trait:

```
#[should_panic(expected = "value must be a valid measurement")]
```

One thing to keep in mind is that you know you are going to create a panic, so the unit test is going to look to see if the panic is generated. This is why you need to make sure you understand what a success condition looks like versus a failure condition. If you get a panic, it may be enticing to believe that the test will be a failure. In fact, the test is looking for the panic, so the panic (error) condition arriving is a success. Running the test case shown here will generate the following results. This is followed by a run of the program, where the main function re-creates the same condition found in the test function. This demonstrates that you will, in fact, get the panic as expected since you can't see the results of the function call. You can't see the results of the function call because the panic gets eaten by cargo rather than being displayed:

```
PS C:\Users\kilro\Documents\unittest> cargo test
    Finished test [unoptimized + debuginfo] target(s) in 0.02s
     Running target\debug\deps\unittest-a51f0af74b0c3317.exe

running 1 test
test tests::test_area ... ok

test result: ok. 1 passed; 0 failed; 0 ignored; 0 measured; 0 filtered out

PS C:\Users\kilro\Documents\unittest> target/debug/unittest.exe
thread 'main' panicked at 'Pre-condition of area violated: value must be a valid
measurement: self . width > 0', src\main.rs:13:22
note: run with `RUST_BACKTRACE=1` environment variable to display a backtrace
```

We created a condition that would generate a panic, the panic is in fact generated, and the test harness built into cargo was capable of recognizing that a panic happened to be able to say the test succeeded. These are, of course, very limited views on developing unit tests, but with the assertions and the ability to look for panics, you have the capacity within Rust natively to write detailed unit tests for all of your programs.

RECURSION

Imagine that you have a collection of boxes, and you are asked to put the boxes in order from largest to smallest, such as the collection of boxes seen in Figure 15.3, for example. You can be sure all the boxes are of different sizes. How are you going to go about addressing this challenge? Well, you're probably going to visually inspect the boxes and identify the largest box, because our brains, fortunately, have that comparison capability built in. You will separate that box from the others and then return to the collection of boxes, perform the visual comparison again, separate the next largest box, and then continue to repeat the process until you have the boxes in the right order.

This process of taking a collection of information, passing that entire collection into something of an algorithm, removing some of the information, and then passing the collection with one less item back into the algorithm is called *recursion*. Recursion is the process of calling the same function over and over with a reduced set of information each time you call the function. From a mathematical perspective, you can think about recursion as being defined by two factors: a base state that does not require recursion to solve along with a set of steps that reduce the collection provided down to the base state. There are a number of problems in mathematics and, by extension, computer science that require recursion to complete.

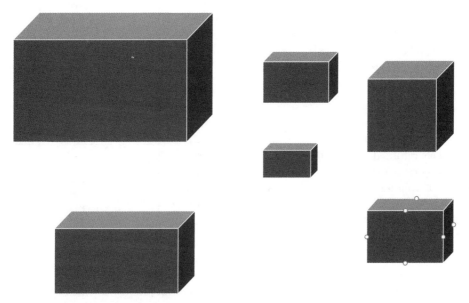

FIGURE 15.3: Boxes needing sorting

A simple problem that can make use of recursion is calculating a factorial. A *factorial* is taking a set of all numbers from 1 to *n* and multiplying them together. The factorial symbol in math is !. This says take a factorial calculation of the number before the exclamation point. As an example, if you want to calculate 5!, you multiply $5 \times 4 \times 3 \times 2 \times 1$. The last digit isn't technically necessary since any value multiplied by 1 is that value. However, for completeness, it's shown in the calculation. As noted already, this is something we can write in Rust. Following is the simple program that makes use of recursion to calculate the factorial of a number:

```
fn fac(n: u128) -> u128 {

    if n > 1 {
        n * fac(n-1)
    }
    else {
        n
    }
}


fn main() {
    println!("The result is {}", fac(10));
}
```

This is a very simple program. We have the `fac()` function to calculate the factorial. If the value passed into the function is greater than 1, we multiply the current value that was passed into the function by the result of calling the `fac()` function with the current value minus one. If you remember that each time you call a function, a frame goes onto the stack in memory with all the data associated with that function, you may find it easier to see recursion by looking at a simplified call stack in Figure 15.4. Remember that we start with the call to `fac()` with the number we want to calculate the factorial on. As an example, if we wanted to calculate 5!, we would start with `fac(5)`. If we look at the call stack beginning with this call, it will be on the bottom.

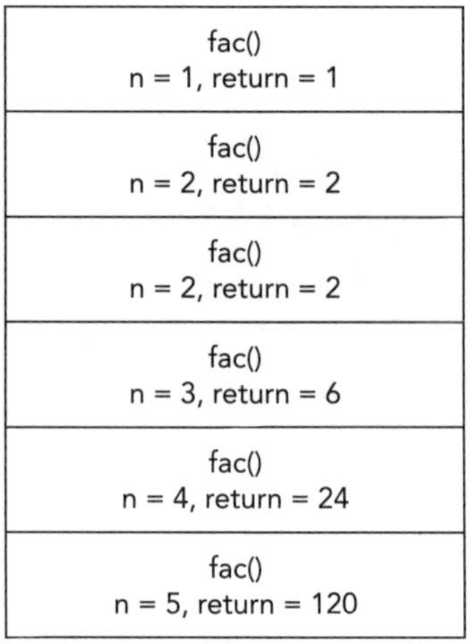

fac() n = 1, return = 1
fac() n = 2, return = 2
fac() n = 2, return = 2
fac() n = 3, return = 6
fac() n = 4, return = 24
fac() n = 5, return = 120

FIGURE 15.4: Factorial call stack

The next call is to `fac(4)`, then `fac(3)`, and so on. We don't start unwinding the stack until we get to `fac(1)`. As the value of n is 1, we return 1. This gets returned to the call `fac(2)`. The return from this is 2 * 1. This gets returned to `fac(3)`. The return from this is then 3 * (2 * 1). This continues until we end up with the complete calculation of 5 * 2 * 3 * 2 * 1. The very last calculation, because all the intermediate ones have been happening as we pop functions off the stack, is 5 * 24. This means the result of 5! is 120.

By comparison, you can do the same thing with a loop in Rust so you don't have to use recursion. Following is a simple program that will calculate a factorial value. This shows that it's not necessary to use recursion to solve the factorial problem. While this problem can be solved without using recursion, there is sometimes a bias toward using recursion for problems. This is because recursion is somewhat attached to functional programming. This type of programming uses functions to achieve tasks. With functional programming, it's thought the program can be proven, because in functional programming you don't get side effects since there are no statements that can change the state of the program. You may notice in the recursive approach to the factorial problem that no value in the program is altered, unlike the case of the loop approach. In the loop approach, we have to create an identifier to store the accumulation value. In the functional approach, everything is transitory. The value that comes back from each successive function call is never stored. It's used to multiply against another value that is coming back from a function. Even presenting the results from the calculation doesn't take an identifier. We pass the result straight into a `println!()` statement:

```
fn main() {
    let mut n = 1;
    for i in 1..10 {
        n = n * i;
    }
    println!("The final value is {}", n);
}
```

Another problem that can be solved using recursion but can't be solved with a loop is calculating Fibonacci numbers. If we wanted to know the 15th number in the Fibonacci sequence, for instance, we could use recursion to find it. The Fibonacci sequence is a list of numbers that are calculated by adding the last two values to get the current value. The first few numbers of the Fibonacci sequence are 0, 1, 1, 2, 3, 5, 8, 13, 21. We start with 0 and 1 because moving on from 0 isn't possible without another seed, since you are adding the last two values in the sequence. If you only start with 0, there isn't another value to add in. Following is a function that will calculate the *n*th Fibonacci number by passing in the value n to the function:

```
fn fib(n: u128) -> u128 {
    if n <= 1 {
        n
    }
    else {
        fib(n-1) + fib(n-2)
    }
}
```

This is similar to the factorial function. The difference is that we are calling the function we are in twice for every pass through the function. The return value for most calls to the function is the return from a call to the function with the current value minus one plus a call to the function using the current value minus two. We don't get to the end of the call stack until n is either 0 or 1. This gives us the ability to handle the case of n equaling 2. A call to `fib(n-2)` where n is 2 results in `fib(0)`.

One final look at recursion is the game Towers of Hanoi. You can see an example of this game in Figure 15.5. The goal of this game is to take a stack of disks that are of decreasing size from bottom to top and move it from the rod on the left to the rod on the far right. The rule is that you can never stack a larger disk on top of a smaller disk as you are moving them. There is a third rod that you can move disks to as you are migrating.

FIGURE 15.5: Towers of Hanoi Image by Ævar Arnfjörð Bjarmason, Creative Commons

This is a problem we can solve using recursion. This is not a case where we rely on the return value from a function call to calculate some final value. Instead, we make a pair of successive calls to the function we are in by passing in one less than the current value as well as a different order of rods. The order determines the rod the disk being moved will come from as well as the rod that will receive the disk. We have to pass in all three rods since subsequent calls will make use of them, so we pass in the unused rod as the third value. What you will receive when you run the program that uses this approach is a set of moves that will solve the problem given some number of disks provided in the call to the function. Following is the function that solves the Towers of Hanoi for you:

```
fn towersolve(n: u16, from: char, to: char, other: char) {
    if n == 1 {
        println!("Moving disk 1 from rod {} to rod {}", from, to);
        return;
    }
    towersolve(n-1, from, other, to);
    println!("Moving disk {} from rod {} to rod {}", n, from, to);
    towersolve(n-1, other, to, from);
}
```

This is a deceptively simple function. Really, it's two calls with a `print` statement in between. The only case where we aren't calling two functions and printing between them is when the disk number becomes 1. The number of disks seen in Figure 15.5 is eight, but you may see games with fewer than that. Solving the problem with only four disks and three rods requires moves as you can see in the steps that follow. Four disks can be solved in 15 moves, which is n^2 – 1. If you have eight disks, it should take you 63 (8^2 – 1) moves:

```
Moving disk 1 from rod A to rod C
Moving disk 2 from rod A to rod B
Moving disk 1 from rod C to rod B
Moving disk 3 from rod A to rod C
Moving disk 1 from rod B to rod A
Moving disk 2 from rod B to rod C
Moving disk 1 from rod A to rod C
Moving disk 4 from rod A to rod B
Moving disk 1 from rod C to rod B
Moving disk 2 from rod C to rod A
Moving disk 1 from rod B to rod A
Moving disk 3 from rod C to rod B
Moving disk 1 from rod A to rod C
Moving disk 2 from rod A to rod B
Moving disk 1 from rod C to rod B
```

There are a lot of problems that can be solved by recursion. When you approach a situation, you can think about whether you need to cut the data you are working with into smaller bundles or at least shave off a piece of data at a time. If that's true, you can potentially use recursion. Sometimes you just need to call the same function over and over again to obtain the result you need. This is also recursion. It can be a powerful programming technique, although it can be hard to keep track of where you are in the successive function calls if you haven't fully planned out how your program is going to work.

MACHINE LEARNING

This is probably a term you have heard a lot. You may also have heard another term that is sometimes mistakenly used in its place—*artificial intelligence*. In reality, *artificial intelligence* is an umbrella term that encompasses several types of programming practices. Machine learning is just one type of approach to giving a computer the ability to present autonomous results from a program. This means the program is capable of deriving results where the results may be determined by means not explicitly provided by a programmer. Machine learning has a lot of possibilities, simply because really complex problems can be hard to write clear programs for. As an example, find a plant out of all of the objects in Figure 15.6. You can, of course, determine where the vegetation is as compared to the fence and rocks and other objects. How do you tell a computer what a plant looks like? What does a program that identifies a plant look like? How about any other type of object?

FIGURE 15.6: Find the plant

You'll run across these problems all over. One common place to find this type of problem is in self-driving cars. Even without the self-driving part, cars that are capable of doing some driving on their own have to do a lot of identification of objects in their environment. The Tesla, for instance, continues to add capabilities of object recognition. In one of the updates in the last few months at the time of this writing, a Tesla car can let you know when traffic lights turn green. This requires that it is able to recognize not only traffic lights but also colors in the traffic lights. The car needs to be able to distinguish red from yellow from green, and be able to see those colors in small circles at a distance. As it turns out, the car is very successful at making those determinations.

In addition, Tesla says it is adding the ability to detect speed changes based on traffic signs. This is to supplement what it knows from global positioning satellite (GPS) data that tells the car where the roads are and what speed limits on those roads are. This means the car needs to be able to see a sign and know it is a traffic sign indicating what the speed is. As with the other types of image detection discussed, this is a difficult thing. The car needs to see a sign and then be able to recognize it is a speed limit sign. Finally, it needs to be able to read the number on the sign and tell the driver about the speed limit. On the display in the car, as with so many other navigation system displays, you get a small sign indicating what the speed limit on the road is. The Tesla will update that information as it reads speed limit signs on the side of the road. In places that are under construction with new roads or new subdivisions, the GPS data in the map display may not be able to keep up with changes that are happening with roads. The recognition system can make sure the latest information is always available to the driver.

This is not to say that this is a new set of challenges. Artificial intelligence started as a concept as far back as at least the 1950s. At that time, the LISP language was developed to be able to help computers exhibit behavior that at least mimicked human intelligence. One of the leading lights in artificial intelligence was the Massachusetts Institute of Technology (MIT). John McCarthy and Marvin Minsky were professors there, and both were early and active developers of artificial intelligence capabilities. McCarthy was the developer of LISP, and Minsky encouraged students to take on projects that could enhance artificial intelligence capabilities. One of those projects was a chess program written in LISP. Other projects included visual recognition capabilities. There is a story, perhaps apocryphal, about a robot arm being taught to play ping pong and nearly taking off Minsky's head—he was bald, and in the bright lights of the room being used, perhaps his head looked like an overly large ping pong ball.

Chatbots

Alan Turing, the man played by Benedict Cumberbatch in the movie *The Imitation Game*, proposed something he called the *imitation game* (thus the name of the movie) that was later called the Turing test. The original game proposed that you have three people: an interrogator in one room and two other people, perhaps in the same room or perhaps in separate rooms by themselves. The interrogator, using a text-only channel, asks questions to determine the sex of the two participants. Turing extended the original idea to ask whether a digital computer could exist that could take the place of one of the participants in the imitation game. The game then turns into whether the interrogator can determine which of the two participants is a computer and which is a human. Turing, as indicated in a speech in the movie, believed that determining whether a computer was thinking wasn't a useful endeavor because of the difficulty in defining what it means to think.

The Turing test has long been considered a goal of artificial intelligence to the extent that in the 1960s, there were several attempts to write programs that could masquerade as a human to have a conversation and fool someone communicating with the program. As indicated earlier, communication in the imitation game is text-based, so typing at a keyboard works well. One such program, called Eliza, was written by Joseph Wiezenbaum when he was at the MIT Artificial Intelligence Lab. Eliza is meant to replicate the experience of talking to a Rogerian therapist in the sense that this type of therapy often turns the question back on the patient. This was a program I discovered on a Digital Equipment Corporation (DEC) PDP/11 in high school in the early 1980s. I had lengthy conversations with Eliza. Today, looking at Eliza, it seems very rudimentary. In fact, once you saw the source code and understood how it worked, the charm of it quickly wore off. Following is a short example of a conversation with Eliza:

   * Hi I need help

   > It is nice to be chatting with you.

   * Thank you. I need help.

   > Oh. . . Let's move on to something else for a bit. You need help?

* Yes, can you help me?

> Don't you believe that I can help you?

* No, I think you are useless

> Perhaps you would like to be useless?

* I feel useless. How do you feel?

> Tell me more about such feelings.

There were several others, including a program called PARRY, meant to model a paranoid personality who had a gambling problem. A much more successful implementation of this is the program ChatBot, which you can find implemented on the ChatBot website.

If you want to see how Eliza works, we can write a very simple example in Rust. The capabilities of this program are fairly limited, although it would be easy to extend the capabilities presented here. Following is the source code for an implementation of an artificial intelligence along the lines of what Eliza was. In Eliza, the mappings of expected input to output were stored in the program itself. In this case, all the mappings are in a text file with the keys separated from the responses by a tab. This makes it easier to introduce additional conversational items without changing the program at all:

```rust
use std::fs::File;
use std::io::{self, Read, BufRead};

struct ChatResponse {
    key: String,
    response: String
}

fn main() -> io::Result<()> {
    let filename = "chatresponses.txt";
    let mut response_vector = vec![];

    let file = File::open(filename).expect("unable to open file");
    let lines = io::BufReader::new(file).lines();
    for line in lines {
        let line = line.unwrap();
        let mut split_line = line.as_str().split('\t');
        let r = ChatResponse {
            key: String::from(split_line.next().unwrap()),
            response: String::from(split_line.next().unwrap())
        };
        response_vector.push(r);
    }

    println!("Hi,my name is Zelia, what can I do for you?");
    loop {
        let mut query_input = String::new();
        let mut found: bool = false;
        match io::stdin().read_line(&mut query_input) {
            Ok(_) => query_input = query_input.trim().to_string(),
            Err(error) => panic!("Error: {}", error),
        }
```

continues

(continued)

```
            for resp in &response_vector {
                if query_input.contains(resp.key.as_str()) {
                    found = true;
                    println!("{}", resp.response);
                    break;
                }
            }
            if !found {
                println!("I'm not sure what you are saying");
            }
        }
    }
```

We aren't going to do anything fancy, so no external crates are necessary. The functionality we are going to import in use statements will be based around input/output. We're going to store our mappings between keywords and responses in a struct called `ChatResponse`. This struct contains two identifiers: `key` and `response`. The key is going to be the value that we'll be looking for in the input from the user. Essentially, we are creating a dictionary. The key found in the input from the user will trigger the response being printed out to the user.

The first part of the program is reading in the dictionary that is stored in the file `chatresponses.txt`. This is something we have done in previous chapters, so we can skim through it quickly. First, we open the file and then read in all the lines to a Vector of `String` values. Each line will contain a key followed by a tab character and then the response. We can iterate through all the lines in the file. We will use the `split()` trait to break the line into two separate values. The first value gets stored into the `key` portion of the struct. Because the `split()` trait returns a vector, we need to use an iterator (the `next()` trait) to get to the values that are returned. Once we have an instance of our `ChatResponse` struct, we can push that instance onto the vector of structs that was created. At the end, we have a vector that we can iterate through for every set of input we get from the user. To start the conversation, we send a message to the user. Next, we start up a loop, which you can see here:

```
loop {
    let mut query_input = String::new();
    let mut found: bool = false;
    match io::stdin().read_line(&mut query_input) {
        Ok(_) => query_input = query_input.trim().to_string(),
        Err(error) => panic!("Error: {}", error),
    }
    for resp in &response_vector {
        if query_input.contains(resp.key.as_str()) {
            found = true;
            println!("{}", resp.response);
            break;
        }
    }
    if !found {
        println!("I'm not sure what you are saying");
    }
}
```

First, we create a new `String` instance to take the input from the user. We also need to keep track of whether we got a hit as we went searching for keys in the input. If we never find anything, we need to let the user know in some way that we didn't understand what was being said. Once those are in place, we can take input from the user using `io::stdin().read_line()`. If we get input, we're going to strip the newline off the end, although that's not strictly required. If there is a desire to extend this program to repeat the input from the user, stripping off the newline character will help when it comes to writing the string back out.

We can use an iterator from the vector of responses to run through all of them. Each instance of `ChatResponse` will get pulled off the vector. We can take the `query_input` identifier and see whether the word is stored in `resp.key`, meaning each key value in the vector is included in the input from the user. If the key value is in the input, all we need to do is print out the response that maps to the key value. This makes it look like the computer has understood the user because it is presenting an appropriate response. It's very simplistic, but in many cases, depending on the response provided, it will look a bit like the computer is trying to carry on a conversation.

There is barely any learning being done here, which is why artificial intelligence and machine learning are far from synonymous. Any "learning" or training requires someone to extend the text file that provides the responses to anyone running the program. The program is always going to be limited by the responses that have been provided to it.

Neural Networks

One type of machine learning is implemented using something called *neural networks*. The thing about the human brain is its complexity. All knowledge, in whatever form, is stored using the connections between the roughly 86 billion neurons in the human brain. These connections come in the form of synapses. We don't understand in any meaningful way how the neurons and synapses actually store memory and knowledge, although we have some idea where different components of memory and knowledge are stored, including the things we do that are mostly automatic—meaning they are implicit memories rather than explicit memories. Implicit memory is all the things you know and do without thinking about them. Explicit memory requires an attempt to recall the information, meaning the memory is reconstructed from the connected neurons and synapses.

Taking the term *artificial intelligence* very literally, some researchers have thought that replicating the way the brain works would allow a computer to think and learn like a human does. A neural network constructs a network of neurons that work together to make connections, developing an understanding that would be very hard to teach the program using traditional programming methods. Using neural networks, you can feed a corpus of data to a program and then let the neural network train itself. If you want to understand more of how neural networks train themselves, there are a lot of places to read up on that. Some of them are listed in the "Additional Resources" section at the end of the chapter.

While there aren't nearly as many machine learning or neural network implementations in Rust as there are in other languages, there are some. We can use the crate `neuroflow` to implement a very simple neural network. The potential uses for neural networks are probably limited by your imagination and the implementation of a neural network you are using. The implementation we are using, or at least the program we are writing, is going to train based on a lot of random data. The neural network is going to try to construct a correlation between one set of data and another set of data. Following is the program that implements that correlation mapping:

```
use neuroflow::FeedForward;
use neuroflow::data::DataSet;
use neuroflow::activators::Type::Tanh;
use neuroflow::io;
use rand::Rng;

fn main() {

    let mut rand_generator = rand::thread_rng();

    // defines the number of layers and the number of neurons in each layer
    // first value is the number of neurons in the input layer
    // last value is the number of neurons in the output layer
    let mut neural_net = FeedForward::new(&[1,7,8,8,7,1]);

    let mut data = DataSet::new();

    for _x in 1..15000 {
        let val1: f64 = rand_generator.gen();
        let val2: f64 = rand_generator.gen();
        data.push(&[val1], &[val2]);
    }

    neural_net.activation(Tanh).learning_rate(0.01).train(&data, 5000);

    let new_val: f64 = rand_generator.gen();

    let check_val = neural_net.calc(&[new_val])[0];
    println!("Calculated value: {}", check_val);

    io::save(&neural_net, "fakecorrelation.flow").unwrap();
    // let mut new_neural: FeedForward = io::load("fakecorrelation.flow").unwrap()
}
```

We're going to import functionality from the neuroflow crate as well as the rand crate. Both of those crates will need to be added to the Cargo.toml file. The first thing to do in the main() function is to initialize the random number generator. This is done using rand::thread_rng(), returning an instance of the random number generator into the identifier named rand_generator. Then we need to create an instance of a multilayer perceptron network, where a *perceptron* is an algorithm for supervised learning. Each layer needs to have some number of virtual neurons in it. In the line that calls the FeedForward::new() function, we pass in a set of values indicating the number of neurons in each layer. The first number indicates the number of neurons to use in the input layer. The last value is the number of neurons to use in the output layer. Unfortunately, the documentation does not make clear what the other values mean or should include. This particular data set is in the documentation, and it works. Reducing the number of values in the data set seemed to generate errors, so I left it alone here.

Once we have our perceptron network in place, we can start building a data set to train the neural network with. We're going to use a for loop to build that data set once we create the instance using

`DataSet::new()`. The loop is going to generate a pair of random floating-point values. We'll push these as a pair onto the `DataSet` instance. The important part of this program is the line that follows. This is where the neural network is trained using an activation function. The *activation function* is a mathematical algorithm that helps the neural network determine which neurons should be triggered (turned on or off). There needs to be a determination when it comes to generating output (a predication) of whether the neuron is part of that prediction or not. The activation function helps with that. In this case, we're going to use the Tanh activation function. This is the hyperbolic tangent function. If you are unfamiliar with geometric functions, the tangent is a line that touches a circle at a given point. The hyperbolic tangent is the line that touches a hyperbola rather than a circle:

```
neural_net.activation(Tanh).learning_rate(0.01).train(&data, 5000);
```

There are three aspects to this line of code. The first is the activation function. As indicated previously, we're going to use `Tanh`. The other activation function supported is sigmoid (`sigm`) as well as the derivative function to the hyperbolic tangent (`der_tanh`) and the derivative function to sigmoid (`der_sigm`). We also need to set the learning rate. This is the rate of adjustment that may need to be made on each pass through the activation function. Finally, we can train the neural network. We need to pass in the data set as well as the number of training iterations. We're going to use 5000 iterations, but you can run through the training many more times and perhaps get better results from your neural network.

Once we have trained the network, we should check our results. In this case, we're going to see if it can predict the paired value based on some given input. We've trained this neural network with random numbers. If we don't have a very good random number generator, it's possible that the values could be predicted. So, we can check the mapping between one random number and another. We generate a new random number and get a calculated value back using the following line:

```
let check_val = neural_net.calc(&[new_val])[0];
```

This is going to give us a predicted value that is stored in the identifier `check_val`. The identifier `new_val` is the random value that was generated that is being presented to the neural network as input to calculate a value from.

You don't have to lose your trained neural network once you've created it. You can save the data set using the following line. After that is the line—commented out so it doesn't run but is in the program—that will read the stored data set back in:

```
io::save(&neural_net, "fakecorrelation.flow").unwrap();
// let mut new_neural: FeedForward = io::load("fakecorrelation.flow").unwrap()
```

This is a trivial example of creating a neural network, but it demonstrates the process. If you have some data, you can feed it into a neural network like `neuroflow` and have the neural network predict output values based on an input to compare it against or calculate on.

SUMMARY

There are a number of types of testing to be considered when writing software. As a software developer, the most important type of testing is unit testing. This is where you write a new function that calls the function you really want to write to extend the capabilities of the program you are writing or working on. The unit test function should try to push the primary function to do what it should do and then validate that it did it correctly. We do some of the same sorts of things when we are writing in a design by contract, especially since we are probably using assertions when we write unit tests in Rust.

Rust provides a test harness. This uses the `unittest` crate. You create a module that contained all your tests. We end up having a namespace problem in this case since all the `main` functions are in the namespace outside of the testing module. This means we need to import `super::*` to pull the namespace of the main program into the unit testing module. We will use the `cargo` program to run the tests. Each test can be run individually by specifying the function name to `cargo` when telling it to run tests. Every function you write, especially when it comes to writing large-scale programs, should have at least one unit test function. Ideally, some of the unit tests should include misuse cases, meaning trying to do something the function wasn't necessarily designed to do in order to make sure it handles the input or call gracefully. In addition to just using assertions, the `unittest` crate allows you to use an attribute indicating that a panic should be expected from the called function. This lets you test that your program is failing as you expect it to.

Recursion is a way of solving problems using functions rather than other elements of a programming language like a loop. Sometimes there is elegance involved in using recursion rather than a loop. Sometimes it makes reading the program easier because it's clear what is happening. A recursive function is one that keeps calling itself over and over until the problem is solved. There are many types of problems that are commonly solved using recursion. The factorial calculation, for example, can be performed using a recursive technique. The Towers of Hanoi game can be solved using recursion.

Artificial intelligence has almost become a meaningless term because its meaning has been stretched so thin over so many different ideas. The Turing test is commonly used as a measure or at least a validation of whether a computer is thinking or interacting with a person as another human might. Turing himself didn't necessarily believe you could prove a computer could think, because he felt it was hard to clearly define what thinking meant, especially in the context of a computer. A number of attempts at what we now call chatbots were attempted going back to the 1960s in an effort to fool people into believing they were communicating with another human. In reality, some of these programs were using simple mapping practices to look for keywords in user input and then generating a response that was relevant to the keyword found in the user input. They rapidly fell apart when there weren't enough keywords to take enough varied input from someone interacting with the program. This can be easily implemented in Rust using a vector of keywords and responses, looking for the keyword in user input and then providing the response associated with the keyword.

Another type of artificial intelligence, and one used in a number of different applications today, is machine learning. This is where the program is provided with a way to learn from a data set. This is commonly called *supervised learning* because there may be guard rails set up around the learning process, as well as a curated data set. This approach is often used to have computers or programs identify complex patterns, including identifying objects from pictures, for instance. One type of machine learning implementation is a neural network. This is a way of mimicking a human brain by creating a collection of neurons implemented in software that then determine how they are going to generate connections between themselves based on the data set and the output that may be expected.

While there aren't a lot of machine learning crates available for Rust, one that is available is `Neuroflow`. It may not be as capable as one that is used on a larger number of platforms, like TensorFlow, but it is much easier to set up and get working with than its more capable counterpart.

1. Change the factorial portion of the program to accept a value on the command line and calculate the factorial value of that.

2. Change the Towers of Hanoi function to keep track of the number of moves that are made. Print the value at the end.

3. Change the chat program to allow the user to say they are ending the program.

5. Move the functionality from the neural network into functions. Write unit tests for the functions.

ADDITIONAL RESOURCES

Introduction to Neural Networks - `www.explainthatstuff.com/introduction-to-neural-networks.html`

"How Do Neural Network Systems Work?" - `computerhistory.org/blog/how-do-neural-network-systems-work`

"Understanding Neural Networks" - `towardsdatascience.com/understanding-neural-networks-what-how-and-why-18ec703ebd31`

Eliza Implementation in JavaScript - `psych.fullerton.edu/mbirnbaum/psych101/Eliza.htm`

When Eliza Met PARRY - `www.theatlantic.com/technology/archive/2014/06/when-parry-met-eliza-a-ridiculous-chatbot-conversation-from-1972/372428`

INDEX